4835552

MOVING MILLIONS

ALSO BY THE AUTHOR

Uptown, Downtown—A Trip Through Time on New York's Subways
Gordie Howe
Hockey! The Story of the World's Fastest Sport
Stan Mikita—The Turbulent Career of a Hockey Superstar
Strange But True Hockey Stories
The Flying Frenchmen—Hockey's Greatest Dynasty
   (with Maurice "The Rocket" Richard)
Up from the Minor Leagues of Hockey (with Shirley Fischler)
Power Play
Slapshot
Bobby Clarke and the Ferocious Flyers
Slashing!
Fischlers' Hockey Encyclopedia (with Shirley Fischler)
This Is Hockey
   (photography by Dan Baliotti)
Those Were the Days
Power on Ice (with Denis Potvin)

MOVING MILLIONS,

An Inside Look at Mass Transit

Stan Fischler.

Stanley I. Fischler

Research Editor: David Rubenstein

Research Assistants: Sharon Eberson, Kevin Kenney

HARPER & ROW, PUBLISHERS
New York, Hagerstown, San Francisco, London

Copyright acknowledgments appear on page 301.

MOVING MILLIONS: *An Inside Look at Mass Transit*. Copyright © 1979 by Stanley I. Fischler. All rights reserved. Printed in the United States of America. No part of this book may be used or reproduced in any manner whatsoever without written permission except in the case of brief quotations embodied in critical articles and reviews. For information address Harper & Row, Publishers, Inc., 10 East 53rd Street, New York, N.Y. 10022. Published simultaneously in Canada by Fitzhenry & Whiteside Limited, Toronto.

FIRST EDITION

Designer: Stephanie Winkler

Library of Congress Cataloging in Publication Data

Fischler, Stan.
  Moving millions.
  Includes index.
1. Local transit. 2. Urban transportation.
3. Local transit—United States. I. Title.
HE305.P58 388.4 78-2133
ISBN 0-06-011272-7

79 80 81 82 83 10 9 8 7 6 5 4 3 2 1

To the memory of my parents, Molly and Ben Fischler, who demonstrated to me, early in life, that mass transit was the only way to travel; and proved it by never buying a car

Contents

Photographs follow pages 110 and 206.

Acknowledgments

The author wishes to express his particular thanks for the invaluable assistance of the Electric Railroaders' Association for the use of their library, as well as the contributions made by individual members who helped in various ways with the manuscript.

In addition, the author was inspired by a number of previous books in the field. They include the innumerable works of William D. Middleton, Brian Cudahy, John Anderson Miller, John F. Bromley, Jack May, Alan R. Lind, and Commander E. J. Quinby, as well as the editors of *Headlights*, the official publication of the Electric Railroaders' Association.

Not to be overlooked was the generous assistance provided by Stephen D. Maguire, columnist of *Railroad* magazine, and Don O'Hanley, one of the truly unsung heroes of mass transit.

The author is no less indebted to the assistance provided by Rich Friedman, Dr. Ira J. Sheier, Don Harold, Dennis Wendling, Ed Silberfarb, Hugh Dunne, Joe Spaulding, Len Ingalls, Bob Leon, Becky Morris, Karen Robertson, Anne Coughlin, Sharon Eberson, Jeff Hasen, Leah Sperry, Barbara Grano, Howard and Suzanne Samelson, Chuck and Joetta Walton, George Horn, John Mesagno, Reuben Guttman, Kevin Kenney, Nate Salant, and Jim Sterngold.

Not to mention special gratitude to the likes of Brad Snell, E. E. Van Ness, and Clint Page, among others, who have fought the good fight for the improvement of mass transit.

Last, but certainly not least, the author wishes to express his gratitude for the encouragement supplied by editor Joe Vergara, Russ Mack, Rhoda Dreifus, copy editors Buddy Skydell and Mary Jane Alexander, and indefatigable researcher David Rubenstein.

Foreword

The Trouble with Mass Transit

The crusade for a sensible mass transit policy in the United States was derailed long ago in Detroit and has yet to get back on the right track. Considering this nation has been able to dispatch a man nonstop to the moon, it is appalling to realize that a New Yorker riding to Bay Shore on the Long Island Rail Road still can't get there without changing at Jamaica!

Actually, it is something of a miracle that the Long Island Rail Road, let alone any of America's other electric commuter lines, still is running, considering a half-century of benign neglect of trains from Syracuse to San Francisco.

Decades after the nation succumbed to the internal combustion engine, we are coming to the realization that urban public transportation policies are a shambles. It is imperative to question why there has been a militant lack of interest in Washington on the subject of transportation.

The answers are basic. For starters, transit was not, is not, and never will be a sexy issue. Washington has to admit that mass transit and intercity rail policies are abysmal. If that means stepping on a few toes and doing away with old concepts, then let us start stepping.

Since World War II approximately 95 percent of all federal transportation dollars has been spent on the building of highways. The remaining 5 percent was divided between airports, waterways, and mass transit. We have the best highway system in the world because we paid for it. We have no rail transit because we have spent nothing on it.

The federal government must reshape its funding if mass transit is to be improved. If we leave it to the state and local communities to resolve their transportation problems and promise that, whichever approach they use, the federal government will finance 90 percent of it, mass transit will come into its own. Today only highways receive that treatment. Until now Congress has viewed highways as synonymous with transportation. When Capitol Hill boasts that it is spending $7 billion "on transportation" this year, it sounds great for mass transit advocates. The catch, unfortunately, is that "transportation," in Congress' eyes, consists of nothing but highways. It is sheer folly to funnel $7 billion indiscriminately into highways when useful enterprises such as Amtrak, Conrail, and urban mass transit projects are ignored.

There are those, I am aware, who insist that Joe and Jane America simply are not interested in mass transit; that they are irrevocably committed to the automobile. I disagree. I am convinced that we can get people out of cars by making mass transit work. But first it must be made competitive by being fast, accessible, and comfortable. That requires money.

In the meantime, Americans have become overdependent on the automobile. Certainly it is understandable that people have a desire for individual transportation; but is it necessary for a family to have four cars in its driveway? Every time people move, must it be by car? An energy-conscious nation is mandated to say no.

One of our biggest self-delusions is that the automobile is a cheap acquisition. A car, in fact, is enormously expensive. We only look at what we pay for the car when we make the purchase. However, the hidden costs of running a car are enormous; parking, roads, law enforcement—all require subsidization. Consider air pollution. Detroit's car builders use every excuse they can get—including the energy crisis—to evade clean air standards. They had the gall to give us a "choice"—energy or clean air. Never once has Detroit assumed the responsibility for *not* having made pollution-free cars before government compulsion. Social responsibility is not in the vocabulary of car builders.

For reasons of energy, environment, and mobility, it is imperative we recultivate an appreciation of rails. Fortunately, some cities such as Boston, San Francisco, Philadelphia, and Pittsburgh never completely abandoned their trolley car networks. Further, the United States Urban Mass Transportation Administration is in being to switch car owners over to mass transit.

But all this will take time—considerable time—and money. To this end I have teamed up with Senator Ted Kennedy in an effort to divert monies from highways to mass transit. We have already seen from the response that communities, if provided adequate funding, will opt for modes of people-moving other than the automobile. The time for the anticar bloc has come. This book could not have come at a more appropriate time.

—SENATOR LOWELL P. WEICKER, JR.
WASHINGTON, D.C., 1979

Introduction

My love affair with the trains and public transportation began in 1936 when I was four years old. In New York, the IND's GG (Brooklyn-Queens crosstown line) was being completed directly below our brownstone house on Marcy Avenue in Brooklyn. In fact, the Myrtle-Willoughby station sat adjacent to the cellar of the house. On any night I could not only hear the GG local entering and stopping at the station, but, with my head pressed to the pillow, hear the sounds of the doors opening and closing as well.

Just a half block away, at Myrtle Avenue, loomed the spindly steel superstructure of the ancient Myrtle Avenue el, which was built in 1888. The el had a romantic air all its own. In those days, the el's rolling stock consisted of wooden cars dating back to the turn of the century. They had open platforms with iron gates for entry and exit. A conductor yanked the gates open by tugging on a large handle.

The Myrtle Avenue el ride cost only five cents but it was worth five dollars to me. In summer, the front door of the lead car would be swung open, and I would stand next to the motorman's cab sopping up the breezes. There was only one drawback: the Myrtle el moved at a distressingly slow pace and rarely—except on slight hills—sped along the tracks in the manner to which I was accustomed on the faster subways.

Fortunately, the Myrtle Avenue el's wooden cars remained in use until 1958; and I enjoyed a number of good years riding those delightful, rickety old cars. In fact, there was a time during World War II when the el trotted out a fleet of 1905-era "convertible" cars for summer use only. These trains were completely open along the sides except for strong metal bars that prevented passengers from falling. On the hottest days these dandy convertibles made air conditioning unnecessary.

Just about the time I discovered the subways and els, I was given my introduction to trolley cars. It was inevitable. My father did not own an automobile—fortunately, he never acquired one—and most of our traveling was done on subways, els, and streetcars.

We were literally surrounded by trolleys. The Myrtle Avenue trolley (which, incidentally, nearly killed me at age eight when I ran out from behind a truck after buying the evening papers) ran under the el. A block away in either direction were the Nostrand and Tompkins Avenue lines, not to mention the important Lorimer Street trolley, which rolled directly to Ebbets Field, home of the baseball Dodgers.

Just a few blocks away, another fleet of streetcars was available and frequently used. These included the cars of the Flushing and Graham Avenue lines (they had a remarkably pregnant look about them), the DeKalb Avenue route to downtown Brooklyn, and most important, the Franklin Avenue line (an alternate route to Ebbets Field), which linked my neighborhood with the Parade Grounds at Park Circle, where we occasionally went to play baseball.

Each of these lines offered a certain purely aesthetic appeal to me, although most of them were utilitarian as well. But by far the most coveted ride of all (partly because it was not that readily available) was on one of the BMT's many outdoor runs, especially the Brighton Beach ride to Coney Island.

For a kid in his preteens there was much to commend the Brighton BMT. Most important of all, the Brighton's standard car was the best hunk of rapid transit machinery built anywhere. They called it the "67-footer" since the car measured sixty-seven feet from stem to stern. The interior was extra special because the conductor operated a large console of buttons from the middle of the train, and these buttons were available for pressing by kids like me when the conductor was in another car (of course we didn't have the pass key that activated the mechanism).

The 67-footers were trains with seats that could hold up to four passengers (most subway seats held only two at a time) and several other curious seat arrangements that proved of inestimable value to a new rider. The most valuable seat of all was a "jump" cushion located directly to the left of the front window. The jump seat was usually in the open or seating position, which allowed a small boy of, say, four years to stand on the jump seat, open the front window, and peer out into the fresh air.

Because the Brighton run had exceptional variety, it was my favorite. Usually, I'd get on the express at the Prospect Park (formerly Malbone Street) station and ride it all the way to Coney Island. At Prospect Park the train emerges from the tunnel and rolls in an open cut through Flatbush to the Newkirk Avenue express stop. From there it climbs a rather steep grade to Avenue H and then speeds along an embankment south to the ocean.

The combination of speed, road bed (earth and ballast), and the distance between rails produced a very special rhythmic click-clack that captured my imagination. I also discovered that the click-clack could be effectively reproduced by quick movements of the tongue over a tightly closed mouth (only occasionally opening). At the time I considered it one of my most commendable discoveries. The mouth click-clack would be altered to suit the various lines. For example, the Myrtle Avenue el, being a much slower train, produced an almost languorous sound, while the newly built IND—its rails tightly bolted—had almost no click-clack at all. That was a big strike against this subway.

Some extra added attractions were also available. Nearby was the Long Island Rail Road's Brooklyn branch, which ran above Atlantic Avenue. Riding the LIRR was a very special treat because it developed much greater speed than the IND, BMT, and IRT, yet had many of the subway's familiar trappings. The Hudson Tubes (Hudson and Manhattan Railway) to Jersey City, Hoboken, and Newark had a similar fascination.

I depended upon public transit for almost every trip I took from age five until manhood. Mostly, though, the IND was *my* subway because it ran right beneath our house. Every Sunday afternoon my friend Larry Shildkret and I would take the GG local to Hoyt-Schermerhorn Street, change for the A express, and head for the hockey games at Madison Square Garden. Unlike the BMT 67-footers, the IND's 60-footers had a wide front window but one that could *not* be opened. This, of course, was a big minus for the GG, A, E, F, and assorted other Eighth Avenue runs.

Curiously, the IRT remained a relatively "foreign" subway to me for much of my youth, mostly because it serviced the Bronx and areas of Manhattan that I never frequented. I never liked the IRT rolling stock either. Nearly all IRT lines used the Low V (low voltage) cars, which, like the IND's, had nonopening front windows and, even worse, grated the cars with a groaning motor that was at its worst on the upgrades. It wasn't until I moved uptown to Manhattan and rode the IRT #1 local and #2 express that I came to appreciate the city's original subway.

By the time I was seven years old, in 1939, I was convinced that the best job in the world was that of subway motorman. I mentioned that to my father one day and he startled me with his unenthusiastic response. "You don't want to be a motorman," Dad insisted, "because they don't make enough money."

I had no idea what salary the average motorman took home with him. "What do they make?" I asked.

"Only thirty-five dollars a week," my father said offhandedly as if that should have ended the discussion.

I couldn't believe it. My guess was that motormen were paid about $20 a week. Or perhaps they did it for nothing; after all, I would gladly have worked as a motorman for no salary at all. How could my dad have the audacity to tell me that $35 a week was *not* enough money?

Obviously, my father and I did not share the same set of values. But I must give him—and my mother—credit. They enjoyed riding the subways as much as I did. Every Saturday morning Dad and I would climb aboard the GG and then the A for a very important shopping trip to downtown Manhattan.

Dad bought his weekly supply of cigars at a place called Joseph Jonas, Inc., on Nassau Street near the financial district. Then we'd traipse over to Callanan's, a wonderful, musty cheese and meat market where my father purchased a smelly collection of exotic cheeses. During the 1939–40 season of the New York World's Fair at Flushing Meadow in Queens, the IND ran a special branch of the GG to the fair grounds. That was an early favorite, purely out of curiosity value. Another that I got to like was the BMT's summer-only Franklin Avenue express that ran from Franklin and Fulton streets to Coney Island. That one has enormous historic value since it took the notorious Malbone Street curve (scene of the 1918 disaster that killed ninety-seven persons) and always threatened to fly off the track.

I deeply regretted that nobody in our family (and that includes uncles, cousins, and even second cousins) worked on the city's transit system. Being rather bashful, I was unable to strike up any acquaintanceship with a motorman on the subways, and it wasn't until I reached the age of twelve that I befriended my first transit employee.

It was the winter of 1944–45. I was taking Hebrew lessons prior to my bar mitzvah at a synagogue in the Bedford Stuyvesant section of Brooklyn. This meant that I had to take the Tompkins Avenue trolley every Sunday morning at 6 A.M. to arrive in time for the 6:45 A.M. lesson.

Frequently I was the only person riding the trolley at that time of day and inevitably I sat in the seat immediately next to the motorman. Week in and week out I would ride with the same motorman and we became friendly, although not what I would call bosom buddies. Nevertheless this was a big breakthrough for me, and by the time I was bar mitzvahed, I believed that I had learned how to operate a trolley car as well as any motorman in Brooklyn.

One ride during the Tompkins Avenue era was memorable. It took place on a Sunday morning in early January 1945. The temperature hovered around five above zero and the first signs of a blizzard were already apparent as swirls of windswept snow blew across the avenue. The trip had a delightfully eerie quality about it. Nobody got on the trolley from the beginning to the end of the trip (about two and a half miles), and, miracle of miracles, we rolled along, making nearly every green light on Tompkins and Kingston avenues. In those days it was quite an accomplishment.

At that point, in 1945, my allegiance to subways first wavered, and I became an enthusiastic trolley fan, wanting only to be a streetcar motorman. Once, I nearly had my wish fulfilled. It was the summer of 1945, and my closest friend, Howie Sparer, was spending August in Sea Gate, the westernmost tip of Coney Island. At one time Sea Gate had a regular trolley line running from one section to the other but now the Sea Gate tracks were used only to store the streetcars. Nevertheless, the tracks remained and the overhead wires still had juice in them.

"Let's borrow a trolley," I suggested to a rather incredulous Howie. "I know how to operate it."

All we had to do, I thought, was connect the trolley pole with the overhead wire. I pulled on the rope, unhooked the pole, and led it toward the wire. At last the little wheel atop the trolley pole made contact with the live wire and, suddenly, the motor inside the sleeping streetcar began vibrating. It was awake and waiting to be taken for a ride.

The two of us raced to the front of the tram and climbed aboard. I was sure that driving it around the Sea Gate tracks would present few problems. The controller was where it was supposed to be and so was the brake. But, alas, the removable brake handle was not in its accustomed place. Without a brake handle, the brakes could not be operated; and without brakes I could not stop the trolley. Needless to say, I was tempted to take the trolley out for a ride anyhow, but discretion proved the better part of childishness and Howie and I climbed off the trolley. The adventure was called off.

Once it had become apparent that I would never be a full-time, paid motorman, I began approaching the subways on a different level. In August 1955 I was hired by the New York *Journal-American* as a reporter and, by sheer coincidence, was almost immediately assigned to cover the Transit Authority on a weekly basis.

One of my first news assignments was to report on a speech made by the then TA chairman Charles "Big Charlie" Patterson about the expansion of subway service in Queens. I knew immediately that the subway beat was just for me. Every Tuesday thereafter, I attended the TA press conferences (and ate their delicious pastrami sandwiches with fat juicy pickles) and wrote more subway stories than anyone else in the *J-A*'s history. (This, of course, is an unofficial record.)

The TA publicity department boasted many colorful directors. However, I never got to know Leo Casey, an old-line newsman turned publicist. Casey's successor, Syl Pointkowski, was a huge, boisterous, and thoroughly lovable man who did me one of the best favors imaginable. This was in December 1962, when the *Journal-American* and all the other New York dailies went out on strike for what seemed an eternity. (Actually, the strike lasted 114 days.) Point kowski hired me as well as the other TA beat men as "consultants." We were paid more than what we were getting as newspapermen and were assigned to write the TA's tenth anniversary report.

Len Ingalls of *The New York Times* captained our team, which included Ed Silberfarb of the *Herald Tribune,* Ed Ross of the *Daily News,* Manny Perlmutter and Ed Clark of the *Times*. Each of us was given a special area of expertise for which we were required to write a 5,000-word report. My assignment was surface transit, and it was a difficult one at that, difficult from the emotional end.

The season at the TA also opened my eyes to the world of the train buff. Until then I had been unaware that others were as obsessed—even more so—with trains as I was. I learned about the Electric Railroaders' Association, a splendid group, and the Trolley Museum in Branford (New Haven), Connecticut, where many pieces of subway and surface rolling stock are on display.

When the strike finally ended, my relationship with the TA began to wane—in 1964 I began covering sports and did fewer and fewer subway stories. The TA, coincidentally, began to cut down on its press conferences, presumably on the theory that the less probing newsmen did, the less dirt they would unearth. (The TA was right, this time.) Interestingly, two members of our consultants team, Ingalls and Silberfarb, were hired by the TA. Ingalls became head of the PR sector and Silberfarb soon went to work for him, thereby giving the press bureau a surplus of professionalism.

The TA had completely eliminated streetcars as well as trolley buses by then, decisions that appalled me. And the very individuals who were responsible for the new directions were the people with whom I had worked during the period as TA "consultant." I was very anxious to confront the surface transit chief, one Hyman Feldman, over the issue of nonpolluting electric vehicles with long life spans verses polluting buses, which use noxious diesel fuel. Finally, Feldman and I had our confrontation. "The diesels," he insisted, "are cheaper to operate." I came away from my meetings with the bus-philes convinced that they did *not* believe buses were better. It all smelled bad!

On the positive side, the "consultant" era enabled me to explore areas of the subway system that I had never realized existed. We rode the rail-grinder at three in the morning and even inspected the Bronx car shops, where Silberfarb was nearly electrocuted when he tried to touch a live power shoe. The total experience, combined with my earlier love of transit, distilled in me the desire to write this book.

I

EARLY HISTORY

FROM THE BEGINNING
TO WORLD WAR I

1

How It All Began

It all began somewhere in southwestern Asia; neither the place nor the person is known. But in the very distant prehistoric past the wheel was invented. Naturally, the wheel created a rut—or track—which, if followed, kept the wheel from moving aimlessly about; and, ultimately, the earliest transit designers (likely the Sumerians) etched ruts in stone and ran the wheels in these ruts. During Pericles' time heavy monuments were transported by the Greeks along stone ways. The Grecian transit masters thoughtfully provided for a secondary route to allow one carrier to pass another. Thus, the siding—commonplace on contemporary railroads—was introduced and refined. In time the Romans refined the groove road and constructed more improved stone ways, including one on the site of a Victorian-style railway station in England.

Only minor improvements were made, and these extremely slowly, until the sixteenth century; the roots of modern mass transit can be traced to the mining country in both Great Britain and Germany. Teuton inventors produced the flanged wheel, the counterpart of which can be found on any subway, trolley, or commuter train in the world today. Meanwhile, English and Welsh coal barons sought ways and means of trimming the sizes—and costs—of horse teams carrying minerals from the mines. If some means could be devised to ease the bumpy path from the pits to the platforms, fewer horses would be necessary.

Wooden rails proved to be the panacea. By the seventeenth century, wooden railways dotted the mining districts of Great Britain. Significantly, the original English horse-drawn coal train rolled on rails 4 feet 8½ inches apart, the precise gauge employed today on such railroads as the New York City subway and others. Inevitably, iron mines produced the material for strapping the wood with protective metal as well as flanged iron wheels. And it wasn't long before the iron wheels-on-track found a strategic use. According to author-historian Hamilton Ellis, this was discovered in 1745, when the coal-carrying Tranent and Cockenzie Waggon-Way became the centerpiece of the Battle of Prestonpans. Writing in *The Pictorial Encyclopedia of Railways*, Ellis observed: "General Sir John Cope, commanding the Government forces, called it 'a narrow cartroad' and tried to hold it, as an incidental fortification, against the Jacobite army. . . . They did not know, nor had they time to care, that their general had just become the first soldier to make strategic use of a railway."

By the early eighteenth century, Great Britain became the pacesetter in the realm of railway development, although still on a most primitive scale. The first railway viaduct—Causey Arch in County Durham—was in use by 1727, and on June 9, 1758, Parliament approved a railway from Middleton to Leeds. All that was needed now for this ever improving rail system was a first-rate means of propulsion to replace the horse. That honor would go to a native of Cornwall by the name of Richard Trevithick. Soon to be revered as "the Father of the Locomotive," Trevithick developed a relatively small, high-pressure engine and in 1804 constructed a "portable fire engine," or steam passenger coach. For reasons known only to Trevithick, he chose not to run his steam engine on rails. But one of Trevithick's locomotives, "Black Billy," caught the attention of George Stephenson, a young enginewright. In 1825 Stephenson built the first steam railroad and, from that point on, the world of transportation never was the same.

The railroad revolution spread as fast as John Birkinshaw's Bedlington Ironworks in Northumberland could manufacture rolled iron rails. The Liverpool and Manchester Railway followed in 1830, replete with mechanical traction, timetables, signals, and formal stations. It was enough to cause a Londoner to wonder why these newfangled machines couldn't, somehow, untangle the knot of traffic on the streets of the burgeoning British capital. One of the first suggestions for a solution surfaced in the 1830s when a plan for an underground railway from King's Cross to Snow Hill reached the desk of Charles Pearson, who eventually would become city solicitor, as well as John Hargrave Stevens, a prominent Londoner who eventually attained the post of city architect and surveyor. Between them, enough energy was directed toward the eventual construction of an underground railroad within London's city limits to make it merely a question of whether London would build a subway before Paris, Moscow, Berlin, Budapest, or its rivals across the ocean, Boston and New York.

By 1851 adventuresome London planners and investors had begun moving in earnest toward construction of a better mode of transport and, two years later, Parliament approved the building of the North Metropolitan underground rail line.

A series of temporary setbacks—the Crimean War caused a shortage of money—delayed the start of actual construction, but by 1855 it was clear that London would be the first city in the world to construct a workable subway. The technique employed was the "cut-and-cover" construction, in which a great trench was cut for the railway and afterwards roofed over, leaving the line in a subway or covered way. Once the trench was roofed either a road or building could be built over the subway. "To save disturbance of property, as much of the Metropolitan Railways's trench as possible was dug along the line of existing streets," wrote John R. Day, historian of the London subway. "This had some disadvantages because beneath the surface of the roads lay nests of pipes—water, gas, and sewerage in particular as well as, even in those days, the electric telegraph. All these had to be diverted before the trench for the railway could be made."

A vivid description of the start of this momentous project was provided by author Frederick S. Williams in his historical piece "Our Iron Roads." Williams observed:

A few wooden houses on wheels first made their appearance, and planted themselves by the gutter; then came some wagons loaded with timber and accompanied by sundry gravel-coloured men with picks and shovels. A day or two afterwards a few hundred yards of roadway were enclosed, the ordinary traffic being, of course, driven into the side streets; then followed troops of navvies, horses and the shafts. The exact operations could be but dimly seen or heard from the street by the curious observer who gazed between the tall boards that shut him out; but paterfamilias, from his house hard by, could look down on an infinite chaos of timber, shaft holes, ascending and descending chains and iron buckets which brought rubbish from below to be carted away; or perhaps one morning he found workmen had been kindly shoring up his family abode with huge timbers to make it safer. A wet week comes, and the gravel in his front garden turns to clay; the tradespeople tread it backwards and forwards to and from the street door; he can hardly get out to business or home to supper without slipping and he strongly objects to a temporary way of wet planks, erected for his use and the use of passers-by, over a yawning cavern underneath the pavement . . . but at last, after much labour and many vicissitudes, even the Underground Railway was completed.

An immediate complication developed over the gauge of track to be used. In advance of construction an agreement had been made permitting both the Great Western and Great Northern Railways to have use of the Metropolitan's tracks. Since the Great Western employed broad gauge (7 foot, ¼ inch) and the Great Northern used standard gauge (4 foot, 8½ inch) track, it was decided to use three rails, the outer one to accommodate the Great Western trains. This, of course, necessitated building a wider trench than one which would have accommodated just standard gauge. Thus, the original trench and the overhead span of the elliptical brick arch measured 28 feet 6 inches across (instead of the 25½ feet which would have been used for standard gauge only).

The first subway construction was not without mishap. In June 1862 the Fleet River, then funneled through a lightly built brick sewer measuring only ten feet in diameter and resting on rubble in the old river bed, seeped through the underground's retaining wall and flooded the subway construction site to a depth of as much as ten feet. The Metropolitan's engineers subsequently were more diligent and managed to avert further disaster.

Executives of the corporation had a devil of a time deciding which means of propulsion to use when the project was completed. Electricity was unknown as a practical means of moving vehicles, but cable railways had worked on a limited basis. Other ideas—some cockeyed—crossed the desks of London's subway barons, but ultimately they chose to go with the traditional, although troublesome, steam locomotive. The trouble, of course, lay in dissipating the engine smoke. After several experiments the Metropolitan commissioned Daniel Gooch, locomotive superintendent of the Great Western, to design the official subway locomotive. The result was a 2-4-0 tank design with 6-foot coupled wheels and outside cylinders 16 inches by 24 inches. A decisive trial run was held in October 1862. The engine, pulling a 36-ton train, ran from Farringdon Street to Paddington in twenty minutes and was pronounced a success.

The gas-lit coaches were well appointed, long, and impressive enough alone to attract passengers. Starting on January 3, 1863, they were put through dress rehearsals. Apart from minor difficulties that were easily remedied, the subway was pronounced fit and, on January 10, 1863, the Metropolitan opened for business. Chugging along a 3¾-mile-long route, the subway connected Bishop's Road, Paddington, and Farringdon Street at the City boundary.

To the Metropolitan's shareholders, all the spit and polish was secondary to the bottom line—profits. Would Londoners forsake traditional means of transportation for the new underground marvel? The answer was supplied the very first day. By the time the last locomotive pulled in to Farringdon Street station more than £850 worth of fares had been collected. That it was no mere novelty was proven in just a few weeks. Within two months the Metropolitan was carrying passengers at the rate of 2,750,000 a year for every mile of track. And in the first half-year of operation the subway was carrying an average 26,500 passengers *daily*. Clearly, the London underground was there to stay.

During the early decades of the nineteenth century, when London planners began the Metropolitan, there was no talk in New York City about building a subway. But New York proved a mass transit pioneer in other respects. What made public mass transportation imperative on the island of Manhattan was the rapid growth of the city northward from the southern tip (Bowling Green and the Battery), and the obvious fact that New York was becoming one of the largest cities in the world. In 1827 Abraham Brower realized that the more than 200,000 New Yorkers had no public vehicles within the city limits.

Brower's plans were more prosaic than an elaborate underground subway. He merely wanted to supply his fellow burghers with local passenger transportation. He designed a special vehicle pulled by horses which would seat a dozen passengers and brought it to the coach-making firm of Wade & Leverich. Not unlike an open-sided stagecoach, the Brower-designed vehicle was labeled the "Accommodation" and entered revenue service in 1827. Its route was north and south along Broadway, Manhattan's main thoroughfare, then as now. Brower charged a fare of one shilling and discovered that he had a ready and willing clientele. Armed with his profits, Brower returned to Wade & Leverich for an improved coach—seats running lengthwise, the door placed at the rear instead of the side—and dubbed it the "Sociable."

Sociability was not the prime desire of potential passengers, but regular service and reliability (of sorts) were imperative. Ephraim Dodge of Boston attempted to fulfill these requirements in 1829 when he launched a hack service between Boston and South Boston. Dodge charged a fare of 12½ cents and America was on its way—albeit slowly—to a form of surface transport second only to the vehicles already in vogue across the Atlantic.

Parisians were accustomed to seeing passenger diligences operating at five sous per rider as early as 1819. An English-born coach builder added to Paris' reputation as a leader in surface transport when George Shillibeer developed a vehicle called an omnibus. The origin of the name lay with a French officer named Baudry, who operated a coach between Nantes and some baths he owned in the neighboring town of Richebourg. "At first," wrote John Anderson Miller in *Fares, Please!*, "he called his vehicle simply the 'Richebourg Baths Coach.' Then, one day when he was passing a store kept by a man named Omnes, he noticed a sign over the doorway reading 'Omnes Omnibus,' or 'Omnes for all.'

"This so tickled Baudry's fancy that he immediately renamed his vehicle 'l'Omnibus,' and the word was soon adopted by the operators of other local coaches."

Since no enterprising Londoner had seized the opportunity, Shillibeer sold his Parisian business and returned to his homeland where he launched a surface transit system in London from Paddington Green to the Bank of England. The British omnibus won no plaudits from hackney coachmen, who saw it as competition. They were right. Londoners flocked to Shillibeer's vehicle in such numbers that he was compelled to press more vehicles into service until he had fattened his fleet to twelve omnibuses in all.

There was, however, one major hitch that curbed growth: the city of London enforced an ordinance that forbade the picking up and setting down of passengers. Aware of the penalty, omnibus drivers chained themselves to their coach seats to keep from being jailed. Vigorous enforcement coupled with equally vigorous protest eventually compelled the city fathers to pass the Stage Carriage Act in 1832. This proved to be a milestone in mass transportation law. A new form of service was recognized, and both drivers and conductors were forced to obtain licenses to pursue their business. So, at the very beginning of public transportation, the principle of public regulation was established.

Abraham Brower, the father of New York City's public transportation system, knew a good thing when he saw it; the good thing was Shillibeer's omnibus, better than anything Brower had rolling up and down Broadway. Brower had John Stephenson build the original Manhattan omnibus and he built it well. The fee was 12½ cents for a ride along the route that stretched from the tip of Manhattan (the Battery) to Bond Street. Again, a success. Within four years more than a hundred omnibuses were crisscrossing the streets of Old New York.

"The practice of having a boy collect fare was soon given up," related John Anderson Miller, "and the money was deposited in a box beside the driver's seat. Change up to the amount of two dollars was supposed to be furnished by the driver on request. This was passed back to the passenger in an envelope through a small hole in the roof. Not all drivers, unfortunately, were careful that the change in the envelope was correct. A passenger who was shortchanged might storm and rage, but there was not much he could do about it, as it was practically impossible to talk to the driver through the hole in the roof. Usually the victim's predicament aroused more amusement than sympathy among the other passengers—a fact well known to the drivers, who took advantage of it and ignored all but the most vigorous protests." Some say 140 years later that this rudeness remains *de rigueur* on New York City's buses.

Similarly, then as now adherence to traffic laws was not a hallmark of the omnibus drivers. In fact, their reckless behavior inspired some sharp newspaper editorials. A typical journalistic attack against the early omnibus operators went as follows:

The character of the omnibus drivers has become so brutal and dangerous in the highest degree. They race up and down Broadway and through Chatham Street with the utmost fury. Broadway, especially, between the Park and Wall Street, is almost daily the scene of some outrage in which the lives of citizens riding in light vehicles are put in imminent hazard. Not content with running down everything that comes in their way, they turn out of their course to break down other carriages. Yesterday a gentleman driving down Broadway, and keeping near the west side, was run down by an omnibus going up, the street being perfectly clear at the time, the omnibus leaving full twice its width of empty space on the right of its track. At the same spot a hackney-coach was crushing between two of them the day before. . . . A ferocious spirit appears to have taken possession of the drivers, which defies law and delights in destruction. It is indispensable that a decisive police should be held on these men or the consequences of their conduct will result in acts which will shock the whole city.

Such carping did little to curtail growth of the public transportation services, and soon other cities took note of the New York system. Abraham Brower and others emerged with omnibuses in Philadelphia (1831), Boston (1835), and Baltimore (1844). But New York City, the pioneer, put more omnibuses on the streets than any North American city. Broadway, at one point, saw an average of one horse-drawn omnibus passing City Hall every fifteen seconds.

In London, such outrageous congestion inspired construction of the world's first subway; but not so in New York City. That there was need for a subway was clear, asserted the newspapers. On October 2, 1862, the New York *Herald* observed: "Modern martyrdom may be succinctly defined as riding in a New York omnibus."

"The answer to New York's traffic problems," said transit promoter Hugh B. Willson, "is a subway line under Manhattan."

Willson put up $5,000,000 and launched the Metropolitan Railway Company.

"Our subway," said Willson's chief engineer, A. P. Robinson, "will signal the end of mud and dust, of delays due to snow and ice. The end of the hazardous walk into the middle of the street to board the car, the end of waiting for lazy or obstinate truckmen. Everything will be out of sight, out of hearing. Nothing will indicate the thoroughfare below."

But Willson's subway never got off the drawing board or under the ground, mostly because of William Marcy "Boss" Tweed, the notorious emperor of New York's Tammany Hall, which controlled Democratic politics (and just about everything else) in Manhattan. Since Tweed was working hand-in-glove-in-wallet with the omnibus interests, a subway could only hurt his bankroll. And since the Willson plan required state legislative approval, Tweed coerced the Democratic politicians in Albany to reject the underground railway.

While New York subway promoters became enmeshed in Boss Tweed's machinations, Londoners loved their underground enough to encourage expansion of the Metropolitan, and more routes were added in the Sixties. Word of the British advances inspired a New York inventor, Alfred Ely Beach, to revive the idea of a line under Manhattan's teeming Broadway. Renowned as the creator of the world's first practical typewriter, Beach had also invented the cable railway, the pneumatic tube, and a piece of hardware that would prove essential for his subway project: a hydraulic tunneling bore.

Much as he admired the London subway, Beach was repelled by the unaesthetic vision of smoke-filled tunnels, a corollary of any steam-operated subway line. Beach chose pneumatic power as his means of propulsion and, following several experiments, was convinced that his pneumatic subway would be practical as a means of transportation and salable to the public. However, like the Willson project, the Beach subway would not be salable to Boss Tweed.

No matter. Beach believed in the theory of the fait accompli. Instead of seeking Tweed's approval, Beach would surreptitiously build his subway at night only, complete the project before Tweed's henchmen discovered what had happened, and then open the pneumatic railroad to a cheering public. The scheme was filled with improbabilities: How, for example, would Beach find a place from where to dig his bizarre subway without escaping public—let alone Boss Tweed's—detection?

A man ingenious enough to invent the typewriter surely could find a solution; and he did. He rented the basement of a clothing store at Broadway and Murray Street, carted his hydraulic tunneling shield to the site—at night, of course—and launched the subway project in the cellar of the Devlin clothing shop, which, fortunately, had never been patronized by William Marcy Tweed.

Each night Beach, his son, Fred, and their corps of construction workers hacked away at Broadway's subterranean sand, piling the debris in a corner of the clothing store basement. The project, costing Beach $350,000 of his own funds, proceeded with significant but surmountable obstacles until completion in 1870. Considering the near-impossible working conditions, the results of Beach's labors were, to be modest, remarkable. When the dust had cleared, his station could boast a waiting room 120 feet long, sprinkled with such Victorian niceties as a fountain (which worked), a grand piano, a goldfish tank, and innumerable paintings. Although Beach's experimental tunnel measured only 312 feet under Broadway, he was determined that the line be so totally appealing that rejection by the public—and Tweed—would be next to impossible. Thus, he installed zircon lamps for illumination and adorned the lone subway car with fittings to make contemporary transportation pale by comparison.

Neither Boss Tweed nor any other New Yorker, except for Beach's highly secure work force, was aware that New York City's first, experimental subway was about to make its world premiere. But on February 26, 1870, a select group of newspapermen and public officials were invited to Devlin's Clothing Store, where they were presented with not a suit of clothes but a subway running from Warren Street to Murray Street and back.

Not only was Beach's pneumatic subway beautiful in all its underground trappings, it worked and won instant raves. "Fashionable Reception Held in the

Bowels of the Earth!" proclaimed a headline in the New York *Herald*. The New York *Sun* observer was equally impressed. "The waiting room," noted the *Sun*, "is a large and elegantly furnished apartment, cheerful and attractive throughout."

Galvanized by the response, Beach promised to extend his subway northward under Manhattan for five miles until it reached Central Park. Upon learning of the Beach plan, Tweed vowed that the subway would not even reach a block beyond Murray Street. As usual, Tweed prevailed. His clout in the state legislature was enough to halt approval of the Beach subway. And even after Tweed was indicted for corruption, Beach, already dazed by his political opposition, faced new foes among engineers who asserted that his hydraulic shield was filled with flaws.

In 1873, when London transit barons were sketching still another expansion of the world's first subway, Beach permanently threw in the towel. His experimental line would remain virtually intact (though sealed at both ends) until workers accidentally bored through the side of the Beach tunnel in 1912. Surprised by their find and amazed at its mint condition, the construction men (who were building the city's new official Broadway subway) eventually came upon Beach's twenty-two-seat subway car, also intact.

For the nineteenth century, at least, New York City would not enjoy the benefits of underground rapid transit, as was London, followed by Glasgow (1886), Budapest (1896), and Boston (1897). By the 1850s more than 500,000 people filled New York City from the Battery to the city line near what is now Times Square. These people had to be moved, and they were—slowly, but expeditiously, on rails.

The birth of the horsecar in 1831 opened a completely new frontier for urban transportation and would forever change the face of the largest American metropolis as well as the complexion of every city in the world.

2

Horsecars–Prelude to the Trolleys

At their very smoothest, the streets of New York City in 1831 provided a less-than-comfortable ride in the omnibuses built by Manhattan carriage maker John Stephenson. Cobblestoned streets around City Hall and such centers as the Bowery and Wall Street guaranteed a bone-rattling ride and a relatively short life for the vehicle involved, although the Irish-born Stephenson did put out a quality coach. But how could one improve on the means of transport?

The answer had been supplied in 1826 when America's first railroad, the Granite Railway in Boston, began plying a short nonpassenger route on rails with a single horse doing the hauling. If nothing else, the Granite Railway demonstrated the value of placing a horse-drawn vehicle on rails. As the Boston *Daily Advertiser* noted: ". . . the horse moved at ease in a fast walk. It may, therefore, be easily conceived how greatly transportation of heavy loads is facilitated by means of this road."

If the hauling of granite could be facilitated, why not do the same for passengers? Railroads pulled by primitive steam engines already were the talk of New York, thanks to the recent performance of the Mohawk and Hudson Railroad's new locomotive DeWitt Clinton between Albany and Schenectady. Though the passengers were frightened out of their wits, the engine hauled three carloads of them without permanent damage.

Surely the same principles could be applied on the streets of New York, thought one of Manhattan's most eminent citizens, John Mason. President of the Chemical Bank of New York City and a wealthy merchant to boot, Mason was convinced that coaches mounted on wheels rolling along rails embedded in the streets, and *not* omnibuses, would come closer to providing the kind of ride New Yorkers needed and deserved. Mason founded the New York and Harlem Railroad and on April 25, 1831, became its president. Tracks were laid along the Bowery (now part of the city's Lower East Side) from Prince Street to 14th Street. For rolling stock, Mason turned to coach builder John Stephenson and ordered a pair of cars, fitted with cast-iron wheels and magnificently decorated, to be drawn by horses.

The far-thinking Mason expected that his streetcar line would ultimately become a traditional railroad, linking New York City with the state capital at Albany, but, for the moment at least, his line first had to prove itself on the demanding streets of Manhattan. As expected, Stephenson turned out a pair of appealing vehicles. After examining them, a critic noted: "They resemble an omnibus, or rather several omnibuses attached to each other, padded with fine cloth and with handsome glass windows, each capable of containing outside and inside fully forty passengers."

Mason's horsecar line made its first official run on a nippy afternoon, November 14, 1832, before a crowd of sixty well-chosen guests who turned out in top hats and satin dresses. Mayor Walter Bowne was surrounded by members of the City Council, not to mention a horde of journalists. The gentleman from the *Morning Courier and New York Enquirer* was among them and reported:

Officials of the New York & Harlem Railroad, with Mayor Walter Bowne and others of distinction, left the city hall in carriages to the depot near Union Square where two splendid cars, each with two horses, were in waiting. The company was soon seated and the horses trotted off in handsome style, with great ease, at the rate of about 12 miles, followed by a number of private barouches and horsemen. Groups of spectators greeted the passengers of the cars with shouts and every window in the Bowery was filled.

A stagecoach driver of considerable experience, one Lank Odell, piloted the first horsecar, while the second of Mason's two-car fleet was driven by a Manhattan hackman who had been especially recruited for the car line's debut. Amid appropriate fuss and fanfare, the cars took off while bigwigs and spectators cheered. Mason's sidekick, John Lozier, then thought it was a worthwhile moment to demonstrate how much "safer" the horsecars were than traditional omnibuses and hacks. In his excellent volume *Fares, Please!*, John Anderson Miller described the episode that followed:

The plan was for him [Lozier] to stand at the corner of Bond Street and give the drivers a signal, at which they would bring their cars to a quick stop. With the cars approaching at a fast trot Lozier raised his arm and gave the signal. The veteran Lank Odell, driving the first car, performed admirably and brought his vehicle to a quick halt, but the local hackman driving the second car forgot to apply the brake and tried to stop by simply pulling on the reins and shouting "Whoa!" The horses did their best to arrest the progress of the rapidly moving vehicle, but its momentum was too great for them to accomplish it without the mechanical aid of the brake, and the tongue crashed into the rear of the leading car in the first street-railway accident on record.

Fortunately for Mason, Lozier, and the New York and Harlem Railroad, nobody was hurt and the ceremonies continued without further incident. Politically, the horsecar's debut was a triumph simply because Mayor Bowne was tickled with Mason's idea. "This event," said Bowne, "will go down in the history of our country as the greatest achievement of man."

A reporter watching the proceedings was less ebullient but more accurate when he declared: "The completion of the road will make Harlem a suburb of New York!"

And so it did.

Once drivers learned how to master the horsecar's brakes, it was clear rolling for the New York and Harlem. Patrons flocked to the horsecars, providing Mason with the inspiration to continue building the line in the direction of Harlem. He commissioned Stephenson to build three new cars, the Mentor, the For-

Get-Me-Not, and the President, and arranged a fifteen-minute headway for his vehicles.

Inexplicably, the horsecar idea failed to catch on in North America at first, except in New Orleans, where two lines opened in 1835. It wasn't until the early 1850s that a streetcar boom began, starting with the Brooklyn City Railroad (1853), followed by the Cambridge Railroad (1856), Philadelphia (1858), and Baltimore, Pittsburgh, Cincinnati, and Chicago, each of which had horsecar lines operating in 1859.

A battle which presaged the conflict between taxis and trolleys soon erupted between the horsecar interests and hack drivers and omnibus operators, the latter of whom strenuously objected to the havoc streetcar tracks played on their nonrail vehicles. In Philadelphia, for example, the city's *Sunday Dispatch* wrote scathingly about the impending death and destruction that horsecars would inflict on the City of Brotherly Love.

"It is perhaps scarcely worthwhile to allude to the fact that in New York City they kill one person each week on city railroads and mangle three or four on an average in the same space of time," commented the *Sunday Dispatch*. "Human life is really of little value nowadays."

One especially vehement horsecar foe went as far as the courts, attempting to obtain an injunction against the vehicles on the grounds that they constituted a public nuisance. The judge was sympathetic—to a point. His reply to the bid for an injunction asserted that while a horsecar line "may occasion loss or inconvenience, and may depreciate the value of property and render its enjoyment incommodious and almost impossible, yet this is a *damnum absque injuria*," which told the complainant that he was suffering "damage without injury." So sorry, but the injunction was refused.

Opponents of the horsecars were less discreet north of the border. When the Montreal City Passenger Railway opened in 1861 it was almost run off its tracks by furious foes. "Cab drivers and carters hooted and yelled at the street railwaymen," noted William D. Middleton in *The Time of the Trolley*, "stoned the cars, and placed obstacles on the tracks. Stern measures were taken to repress such ruffianism."

Luckily, the streetcar interests were supported by the august Montreal *Gazette*. After one antihorsecar episode, the *Gazette* made it clear that punishment would fit crimes against public transportation. "As a warning to those who have by placing [sic] obstructions in the track and otherwise interfered with the running of the cars, we have to state that Hermidas Racette was yesterday committed to gaol by Mr. Coursol on a charge of felony, the prisoner having placed a stone upon the track upon the approach of the cars."

As more lines opened—by the 1860s horsecars were operating in London and Paris—refinements appeared on the rolling stock. New York City proved the pacesetter, and in 1871 the Pullman Palace Car Company turned out a richly upholstered drawing-room car for the Third Avenue Railroad, which seemed more appropriate for royalty than commuters. In Winnipeg, Canada, Albert Austin backed the Winnipeg Street Railway by supplying it not only with open cars and closed cars for its debut in 1881, but also with four sleigh horsecars to accommodate the city's inordinately harsh winters. Horsecars there showed a small but consistent profit. In New York profits were bigger. While Winnipeg just managed to stay in the black, the lines of Manhattan recorded more than 188,000,000 passengers between 1855 and 1885.

Apart from the convenience the horsecar provided, riders found a number of faults with it—from its inadequate ventilation to smoky oil lamps. The bobtail-style car required that passengers enter from the rear but make their way to the front to deposit their fare. This caused considerable inconvenience when the cars were crowded. In 1884 this nuisance was eliminated with the invention of the automatic fare collector: an inclined, hemispherical metal strip that conveyed the coins from the rear platform to the driver at the front of the car. Variations on the conduit system of moving coins to the pilot were tried on lines in other cities.

The most trying times for horsecar riders occurred in winter. In Chicago, for example, the only "heat" provided was hay or straw thrown upon the floor, into which the passengers buried their benumbed feet in the hope of finding some comfort and protection from the biting cold. "The main problem," said a historian for the J. C. Brill horsecar manufacturing company of Philadelphia, "was to make the car tight so as to keep out the cold." A similar problem existed in Winnipeg, Montreal, Toronto, Boston, and New York, among other blustery winter cities.

What there were of mechanical trappings were primitive in the extreme. Chicago's horsecars had no headlights and the only identification for night operation was a colored "bull's-eye," placed in front of the coal oil lamps. New Jersey's horsecar system, which paralleled the Hudson River Palisades, was confronted with another problem—height. It was particularly difficult to link the horsecar route between the extensive section in the north, lying along the Hudson, and the desirable section walled off from it by the ramparts of the Palisades and the foothills into which the Palisades merge. It was only after monumental engineering feats that the Jersey City Heights were made accessible to New York. At first it required as many as four horses to drag the cars up the Heights. A major breakthrough occurred in 1874 when the North Hudson County Railway, then operating all roads out of Hoboken, constructed a steam-operated elevator which carried car, horses, and passenger load to the top of the cliffs in just one minute.

Actually, horsecars presented as many problems for pedestrians as they did for passengers. In 1865, *Frank Leslie's Illustrated Newspaper* carried a drawing of a Manhattan horsecar spilling pedestrians left and right. Similar pictures of newsboys, mothers, children, and gentlemen being bowled over by the vehicles were common in publications of the late 1800s.

The care and feeding of the horses remained a prime concern for operators, not to mention the question of whether horses or mules made more economical employees. A survey by the *Street Railway Journal* suggested that a pair of mules could be fed as cheaply as one horse. What's more, two mules could do one-third more work than a single horse. The mule could handle the cold as well as the horse and stand the heat better. "One drawback," noted John Anderson Miller, "was that a mule had practically no resale value when he got too old to pull a car, whereas a horse could be sold for about three-fourths of the original cost."

Horses cost about $125 apiece and averaged three to five years of service. The vehicle itself cost approximately $750. Since several shifts of horses were required for each car, nearly 40 percent of a horsecar line's operating costs were devoted to dobbin. Occasionally, a horse of a different color would emerge, proving that dobbin is virtually indestructible. Just such an animal made its appearance on the Chicago City Railway in 1863. The horse was called "Old Crooked Tail," and it plied the streets of the Windy City for twenty-one years and five months, working seven days a week and *never missing a day*. It was estimated that Old Crooked Tail clip-clopped some 120,540 miles while making 17,090 round trips for the Chicago City Railway. Obviously Old Crooked Tail was more than fortunate. Other horses were burdened with too heavy loads and, sometimes, disease.

Many operators debated ways to make life more livable for the horses. Subjects such as the proper horseshoes resulted in lengthy discussion. The American Street Railway Association once suggested that horseshoes weren't necessary. "When the horse was created," asserted a member of the Association, "didn't he work without shoes?"

The logic failed to impress Brooklyn City Railroad official W. H. Hazzard, who snapped back: "So did man, when he was created without shoes, but could you pull a car barefooted on cobblestones?"

To ease dobbin's burden several inventors applied themselves to the problem of getting the car, so to speak, to help the horse. William D. Middleton mentioned one such device in *The Time of the Trolley*—a "car starter" developed by A. R. Witmer of Safe Harbor, Pennsylvania, in 1886. "It consisted of springs coiled about the car axles and a clutch arrangement whereby the springs were wound up by the momentum of the car in stopping. The spring tension was used to help start the car."

The most intense concern over the horses' health focused on the fear of disease. Early in the 1870s epizootic aphtha, a horse disease, reached epidemic proportions. This "Great Epizootic" infected stables in Montreal and Toronto in 1872 and swept through cities in the eastern United States, decimating the stables of streetcar companies as thousands of horses perished. Boston lines were completely without horses. Service continued, however, thanks to the cooperation of drivers and riders, who combined to pull the cars by hand.

Devastating as the Great Epizootic was to the horsecar industry up and down the Atlantic seaboard, it could not stem what had become a boom business tide for the horsecar barons. When the American Street Railway Association held its first convention in the late 1880s, more than 100,000 horses and mules were then pulling 18,000 streetcars on 3,000 miles of track throughout the United States.

Encouraging as they were, the figures failed to deceive horsecar operators, especially those in hilly cities such as San Francisco and Seattle. Plying a steep grade was hell on the horses and convinced the operators that it was necessary to switch from animal to mechanical motive power. Several steam locomotive experiments failed, as did such esoteric ideas as naphtha-powered streetcars, a low-pressure compressed-air tram car used in London, and a gas motor car, which failed to persuade streetcar operators in Brooklyn or Elizabeth, New Jersey.

But the search for an alternate power source continued and eventually dobbin would lose out to a piece of cable and an engine powered by steam.

3

Cables and Steam

It had become clear that steam was an effective means of motive power long before Andrew S. Hallidie had left his native London to establish a business base in San Francisco. Steam locomotives had become as much a part of Americana as the covered wagon. Their application to street transport was simple enough: attach a tiny steam locomotive to a pair of horseless horsecars and have it operate along the regular horsecar route. In some cities the appearance of a small but raucous locomotive running along a regular urban thoroughfare had devastating effects (on the eyes and ears of humans and horses alike). A partial solution was devised in San Francisco, where steam dummy locomotives—looking conspicuously unlike engines—had a more calming effect on dobbin. Where other metropolises merely experimented with the steam dummies, San Francisco built an impressive fleet of locomotives, including one line that plied Market Street, the city's main drag.

But smoke, soot, and substantial economic problems militated against widespread use of the steam dummies. San Francisco's steam dummy locomotive on Market Street was forced to give way to a horsecar less than a decade after the steam engine was put to use on the thoroughfare. However, Hallidie remained persuaded that steam could be effective if it could be melded with another hauling product: wire rope. (He just happened to be the owner of that product, since his father had been its inventor.) The wire rope, or cable, had already been applied successfully to such uses as pulling elevators or carrying goods on lifts that hauled metal off the Sierra–Nevada range. Barge canals and coal mine cars were also pulled by cable. Hallidie figured the steam engine with a steel cable could haul streetcars around San Francisco.

The plan was to install a huge stationary steam engine and connect it with an endless wire rope which would slide over rollers in an underground trench. A special grip attached to the underside of the car would enable it to snare the moving cable and move at speeds determined by the operator or, in this case, the "gripman."

It is a tribute to Hallidie's tenacity and persuasiveness that he was able to persuade the city fathers of San Francisco to sanction the experiment. They did, and on August 1, 1873, the cable car made its world premiere on the Clay Street hill. The experiment was a success.

Hallidie never dreamed on that misty day in San Francisco that his invention would take off like a Fourth of July rocket. But it did, capturing the imagina-

17

tion of the man in the street as well as the men in the boardrooms. San Francisco built more lines, followed by Chicago (1882), Philadelphia (1883), and New York City (1883), where a cable car line plied the then-new Brooklyn Bridge. And after a year of operation the Brooklyn Bridge cable line had successfully carried more than 9,000,000 passengers.

Cable railways were spreading across the continent, from Washington, D.C., to Denver; and for good reason, because they not only worked but boosted real estate values as well. H. H. Windsor, secretary of the Chicago City Railway, enthused over the advantage of

its immediate and lasting effect upon the value of real estate. Within six months after the conversion of this company's lines from horse to cable power, property along those lines rose in value from 30 to 100 per cent, and on adjoining and contiguous streets in amounts proportionate to its distance from the cable lines. So well established is this fact, that the mere announcement that this company was considering the construction of a cable line on any street in the city, would be sufficient to put values up at once. One of Chicago's earliest, most successful and best-known financiers said, "Only let me know six weeks in advance where the City Railway intend building a cable line, and I will make an independent fortune every time." The enhanced value of property in the South Division of Chicago due wholly to the construction and operation of cable lines will not fall short of $15,000,000.

That was the good news. The bad news was that the cable operation could be complicated in the extreme and, when it came to operating the cars, a matter of extreme muscular endeavor. Gripping the car was not a job for the frail or inattentive. It required power and vigilance—and a little bit of luck when a loose cable strand wrapped around the grip and dislodged the grip from the release.

The excitement of riding the cable cars varied from city to city. In Seattle, for example, trestles were so long and high that even if they had been solidly built (which they weren't) a ride would have tested the courage of the bravest. Seattle's wooden Jackson Street Trestle, built in 1888, reached a height of 140 feet above ground. Its gradient was 15 percent and it required 330,000 board feet of lumber before completion. Just one block to the north loomed the Yesler Way Trestle, spanning a gorge just east of the cable railway's power station. The rickety, hastily built trestle measured 500 feet long and soared 200 feet above ground at its highest point. Built in two sections, the span was divided by a steep hill. The second section took the cars down a 15 percent grade to the power house and, finally, to the eastern terminus at the lake shore.

For the first two years luck was with the cable car company, but on August 17, 1890, a gust of wind struck an inbound car near the top of the grade. According to the Seattle *Telegraph*, the spidery structure began swaying violently, spreading the track and putting the car on the wooden ties. Passengers panicked and leaped from the moving vehicle, only the railing on either side preventing them from plummeting to the gorge below. The gripman stuck valiantly to his post, with the car careening wildly down to the lake front where it was finally stopped by ties hurriedly thrown across the tracks.

Seattle's cable cars were the first in the Northwest and, as Leslie Blanchard, Seattle street railway historian, noted, a source of civic pride and a novelty. They baffled many of the rough-hewn lumberjacks, threshermen, and other migratory laborers who visited Seattle in their off-seasons. One such hick from the Washington boondocks was stunned when he saw the Seattle cable cars for the first time. Seattleite Floyd A. Fassler described the scene in the Seattle *Star*.

"This hick," wrote Fassler, "his first morning in town after a very, very rocky night, stood on the corner of Second Avenue and Yesler Way, near the Guy Drug Store corner. As he stood, weaving uncertainly, a grimy paw occasionally rubbing an aching head, a bright red cable car came up Yesler and passed him. He gazed after it until it disappeared over Yesler Hill.

"In ten minutes, another came by on the single-track, one-way route. Then a third and a fourth. The tenth car was passing when a friend appeared.

" 'How,' asked the friend, 'do you like our new cable cars?'

" 'Wunnaful . . . Simply wunnaful . . . An' I think ya have a wunnaful company. Been standing here for two hoursh and seen ten bran' new carsh go by. None of 'em ever come back. Mush sen' a new car ev'y trip.' "

More inebriates gaped at cable cars in Washington, D.C., when the Grand Army of the Republic held its 1892 convention in the nation's capital. One day during the convention the Washington and Georgetown (cable) Railroad carried 170,000 riders, four times the line's daily average. Other cities, such as New York, found the cable car equally effective in other ways. On October 1, 1895, the Third Avenue (Manhattan) Railway inaugurated cable car mail service for the Post Office Department. Ten special mail cars began groaning and wobbling up and down the streets of New York, eventually delivering their cargo to a special siding at the main post office.

Kansas City favored the cable cars for other reasons. One local newspaper observed in the 1880s: "The value of their [cable cars'] services in the development, expansion and upbuilding of the city is universally recognized. They attract the admiring attention of visitors and sojourners. They are the pride of the citizens."

Nevertheless, the cable car industry was already being threatened with extinction at a time of its most vigorous growth. There were two distinct problems: the cable cars' inherent shortcomings both mechanically and economically, combined with the emergence of electricity as a motive power for streetcars.

In the case of the Washington, D.C., cable car operation, it died when a huge fire wiped out the company's chief power station in 1897, burning down the general offices, repair shops, and power plant. In order to maintain service without the power, horses were rented and began pulling the cars as they had in yesteryear. It was, of course, a stopgap measure, but the board members had sufficient time to realize that they should switch from cable operation to electricity. Other cities with cable cars either had suspended operation just before the turn of the twentieth century or were about to do so in favor of electric trolleys. "By 1902," observed John Anderson Miller, "the mileage of the cable railways in the country had dropped to half of what it was in 1890. Chicago, which once boasted the second (to San Francisco) largest cable car network in North America, threw in the towel in 1906."

While other cities gave up on the cable cars, San Francisco and Seattle remained true to the bouncy, jouncy little vehicles. Despite benign neglect on the part of the Seattle Transit System, the city's three cable car lines continued operating on a regular basis through the 1930s. *Finis* was written for cable car operation in the Northwest in 1940. On August 10 of that year gasoline-powered buses replaced the famous grip cars that had plied the hilly Yesler Way route for fifty-two years.

That left San Francisco as the last remaining cable car municipality in North America. For a time it appeared that the California city would take its cue from Seattle. As the 1940s, 1950s, and 1960s passed, San Franciscans were reminded time and again that their cable cars could bankrupt the city. By 1976 the financially troubled Muni Railway, as the public transportation system there is called, spent $5,100,000 a year on its thirty-nine cable cars. All of the antique cars were handmade and require meticulous care from five full-time mechanics, who make as well as install all the replacement parts needed. The anti-cable car bloc also claim that they are more accident-prone than traditional forms of transit. But try as they may, cable car foes have been unable to force San Francisco to abandon these vehicles.

The clanging, rumbling, careening vehicles were declared a national landmark, and the San Francisco City Charter now provides that cable car service cannot be halted unless the step is approved in a city referendum. "The cable cars were here when this town was really magic," said Herb Caen, columnist of the San Francisco *Chronicle*, "and we look at them now with adoring eyes. They can do no wrong. They're like old people tottering around on the hills costing us a fortune, but without them we'd be lost."

To which Curtis Green, manager of the city's transportation system, added in 1976: "No expense for cable cars is too extraordinary."

Ironically, the very popularity of San Francisco's cable cars has been their biggest problem. Wear and tear increased as the number of passengers climbed to 12 million a year in 1978. Cables, which once were replaced yearly, now have to be changed every sixty to a hundred days. And the cost of cable has doubled since 1974. But Muni officials accept these economic facts of life, shrug their shoulders, and rationalize. "San Francisco is a great tourist center," said one Muni official, "and the number one attraction we have is the cable car. You can bet your bottom dollar that they bring in more than their weight in gold and tourist revenue. The future of the cable car is as sure as the future of San Francisco!"

This love affair with the cable cars is emphasized by the willingness of visitors to ride the extraordinarily frightening Powell & Hyde car, which mounts and descends the steep Hyde Street hill, overlooking San Francisco Bay. In the autumn of 1964 a cable car climbing the hill broke loose from its connection and rolled backward down the hill out of control. Only a last-second use of the slot brake prevented a major disaster.

Several years later brakes failed on another car, which began a perilous, brakeless rush down the hill. The driver had no way of knowing whether the cable car would smash at the bottom of the hill or jump the tracks and cables.

Instead of shrieking in panic, the passengers yelled happily. "They reacted," said a *New York Times* reporter, "as if it were a carnival ride."

Somehow, the cable car managed to negotiate the hill, holding the tracks without mishap. When the car finally came to a safe stop, the riders pleaded with the driver: "Do it again! Do it again!"

4

Of Trolleys and Trolley Dodgers

It had become apparent in the second half of the nineteenth century that neither horsecars, omnibuses (pulled by horses), nor cable cars could provide a panacea for public transportation problems in burgeoning cities such as New York, Baltimore, and Richmond. The Great Epizootic of 1872 signaled the death knell for horsecars, although some lines continued operating well into the twentieth century. Surprisingly, the Bleecker Street horsecar line in Manhattan remained in revenue service until July 26, 1917.

Even before the Great Epizootic, numerous attempts had been made to produce a more economical and efficient means of moving the vehicles than horses or cables. Assorted experiments had been conducted in Vermont, New Hampshire, and Edinburgh, Scotland, to move cars by means of electrical energy derived from batteries. While success was evident, it also was too modest to be significant.

One of the most exciting battery experiments was conducted at Bladensburg, Maryland, near Washington, in 1851 by Professor Charles G. Page of the U.S. Patent Office. Using track of the Baltimore and Ohio Railroad, Page's battery-run car achieved a hitherto unthinkable speed of 19 miles per hour, considerably better than the speed of horsecars or even the primitive steam locomotives. Professor Page's triumph was the forerunner of still more experiments through the 1860s. It was only a matter of time before some ingenious creator produced a thoroughly practical electric railway.

In his book on public transit, *Fares, Please!,* John Anderson Miller wrote that American inventor Thomas Edison at first was involved with the idea of electrifying steam railways but then turned his attention to electric lighting.

By this time [wrote Miller], it was clear that electricity could be harnessed successfully as a motive-power for railway cars. What practical use to make of such an arrangement was another question. The longest distance over which electrical current could be transmitted was not yet very great, and it seemed likely that the largest field of usefulness of the electric railway would be in city transportation where no part of the line would be more than a few miles away from the power-generating station.

Of all the problems faced by the early electric-railway builders the most troublesome was that of conveying electric current from the dynamo in the powerhouse to the motors of cars moving along the track. The easiest solution of this problem was the use of an electrified third-rail from which the cars could obtain power through a sliding contact of some sort. That was all right where the track was on private right-of-way, but it was no good in city streets where a charged third-rail might electrocute men and animals.

A major breakthrough occurred in 1884 when Edward M. Bentley and Walter H. Knight inserted a third rail in an underground conduit to power the East Cleveland Street Railway, the first commercial electric railway in America. The Cleveland *Herald* commented favorably about the attempt. "It was amusing to watch the passengers who boarded the car," said the *Herald*. "Some took the invention as a matter of course, while others, especially the ladies, evinced great curiosity. An unexpected drawback is the fact that half the horses that pass the car are frightened by it. There is nothing unusual in the appearance of the car. But even old plugs were frightened; and one passenger opined that the horses, jealous of loss of business, had combined to express their disapproval of the invention."

Despite the good notices, the Cleveland underground conduit line closed down after a year of operation. High costs were cited for its demise, coupled with mechanical problems. Cleveland's bitter winters presented a problem as snow and ice seeped through the open conduit, causing short circuits. Trolley historian Michael R. Farrell, author of *Who Made All Our Streetcars Go?*, noted that the Cleveland transit arrangement, while interesting, left much to be desired. "Neither this [Cleveland] nor any other early line," said Farrell, "can be classed [prior to 1888] as successful."

Following the East Cleveland Street Railway experiment, attention among transit planners moved east to Baltimore, where a milestone in surface transportation was achieved by Professor Leo Daft in cooperation with the Hampden Line of the Baltimore Union Passenger Railway. Otherwise known as the Baltimore and Hampden, the horsecar line had begun operation in 1876 on a route running from Charles Street and Huntingdon Avenue in Baltimore to Roland and 36th Street in Hampden. It was an ordinary horsecar operation except for some difficult grades that necessitated use of mules rather than horses to pull the cars. T. C. Robbins, general manager of the Baltimore and Hampden, became aware of Professor Daft's genius when the inventor was exhibiting an experimental electric railway at Coney Island in Brooklyn.

Daft, who was the founder of the Daft Electric Company of Greenville, New Jersey, had become convinced that the electric motor could replace the horse in street railway operation and set about proving this to the rest of the world. First, he conducted tests at his factory and then launched his crusade in Saratoga, New York, in Boston, and ultimately, at the Iron Pier in Coney Island. Robbins liked what Daft had to exhibit and wondered whether the electric motor would enable his cars to climb the Hampden hills more easily. After considerable discussion, Daft agreed to visit Baltimore and evaluate the Baltimore and Hampden line. "He was not overly enthusiastic with what he found," wrote Farrell. "Still, no other company had shown any interest in this equipment, so he agreed to tackle it."

Daft's decision would, in time, result in the operation of the first successful commercial electric railway in the United States. The Baltimore and Hampden commissioned Daft to make the electrical installation. However, the streetcar company's directors were more dubious than their general manager, Robbins, and inserted a clause in the contract asserting that Daft would not be paid until the line had been in operation for a year. Convinced that he could make it work, Daft agreed to the demand.

The professor's okay didn't seem to be enough for the directors. "The management," wrote Farrell, "had second thoughts about the experiment. Some of the directors sought other advice."

At the time there was, in fact, so much skepticism about the ability of electricity to handle such a Herculean task that the management had no trouble obtaining criticism of Daft's plan. "The man who undertakes to operate this section by electricity," said one expert, "in the present state of the art is either a knave or a fool!"

More criticism of Daft's plan poured in until the Baltimore and Hampden's directors notified the professor and general manager Robbins that the deal was off. With that, Robbins courageously shot back that if the contract was broken he (Robbins) would quit. The general manager was so emphatic—and persuasive—in his stand that the directors backed off and agreed to allow Daft to proceed with his work. A pair of dynamos was installed at the car barn located at Oak Street and Huntingdon Avenue (now Howard and 25th), and by June 1885 daily tests were being performed on the electric line. Writing in *Who Made All Our Streetcars Go?*, Farrell explained the nature of America's first electric railway, developed by Professor Daft:

Ordinary passenger cars were pulled by separate motor cars, which were simply dummy cabs equipped with series motors grouped by commuted fields. They were given names, the first being Morse, and succeeding ones, Faraday and T. C. Robbins and Keck. Power was supplied by an Atlas engine connected to two Daft dynamos which were in series and supplied 250 volts.

What fascinated electric railway officials was the manner in which Daft would feed the voltage to the streetcars. Would it be a conduit system like the one used in Cleveland, or would the professor opt for another technique? Daft decided that the most practical method would be to feed the voltage into a third rail, located in the center of the tracks and supported by insulators.

Having a bare third rail sitting between the tracks inspired considerable fear among the local populace, and justifiably. Livestock that made contact with the live rail would instantly become late livestock! Several humans received shocks when accidentally touching the rail, though, according to Farrell, no fatalities were recorded. To protect livestock and humans, the Baltimore and Hampden installed wooden protective coverings in certain dangerous areas, and these apparently worked.

So did the line. It began regular revenue service in mid-August 1885 and, within a year, was averaging 29,000 passengers per month. "This," said Farrell, "was not bad for what was strictly a suburban line."

That it was successful could be attested to by the company's decision to buy the motors and electrical equipment from Daft and place an order for two new dynamos. Directors of the Baltimore and Hampden went so far as to suggest that the line, rather than continue with the surface-level third rail, employ an overhead wire, using equipment made by Professor Daft's company. After due consideration, the company decided to leave well enough alone and continue using the ground-level third rail. In so doing the Baltimore and Hampden officials inadvertently lionized Frank Sprague, a man who already was fast becoming a hero of the surface transit industry.

Born in Connecticut and a graduate of Annapolis, Sprague did more to popularize the electric trolley car than any other score of men involved in the transportation business, here or abroad. "Measured against today's space-age standards," said transit analyst Brian J. Cudahy, "Sprague's work may seem crude and unimpressive; but the technical and engineering difficulties he faced were genuine and real in the 1880s. His success in overcoming them should not be discounted." Sprague's success actually was rooted in his stewardship as a U.S. Navy officer, which had taken him to London. While there he rode the poorly ventilated underground, which then was employing only smoke-billowing steam locomotives. Sprague was appalled to learn that a passenger had died hours after having taken a ride on the underground. A coroner's jury declared that his death, while due to natural causes, had been "accelerated by the suffocating atmosphere of the railway."

After completing a year's tour of duty with the navy, Sprague got himself a job with Thomas Edison, then struck out on his own, organizing the Sprague Electric Railway & Motor Company. Sprague was the right man with the right goods at the right time. Shortly after opening for business, he was notified that the Union Passenger Railway was building a line in Richmond, Virginia, and that it was contemplating use of electricity. Sprague leaped at the opportunity to get a foot in the door and worked out a deal to outfit the Richmond line with a power plant, a complete system of current supply, and forty cars, each equipped with two motors. Sprague was given a warning—Richmond had hills that would test both his ingenuity and the quality of his apparatus and could conceivably ruin it in no time at all. After checking out the Franklin Street incline, Sprague realized that the warning was understated. He feared that the electric motors would burn out on the precipitous Franklin Street hill. His first inclination was to drop the idea and employ a more traditional, if less powerful, use of motive power. But his aides urged him to give it a try and he went along with their suggestion.

Sprague decided that he himself would pilot the experimental streetcar. Its initial moves were satisfactory, but when Sprague drove the car to the foot of the Franklin Street incline, he peered at the hill ahead and turned to an aide. "It doesn't look good to me," he said.

The retired naval officer realized however that he had no choice and pulled on the controller. The steel wheels spun against the rails; the motor groaned and, sure enough, the vehicle began to negotiate the hill. Slowly but relentlessly, it reached the brow of the incline and turned the corner into City Hall Square, where it was greeted by a horde of theatergoers departing from a play. Never having seen such a vehicle as Sprague's, they circled it with a mixture of astonishment and curiosity. Sprague could have done without this; he could smell the odor of an overheated motor and realized there was a short circuit. While the onlookers gaped, Sprague turned to his assistant and snapped: "I think there is some trouble with the circuits and I'd like you to get the instruments so we can make a check."

Nodding with understanding, the aide turned and walked away, ostensibly in search of the missing instruments. At that point, Sprague flicked off the lights and reclined on one of the streetcar's seats while the unexpected audience drifted home. Shortly thereafter, Sprague's assistant returned with several thousand pounds' worth of repair equipment disguised as a team of mules to haul the rundown streetcar to its shed.

The episode reeked with symbolism because, time and again in the next few months, Sprague and his streetcars would be bedeviled with problems. Tenaciously Sprague and his assistants attacked each dilemma—especially the knotty problem of burned-out motors—until the line finally opened for regular service in February 1888. It was less than a smooth operation. Track work was shabby. Child vandals frequently placed obstructions on the rails. And motors continued to lack efficiency and consistency. But, more often than not, the streetcar worked.

According to John Anderson Miller, a black man, watching the trolley climb Franklin Street, commented: "Fo' Gawd, what am de whitie folks a-gwine do nex'? Fust dey freed de darkey, an' now dey freed de mule!" One writer alluded to the trolleys' performance as Sprague's "incredible adventure in Richmond." Whatever it was labeled, the electric trolley attracted the attention of streetcar barons up and down the East Coast. One of them was Henry M. Whitney, president of the West End Street Railway Company of Boston, which then boasted the world's largest horsecar operation, with eight thousand horses in its stables. Whitney had decided that the horses had to go; his question was whether to replace them with cable cars or some other form of surface transportation. Sprague's electric trolleys, of course, now became a distinct possibility. Whitney visited Richmond and inspected the new trolley lines with his general manager, Daniel F. Longstreet, who openly favored cable cars rather than electric trolleys.

Sprague wasn't concerned about persuading Whitney, but he knew he needed a show stopper to win Longstreet to his side. The inventor invited the two Bostonians out to Church Hill late one night when most citizens were asleep. There, Whitney and Longstreet were confronted with the sight of no fewer than twenty-two trolleys lined up at the base of the hill. At Sprague's command, the motormen pulled on their controllers and, one by one, the cars started up

Church Hill. Each and every one of the trolleys made it to the top, and Whitney and Longstreet returned to Massachusetts, convinced. "No sooner were Sprague's electric cars running in Richmond," observed historian Ruth Cavin, "than orders began to pour in from all over the country."

Cavin, author of *Trolleys*, traces the term "trolley" to the Middle English "trollen"—to roll or ramble. Sprague connected his cars to the power supply with overhead wires and a pole on the car roof. "At the top of the pole," said Cavin, "was a small wheel that ran along the wire. This wheel was a descendant of a little four-wheeled wagon called a 'troller,' which connected an earlier car to the wires, [and] was named 'trolley.' "

In no time at all the word "trolley" would be on the lips of hundreds of thousands of Americans as city after city—Pittsburgh, St. Louis, Tacoma, Cleveland, St. Paul, and Minneapolis—chose to follow the Richmond route.

The results were invariably successful, especially in Boston, where Oliver Wendell Holmes took pen in hand and wrote a poem about the trolleys for the *Atlantic Monthly* called "The Broomstick Train or the Return of the Witches."

They came, of course, at their master's call,
The witches, the broomsticks, the cats, and all:
He led the hags to a railway train
The horses were trying to drag in vain.
"Now, then," says he, "you've had your fun,
And here are the cars you've got to run.
The driver may just unhitch his team,
We don't want horses, we don't want steam;
You may keep your old black cats to hug,
But the loaded train you've got to lug."

Since then on many a car you'll see
A broomstick plain as plain can be;
On every stick there's a witch astride—
The string you see to her leg is tied.
She will do a mischief if she can,

But the string is held by a careful man,
And whenever the evil-minded witch
Would cut some caper, he gives a twitch.
As for the hag, you can't see her,
But hark! You can hear her black cat's purr,
You may catch a gleam from her wicked eye.

Often you've looked on a rushing train,
But just what moved it was not so plain.
It couldn't be those wires above,
For they could neither pull nor shove;
Where was the motor that made it go?
You couldn't guess, *BUT NOW YOU KNOW!*

Poems were not the only testimonials to the trolleys. For Sprague, there could be no greater endorsement than the growing list of streetcar operators seeking his service. Within two years of the Richmond debut, more than 150 electric trolley systems were flourishing, and the demand was for electrically powered vehicles above the ground as well as on the surface. If streetcars could be moved by voltage, why not elevated lines such as those now powered by steam in New York City?

5

Looking up to the Els

During the 1860s, street traffic in Manhattan had become so congested that a New York *Herald* editorial of October 2, 1864, declared:

Something more than streetcars and omnibuses is needed to supply the popular demand for city conveyance. Modern martyrdom may be succinctly defined as riding in a New York omnibus. . . . It is in vain that those who are obliged to ride seek relief in a city railway car. . . . It must be evident to everybody that neither the cars nor the omnibuses supply accommodations enough for the public, and such accommodations as they do supply are not of the right sort.

Manhattan residents were becoming fed up not only with the inadequacy of the horse-drawn transportation system but also with the treatment they received at the hands of the surly drivers who ran down pedestrians in pursuit of more passengers, swore at their customers, and openly shortchanged them. City fathers knew that something had to be done to prevent the devastating social and economic effects that the overcrowding would ultimately produce. Already, businesses and residents had begun leaving Manhattan's crowded streets for Brooklyn and New Jersey.

Numerous solutions to the city's traffic problems, notably Hugh B. Willson's plan to build a subway under Broadway from the Battery to 34th Street, failed to gain the approval of the New York State legislature, largely through the machinations of Boss Tweed. Tweed, a member of the New York State Senate, commissioner of public works in Manhattan, and boss of the Tammany Hall Democratic gang, dominated the stagecoach and horsecar companies and, furthermore, had his own rapid transit proposal, the Viaduct Plan, a railroad that would run the length of Manhattan on an elevated masonry arch.

It is hard to imagine how inventor Charles T. Harvey's plan for an elevated cable car to be erected on Greenwich Street in downtown Manhattan escaped the watchful eyes of Tweed. Tweed may have been convinced that Harvey's scheme was just another foolish proposal, but in 1866, an amendment to the state's railway law allowed Harvey's West Side & Yonkers Patent Railway Company to begin construction on Greenwich Street. On October 10, 1867, the first column of the line was erected. By the end of the year, Harvey's successful trial of the first quarter-mile of the track proved that the el was here to stay.

Harvey knew that his elevated railroad would make money if it could be extended as far as 30th Street to connect with the Hudson River Railroad Terminal, especially since, by horsecar, a trip to the important depot could take as long as an hour. Although the West Side & Yonkers Patent Railway had official approval to continue expanding, it was threatened by severe financial difficulties in the Great Depression of 1869. Harvey's quest for backers was not entirely unsuccessful, so construction continued. By autumn of 1869, when the el was just a mile away from the railroad terminal, Harvey went broke.

The West Side & Yonkers Patent Railway did reach the Hudson River depot at 30th Street, but only after Harvey had relinquished control of his invention to a group of backers who offered a loan to complete construction. On February 14, 1870, with fares at ten cents, regular passenger service began, running from the lower Manhattan Dey Street station to a Ninth Avenue and 29th Street terminal. The company used drop-center "shad belly" cars, whose low center of gravity overcame passengers' fears of tipping over.

The first months of operation revealed that the el was mechanically deficient. Periodically, the cable would snap, and emergency crews, with the help of a team of horses, were forced to haul the stranded car and passengers to the end of the line. Service was then disrupted while the entire railway was shut down for repairs. However, to the chagrin of Boss Tweed, it seemed that the el would ultimately be a success.

In 1871, when Tweed obtained a charter for his Viaduct Plan, he began his campaign to close down the West Side & Yonkers Patent Railway permanently. A few years later, the New York *Herald* would report:

In the days of the Tweed Ring, the corruptionists went so far as to try to indict the Greenwich Street Elevated railroad as a nuisance: they boasted that they would not only tear down the road, but would fine and imprison the enterprising citizens who advanced money to try this important and now entirely successful experiment. Engineers and newspapers were hired to assert that the road would not stand; that it was dangerous to the lives of passengers; that it would cause constant runaways of horses; that it would destroy business; and attempts were even made at one time to incite mob violence against it.

Tweed, not satisfied with these behind-the-scenes tricks, sponsored a bill in the Senate that branded the el a public nuisance and authorized him (as commissioner of public works) to level it within ninety days. Tweed's henchmen pushed the bill through the New York State Senate. However, Harvey also had a friend in Albany, a friend who owed him a favor. Erastus Corning, a powerful figure in New York State politics, had, years earlier, been involved in a canal-building project which seemed doomed to financial ruin until Harvey came up with a device that allowed construction to be completed. Not afraid to stand up to the infamous Tweed, Corning, now seventy-eight years old, defended his friend's elevated railroad before the New York State Assembly, and the el was allowed to stay.

The political triumph of the West Side & Yonkers Patent Railway did nothing to ease the company's financial worries. In November 1870, the combination of cable failures and financial troubles forced the line to close down. The company was auctioned off for $960 to a group of bondholders. The new company abandoned the use of cable vaults. When the line reopened after the defeat of Tweed, steam locomotives were used to pull the original cable cars. To prevent them from frightening horses in the street below, the engines were disguised as passenger cars. The optimism produced by the success of this innovation was partially dispelled by new financial difficulties. In 1871, the company was again auctioned off to another group of bondholders for $5,000 and was reorganized as the New York Elevated Railroad Company.

Although Charles Harvey was no longer involved in the management of the company, he had the satisfaction of watching his el prosper. With the opening of the Little West 12th Street station, service was no longer limited to a single track. A passing track was installed, allowing trains to roll in both directions, an improvement over the original system with just one train running back and forth. Stations were opened at Morris and Franklin streets, with running time over the entire route averaging twenty-eight minutes.

During the 1870s, the el continued to grow. In January 1876, the el was an impressive five miles long and was averaging 5,600 fares daily. In 1878, the evident prosperity of the company, now averaging 8,500 passengers each day, inspired a competitor, Dr. Rufus H. Gilbert, to begin work on a Sixth Avenue elevated line.

Gilbert, a former medical practitioner, had obtained a charter for his own brand of elevated as early as 1872. He planned to construct tubular iron roadways suspended above the streets from Gothic arches. The financial panic of 1873 forced Gilbert to suspend the execution of his system until 1878, when he and his associates reorganized as the Metropolitan Elevated Railway Company. The Sixth Avenue el was not constructed according to Gilbert's original plan, however, but was steam-powered and followed traditional design.

Property owners were not so enthusiastic about the els as the crowds of passengers, who were especially anxious to ride the trains between 5:30 and 7:30 A.M. and 5:00 and 7:00 P.M., when fares were lowered to five cents. Each time a new line was proposed, a clamor arose, denouncing the el as a nuisance and a menace. The opposition claimed that horses would be frightened, pedestrians would be burned by falling ash, and fires would be started by sparks from locomotives. Despite these objections, the Manhattan el flourished during the 1880s, and other cities started to build their own elevated structures.

The development of elevated railroads in rural Kings County, better known today as Brooklyn, differed from that on neighboring Manhattan Island. The lure of Coney Island's clams, beer, and beaches created a demand for a rapid transit system to connect the populous northern section of Brooklyn with the beaches on the southern tip. In 1867, the Brooklyn, Bath & Coney Island Railroad, Brooklyn's first major steam line, reached Tivoli's Hotel in Coney Island. Known as Dummy Road because of the steam dummies used to supply power, the line connected with the Brooklyn horsecars and with the ferry boats to Manhattan.

Two more steam lines were constructed to transport passengers from Brooklyn to resort hotels in Coney Island. Andrew Culver established the Prospect Park and Coney Island Railroad (steam), which provided a twenty-minute journey from a northern depot at Prospect Park, at 20th Street and Ninth Avenue, to Cable's Hotel in the West Brighton section of Coney Island. In 1878, the Brooklyn, Flatbush & Coney Island Railroad opened, following a route from Atlantic Avenue, where it connected with the Long Island Rail Road, to Coney Island's Hotel Brighton. Both lines enjoyed such a brisk summer trade that soon another railroad was constructed to connect the communities of Brooklyn with the Atlantic. By 1879, the New York and Sea Beach Railroad was carrying pleasure seekers from 65th Street in Bay Ridge to the Sea Beach Palace Hotel in Coney Island.

By 1880, the seemingly endless demand for fresh-dug clams, beer, and salt breezes led to the construction of Brooklyn's first elevated line. Although the line was more a long trestle than an authentic elevated railway, it was built above the street on wooden columns with iron bridges at road crossings. Erected within view of the Atlantic, the Coney Island Elevated Railway was a mile long, connecting the Hotel Brighton with a terminus near the Culver Depot in Coney Island. Passenger cars, pulled by a steam engine, ran only during the tourist season.

On September 24, 1883, four months after the opening of John Roebling's Brooklyn Bridge, rapid transit came to Brooklyn, as cable-powered cars began shuttling over the bridge from Park Row in Manhattan to Sands Street in Brooklyn. Business on the railway was lively (during the first year of operation, it carried more than 9,000,000 passengers) and soon would prove even more so as plans were made for the erection of Brooklyn's first conventional el.

The Brooklyn Elevated Railroad Company, accompanied by the cheers of spectators, commenced operation at 2:00 P.M. on May 13, 1885. The train ran east from a terminal at Washington and York streets, then south on Hudson Avenue, east on Park Avenue, south on Grand Avenue, then, finally, south on Lexington Avenue to a depot at Broadway and Gates Avenue.

From the late 1870s to the early 1900s, it seemed as if the elevated lines of Brooklyn and Manhattan would never stop expanding. By 1888, three els had been erected in Brooklyn and, within six years, two more lines were running eastward and southward to the city's limits. The Brooklyn elevated network covered a distance of 157 miles by 1910, carrying 170,752,487 passengers in 928 cars. And, by 1917, Manhattan's Third Avenue el reached 177th Street in the Bronx, with an express track that served southbound traffic in the morning hours, northbound traffic in the evening.

The early elevated railroad owners had discovered that steam locomotion was neither economical nor completely safe. The original steam dummies did not provide sufficient motive power, and pedestrians complained strenuously about the hot coals and sparks that showered from the trains. Pennsylvanian Matthias N. Forney, a locomotive designer, devised a small double-end tank engine that could haul up to six or seven cars while maintaining a 12-mph schedule, including stops. Manhattan's elevated lines quickly adopted the Forney because of its superior hauling and tracking capacities and reduced maintenance costs. By the early 1890s, more than 500 Forneys were in service, as Brooklyn and Chicago followed Manhattan's lead.

The search for a better form of locomotive power did not end with the Forneys. In 1881, the experimental Hardie air locomotive, looking much like the steam locomotive of the day, was tested on New York's Third Avenue Elevated. The air locomotive was equipped with four large air reservoirs, which were charged to a pressure of 600 pounds per square inch. As the train started its run, air was released through an expansion valve and passed through a boiler, driving the locomotive by means of reciprocating machinery. However, this and similar devices never progressed beyond the experimental stage.

Interest in electric power began to develop during the 1880s. Although several experiments using electric traction were carried out on Manhattan's elevated lines, the first el to operate with electric power was Chicago's Metropolitan West Side Elevated Railway, which opened on May 17, 1895. With power supplied by a third rail system, this method was certainly superior to steam locomotion. However, the locomotive-powered train system with its restricted train size and schedule speeds was still in use. The development of the multiple-unit system by Frank J. Sprague, hero of Richmond's electric trolley car, would soon overcome the limitations of the locomotive.

Although Sprague, along with Leo Daft and Stephen D. Field, had experimented with electric power on the New York Elevated during the mid-1880s, he had abandoned those efforts to work on the development of an electric elevator. In 1893–94, Sprague installed an elevator system in New York's Postal Telegraph Building. A single control switch regulated the movement of any elevator, and the movement of all of them in unison. Sprague was inspired. Applying his control concept to the problem of train operation, Sprague realized that a train could be made up of a number of cars, each provided with its own motor and main control, but all controllers capable of being operated from a master switch on any car. This theory would allow a train of any length to perform as a single car.

After the Manhattan Railway rejected Sprague's offer to install his system on their elevated line at his own expense, the multiple-unit concept was put into practice when Sprague won a contract to design 120 cars for the South Side Elevated Railroad in Chicago. The installation process was beset by difficulties, some of them arising from the rigid terms of the contract, which required Sprague to provide six test cars within two months. On July 26, 1897, the successful operation of the six-car train by Sprague's ten-year-old son convinced South Side officials that Sprague's theory was sound, and the remainder of the contract was put into execution. The experiment was threatened, on the following April 20, by a short circuit of the control line, which put seventeen of the twenty cars, one of them in flames, out of operation. Sprague circumvented this problem by connecting the contacts of the cars with a power line that made power available to all as long as one car was in contact with the third rail. In the spring of 1898, all 120 cars were running, and steam operation was abandoned by the South Side Elevated Line. The use of electricity to power the rapid transit line was so successful that the railway's stock trebled in value.

The multiple-unit system was quickly adopted by other Chicago elevated lines. In 1898, the Brooklyn els followed suit and discontinued use of steam operation in favor of electric power. Boston's first authentic rapid transit operation commenced in 1901, when the Boston Elevated Railway introduced a combined subway-elevated system following Sprague's design. Manhattan was the last to install the multiple-unit control concept, but, by 1903, all the New York City elevated lines were converted to electric power.

Although the Chicago Loop, erected in 1897, remains, public opposition to elevated railways forced the removal of many New York and Boston lines. When public opinion finally became reconciled to the notion of an underground railway, subways rapidly usurped the dominant position of the elevated lines, which, until the construction of America's first subway on Tremont Street in Boston in 1897, provided Americans with their only means of rapid transportation.

6

Origins of the Subway

Traffic and congestion become problems when villages grow into towns and then cities, paths into lanes and then thoroughfares. The great cities of all advanced civilizations have had to deal with the same "urban" headache—traffic jams. The Romans were master roadbuilders who overcame the problems of access with permanent stone highways. But that represented only part of the problem. Narrow roads, no matter how well constructed, provided limited space for a swelling tide of people and their vehicles.

During the Renaissance, the rapidly growing port of Milan decided, as part of a massive reconstruction effort, to alleviate the chaos on its hopelessly choked roadways. Milan was fortunate that it was no less a personage than Leonardo Da Vinci who thought up the most "modern" solution. Da Vinci proposed underground thoroughfares for commercial traffic, out of sight of the streets, where strollers and light traffic could travel easily. The Milanese rejected the idea, and for three hundred years surface traffic continued to congest every growing city, a problem that seems synonymous with urban life.

Da Vinci would have finally been impressed had he been in London during the winter of 1863. On the tenth day of January of that year the world's first subway, an underground steam train, puffed its way along three and three-quarter miles of track on the Metropolitan Line before curious throngs. By the end of that summer more than one and a half million passengers had traveled on the subterranean rails.

The London subway ran only a few feet below ground (not unlike Da Vinci's double-deck sunken roadway), with riders occasionally gasping from the steam, cinders, and smoke produced by a coal-fired locomotive. The sudden discharge of smoke from the street-level "blow holes"—when the locomotive passed below—frightened horses and pedestrians alike. Despite these bugs, ridership increased and, almost immediately, new lines were proposed. The underground subway had been born and would soon, literally, begin digging its way into the heart of nearly every major urban center of the world.

From the start, development of subways depended in equal part on the twin pillars of human social progress, technology and chutzpah. The first steam railroads began doing business in England earlier, in 1825. Steam and railroad technology were part of the necessary ingredients for the first subway, and almost immediately plans were put forward for underground lines. There were at least two proposals put before Parliament in the 1830s to locate terminals inside busy London with the trains underground. These proposals all failed; but they did give the subway its second necessary ingredient by stirring the fancy of an ambitious man, Charles Pearson, who would become a tenacious subway promoter.

Pearson, abetted by architect John Hargrave Stevens, was to persist for twenty-five years. His rewards would be approval for his "Metropolitan Railway": Paddington and Great Western Railway, the General Post Office, the London & North Western Railway, and the Great Northern Railway.

At first, these two promoters had considered pneumatic, or "atmospheric," propulsion for the system, certainly a clean form of transit. With a famous experimental disaster in 1848 known as the Atmospheric Caper, these plans were dashed. Pearson and Stevens returned to conventional and reliable steam power, already running England's burgeoning railroads.

By this time, many of Britain's intercity train lines were knocking at London's doors, clamoring for terminals and more connecting routes to expand services. Many new promoters joined Pearson and, with the increased salesmanship, a measure finally passed Parliament in 1854. More time was needed to overcome financial and other hurdles, with the drama drawing to a climax at ground breaking in 1860.

But in heavily built-up areas, such as central London, the subways would require a different method from the Metropolitan Line's cut-and-cover construction if they were to deviate from established road patterns or to cross undeveloped areas. The tube—deeply sunk tunnels—was the next method developed by London's expanding underground network. These deeply bored routes left the surface unmolested; and they were to become the standard mode of construction in London, especially when it came time to traverse the Thames.

As early as 1798 a proposal had been drawn up for tunneling under the Thames. In 1802, a second scheme was passed, and Cornish miners built a narrow shaft, completing 1,000 feet of its proposed 1,200-foot length before the Thames crashed in and destroyed the works. Another advance came in 1818 with engineer Marc Brunel's tunneling shield, a contraption for inching the way underground through London's clay and rock. A deep tunnel was finally completed in 1841 by Brunel's son, and although this shaft was never more than a pedestrian walkway because of financial failures, it signaled the start of other ventures that would ultimately succeed.

The first of these was Peter Barlow's tiny and short-lived subway, which carried only about a dozen passengers, in 1870. It ran successfully for a few months before folding because of persistent mechanical problems and financial collapse. Twenty years later a more enduring success came with the opening of a line on November 4, 1890—London's first modern tube.

This new line incorporated another major technological advance which was to become a fixture in nearly every subsequent subway system: electric traction. Only eleven years earlier, in 1879, the first electric railway had been exhibited in Berlin. This idea for a clean and quieter system was quickly seized upon by the English subway barons and developed over the years.

London's subways having shown the way, the rest of the world was clearly not going to pass up an obvious winner. Scotland's booming industrial capital, Glasgow, opened its first underground link in 1886. By 1900 Budapest, Boston, and Paris had joined the growing subway elite. In 1927 Tokyo opened Asia's first underground transit system, with South America's premier subway coming a year later in Buenos Aires. Australia was operating its tubes in 1932 and the pioneering Moscow underground began business with a majestically artistic and technologically advanced setup in 1935. One of the most complex and interesting developments was New York City's subway, the first link opening in 1904. From modest beginnings, New York's has grown into one of the largest, most heavily traveled, most reliable, and noisiest systems to be found anywhere.

New York's underground debut had to wait for both the appropriate technology, and ardent promoters to fight for it. It was evident as early as 1862 that the city's hopelessly snarled traffic had to find some form of relief.

But with the failures of Hugh B. Willson and Alfred Ely Beach, New York had to continue to rely on its extensive network of unsightly elevated railroads while the rest of the world's great metropolises turned to subways. Then the unanticipated and explosive growth of Manhattan during the waves of immigration near the turn of the twentieth century intensified the issue.

The advantages of the subway could not be ignored forever, and after another daring attempt and failure—a futuristic train much like the modern monorail—multimillionaire August Belmont broke ground in 1900 for what would be New York's IRT. Belmont planned the project on a grand scale with thirteen miles of underground and a few more of elevated extensions. After a late start, New York would not be long in catching up to London, Glasgow, Budapest, and Boston.

There were construction mishaps, and shopkeepers suffered while the streets were temporarily dug up by the cut-and-cover technique then employed. There were numerous geological formations that had to be tackled one by one. The tracks did advance slowly and before the close of 1903 about 90 percent of the work had been completed. The achievement was monumental: 10,000 workers had excavated 3,508,000 cubic yards of earth. On opening day, October 27, 1904, one could ride the brand-new trains for a nickel. That first evening 150,000 people alone paid their five cents to have a try.

The IRT continually expanded its rails like tentacles across the boroughs of the newly created composite that was the City of New York. The first major new line to enter the scene was the Brooklyn Rapid Transit, or BRT line. Opened in 1915, this was from the start a flashy and sleek operation, pioneering in the area of rolling stock. With names like Bluebird, Green Hornet, and Zephyr, the BRT (later BMT) cars covered the tracks from Coney Island to the southern end of Manhattan at Chambers Street, adjacent to City Hall. Like London's subways, the IRT and the BMT both had to bore under rivers, and employed every advance in electric train technology.

New York's third major line, the IND, broke ground in 1925. This was to be a showcase, built with the most modern equipment and emphasizing safety as well as beauty.

When the IND premiered in 1932, its engineering statistics, as well as costs, were staggering—22 million cubic yards of earth excavated, 1 million cubic yards of concrete poured, 150,000 tons of steel erected. Indeed, subway technology had progressed by light-years from the days when five miners struggled a few feet at a time under the Thames River in the nineteenth century.

From their modest origins, subterranean railways have assumed a significant role in the fabric of every city. Like other forms of contemporary mass transit, subways developed partly out of necessity, but the manner in which they have grown and the turns they have taken have been a product of political and economic judgments, sometimes whims. As we shall see, these political and monetary factors and clashes determined their future, and will continue to do so.

7

Ominous Omnibus

It would be decades after the first successful streetcar lines began operating along the East Coast before traction barons realized that they would be getting a run for their passengers' money from a noisy, smelly, uncomfortable means of transportation called the omnibus. Offspring of the automobile, the original buses were merely glorified autos—taxis, if you will—but they did present enough of a challenge to tram interests as early as 1900 to warrant comparison. One such auto stage line in Cleveland drew the following comment from the *Street Railway Journal:* "It is not thought, however, that automobiles can ever practically compete with electric cars in Cleveland." Not for a while anyway, but as the automobile became a sturdier, more powerful product, its possibilities as a money-making passenger carrier increased. The first battleground was Los Angeles, where the five-cent-fare auto (alias the jitney) achieved craze proportions just as World War I broke out. The vehicular battle was won by the trolleys—though not without considerable wounds—but jitneys continued to make inroads into the traction passenger business across the country.

What irked the lords of the streetcar industry as much as the pesky nature of the jitneys was the fact that they operated completely without municipal regulation. If ever there was an example of rugged individualism at work, the jitneys provided it; hustling each other for passengers, flitting like waterbugs in and out of traffic and off their chosen routes if necessary, and then speeding back to the heavily traveled (trolley) routes for more business.

The jitney had obvious advantages over the rail-bound trolley. Rubber-tired and flexible, it could deliver passengers considerably closer to their homes, if not right up to the doorstep. Americans had also become infatuated with the automobile. As one observer put it: "Everyone wanted to have a car in his garage. If he couldn't fulfill that part of 'The American Dream' the next best thing was riding the jitney." Except that the jitney, like so many crazes, soon spent itself, partly because of its space limitations and partly because the operators discovered that it was difficult to make a profit. What the industry needed was a vehicle similar in relative size to the streetcar but rubber-tired and with a large power plant. Frank and William Fageol, brothers who had dabbled in the auto-bus transportation business, decided in 1920 to replace jitneys with a genuine, up-from-the-ground, gasoline-powered omnibus. When the Fageols finished work at their Oakland, California, workshop, the face of American surface transit had reached a significant turning point.

39

Frank and William dubbed their creation "the Fageol Safety Coach." It had better springs than the earlier buses, which used truck chassis, and was designed so that the superstructure was close to the ground with a low center of gravity. This allowed passengers to alight and depart considerably more quickly than they could from the earlier prototype buses.

Fageol's Safety Coach won immediate acceptance wherever it was tried and, with additional revenue to invest, the brothers set about the business of further improving the omnibus design. Dabbling on the blueprint board, they decided to tuck the proboscis-looking engine snout out of view, placing it inside the body rather than under the hood, as was the tradition with automobiles and trucks of the era. Once again, the Fageols were pacemakers for the industry.

There were, of course, others to jump on the bus bandwagon as well as people who had been in the coachmaking business for years who tried their hands at omnibus building. The St. Louis Car Company, for one, which had gained nationwide acclaim for the excellence of its electric traction vehicles, had entered the bus derby as early as 1913, building a pair of vehicles for the New York Motor Bus Company. One of its earliest products was an unusual double-deck motor coach with an open top and a combination open and closed lower deck, developed in 1914 for the Pacific Motor Coach Company in California.

Although Fageol had proven that the hidden engine design was practical, it did not receive widespread acceptance. St. Louis Car Company, for one, continued with the traditional hooded engine in front. Its 1924 model, built for the Houston Electric Company (now, there's an irony), had a hand-cranked engine, similar to the cranked motors used on passenger cars.

The speed with which auto manufacturers leaped into the bus business signaled the trolley lords that they were in for a long war to the death. The only solution to the conflict appeared to be compromise; that is, the traction companies were urged to get into the bus business and supplement (or replace) tram operations wherever possible. The *Electric Railway Journal* got to the nub of the problem when it editorialized: "The question now is will the railways grasp the opportunity while it exists? Neither coordination nor monopoly is likely as a natural course unless the development of the bus is guided in that direction. This 'guiding' means that the railways should inaugurate the use of buses themselves where there is a field for them. This will avoid the development of a competitive situation, costly to all, and will satisfy the desires of the public."

Grasping the relevance of the message, traction companies plunged into the omnibus business and by 1929 some 390 trolley firms were handling more than 13,000 buses.

Nowhere was the gasoline-powered product in a qualitative league with the formidable trolleys turned out by the likes of J. G. Brill, St. Louis Car Company, and other tram builders. Not only did the buses produce a noxious odor and a bumpy ride but they were considerably less durable than the cheapest tram. During the late twenties it was estimated that the average life of a bus was five years, whereas trolleys were good for a minimum life of twenty years or more. This led to the development of the gas-electric bus, in which a gasoline engine was directly linked to an electric generator. In turn, the generator produced electric current for electric motors that drove the rear wheels. When the gas-electric concept proved practical it eliminated the need for the gear shift, a major source of wear and tear on the monsters. This was followed by the diesel-electric, which scored its first major success in 1937 with the massive Public Service of New Jersey operation.

Fageol was still at the forefront of transit design in the thirties. In 1938 the brothers introduced an articulated "long" bus by joining two standard bus bodies together with a flexible coupling. The result was a single-deck bus with the capacity of a double-decker. The articulated vehicle could accommodate fifty-eight passengers, a record for a non-double-decker.

Strangely, the Fageol articulated bus remained more a curiosity than a standard means of transportation. Few made their way from factory to boulevard, although the idea would be resurrected in Europe following World War II and again in the United States late in the 1970s. The basic competition for the trolley was the ominous single-level omnibus, which, despite its flaws, proved a lethal competitor. Whether the decision to change from electric traction to gasoline-power bus was logical or not, the fact remained that by 1937 approximately 30,000 buses were moving more than three billion passengers a year. The jitney had come of age!

II

THE GOLDEN AGE

WORLD WAR I TO
WORLD WAR II

8

The Golden Age of Trolleys

When Andrew Hallidie introduced the cable car to the dales and hills of San Francisco there were those who believed that the pollution caused by the four-legged tuggers of horsecars was permanently erased from the streets of North America. As it happened, Hallidie's invention was good, but not good enough. Alec Dubro, the author, noted that cable cars "required too large an initial investment and were too finicky for widespread use." So, horsecars continued to ply and deface the communities they serviced until Frank Sprague's electric streetcar proved a success in Richmond, Virginia.

Not long after the Richmond experiment won acclaim, the rush to install electric trams was on. At the turn of the century, the rage became a mania, and by 1917 there were 80,000 trolleys running on 45,000 miles of track in nearly every city and town. Traction expert William D. Middleton described it as "the time of the trolley" and wrote a book with the same name about the subject.

"There was a time in America," wrote Middleton, "when if you went anywhere you took a trolley, for trolleys went everywhere. . . . Clanging, swaying, grinding along, the streetcar created the modern city; rolled two generations of Americans to work, to the suburbs, to the ball park, out to the laughter and bright lights of the Ferris wheels and roller coasters; and carried up to 11 billion persons a year."

The growth of streetcar lines was closely followed by a growth in the trolleys. While the first trolleys closely resembled horsecars in design, utilizing a single truck and four wheels, the golden age of streetcars featured a car with the body supported on two independent four-wheel trucks, pivoted near the ends of the car. A pioneer in streetcar art was the J. G. Brill firm of Philadelphia as well as the St. Louis Car Company. These and other outfits built a brilliant assortment of vehicles which if new today would be a marked improvement in every aspect—from speed to aerodynamics—on the rubber-tired vehicles polluting urban America.

Undoubtedly the burgeoning of trolley empires would have been impossible without the consolidation of many previously independent lines. Typical was the spread of electric traction companies in New Jersey. At the turn of the century the North Jersey Street Railway Company embraced a vast system covering almost the entire upper tier of the state. By 1905 the North Jersey and eleven trolley companies had been swallowed whole by the Public Service Corporation, which operated more than 650 miles of track and represented 108 different street and electric railway properties in almost every part of New Jersey.

Similar marriages of little with big lines were evident throughout the country. In Massachusetts the Bay State Street Railway operated more than 3,000 cars and 500 miles of track, serving all of the eastern portion of the state except Boston. Having done basic training as boss of the New York, New Haven, and Hartford Railroad, Charles S. Mellen put together a trolley system in Connecticut that boasted more than 800 miles of track and 1,800 cars touching almost every important base in the Nutmeg State.

Sometimes [wrote John Anderson Miller in *Fares, Please!*] these street-railway mergers produced companies of considerable financial strength. At other times the larger company was as shaky as the various small ones had been. In any event the mergers added greatly to the attractiveness of the service, as free transfers were given from one line to another and a person could often ride all over the city for a single fare. They also permitted some economics in operation. This was particularly true with respect to power. One large generating station could furnish electric power for a number of street-railway lines at a cheaper rate than several smaller stations could do it. Everything considered, however, the mergers probably did more for the public than for the owners of the properties.

What the owners needed more than anything was some convenient formula for keeping costs from climbing faster than profits, especially after the outbreak of World War I, when the tab for labor and equipment began an upward spiral.

One of several "solutions" was in improved rolling stock. Prior to World War I most streetcars were manned by two employees—the motorman and the conductor, the latter of whom collected the fares. Trolley barons made economies by doing away with the conductor. An engineer, Charles Birney, produced the panacea for this in 1916 when he designed a dumpy—some called it cute—little trolley much like the old horsecar. Instead of the then traditional two-truck trolley, the Birney car featured a single truck with fewer seats but more safety devices; so a motorman could orchestrate the entire operation without help from a conductor.

The idea was that with more service, more passengers would ride the new Birneys. The theory behind the Birney car was persuasive, and soon J. G. Brill and other companies began producing them at a terrific clip. Within fifteen years, more than 6,000 of the Toonerville-looking cars rolled onto the rails and, in many cases, they fulfilled their early notices. The Birneys were inexpensive to operate and because the companies ran them more frequently, the public rode them more. But the Birney bubble soon burst, the car being a victim of its own virtues. "They were somewhat dumpy in appearance," said John Anderson Miller, "and rather prone to gallop. The public soon began to make fun of their looks and gait."

Because it was a one- and not a two-truck trolley, the Birney was victim of more than the usual number of derailments and its pair of 25-horsepower motors gave it the image of a groaning local in contrast to the speedier, more heavily powered two-truck trolleys. Eventually, the brainstorm bulb flashed and a

Birney Safety Car with two trucks and added horsepower was designed in the twenties. Not surprisingly, it also proved a hit, especially since it retained the assets of the original Birney while eliminating many of the liabilities, especially the poor riding qualities. A spate of the tiny Birneys continued to be built until they finally were phased out of production in 1930.

Almost simultaneously with the development of the first Birney car, the commissioner of the Cleveland street railways had designed a modern trolley of his own. The resultant product was so practical in its design and efficient in its operation that the name "Peter Witt car" is a byword in transit circles even today. Cleveland's Peter Witt sought to eliminate the front-of-the-car congestion that had plagued streetcar operators since the nineteenth century. His plan was simple enough: Allow passengers to enter the front doors without having to pay their fares as they pass the motorman. When the riders were ready to leave, they exited via center doors and there paid the conductor.

Expeditious as the plan was, the Peter Witt legacy is more in the car's design than in the clearing of the front portion of the trolley. The drop-center exit of the Witt design would become characteristic of all future Witt-style cars, many of which incorporated others of its features. It still was appealing to transit planners in the late 1970s. Proof of Peter Witt's genius was the car's quick popularity. The J. G. Brill Company, among others, was swamped with requests for them in the early twenties. Major municipalities such as Toronto and Brooklyn chose the Witt car over other designs, and soon it became one of the most ubiquitous sights on city streets.

The Brill Company was doing so well it could afford to publish its own journal (Brill Magazine), which took due note of the purchase in 1924 of one hundred Peter Witts by the Brooklyn City Railroad. "These new cars," the magazine commented, "have been placed in service on lines in Brooklyn serving the most thickly populated sections of the city and where the maximum amount of service is required."

When Toronto received its first Peter Witt car in 1921, the Toronto Transportation Commission was so proud of its new baby that the trolley was placed on the lawn of the Canadian National Exhibition. "Thousands of visitors," said one report, "viewed the all-steel car with great anticipation."

Torontonians had good reason to look forward to their Witts. The excellently designed and well-built car would remain a part of the city's scenery well into the late 1970s.

The basic design of the Peter Witt, though practical in most municipalities, was altered for specific localities. The Peter Witt cars used by the Toronto Transit Commission and the Cleveland Electric Railway, for example, were single-end cars. They carried one trolley pole—in the rear—and returned to service at the end of the line by means of a terminal circle that provided a U-turn and pointed the tram in the right direction. By contrast, Brooklyn's Peter Witts were double-enders, carrying a pair of trolley poles and controllers and brakes at each end. Thus, when a Brooklyn Peter Witt reached the end of the line—as it did at Ebbets Field on the Lorimer Street line—the motorman lowered the rear trolley pole, and engaged the one at the other end, and brought his equipment to the new "front" of the vehicle.

Overhead trolleys were no problem in Manhattan, where power was obtained from an opening in the center rails. The Third Avenue Railway built a number of handsome trolley-less streetcars, as did New York Railways, which, in 1913, introduced a double-decker streetcar known as the "Broadway Battleship."

In the twenties the Peter Witts began to face competition from a number of interesting "modern-design" trolleys. Two of the most productive car-building firms, J. G. Brill and the St. Louis Car Company, each developed an innovative machine. The St. Louis entry was a squarish, yet sleek, lightweight vehicle dubbed the Rail Sedan. Its up-to-date extras included cushioned wheels and a load-equalizing braking system. Cosmetically, the Rail Sedan incorporated an automobile-type spring bumper.

The J. G. Brill car was one of the most popular standardized trolleys of the late twenties. Like the Rail Sedan, Brill's Master Unit trolley was a lightweight car of advanced design and modern appearance. It proved a quick hit throughout the country.

A few cities even indulged themselves in the exotic and the preposterous. Detroit ordered a three-section, 140-seat car that more resembled a subway train than a surface trolley. Premiered in 1924, the Detroit behemoth-on-wheels required a crew of four to operate the four-truck, three-section articulated trolley, reputed to be the biggest tram in existence. The experimental trolley, built by the Cincinnati Car Company, was effective in transporting workers to and from the auto plants at rush hours, but the huge trolleys were starved for passengers during the lightly traveled hours.

Cleveland, which had introduced the Peter Witt car, unveiled a mammoth, two-car articulated entry in 1928. This one, manufactured at home in Cleveland by the G. C. Kuhlman Car Company, could accommodate 100 passengers spread through two 101-foot, 40-ton vehicles. One could tell that they were not quite as large as their Detroit counterparts since the Cleveland "articulateds" required three, not four, employees—one motorman and two conductors.

Throughout the twenties, car builders such as Kuhlman and Brill attempted to redesign trolleys to keep pace with the rubber-tired competition. But by 1923 passenger ridership on trolleys was beginning to decline. There were many reasons, not the least of which was the failure of municipalities to grant streetcars preference over private cars. By 1920 it should have been obvious to city planners that streetcars needed and deserved private rights-of-way in order to function properly. Only emergency automobiles should have been permitted on avenues plied by the trolleys. This, unfortunately, was not to be, and slowly the intrusion of autos on the trolley tracks hampered service and discouraged passengers. In addition, the gasoline bus and trackless trolley proved less expensive in the short run and more flexible than the streetcar in some cities, further curtailing the streetcar's business.

This should not have been enough to put the streetcar industry out of business. Trolley barons were aware of their problems and tried to rejuvenate their industry. By the end of the twenties it seemed they were well on their way to restoring streetcar operation. At the time, though, they could not have been aware of the extensive schemes against them that would boggle the mind when, decades later, they came to light in a Senate subcommittee room in Washington, D.C.

The trolley people actually leaned on the auto industry for some ideas. One was an experimental four-wheel "automotive-type" streetcar, produced by a bus manufacturer, the Twin Coach Company. In its advertisement, Twin Coach boasted: "Automotive Practice Arrives For Street Cars." The Twin Coach tram was built along the lines of the company's buses. The Twin Coach buses sold well, but the experimental trolley never went into revenue service. A year later Twin Coach returned with an elongated version of the same idea, this time with a pair of four-wheeled trucks. The sleek trolley was placed in revenue service in Brooklyn and lasted more than a year, but no one, not even the Brooklyn trolley operators, saw fit to order any more. Meanwhile, costs continued to rise and trolley revenues continued to fall.

Finally, in the autumn of 1929, a semiofficial SOS was sounded throughout the electric railway industry. Something other than experimental Twin Coach trolleys or overlong Detroit trams was needed to pump life back into the streetcar business.

It looked bleak. But at last the Advisory Council of the American Electric Railway Association was convened in Atlantic City. A braintrust composed of Dr. Thomas Conway, Jr., president of the Philadelphia and Western Railway, and Charles Gordon, managing director of the American Electric Railway Association began planning a super tram.

To this end they persuaded the trolley barons to unite under one flag in the crusade to produce the utopian streetcar. These formed the Electric Railway Presidents' Conference Committee, composed of the bosses of twenty-five trolley companies. Each of the participating firms, along with the manufacturers of cars and equipment, contributed to a "war chest." When the battle plan was finally okayed, Professor C. F. Hirshfeld, research chief of the Detroit Edison Company, was hired to orchestrate the campaign.

If ever a vehicle was thoroughly tested, top to bottom, side to side, before being placed on the market, it was the prototype spawned by the Electric Railway Presidents' Conference Committee. And ultimately the result would be known as the PCC car.

Seeking perfection, Professor Hirshfeld ordered his staff to determine the flaws in all contemporary rolling stock of the period. Brooklyn was chosen as the site of the tests. "Street-railways all over the country sent their cars to Brooklyn to be tested," recalled John Anderson Miller. "The volume and character of noise was measured on the street and inside the cars. Tests were made of the amplitude and frequency of vibrations, and their effect on the passenger."

The trolley barons had originally benefited from the plethora of manufacturers, with competition a stimulus for better design and quality. But by the late twenties the high cost of street railway cars was aggravated by the tendency of the master mechanics on each property to specify cars to suit their own particular ideas. Dr. Conway, one of the principal developers of the PCC car, pointed out that modern streetcars were essentially assembled vehicles and that a standardized car would have to be designed.

After a year and a half of intensive testing in their Ann Arbor, Michigan, experimental station, Professor Hirshfeld and his corps of consultants began to see the light. They understood that the perfect tram would be competing with automobiles not only for city space but also for city riders. So they used the automobile as a basis for comparison. One consideration was the auto's ability to start and stop considerably quicker than the trolley car. The Hirshfeld report showed that the speediest tram could roll only 76 feet in the first five seconds; this meant that the fastest auto left it 25 feet behind. Similarly, from a speed of 30 miles per hour the fastest-braking trolley car required some 144 feet to come to a complete stop, whereas the auto needed but 50 feet. "Worst of all," commented John Anderson Miller, "the cars' solid steel wheels conducted impacts, noises, and vibrations into the structures above, necessitating great sizes and weights in trucks and car bodies."

Hirshfeld's answer to the wheel dilemma was design of a resilient wheel with vulcanized "sandwiches" of rubber and steel forming a cushion between rim and hub. One by one, the other problems—acceleration, braking, lightening the truck—were examined and solved. Acceleration was handled by shifting from the standard, herky-jerk nine-step movement to a control with a sophisticated 61 to 260 steps, allowing a smooth, powerful, sweeping start. From a standing start, the PCC car reached a rate of acceleration of nearly 4 miles per hour per second and maintained that rate of acceleration until it reached a speed of about 12 miles per hour. (Even today's highly tested new light-rail vehicles are not capable of this initial acceleration. The PCC car's acceleration rate is better than the LRV 1978 cars until a speed of about 21 miles per hour is achieved.) Braking, achieved with the help of a new magnetic shoe that gripped the rails under each truck, was no less impressive than the PCC's acceleration.

After five years of work and more than a million dollars' worth of expenses, the PCC car rolled out of the test tube and onto the tracks of Brooklyn, where it was put to the test and further modified. The improved PCC streamliner featured a record low weight, a highly efficient engine, and superb braking. Interiors were designed with up-to-date lighting, soft leather seats, and semiprivate motorman's compartment.

The St. Louis Car Company built most of the first fleet of PCC cars. The first major order—101 of the streamliners—was delivered to the Brooklyn and Queens Transit Company in July 1935, and the PCC boom was on its way. "The PCC car," said Alan R. Lind in *From Horsecars to Streamliners*, "is one of the most notable achievements in the history of urban public transportation. In fact there can hardly be any development to compare with its scope or its total influence upon public transportation not only in the United States but around the world." Within five years of its debut on the streets of Brooklyn, more than 1,100 of the dazzling PCC cars had been purchased by transit companies in North America.

Unquestionably, the PCC car was a four-star hit. In some municipalities it brought about a 33 percent increase in ridership. "The Committee," observed John Anderson Miller, "had proved what it set out to prove—that a streetcar could be designed and built that would recapture public favor."

In time the PCC car would so thoroughly dominate the streetcar industry that it would be without competition, but in the thirties a significant few other models made short-lived appearances. Pullman-Standard sold an experimental streamliner, the Blue Goose, to the Chicago Surface Lines in 1934. It featured an aluminum body, cushioned wheels, and magnetic track brakes. The Blue Goose lasted for seven years before being removed from service. Another interesting model was a compact 12-ton, 39-seat streamliner designed and built in Detroit for its trolley lines in 1934. But it failed to draw the attention that J. G. Brill received for its entry in the sales derby, the Brilliner. More functional-looking than the PCC car, the Brilliner had a boxy appearance and arresting circular glass in its doors. It was heavier than the PCC and there were those who contended that it provided a better ride. Acceptance of the Brilliner car was not overwhelming. The Baltimore Transit Company purchased only one and then went back to PCC cars, which took Baltimore's public by storm.

For all its assets, the PCC car in some instances was too good for its own good. In Cleveland, for example, some motormen reportedly were fearful of allowing the PCCs to attain their maximum speed.

The original 1935 PCC model had not reached its full technological potential. One of the most dramatic improvements took place in 1946, when the air compressors and air brakes were replaced by all-electric operation. The air brake was dispensed with in favor of an electromagnetic braking system in which the drum brake was totally enclosed on the motor shaft. Other improvements were made in the smoothness of acceleration and the performance of the General Electric and Westinghouse motors.

Judging by the enthusiastic reviews, the increase in ridership, and the continued improvement in the product, the PCC car appeared to guarantee the survival—if not the thriving—of North American trolleys.

In many communities the PCCs were hailed like the arrival of a newborn monarch. Toronto trotted out its spanking new models to the 1938 Canadian National Exhibition, just seventeen years after it had given the same treatment to the then new Peter Witts. The "dawn of a new era" was the way one Toronto commentator described the arrival of the first streamliners in Canada. Brooklynites, by contrast, were handed multicolored brochures with the cover proclaiming: B.M.T. LINES PRESENT—MODERN STREET CARS. Inside, the booklet listed the many pluses represented by the PCCs. In a sense this was redundant since riders in Brooklyn, as elsewhere, had an excellent basis for comparison.

Compared with the venerable, whining-motored, slow-accelerating Peter Witt cars, the PCCs fairly whooshed along the rails. Their motor noise was virtually inaudible and the brakes—wonder of wonders—never screeched. Orders continued to pour in to the two licensed builders, St. Louis Car Company and Pullman-Standard, while J. G. Brill somehow missed the boat—or tram, as it was—in the PCC derby. The Brilliner, which was sold to the Atlantic City and Shore Railroad as well as the Baltimore Transit Company, failed to click. The Brill firm, which had accomplished so much for the traction industry for decades, never took up PCC production and made its exit from the trolley-development scene before World War II.

Some municipalities never did get around to ordering the PCCs. Albany, New York, for one, employed an antiquated fleet including a number of four-wheeled Birneys which plied North and South Pearl streets—the main drags in the New York State capital—for the United Traction Company. Surprisingly, San Francisco, which had a long and impressive history of supporting surface rail transportation, ignored the PCC car until June 1946, when it ordered ten streamliners. The second and last order for new San Francisco cars was placed in 1951. The twenty-five vehicles were delivered in 1952, marking the last PCC cars built by the St. Louis Car Company.

It is most significant that the PCCs were still in use on the tracks of San Francisco in 1979. Despite their age, the PCCs remain more attractive to the city's riders than the brand-new diesel buses which are also in operation. Alec Dubro, the author, polled passengers in San Francisco and then reported: "Funky as the PCCs are, every passenger I questioned preferred them to buses."

The commuters were asked why they preferred the trolley to the bus. "More space," was a typical reply. Also: "They ride better and faster." "They're smoother and faster." "There's a European charm about them." Or, as Dubro himself explained: "They are, in short, a nice compromise between the mechanistic efficiency of full rapid transit and the chaos of buses."

Nobody expected the PCC car to knock the automobile out of the box but the "Million Dollar Trolley," as it was known, provided more than faint hope for the future of electric surface traction. "It did mean," said John Anderson Miller in *Fares, Please!*, "that a type of car was available that could be used effectively where conditions favored the continued operation of electric railway service. The prevalence of these conditions varied, of course, in different localities."

The auto-oil-tire interests were actively—some charged—working against the PCC cars. But when World War II broke out, the trolleys not only had a chance for survival, they proved themselves supremely able to do the people-moving job throughout the four years of war. After the war it was all downhill for the streetcar industry for reasons cited elsewhere.

In some cases, such as the Washington, D.C., system, the motives behind the changeover from trolleys to buses were extremely suspect. The nation's capital offered one of the finest fleets of PCC cars on the continent when it was operated in the post–World War II years by the North American Company, owner of both Potomac Electric Power Company and Capital Transit. Unfortunately, the Public Utility Holding Company Act forced North American to divest itself of one or the other property. The Public Utility Act, generally, was a move by the

Securities Exchange Commission to have companies that were in the business of generating power to homes but also owned transit businesses divest themselves of one or the other. As a result Capital Transit was sold to a group of financiers headed by Louis Wolfson on September 12, 1949. Alan R. Lind observed:

In short order, the Wolfson group cut deeply into the wartime earnings by declaring large dividends. The group also cut back maintenance on the entire streetcar and bus fleet, and requested fare increases. This action, which many felt to be a reversion to a "public be damned" attitude, reversed the favorable position of the company with its regulators, and infuriated riders and Congress alike.

In addition Capital Transit refused to negotiate with its employees during a 1955 strike unless it received a guarantee of a fare increase from the regulators. On August 14, 1956, Congress revoked the franchise of Capital Transit. This was reasonable enough but what followed was not only curious but downright suspicious. Congress provided a new franchise that called for an all-bus transit system. The absurdity of this demand infuriated financier O. Roy Chalk, who took over the system on August 15, 1956. But he went about the business of saving the trolleys nevertheless. He beautified several trolleys, developed a sight-seeing tram with a female guide, and, with the help of an ardent pro-trolley bloc, hoped to beat the congressional bus edict. Logical as the electric traction campaign was, it could not bend an illogical Congress, which refused to allow the District of Columbia's trolleys to live. Lind made an extremely pertinent observation in this regard in his book *From Horsecars to Streamliners:*

At the same time that Washington was undergoing this forced conversion to bus operation, Congress was considering both the National Capital Transportation Act and the Transportation Act of 1958. Given the fact that regional and national urban mass transportation policy was being written by the same men who had so badly handled local transit in the nation's capital, it is easier to see why federal assistance to urban mass transportation has produced so little of value.

In 1962 trolley operation in Washington, D.C., ceased to exist. By any interpretation, this should not have happened. Even following World War II, transit usage not only was high on the Washington trolleys but showed a profit, while the buses recorded losses. For example, in 1955, the streetcars produced a profit of about $1,600,000, while the bus lines lost about $1,100,000.

While Washingtonians lost their crusade to save the streetcars, citizens of Pittsburgh rallied behind their PCCs just when it appeared that they, too, would be exterminated by the pro-diesel interests. The differences between Washington's experience with trolleys and that of Pittsburgh are especially pertinent since they demonstrate how and why one eastern metropolis retained its electric traction whereas the other was forced to accept—unwillingly, as we have noted—its extermination. Like Washington, Pittsburgh had a long history of PCC usage, starting in 1936.

At one time the Pennsylvania hub operated 666 PCC cars—all made by the St. Louis Car Company—one of the largest fleets of streamlined trolleys in the world. No city used the magnificent PCC car for more purposes per mile than the Pittsburgh Railways. They ran on heavy trunk routes with close headways, on rural interurban lines where high-speed operation was required, and on little-used shuttle lines. No grade was too great for the PCC, a fact amply demonstrated on the 21-Fineview line, where the climb reached a maximum grade of 15.5 percent.

The cars further demonstrated their versatility [wrote Alan R. Lind in *From Horsecars to Streamliners*] by moving with ease from traffic-choked Downtown streets to reserved rights-of-way on bridges, through tunnels, and onto private rights-of-way and across long trestles.

One reason Pittsburgh stuck with the PCC so long was the atrocious condition of many streets in that city and its nearby suburbs. Even today Pittsburgh may have the worst street conditions of any major United States city. In some cases, bridges with paved roadways and streetcar tracks owned by Pittsburgh Railways were the only way private cars and buses could reach many parts of the city quickly. In a real sense, Pittsburgh Railways was subsidizing its competition on these bridges. As far as street repaving projects go, they were used in many cities as the reason (or pretext) for conversion of rail lines to bus service.

Pittsburgh continued receiving large orders of new PCC cars as recently as 1949. The manufacturer was so delighted with the loyalty and regularity of the Pittsburgh purchases that it placed a large ad—OUT IN FRONT WITH ST. LOUIS BUILT—featuring a new Pittsburgh PCC in a head-on view. However, trolleys did not remain out in front as far as Pittsburgh's purchases were concerned. In the 1950s and 1960s several tram routes were abandoned, some for asinine reasons. Route 56-McKeesport via Second Avenue had to give way to a street repair program. Since the repair program didn't include streetcar tracks on the new roadway, the trolley service was killed.

More ominous for Pittsburgh Railways was the competition from an assortment of thirty-one independent and loosely regulated bus companies. In 1964 Pittsburgh Railways threw in the towel, and its properties were taken over by the Port Authority of Allegheny County, later known as Port Authority Transit. Within a year PAT elected to rid itself of all remaining trolley lines, converting them to buses. In 1965 nearly all the North Side lines were converted to bus operation, thanks to federal funds that made the bus purchases possible. By 1967 only twelve routes were operating. A decade later the number had been trimmed to eight.

That Pittsburgh's remaining trolleys were saved can be chalked up to a pair of factors: the determination of some citizens to preserve the valuable trams and the failure of planners to push through a galactic Skybus which would have replaced all remaining trolleys. The Skybus would have included a guided busway using unmanned electrically powered vehicles running on rubber tires on a concrete roadway. A storm of protest erupted when the county commissioners approved the Skybus plan, enough to force a compromise—a paved busway shared by buses and streetcars—and save the remaining trolley lines. Unlike Washingtonians, who faced an insensitive and implacably illogical antistreetcar

Congress, the burghers of Pittsburgh discovered that their pleas to save the trolleys were not falling on deaf ears.

When the Skybus proposal was routed, PAT launched a program of retention and upgrading of its trolleys. "Cars," noted Alan R. Lind, "were rebuilt and painted in dazzling color schemes. Marketing efforts have pointed up the advantages of rail travel and Pittsburghers and visitors are using the cars to a greater extent today."

If any vehicle symbolized the positive trolley turnabout in Pittsburgh it was Car Number 1779, built by the St. Louis Car Company in 1946 and severely damaged several years later.

"That the dented, battered, scarred rusted-out Pittsburgh cars were able to operate at all after most maintenance on them had stopped," said Lind, "is itself a tribute to the design and construction of the PCC. Even Philadelphia's sadly deteriorated PCC fleet is today probably not nearly in as bad condition as the Pittsburgh cars were in the 1960s."

Rather than scrap the streamliner, PAT rebuilt the trolley in 1975 at a cost of $25,000. The dramatic changes include a European-type front end, a boxy rectangular design with a large front window, headlights like an automobile's, and an oversized destination sign. Interior improvements featured seats around a card table, high-intensity fluorescent lighting, simulated wood paneling finish, and a two-way radio. "Once threatened with slow death by attrition," Alan R. Lind commented, "then faced with swift extinction as a result of the Skybus project, Pittsburgh's PCCs today are battling buses on the PATway, but at least seem to have a secure spot in Pittsburgh's future transportation system."

While Washington, D.C., proved a trolley burial ground and Pittsburgh epitomized the compromise, Toronto is clearly the most favorable example for the past, present, and future for streetcars. Not only was the Canadian metropolis one of the first cities in North America to order PCC cars (March 10, 1938) but the model that first hit the tracks of Brooklyn in 1935 was still cruising along Toronto thoroughfares in 1979. And the basic PCC design still retains all the beauty and pollution-free dignity that it offered when it first came to Canada. By 1954, when Toronto opened its first subway, its trolley fleet had 745 pieces of rolling stock. From time to time the Toronto Transportation Commission wavered in its commitment to electric traction and the protram bloc feared that a wholesale extermination—à la Washington, D.C.—was in the works; but public opinion was so emphatically supportive of the trolleys that the TTC became renowned in North America as the archetypal streetcar operator. In 1972 the Toronto system still had 418 operating PCC cars, which comprised 44 percent of the TTC electric vehicle (trolley, subway, electric bus) roster. The TTC's basic rule of thumb was to retain the PCC cars on avenues with medium-density traffic—from 4,000 to 9,000 riders per peak hour in one direction.

The dedication that the TTC has displayed toward its PCC cars is evident to the attentive transit observer. "I have ridden every major transit system in North America," said Alan R. Lind, "and have never found a system that exceeded Toronto for courtesy, efficiency, and dedication to duty among operating personnel. Equipment maintenance is to the highest standard. Cars are thoroughly cleaned inside and out, always kept well painted and, of course, bear no graffiti. The excellent maintenance is a further source of employee pride, and thus a source of better employee–transit rider relations."

While Washington's trolleys are long gone and Pittsburgh's system has been decimated over the years, Toronto has not only rebuilt its newer PCC cars but has ordered 196 new Canadian light rail vehicles (LRVs)—otherwise known as trolleys—which should guarantee streetcar transportation in Canada through the twenty-first century. For Toronto, at least, the golden age of trolleys is still now!

9

Interurbans,
a Splendid Specimen—
and the Sole Survivor

If anything, urbanologist Lewis Mumford was understating the case when he acclaimed interurban trolleys, which fifty years ago moved between towns and cities as ubiquitously as autos do now, as "a total transportation network that met different human needs at different speeds."

Were this a less lazy, less selfish, and more environmentally serious America, the splendidly speedy, deliciously designed interurbans today would be thoroughly de rigueur for the millions commuting to and from suburbia rather than the automobile, whose cost keeps rising, which endlessly inflicts death and destruction both directly and indirectly upon the American countryside and city.

The interurban—an extra-large, extra-fast electric-powered rail vehicle—found a niche in the North American mass transit picture somewhere between streetcars, elevated trains, subways, and omnibuses at one end, and intercity railroads at the other. Writing in *The Electric Interurban Railways in America*, Professors George W. Hilton and John F. Due described the interurban: "railways that shared most or all of the four following characteristics: electric power, primary emphasis on passenger service, equipment that was heavier and faster than city street cars, and operation on streets in cities but at the sides of highways or on private rights-of-way in rural areas."

Another electric railway analyst described the species this way:

Interurban wheels were larger than those on streetcars, motors were 50 to 160 horsepower as against the streetcars' 20 to 40 horsepower, the interurbans ran at about 45 miles an hour more than the streetcars were capable of, their ride was smoother and heavier, and the cars were furnished more comfortably—more like long-distance vehicles than like city transport.

In fact the interurban was many things to many people. At its most inept, it was characterized in print as the "Toonerville Trolley." At its most efficient, the ultimate interurban ran as effectively as a high-speed, on-time railroad. Many interurban lines had rolling stock that sprinted across the countryside at speeds of more than a mile a minute. Ruth Cavin, author of *Trolleys*, said she was told that some interurbans reached 100-mile-per-hour speeds in revenue service. Like Lewis Mumford, Ruth Cavin believes that the rise and subsequent fall of the interurban represented an American transportation tragedy.

The interurbans [wrote Cavin] literally revolutionized the lives of farmers, and they expanded the physical and social horizons of every class, making possible country homes for the urban wealthy, college educations for the small-town well-to-do, larger territories for the traveling salesman, and cheaper and fresher milk and vegetables for those who lived in the cities.

They accomplished this while operating through the countryside at a level of speed, convenience, cleanliness, and comfort that makes it clear why Mr. Mumford and his fellow social thinkers look back on the interurban trolley with something more than nostalgia.

The interurban was the precocious kid brother of the urban trolley car. While the trolley scored its first big hit on the streets of Richmond, Virginia, in 1887, the unheralded "world premiere" of the interurban took place in Minnesota and Oregon. Purists argue over which actually was *the* first, pointing out that the line running between St. Paul and Minneapolis, starting in 1891, was ultimately to become "a long streetcar line," whereas the fifteen-mile East Side Railway, plying a route between Portland and Oregon City—which started operating in 1893—is considered the pure interurban ("between cities"). Transit expert William D. Middleton suggests that Indiana State Senator Charles L. Henry coined the term "interurban" in 1893 and later became a trolley baron, building the four-hundred-mile Union Traction Company in central Indiana. Wrote Middleton in *The Interurban Era:*

The interurbans seemed to fill a travel void for much of America. Aside from what slow, infrequent and grimy local passenger service might be available from the steam railroads, rural America was pretty well restricted to whatever lay within horse and buggy range. The interurbans were bright and clean, stopped almost anywhere, and ran far more frequently than the steam trains, for one car made a train. Once in town the cars usually operated through the streets and went right downtown. They were almost always cheaper than steam trains, too.

All in all it was a terrific parlay; and the proof was in the public's enthusiasm for the vehicles. From Milwaukee to Montreal, lines were constructed and, by the turn of the century, it was evident that a new boom transit industry had been spawned. "These great arteries of commerce," noted the *Street Railway Journal* in 1906, "are stimulating and benefiting to those sections of the country through which they pass."

Although much was made of the benefits the interurbans were having on farm life, the oversized trolley was just as evident in the heavily industrialized Northeast as it was in the Midwest, Northwest, and in Southern California. Typical of the interurbans that graced the New York Metropolitan Area was the North Jersey Rapid Transit Company, built in the shadow of Manhattan's skyscrapers in 1908. The raison d'être for the North Jersey Rapid Transit interurban was typical of its time. E. J. Quinby, founder of the Electric Railroaders'

Association and one of the most knowledgeable students of the American Transportation industry, asserted in *Interurban Interlude* that the elimination of the North Jersey line was one of the most egregious errors of transit planning:

The grandiose scheme to provide the suburbs of New York City across the Hudson River in Northern New Jersey with swift and convenient rapid transit access to the big town was well-founded. It is more of a necessity today than it was back in 1908 for today this increasingly popular suburban area has become much more densely populated. Its transportation problems have become gigantic in the meantime. The frantic efforts to relieve the automotive congestion of its highways by constructing more highways at increasing costs to the taxpayers, serve only to attract so many free-wheeling vehicles that the situation gets progressively worse instead of better. . . . The remedy merely aggravates the malady.

As Quinby noted, the "remedy" actually was developed during the halcyon era of interurban construction. In Indianapolis, home of the country's most elaborate interurban network, the population of the city climbed by 38 percent between 1900 and 1910, according to transit analysts, because of the possibilities created by the interurbans.

"By 1910," said Quinby, "the interurban was the up-and-coming mode of comfortable, convenient and economical transportation between many major cities." So popular were the interurbans that songwriters camped at their uprights and banged out such tunes as "The Pacific Electric [Interurban] Trolley Waltz," "The Trolley Car Swing," and "On a Good Old Trolley Ride."

The North Jersey Rapid Transit Company was one of the first to jump on the bandwagon. Started in 1908, the interurban finally ran all the way from East Paterson (N.J.) to Suffern (New York) over track that was still being ballasted and adjusted in June 1911. Meanwhile, the boom was sustained throughout the country. Rare was the state that didn't boast an interurban, and by 1917 there were more than 18,000 miles of interurban lines and 10,000 cars spread across the nation. Manufacturers, in particular, were enamored of the possibilities of transporting city dwellers to their factories in the suburbs. That is precisely what F. J. Meyers of the Meyers Pump Company did in Ohio, building a thirty-seven-mile section of the Cleveland, Southwestern from Seville to his plant at Mansfield. Likewise, Tom L. Johnson, a onetime mayor of Cleveland, ensured that a trolley line was available to carry Cleveland steelworkers to a plant (now U.S. Steel) in Lorain, Ohio. The interurban did the job time and again.

Simultaneous with the rise of the interurbans was the growth of amusement areas ("electric parks") at the end of the line, or somewhere along the route, where passengers could alight, spend the day, and then return by trolley. In New Jersey, the Hudson River Line boasted the vast Palisades Amusement Park on the Hudson, overlooking West 125th Street in Manhattan. The New Jersey Rapid Transit line serviced Ho-Ho-Kus Race Track. Near Pittsburgh, the wealthy Mellon family erected Kennywood Park as a terminus for its line that ran into the city.

Riding the crest of the interurbans' popularity, owners launched grandiose plans to extend routes far beyond state lines. One of the most extraordinary pro-

motions of all was conjured up by banker Alexander C. Miller, an official of the
Chicago, Burlington and Quincy Railway. Studying the steam railroad routes
from New York City to Chicago, Miller concluded that they were so circu-
itous—and therefore time consuming—that a more efficient means of transporting passengers should be devised. The Miller plan called for a straight run,
employing interurbans averaging 75 miles per hour, that would eliminate between 160 and 230 miles from routes used by competitors. Dubbing it the Chicago–New York Electric Air Line Railroad, Miller got his act together in earnest in 1906 with such vigor that more than ten thousand investors coughed up
nearly $200,000,000, of which $25,000,000 was in shares of common stock. One
of Miller's magnets was *The Air Line News*, which even featured a verse extol-
ling the potential virtues of his interurban over the traditional railroads:

> The moral of this tale is plain
> Let us send our "Air Line" train
> Straight across the continent
> Not follow where some fool calf went
> The twentieth century calls for men
> Who dare to leave the "once has been"
> And shunning calf-paths which they see
> Aim straight and sure for "what's to be"!

The Air Line was transformed from the drawing board to the ballast in 1906
when construction started in Indiana, but both money and enthusiasm soon
evaporated—in that order—and no more than thirty miles of track were laid.
By far the most encouraging outcome of Miller's venture was construction of an
amusement park six miles from LaPorte, Indiana. Suitably named Air Line
Park, the Coney Island of Indiana attracted as many as twelve hundred customers—who, naturally, rode the Electric Air Line's two green cars—on a sunny
Sunday.

Nevertheless, there were enough successful interurban lines within the state
to encourage promoters. Indianapolis was not only the hub of several major
lines but also sported a train shed connected to a large office building and the
Indianapolis Traction Terminal, which housed nine tracks. In nearby Ohio,
there wasn't a community with more than ten thousand residents that lacked
interurban service. The state, during the interurban heyday, had three thousand
miles of trackage. And, despite the fact that the Air Line never fulfilled its
promise, a number of long interurban runs were possible. It was possible to
make an unbroken journey between Cleveland and Detroit (165 miles), Indianapolis and Louisville (117 miles), Cincinnati and Toledo (217 miles), Indianapolis and Fort Wayne (136 miles), Rochester and Syracuse (87 miles), San Francisco and Chico (183 miles), Los Angeles and San Bernardino (58 miles), and
finally, the longest trip without changing cars, from Youngstown, Ohio, to Jackson, Michigan—a total of 440 miles.

By changing cars, even longer trips were possible. For example, it was possible to ride from Elkhart Lake, Wisconsin, to Oneonta, New York, which

amounted to 1,087 miles. If a hardy traveler chose to switch to a steam railroad here and there, it was actually possible to make the run from New York City to Chicago almost exclusively via interurban. All but 187 of the 1,143 miles between the two metropolises were connected by high-speed trolleys.

Although the trips were long in hours—it required forty-five hours for one J. S. Moulton to take the interurban route to Chicago from New York—there were many amenities. Passengers usually received warm, courteous, familylike treatment, and the trolleys themselves provided a surprising number of luxuries, not to mention toilet facilities. The Illinois Terminal Railroad sported a fleet of parlor cars with wicker chairs, tulip-shaped lampshades, and upholstered seats, as well as sleeping cars.

The Illinois Terminal provided regular sleeper-trolley service between St. Louis and Peoria. The interurban departed St. Louis at 11:45 P.M. and arrived in Peoria at 6:35 A.M., and vice versa. Nicknamed the Owl, the sleeping-car trolley advertised itself as a conveyance with "extra long berths, windows in uppers and no smoke, no cinders."

Such ads did little to cement relations between the steam railroads and the electric traction interests, especially when the steam lines took note of the fact that the interurbans had begun to handle significant quantities of express and freight. "The proprietors of the big steam railroads looked with alarm at this growing competition," said E. J. Quinby, "and began to quietly buy up the securities of these upstarts. Thus the New York Central gained control of the interurban lines across New York State just as they were about to forge the last connecting links that would have made it possible to ride by trolley all the way from New York to Chicago."

Wherever possible, the big railroads zeroed in on the threatening interurbans. One of the most promising new interurban lines had hoped to link New York City with Boston along a magnificent "million-dollar-a-mile" track. But the New York, Westchester and Boston Railway never made it to New England. It was purchased by the New York, New Haven and Hartford Railroad once construction workers had laid the track up to Port Chester, New York.

Such interference from the steam railroads cut sharply into the growth potential of the interurbans, but not enough to stop the climb to prominence of three trolley networks: one in the East, one in the Midwest, and the third in the Southwest.

Centered in Los Angeles, the Pacific Electric began its rise at the turn of the century and, at the peak of its popularity, operated more than a thousand miles of track and almost eight hundred route miles. It was the brainchild of Henry Huntington, a millionaire whose uncle, Collis, was boss of the Southern Pacific. In time the Pacific Electric interurbans connected Los Angeles with Pasadena, Glendale, Santa Ana, San Fernando, and Balboa, among other Southern California centers. Before the campaign against electric traction began, the Pacific Electric was an extraordinarily popular part of the woof and warp of Southern California life. As late as the 1940s the Pacific Electric carried so many passengers that it was compelled to borrow extra rolling stock from other cities and haul its antediluvian wooden cars out of mothballs.

Although not as extensive as the Pacific Electric, the West Penn Railways, located near Pittsburgh, sported 339 miles of track spread over three states. The West Penn connected Pittsburgh with West Virginia and Maryland, fortified with a superior signaling system that proved its worth in the West Penn's impeccable safety record.

Business thrived on the West Penn because it served the Pennsylvania and West Virginia coal-mining communities, and the miners found the West Penn the cheapest, most efficient way to get to the pits. "Even in good times," noted Ruth Cavin, author of *Trolleys*, "when these workers had their own cars, they rode the trolley rather than cover the interior of what was a prize possession with the coal dust they had accumulated in a shift's work."

Another formidable interurban operator was the Illinois Terminal Railroad—originally the Illinois Traction Company—which ran as far as St. Louis. Utilizing heavy equipment, the Illinois Terminal had three main lines—from St. Louis to Peoria via Carlinville and Springfield (172 miles); from Springfield east through Decatur and Champaign to Danville (123 miles); and Decatur through Clinton and Bloomington to a junction with the main line Decatur-Peoria trains at Mackinaw (66 miles). Always thinking big, the Illinois Terminal built a trolleys-only bridge across the Mississippi River at Venice, Illinois, near St. Louis. The fifty-foot-high (over high water) span stretched almost a half mile, including its approaches, and cost $3,000,000, an extraordinary sum for an interurban project. The Illinois Terminal's longevity was guaranteed for several reasons, not the least of which were absence of competition from the main line railroads and an energetic freight business.

Freight notwithstanding, passenger service was the core of all interurban operations and, to this end, the entrepreneurs provided the public with a variety of services, not the least of which was the excursion special. More than any line, the Pacific Electric turned the excursion into a veritable art form. It established an agency in New York City to lure riders to Los Angeles and environs. It was not uncommon for Pacific Electric to hustle business by dispatching passenger agents to Salt Lake City and Albuquerque in order to drum up revenue. Interurban historians recall that in 1910 the Pacific Electric operated up to eighty excursion trolleys *every hour* from its station in Los Angeles.

Excursions were popular because they were inexpensive—in Indiana and Ohio, lines charged only a penny a mile—and the "in" thing to do, a fact that did not elude the notice of other promoters, such as newspaper publishers. In Brooklyn, where the trolley had become a way of life, the Brooklyn *Daily Eagle* published an annual *Trolley Exploring Guide*, describing trips by traction as distant as Washington and Chicago. One of the most popular runs was the Boston–New York excursion, which offered a variety of routes. "To publicize Boston–New York trolleying," wrote William D. Middleton in *The Interurban Era*, "the Bay State Street Railway fitted out one of its cars with wicker lounge chairs in 1914 and took a party of electric railway officials and 25 newspapermen on a leisurely two-day junket between the two cities, stopping at New London for the night."

A 1910 edition of the *Electric Railway Journal* extolled the virtues of a meandering four-week trolley tour between New York City and Chicago. The writer E. C. Van Valkenburgh described the 1,163-mile trip with unbridled enthusiasm. "A better way of seeing the country at reasonable cost would be hard to imagine," said Van Valkenburgh, and he was right.

The interurbans were equally popular north of the border, although on a considerably smaller scale. Canada's vastness and less dense population made it economically impossible to provide the successful interconnecting electric networks that proved so efficient in Ohio, Indiana, Illinois, and parts of New England. Most of the Canadian interurban routes were centered in the heavily populated province of Ontario. Others sprouted in British Columbia and Quebec. One of the most popular Canadian interurban lines emanated from Quebec City on the Quebec Railway, Light and Power Company's line, which linked the provincial capital with the Roman Catholic shrine at Ste. Anne de Beaupré. Graced with a bilingual guide-lecturer, the *Chemin de Fer de la Bonne Sainte Anne* operated as a regular interurban until 1958.

In English-speaking Canada, one of the most popular interurban corridors crossed the international border, connecting Toronto with Buffalo. The line, the Niagara, St. Catherines and Toronto Railway, would leave the United States at Niagara Falls, New York, and roll over the old Rainbow Bridge and across the Niagara peninsula to Port Dalhousie East, where a shipside connection with Toronto-bound Lake Ontario steamers was made.

Despite the vastness of the Canadian prairie, in the province of Manitoba two interurban lines provided service out of the metropolis of Winnipeg: the Suburban Rapid Transit Company and the Winnipeg, Selkirk, and Lake Winnipeg Railway Company. The Suburban Rapid Transit operated from 1902 through 1930, while the Winnipeg, Selkirk, and Lake Winnipeg began service in 1904 and stayed in business until 1939.

Farther west, on the Pacific coast of British Columbia, an impressive interurban system operated from Vancouver and through the Fraser Valley for seventy-six miles to Chilliwack. The British Columbia Electric Railway was Canada's largest interurban traction line, even operating a short line emanating from Victoria on Vancouver Island. As was the case in other parts of North America, the rail tributaries not only were useful in the early part of the century but, in a sense, were ahead of their time in terms of the province's future transit needs. As many a British Columbian transit planner has recently lamented, they no longer exist.

The British Columbian interurban empire perished for much the same reasons that other electric traction lines, whether in Indiana or Illinois, headed for the great carbarn in the sky: competition from the automobile and fuzzy foresight on the part of governmental agencies on every level.

At first the interurban industry failed to perceive the ominous threat posed by the auto industry. In a 1915 editorial, the *Street Railway Journal* discussed the potential effects of the car craze and concluded: "Whether this condition will be permanent or whether it will practically disappear, as in the case of the bicycle, is hard to say."

The turning point in favor of the auto, at the expense of the interurban, occurred shortly after World War I. Where once the interurban industry boasted more than sixteen thousand miles of track, the figure was cut by one-sixth before 1920. Even worse, nobody seemed inclined to rescue the dying interurbans, although their value was clear to many. Echoing the sentiments of many traction authorities, Ruth Cavin made an excellent point in *Trolleys:*

We are only belatedly learning that interurban short-haul transportation and motor car travel could have existed side-by-side, providing a genuine alternative for travelers going distances too short for airplanes.

But the automobiles never had the financial burden of securing right-of-way and maintaining track; their government did that for them. The contention that roads are financed by taxes on gasoline is hardly accurate, according to a study a few years ago by Dr. Lyle C. Fitch of the Institute of Public Administration.

Despite the overwhelming—and conspicuously unfair—partiality displayed by the government toward the automobile interests, the interurban industry valiantly attempted to stay alive at the turn of the twenties. Occasionally, a new route would emerge, the last of which was Houston's North Shore Railway in Texas, which made its debut in 1927. Just three years later, Dr. Thomas Conway of the Cincinnati and Lake Erie interurban line challenged an airplane pilot to race one of his newer pieces of rolling stock. The trolley won the race—which was recorded on movie film—and a day later Dr. Conway's interurban was rolling through the streets of Dayton dressed in a huge banner from stem to stern, reading: SEE THIS CAR RACE AN AIRPLANE. The banner noted that films of the race were shown at a Dayton theater.

The trolley's upset victory symbolized what had been an uphill battle to stabilize the interurban industry. Gains were, in fact, made during the late twenties, but whatever progress had been recorded was nullified by the onset of the Great Depression, which extended through the thirties. A handful of interurban lines made it through World War II, but by 1961 only Pacific Electric and three Chicago runs were factors in the dwindling interurban picture. That year Pacific Electric gave way to diesel buses, and within two years only one interurban line was left.

That the Chicago South Shore and South Bend Railroad was able to survive when such giants as Pacific Electric, West Penn, and the Cincinnati and Lake Erie failed is a tribute to the foresight and perseverance of such transit giants as James E. Hanna and Samuel Insull. It was Hanna who organized the line and Insull who later put it into high gear and made the name "South Shore" synonymous with successful interurban operation. "The South Shore alone," wrote William D. Middleton in his history of the line, "among all electric interurbans has achieved the dual feat of survival as an electrically operated railroad, still transporting freight and passengers over the original route envisaged by its founders over 60 years ago, while managing to transform itself into an important short line railroad that now constitutes an integral part of the North American railway network."

The South Shore actually began in 1901 as the Chicago and Indiana Air Line Railway when it opened a 3.4-mile streetcar line between East Chicago and Indiana Harbor, Indiana. It was the start of something big because in 1905 plans were unfolded for the construction of a mammoth United States Steel plant on land that ultimately would become Gary (named for Judge Elbert H. Gary, a member of the company's board of directors), Indiana. The projected growth of the steel city meant that an interurban service was essential, and in 1908 the Chicago, Lake Shore and South Bend Railway was organized to serve Gary. A Cleveland financier, James B. Hanna, organized financial promotion of the line, which soon obtained more than enough funds. Unlike early railroad construction, which ignored safety for speedy completion, the Lake Shore planners designed an exquisitely sound traction line, from power plant to road bed. Trolleys would run at 75 miles per hour wherever possible. Stations were established at South Bend, Michigan City, and Gary.

One of the first major events in this interurban's history occurred on June 30, 1908, when the first Chicago, Lake Shore and South Bend trolley arrived from Michigan City. The missing link, of course, was a direct connection to the Windy City. This was accomplished in 1908 by transferring at Calumet to steam trains of the Lake Shore and Michigan Southern Railway. From South Bend to Chicago, the complete run took approximately three hours.

Although the line's growth fell below expectations as it approached the start of the twenties, it recorded successes in the areas of excursion traffic and freight. But the end of World War I meant the proliferation of new hard-surfaced highways and increased production of automobiles. Like other interurbans, the Lake Shore went to pieces, and by 1925 a savior was needed to bail the route out of its financial morass. On June 29, 1925, the Chicago, Lake Shore and South Bend changed its name to the Chicago, South Shore and South Bend.

While the South Shore's brethren were wolfed up by the auto industry, the Midwest interurban found its angel in London-born Samuel Insull. A colleague of inventor Thomas Edison, Insull already was a wealthy man in 1914 when he unified Chicago's elevated railway system. From that point on he became a pivotal factor in the resurgence of traction development in the Midwest. He took a disorganized North Shore line, revamped its fabric from top to bottom, and made it a money-making interurban. If Insull could do it for the North Shore, why not for the South?

The plan was to infuse money into a variety of areas, beginning with the track and roadbed. Cosmetic moves were made in the area of cleaning and painting not to mention the construction of new bridges and the clearing of the right-of-way as well as installation of new block signals. The insightful Insull understood that one way to lure passengers away from cars and back to the interurbans was by trotting out a new fleet of rolling stock. To this end he ordered twenty-five spanking-fresh steel passenger cars from the Pullman Car & Manufacturing Corporation.

He beefed up every aspect of the freight operation, adding four new eighty-ton electric freight locomotives. And for those passengers who preferred deluxe accommodations, Insull purchased a pair of dining cars and a pair of parlor-observation cars. When the rolling stock began arriving in June 1926, the coaches were hailed as the ultimate in interurban travel. All steel in construction, the Pullmans were sixty feet long and weighed sixty tons. Their interior appointments pleased the most discriminating commuter; the South Shore began to increase its ridership to such a significant extent that the company ordered twenty more cars from Pullman only six months later. With a perceptive touch, Insull chose to place the brand-new dining and parlor-observation cars on exhibit at the South Shore line station in Chicago. Taking ads in all the major dailies, Insull proclaimed: "It is the last word in railroad equipment of this type." And none could accuse him of exaggeration. The dining car, for example, featured fare that would not have been out of place on a transcontinental Pullman. Steaks and milk-fed spring chicken were some of the items on the menu.

Typical of Insull's foresight was his decision to take on the growing competitors in the bus field. He organized the Shore Line Motor Coach Company, employing the gasoline-powered vehicles as feeders for the interurbans. In short, Insull left no stone unturned—be it in the area of safety, public relations, or employee relations—to make the South Shore a better interurban railroad.

Keeping pace with track and rolling stock improvements were terminals for the growing numbers of passengers. Typical of the updated interurban stations was the Michigan City terminal, which accommodated both traction as well as motor coach passengers. It cost more than $200,000, but Insull believed the investment worthwhile. Within a year he was operating more than eighty daily trains, including an hourly service between Chicago and South Bend that began in the early morning and continued until almost midnight.

Occasionally, the South Shore was a victim of its own success. Once it dispatched five special trains to handle crowds for a Notre Dame–Minnesota football game. But the trains became too closely bunched near South Bend, with the result that circuit breakers were blown in the Grandview substation. More often, the line was being commended in one way or another. One of the South Shore's most prized awards was the Charles A. Coffin Medal "for distinguished contribution to the development of electric transportation for the convenience of the public and the benefit of the industry." A committee of the American Electric Railway Association acknowledged Insull's accomplishments. "Within four years," the committee declared, "the Chicago South Shore and South Bend Railroad has moved figuratively from the scrap heap to the front rank among the electric railways of America."

As prizes poured into the South Shore's trophy room, passengers poured through the turnstiles, making 1929 the best year yet. Passenger revenues exceeded the $2,000,000 mark, while freight revenues were considerably more than $1,600,000. The skies over the South Shore route appeared bluer than ever, except for one dark cloud way off in the distance. Late in 1929 Wall Street had laid an egg and the rotten aftereffects were being felt up and down the economic community.

Undaunted, the South Shore continued to pour money into its plant; new shops, new freight houses, new freight locomotives—all concealed any concern about the Great Depression. But the fallout from the stock market crash wafted across the tracks from South Bend to Chicago, and by 1933 the once proud South Shore had been shaken to its very ties by awesome losses on its ledgers. Even worse, Insull's empire was trembling, and when his Middle West Utilities filed for bankruptcy in 1932 Sam Insull was driven from his other companies. The last glimpse of blue skies was gone, and in September 1933 the South Shore went bankrupt. In a sense the defeat was not totally catastrophic. The interurbans continued running and actually began to describe an upward revenue spiral in the mid- and late thirties, climaxing with a reorganization and end to the bankruptcy in 1938.

The leadership baton had been handed to Jay Samuel Hartt, a Chicago consulting engineer who would direct the South Shore with the consummate efficiency of Insull. When the Japanese attacked Pearl Harbor the national disaster turned out to be a blessing for the South Shore. Defense plants in the Gary-Chicago corridor revved up their production and personnel capacities to such a high degree that it was inevitable that war workers would turn to the interurban for transportation in a car-short society. Revenues were like 1929 all over again—only better!

Instead of just sitting back and coining money, the South Shore responded by rehabilitating all its rolling stock. Coaches were lengthened, modernized, and returned to service in spiffy condition. Up and down the line the trappings were altered to suit the burst of business, which, surprisingly, continued well after hostilities had ceased and the boys came home. Naturally, the figures were not so high as they had been between 1942 and 1946, but even in the early fifties the South Shore could boast that it carried somewhere between 4,000,000 and 4,500,000 passengers annually. One of the most unusual boosts to ridership, strangely enough, came as an offshoot of an automobile-oriented improvement, the Indiana Toll Highway.

In the early fifties the Indiana Toll Road Commission had its eye out for available land on which to construct an east-west turnpike across the northern tier of the state. At this time the South Shore had been vexed by insufferable delays moving its coaches through East Chicago, Indiana. Ever since the twenties the rolling stock had moved ponderously along East Chicago's main drag, competing with buses, trucks, and automobiles. At the same time that the Indiana Toll Road Commission was pursuing a right-of-way for its turnpike, the South Shore also had been seeking ways and means of getting around the bottleneck. In a rare marriage of traction and rubber-tired interests, the commission and the interurban merged forces to construct their two routes through East Chicago. Wrote William D. Middleton in *South Shore:*

Under the agreement, 110 acres of railroad-owned land were deeded to the Commission. In return, the Commission agreed to build an elevated, five-mile right-of-way through East Chicago, including all necessary bridges, for the joint use of the toll highway and the South Shore. In addition, the South Shore was paid some $850,000 in cash. With a further investment of only $2,500,000 for track, power, signal, and station facilities, the South Shore was able to complete the construction of a superb high speed, entirely grade separated, electric line that would permit a major improvement to the railroad's freight and passenger service.

For a change, the automobile helped the trolley. Work was finished in the autumn of 1956, at a time when nearly all other interurban lines had gone or were going out of business.

The East Chicago bypass proved a boon to the South Shore's freight revenue in years to come; and a good thing too, for the passenger business on the interurban simply could not provide enough cash to offset spiraling labor and operating expenses. Worse still, new superhighways sliced heavily into the passenger business, and by the early sixties the prospects in the passenger department were, at best, cloudy. For all intents and purposes, the interurban industry in 1965 was kaput. The Philadelphia Suburban Transportation Company was the only surviving interurban east of Chicago, and handling the irrevocable passenger deficits became a seemingly impossible task over the long haul.

Nevertheless, the South Shore kept rolling along through the sixties by taking its freight profits and using them to assuage the passenger wounds. A number of new industrial plants along the right-of-way gave the freight operation a bright outlook and helped inspire the Chesapeake and Ohio Railroad to pursue the purchase of the South Shore. In January 1967, the Chesapeake and Ohio took over the South Shore, gaining 94 percent of the interurban's outstanding stock shares. Business on the freight side remained healthy under the new management, but the passenger dilemma defied the traditional panaceas. As it passed its seventieth birthday, the South Shore survived one attempt by the high command to discontinue passenger service in 1976. By this time the states of Indiana and Illinois realized that a vast infusion of funds from government—similar to New York State's keeping the New York City subways operating—was required to preserve South Shore interurbans through the 1980s.

One of the most depressing aspects of the South Shore's passenger operation was its reliance on the venerable and once magnificent passenger coaches from the Insull era. Although well built, the trains had passed the point of no return in terms of maintenance and rehabilitation. South Shore President A. W. Dudley asserted that the ancient cars were a primary reason why the South Shore had to reduce the number of trains on a frigid day in February 1978 from thirty-nine to six. "The cars," said Dudley, "are simply worn out and border on unsafe."

If the nation's last interurban is to succeed as a passenger carrier it must receive the brand of support provided to mass transit systems in other parts of the country—and auto-truck travel as well—that is, state and federal funding on a grand scale. It is the least that can be done for a traction company that has faithfully served the public for seven decades.

Fortunately, the Illinois and Indiana Rapid Transit authorities have been rallying to the aide of the South Shore line. The service was continued through March 1979 with partial financial assistance from those agencies while "we are encouraged and optimistic that we finally are on a course to a solution to South

Shore's woes," Albert Dudley, president of the line, said. Plans have evolved to scrap the ancient cars, which were particularly unreliable during the stormy months of 1978 and 1979, and specifications are being drawn up for a new fleet of cars.

"The inflationary impact of buying new cars—which is a must—along with day-to-day operating costs and preserving current passenger service, are the problems we are trying to cope with now," Dudley said. "We are talking about millions of dollars, and the complexities of meeting these costs are great."

Dudley was convinced that Illinois and Indiana would not let their interurban die and were prepared to work hard to restore the South Shore, once praised as the best electric railway in America.

In April 1979, the Indiana State Legislature signed into a law a plan to save the South Shore Line. They committed $1.5 million to improving the decaying tracks while the one- to three-year bidding on a federally funded $30 million contract for new cars and equipment was to begin some time before 1980. The struggle to restore the interurban was finally over and South Shore commuters looked forward to the day when the fabled line could once again be hailed as the nation's best.

10

Diesel Buses and
Trolley Coaches

The trackless trolley—or electric bus—was born in the latter part of the nineteenth century and has held considerable promise ever since. In Massachusetts, experimentation with the trolley bus began in 1915 but halted before the year was up. The major breakthrough for the industry, however, took place in the twenties when General Electric successfully demonstrated a vehicle built by the Atlas Truck Company at Schenectady, New York. Other passenger vehicle manufacturers such as J. G. Brill and the Trackless Trolley Corporation of New York would soon follow suit in the bid for this potentially lucrative market.

One of the first major investments was made by the Staten Island (New York City) Midland Railway, which opened two lines totaling seven miles. To service them, the company bought eight trackless trolleys manufactured by Atlas. Another order for fifteen more electric buses gave Staten Island the honor of having the nation's largest trolley bus system, at least for the twenties. Philadelphia, Baltimore, Rochester, and Windsor (Ontario) also took a crack at electric bus operation in the 1920s. Nobody, however, was ever really convinced that the trackless trolley was superior to the traditional tram or the gasoline-powered omnibus.

But a number of forces were working relentlessly in favor of both the electric and the fuel-powered buses. The most important of these were the taxes levied against streetcar companies in most municipalities. Alan R. Lind, in his book *From Horsecars to Streamliners*, summed up the problem quite cogently when he wrote:

Many street railway franchises contained provisions requiring the transit firm to pay for street paving along its lines; other franchises had exorbitant taxes on gross receipts, required free fares for firemen and policemen, or mandated snow removal at the expense of the street railway company. By converting to bus operation under a new franchise, the burdensome provisions of the old franchise could be eliminated or greatly modified. Thus economic forces and political reasons, together with the declining transit ridership, helped to bring about the . . . conversion of street railways to bus operation.

Another factor was the Public Utility Holding Company Act of 1935. "One of the few cities that seemingly escaped the effects of the Act was New Orleans," said Lind, "where until a few years ago a private utility company, New

Orleans Public Service, operated the streetcars and buses as well as the local gas and electric utility business. Fares were, I believe, kept low on the transit system through subsidy from gas and electric utility parts of the operation."

There was no better example of the shortsightedness and callousness of city government toward the streetcar—and in favor of rubber-tired transit—than the case of Salt Lake City, where the Utah Light and Traction Company operated the trolleys.

In the late twenties the city chose to conduct a wholesale street-repaving project, including many avenues on which the trolleys ran. The Salt Lake City streetcar franchise provided that the Utah Light and Traction Company was obliged to pay from one-third to one-half of the entire cost of this paving work. The arresting lack of logic here was noted by many transit critics, including John Anderson Miller, who commented in *Fares, Please!*:

That would have been bad enough by itself, as it meant additional investment without any additional earnings to pay interest charges, but that was not all. Paving improvement was likely to result in greater use of private automobiles, and the average auto driver, wishing to show himself a good fellow, was inclined to pick up anyone he passed who was waiting for a streetcar. Thus the trolley company was being asked, in effect, to furnish a large part of the means of destroying its own business.

Most observers believed that, despite the exceedingly high cost being exacted by the city, the Utah Light and Traction Company would still pay for the paving as well as return the rails and trolleys to the four miles of newly paved street. Considering the city's displeasure with gasoline-powered buses, it appeared impossible that the trolleys would be given the hook. But Edward West, general manager of the Utah Light and Traction Company, remained convinced that the future of surface transit was in trackless trolleys and finally persuaded the city fathers to amend the company's franchise. The city government agreed.

West's campaigning for electric buses proved a benchmark in national transit development. Salt Lake City's success with the vastly improved trackless trolleys—earlier models had solid rubber tires, inadequate springs, and a short wheelbase—inspired Chicago Surface Lines to take a chance on them, and six routes were operating in the Windy City by 1931. Trackless trolley service was also started in Providence, Rhode Island, in 1931, and a year later the pollution-free vehicles made their debut for the Fitchburg and Leominster Street Railway Company in Massachusetts. Bradley H. Clarke, who wrote a history of the line, explained the reasons behind the decision:

The trolley bus would bring several distinct benefits including streets unbroken by tracks, curb loading, ability to swing around route obstructions, quiet operation due to pneumatic tires and silent gearing, rapid acceleration and braking, elimination of track maintenance and lower power consumption. Advantages over the gasoline bus included an unlimited inexhaustible power supply, smoother and faster acceleration due to the absence of gear shifting, quieter operation because there was no engine exhaust noise or gear clashing, effective odorless heat, good lighting, no exhaust odor, less fire hazard due to the lack of combustible fuel, longer vehicle life and lower energy and maintenance costs.

What was to become a standard criticism of trackless trolleys emerged in Leominster, where many prominent citizens expressed concern that the twin overhead wires required for each bus would prove an aesthetic handicap. "Major opposition," said Bradley H. Clarke, "was centered in Leominster because of widespread fear that the second overhead wire, especially on the loop in Monument Square, would adversely affect the appearance of the city."

Despite the opposition, electric buses ultimately won the approval of Fitchburg's City Council, and the last trolleys operated by the Fitchburg and Leominster Street Railway Company ground to a permanent halt on May 7, 1932. In their place was a fleet of forty-seat J. G. Brill-made coaches with a squarish body. After a week of operation the Fitchburg *Sentinel* reported ". . . the riding public is apparently ready to vote the trackless trolleys a decided success." The article added that the faster ride, elimination of turnout delays, and comfortable noiseless operation were the most appealing features.

Better still, ridership increased. Before the year was up, officials decided to expand the trolley coach network, converting gasoline-bus lines to electric bus operation. Those who previously had fought the trackless trolleys were being won over to their side. In August 1932 the *Transit Journal* reported widespread approval in Fitchburg with trolley coach operation. Fitchburg police added that traffic in congested areas had speeded up 30 percent since the start of electric bus service.

Because of the very nature of its reliance on the overhead wires, the trolley bus betrayed limitations. A driver who drifted too far afield from his power source chanced a dewiring. This was the case on October 3, 1932, when a driver—who had piloted a traditional gasoline bus the previous week—forgot that he was dealing with an electric coach. As the Fitchburg *Sentinel* reported, the electric bus descended Daniels Street from Cleghorn. The wire turned left onto Fairmont Street, but the operator steered straight ahead, the coach losing its poles and drifting helplessly away from the power supply. The denouement proved amusing to all but the driver as a large crowd of about 150 children pushed the vehicle back up the hill and under the overhead wire.

Wherever possible the advantage of electric buses over streetcars was pointed out by the Fitchburg officials. When a raging blizzard tied up traffic in February 1934, it was the trolley bus that managed to get through without having to halt operation. Transit experts were convinced that the streetcars could not have matched that performance and noted that gasoline-powered buses "were handicapped."

Although the Fitchburg and Leominster Street Railway Company's electric bus operation was situated in a relatively small community, it received nationwide attention because of its success and the fact that industry publications such as the *Transit Journal* touted its virtues. In one issue *Transit Journal* remarked that six trolley buses in Fitchburg were doing the work formerly handled by seven streetcars—and doing it better.

Such reviews eventually made their way to Boston, where in 1935 the Boston

Elevated Railway decided to eliminate trolleys from its Harvard Square to Lechmere Station line and replace them with electric buses. "The Lechmere line," wrote Bradley H. Clarke, "was rapidly installed during the Winter of 1935 and 1936, and the ease of this construction later proved to be a strong selling point for further trackless trolley installations. . . . The trackless trolleys were fast, comfortable and attractive and were at the time the latest word in modern transit."

In the Midwest considerable attention was given to Chicago's electric bus network, especially the Windy City's Central Avenue line, a fifteen-mile crosstown route intersecting many of the trolley lines. The Chicago trolley bus was as effective as its Massachusetts counterparts, and soon the trackless trolley concept proliferated throughout North America. By 1938 more than two thousand of the silent, nonpolluting vehicles were meandering over some fifteen hundred route miles in sixty cities. Interest also was strong in Europe, where the electric buses sprouted in Great Britain as well as on the Continent.

New Jersey went one better when its Public Service Coordinated Transport melded a gas-electric-drive passenger bus with a trolley coach. The result was a hybrid that utilized the gas-electric power plant but switched the poles up to the electric wire and used the overhead energy source where it was available. After successful experiments were conducted at Weehawken, New Jersey, in 1934, Public Service placed an order for sixty-two dual (trackless trolley, gas-electric) energy system buses. Officials were delighted with the results to the extent of buying more of the same until their fleet boasted 566 such vehicles.

In the years immediately following World War II, manufacturers such as the St. Louis Car Company did a handsome business putting out the vehicles. Chicago Surface Lines ordered forty-five of the trackless trolleys from St. Louis Car in July 1946 but had to wait two years for them. St. Louis Car Company also turned out an excellent electric bus fleet for Brooklyn in the late forties. At the same time, Pullman was building new electric buses for Boston.

The advantages of trolley coaches—low operating cost, quiet and comfortable ride, no pollution—were often not enough to sustain their lives. The vast Brooklyn fleet, for one, was ultimately scrapped in its entirety, as was that of the pioneering New England line, the Fitchburg and Leominster. If the Brill trackless trolleys had served the Massachusetts community so well, why then were they earmarked for the scrap heap in July 1944? Kenneth Hoover, a transit consultant, had several rationales, not the least of which was the greater flexibility of gasoline-powered buses. Trackless trolleys lacked the ability to cope with routing variations.

Without question, the king of flexibility among surface transit vehicles was the gas- or diesel-powered bus, which had undergone innumerable refinements since the mid-thirties. One of the most noteworthy innovations was developed at the Pontiac, Michigan, plant of Yellow Coach, where Colonel George Greene discovered the practical use of hydraulic (automatic) transmission for use on city buses. And bus sales were strong after a splendid performance on New York City's Eighth Avenue route in 1939.

By the end of World War II the future for bus manufacturing appeared rosy, and there were many builders hoping to get a piece of the pie. Apart from General Motors, which led the way, other significant bus manufacturing concerns included Mack, Twin Coach, White, and ACF-Brill. Their prospects were bullish because petroleum was once again plentiful worldwide and, more important, cities that had once prided themselves on their streetcar networks now for curious reasons were rushing to wipe out the trolleys and install gasoline- or diesel-powered omnibuses. No city more epitomizes this situation than San Diego, California, a municipality with a tram heritage dating back to the nineteenth century, when San Francisco sugar and shipping magnates developed San Diego's magnificent trolley empire.

Unlike metropolises that ceased trolley construction by the 1920s, the San Diego Electric Railway system had strung a new line to Mission Beach and La Jolla in 1924. Faith in the trolley's value continued into the 1930s, when San Diego quickly grasped the importance of the new PCC trolley cars and ordered twenty-eight such streamliners, which began operating in 1937. Nevertheless, San Diego had been featuring bus service of an assortment of varieties, dating back to the early part of the century, when Stanley Steamers were the backbone of the Big Ben Stage fleet.

Before World War II San Diego boasted a formidable array of buses. When the war ended, San Diego invested heavily in buses and the phasing out of trolley lines accelerated. On June 1, 1947, three streetcar lines were replaced by two bus lines. Soon the Imperial Avenue carbarn was razed and replaced by an open storage lot for buses. With that, only three streetcar lines remained.

Despite the fact that only three trolley lines survived the general tram wipeout, it was believed that these would remain a part of the San Diego landscape. As P. Allen Copeland noted in the September 1975 issue of *Motor Coach Age*, all three trolley lines "had heavy traffic and an apparently indefinite future." In his history of San Diego's mass transit system, Copeland added: "The company stated that while the streetcars cost more to operate, the system had been rationalized to the point where each type of vehicle was being used in the most economically effective way."

But the hope was ephemeral, especially after the estate of John D. Spreckles sold the San Diego Electric Railway to Western Transit Systems for a price estimated at $5,500,000. At the time, San Diego's people-moving roster included 78 streetcars and 284 buses. The name of the operating company was changed to San Diego Transit System on November 17, 1948, and it was announced that the three streetcar lines would be converted to diesel buses as soon as possible.

Jesse L. Haugh became the orchestrator of Western Transit Systems. In no time at all Haugh ruled that the three trolley lines had to go and forty-five General Motors buses were ordered. Upon their delivery in April 1949, San Diego's long and successful streetcar era had ended. San Diego's General Motors buses hardly proved a panacea. "The typical experience on other lines," wrote P. Allen Copeland, "during the late 1950s and early 1960s was slow but steady deterioration of the service. There were few actual abandonments, but a good deal of weekend service was given up and weekday headways were widened.

San Diego Transit System ended 1964 with an estimated loss of $40,000. . . .
The loss brought about further service cuts and layoffs."

In contrast to San Diego, Houston was a city with limited streetcar operation.
The trolleys in the Texas city dated back to June 1891, when electric cars were
introduced on the South End line. Houston Electric Company, which assumed
control of the streetcar operation early in the 1900s, maintained thirty-five
miles of track and continued operating trolleys through the 1920s, although the
company signaled its future intentions when it organized Texas Bus Lines as a
subsidiary in August 1928. While Houston continued growing, its tram system
remained stagnant. Buses, on the other hand, were added to the transit roster
until in 1938 Houston featured only 7 rail lines but 19 local, 22 express, 3 crosstown, and 6 shuttle-bus services.

On June 8, 1940, the last cars pulled into the Houston trolley barns and Houston became the largest all-bus city in the United States. Unlike cities that leaned
heavily on General Motors for their rolling stock, Houston spent heavily for
both White and Mack buses, providing the city with a pleasant difference in
style. The Whites, in particular, were large, formidable vehicles and, although
the company eventually discontinued its manufacture of buses, Houston kept
them in business until after World War II. Other models in use after the war included Twin Coach and Brill. General Motors' first diesels appeared in Houston
in 1948, and by this time hardly anybody remembered the trolleys.

No area better revealed the trend from trolleys to buses than the state of Connecticut. In 1924, the Connecticut Company's trolley adjunct had a track mileage of 834 miles (the entire state had 1,024 miles of track at the time) and no
fewer than 1,640 passenger cars. Until then, the Connecticut Company had a
modest roster of buses including Reos, Whites, and even some rare Pierce-Ar-
rows.

The turnabout away from electric traction began in the late 1920s, when
lightly patronized suburban and interurban trolleys were replaced by buses. By
the time of the Great Depression the pace had quickened. By 1935 the company was down to 968 streetcars and going fast. Replacements ran the gamut
from General Motors' products to Macks to Brills. By the end of World War II
the victory of bus over trolley was virtually complete, with just a handful of
mop-up operations to be completed in the next few years.

By the 1970s the rubber-tired buses—be they diesels or electric coaches—had
virtually wiped trolleys off the map of North America. Likewise, some significant competitors to General Motors had disappeared from view. Such bywords
in the bus business as Mack, White, and Brill were likely to be found in the junk
heap rather than on a revenue route.

How, then, did the contemporary bus compare with its predecessors and
competitors? Fresh from the showroom, the new diesels were eye-catchers. In
use, however, it was another story. The broad windows, which afforded the vehicle a "modern" look, provided little fresh-air space for those lucky enough to
find a way in which to open them. Unlike the PCC trolleys, the diesels not only
spewed fumes but often betrayed a noisy whine, courtesy of the engine. Com-

parisons of diesels with modern streetcars suggested that while it may have cost less to buy diesel buses than a trolley network, the buses cost more to maintain. The diesels depreciate much more rapidly because of chronic vibrations.

While flexibility, comfort, and attractiveness were supposedly among the assets of the 1970s city bus, critics of the transit industry found substantive flaws. New buses running on New York City's streets in 1978 and 1979 suffered loose (or fallen) bumper parts and inner workings, which indicated shabby construction. Air conditioners, after a few months' use, seemed to be out of order or bordering on useless. Despite the presence of air conditioners, windows could be forced and inevitably *were* opened by passengers, further negating the value of the air-cooling devices.

Even if the contemporary diesel bus were thoroughly efficient, it is as the *Village Voice* authors Brian Ketcham and Stan Pinkwas observed, "a notoriously filthy machine." Ketcham and Pinkwas pointed out that diesel engines release fifteen to sixty times as much pollutant matter into the atmosphere as gasoline engines, yet diesels are being promoted because they get better mileage. "Diesels," they went on, "may prove to be the most dangerous producers of pollutants in the urban environment."

The diesel bus may have won the big battle over the streetcar; but if pollution increases in cities that operate the notoriously filthy machines, we all will have lost the war for survival.

III

WAS THE MASS TRANSIT INDUSTRY SYSTEMATICALLY DESTROYED?

11

The Tragic Story of Trolley Cars in North America

Judging by headlines in assorted North American cities during 1978, a visitor from another planet could be excused for believing that the trolley car was the favorite means of urban transportation in Canada and the United States. On the West Coast, Seattle civic leaders exulted over their city's purchase of a fifty-two-year-old Melbourne, Australia, streetcar for use on new trackage to be laid along the Seattle waterfront. On the other side of the continent, in New York City, members of the Big Apple's planning commission mulled over a proposal to install a trolley line along populous 42nd Street, running from the East River to the Hudson. Meanwhile, north of the border, in Toronto, Canada, citizens eagerly awaited delivery of a spanking new fleet of Canadian-built trolleys to augment an expanding tramway empire.

Yes, a newcomer could have mistaken 1978 as the time of the trolley. This, however, was hardly the case because the street railway had long ago become virtually an extinct species in the United States. Special interests had assiduously worked toward the systematic extermination of trams even before the advent of World War II. The elimination of the tram is both an awesome and an appalling story.

Only a confirmed trolley buff would dare claim that the electric streetcar was the perfect mode of municipal transportation. Compared to the gasoline-powered bus and, for that matter, the trackless trolley, the streetcar on rails had its limitations. Leaders within the electric tram industry realized that themselves and developed a marvel of transportation in the thirties, the Presidents' Conference Committee (PCC) car, which won the hearts of commuters from Brooklyn to Los Angeles. Based on the PCC car's rave reviews, there was every reason to believe that the trolley industry would survive. But it didn't. Production of American-made streetcars ended in 1951, and by the late sixties trolley fleets remained only in San Francisco, Boston, Philadelphia, Pittsburgh, Toronto, Cleveland, Newark, New Orleans, and El Paso.

To the average straphanger in Seattle, Chicago, New York, and San Diego, the departure of the trolley was a puzzle; "progress" was the catchword inevitably heard by those who questioned the changeover from electric streetcar to diesel bus. Unfortunately, the average straphanger never had the opportunity to vote on *his* choice of transportation—almost always it was inflicted upon him—

nor did he have the resources to probe behind the choices, so that a determination could be made as to whether or not the good of the rider as well as the good of the municipality was being served. But early in 1974 hearings before a United States Senate Antitrust Subcommittee unearthed testimony strongly suggesting that the trolley was, in fact, a victim of genocide and that the assassins—no surprise—were based in Detroit and assorted petroleum centers. The most powerful declaration presented to the Senate was a five-year study of ground transportation by Bradford C. Snell, who became an assistant counsel to the subcommittee.

Writing in New York's *Village Voice* on March 7, 1974, analyst David Gurin observed: "The Snell report records in detail the planned extermination of sensible, energy-efficient and non-polluting modes of transport."

The essence of the study alleged that General Motors, along with oil, tire, and highway interests, more than fifty years ago deliberately began to wreck the mass transport systems of this country in order to increase sales of their products. The suggestion, right or wrong, was that GM tried to wreck the mass transit system.

"This explanation of the sickness of American transportation might once have been dismissed as the paranoia of mass transit advocates," said Gurin. "But its reality was thoroughly documented in hearings before the Senate Antitrust Subcommittee."

If the public were privy to the facts involved in the purchase, use, and life of mass transit vehicles, it is doubtful that the average commuter ever would cast a vote for the diesel bus. In determining which vehicle is best for the job, one should determine which type most nearly meets such criteria as: has few points of wear; operates at a low temperature; is capable of greatest turning effort at zero engine rpm. Further, as Seattle transportation engineer E. E. Van Ness noted: "The prime mover (motor) must: 1. Not carry its fuel on board; need no transmission and travel the farthest per cost of fuel consumed." Van Ness argued that diesel buses should have been rejected in favor of electric streetcars or trackless trolleys since "the motors for the gasoline or diesel buses share one thing in common—they have hundreds of points of wear. There are 30-year-old traction motors with only ten points of wear. The more points of wear, the higher the maintenance costs and the poorer the fuel utilization."

Considering the drawbacks of the diesel, it is no wonder that the vehicle required an exceptional push to claim the territory of the trolley and electric bus. "The internal combustion bus," wrote Van Ness, "partly due to its many points of wear has very poor efficiency: about 10 percent at the wheels. This means that for every $10 spent on bus fuel, $9 goes out the tailpipe. Only $1 goes toward moving people. The electric trackless trolley, on the other hand, has a wheel efficiency of about 83 percent which means that for every $10 spent on kilowatt hours only about $1.70 is wasted. All the rest—$8.30—goes toward moving people."

Inefficiency of the internal combustion engine is cited in point after point; for example, the internal combustion engine must be turning at high speed before it can develop its rated torque whereas the electric motor develops highest torque at zero rpm. "This," Van Ness explained, "not only increases efficiency but it means that the electric does not require a transmission."

With these facts in mind, one might justifiably wonder why a city such as New York, which once boasted the most extensive streetcar network in the world, was persuaded to forsake the trolleys in favor of the gasoline-powered omnibuses. Gurin argues that the buses were the beneficiary of a Madison Avenue hype abetted by easily persuaded journalists and headline writers. "In the media," said Gurin, "buses were always 'sleek' or 'streamlined,' trolleys always 'Toonerville' or 'lumbering,' despite the trolley industry's development in the mid-thirties of remarkable new trolley cars. They were swift, comfortable and capable of much smoother stops and starts than 1974 buses. And, of course, the new trolleys were also odorless. To those who complained about bus fumes in 1939, General Motors promised cleaner engines in a year or two."

The pro-bus hype was helped by two key New York power brokers who had been passionately prorubber and antirail: transit czar Robert Moses and Mayor Fiorello La Guardia. For debatable reasons, La Guardia in 1939 ordered the Third Avenue Railroad Company—owner of the heavily used Broadway line and others—to completely motorize its routes with "modern, up-to-date buses" or lose its franchise!

Those who protested La Guardia's decision were confronted with a City Hall version of "Let them eat cake!" which, translated, came to "Buses are better," a theme dispensed by the General Motors public relations department. Following World War II, when, one by one, New York City's trolleys were wiped out, an even more extraordinary event took place. The Board of Transportation selected Brooklyn as the site of a vast new trolley bus network. A fleet of quiet, speedy electric buses manufactured by the St. Louis Car Company graced many lines that previously had seen gasoline-powered polluting buses virtually break down overnight, and it appeared that a new dawn was breaking in electric transit throughout the borough. But the trolley bus—with much of the flexibility of the diesel—lasted less than a decade and was replaced by diesel buses. In a horrendous touch of irony, soon after the Brooklyn trolley coach plant was dismantled and the electric buses disposed of, a master report on air pollution in New York City was published. One of its essential points was that to eliminate air pollution *New York should invest in electric buses!*

But the slaughter was complete. No matter how vivid the facts may have been, no matter how effectively Snell's report may have supported electric transit, the job had been done. Whatever persuasive chapters and verses were transmitted to mayors, governors, planning commissions, and city managers, the unvarnished fact was there, as plain as a paved-over trolley track: too many millions and billions of dollars would be required to bring the trolley and electric buses back from the dead.

The news in 1978 that Seattle had purchased a pair of fifty-two-year-old Australian streetcars and New York City was contemplating a trolley line along Forty-second Street merely confirmed what most analysts in the transit industry already knew. Auto interests had lost a battle but won its half-century-long war against the trolley.

12

Exposing the Trolley Killers

The transit planners who painfully watched the decline and fall of the street-car-interurban industry would finally marshal their resources for a counterat-tack. And what amounted to a two-pronged counterattack—by Senators and municipal officials such as San Francisco mayor Joseph Alioto—reached its peak of effectiveness in the spring of 1974.

Act One, Scene One was set before Michigan Democrat Philip A. Hart's Sen-ate Antitrust Subcommittee. It was at a time when the energy crisis was Topic A in Washington and politicians were desperately in search of those responsible for the eventual dearth of oil and petroleum reserves. At first the accusing fin-ger was pointed at the oil companies, the government, and the consumer. But, then, in a series of surprising developments, blame was redirected at Detroit, and auto interests in particular. Informed witnesses testified that by killing off other forms of transportation in the past, Detroit car makers stimulated the use of autos and thereby contributed to the fuel shortages of the seventies.

Alioto, who had also been an antitrust lawyer, was among the more promi-nent speakers against the auto combine. "A demonstration of the terrifying power of the automobile monopoly," Mayor Alioto related to the Senators, "oc-curred in the demise of the Key System that once linked San Francisco to Oak-land and other communities of the East Bay region." The Key System, as he tes-tified, once operated a total of 230 electric streetcars and trains. Because they ran on electricity, the cars produced no smog. And because they ran on their own private tracks, they did not contend with automobile traffic.

The Key System was not financially well off when, in 1946, a controlling in-terest in its parent company was acquired by National City Lines. National City Lines was a holding company that had been organized by General Motors, which was joined by Standard Oil and Firestone in its financing. The Key Sys-tem needed to change to survive, and the new holding company was not long in making those changes.

As Mayor Alioto explained, "A scant two days later, GM's newly acquired transit company announced that streetcars would be replaced by buses. The buses, a fleet of two hundred vehicles, were purchased during the next two years from GM." This was just the beginning. Key also announced in 1954 that its bridge trains would stop running and be replaced by buses. Train tracks were soon torn up and an additional auto deck was created on the bridges.

The timing of this decision was crucial. In 1958 the Bay Area Rapid Transit

(BART) Commission was already discussing plans for crossing the bay with its own trains, and, as Mayor Alioto pointed out, "it could have used the Key System bridge right-of-way." The result was to make it that much more expensive and difficult. "Ultimately, BART was forced to spend $180 million to make a trans-Bay tube connection. Meanwhile, automotive traffic rolls on the paved-over bridge right-of-way that would have been the least expensive and most logical connection."

San Francisco's experience was not unique. As Mayor Alioto testified, "In all, General Motors, acting through subsidiary mass transit companies, acquired forty-six streetcar systems in forty-five cities and converted all to smog-producing bus operations." Some claimed that the failing streetcar companies were only succumbing to a natural, not premature death. Senator Roman L. Hruska of the subcommittee contended that the "streetcars were inordinately inefficient." Mayor Alioto's response, in question form, was more to the point. "If it is true," he asked, "that the streetcar companies were breaking down of their own weight, why was it necessary for General Motors to join with Standard Oil and the tire company to go in and buy the systems and tear up the tracks?"

Mayor Alioto also discussed a second case of an alleged cabal at work in his own city. Alioto charged that expensive lobbying and advertising financed by the automotive giants was aimed at nipping the BART system in the bud, the auto's only possible serious competitor in the Bay Area.

Inflation, cost overruns, and other setbacks had exhausted the BART treasury long before its first trains were in operation. BART's backers organized then, in 1970, to put on the general ballot a measure that would divert gasoline tax money to mass transit developments. Besides aiding completion of the rapid transit system, the funds would be diverted to combat smog.

The statewide ballot battle was lost. A prime factor in the margin of 700,000 votes by which the auto interests won was, in the mayor's eyes, the disproportionate spending for advertising by the two sides. The pro-mass-transit group spent $15,275. Opponents, on the other hand, collected $348,000 and spent $333,000. It was not until after the loss that the actual source of the winners' funds became known. Certainly the public could not know from whom this support was coming when going to vote.

Those interests preferred seeing a half-completed rapid transit system crunch to a halt, to "remain a hole in the ground rather than a threat to their profits." Mayor Alioto observed that "they had the money to beat us at the polls every time we started to try to get the gas tax funds or transportation funds diverted for rapid transit. They can beat us every time."

The San Francisco experience exemplified the organized bullying mass transit has had to face at the hands of powerful auto interests. Like fish killed off by a swiftly polluted river, Mayor Alioto was saying, the streetcars and electric trains did not perish simply because of a lack of flexibility to changing "realities." "If we don't take action," the mayor pleaded, "we are going to lose the struggle to save the cities from congestion and pollution. I think it is that simple."

The simplicity and yet utter magnitude of the problem was further underlined by Los Angeles Mayor Thomas Bradley, who had been invited to attend the hearings for several reasons, not the least of which was the fact that, as one of the senators pointed out, "no other city in the United States has become more a symbol of the pervasive influence of the automobile in our lives than has Los Angeles." Likewise, no other city has suffered as much from the suffocating effects of pollution and the attendant problems of highway construction.

Although Bradley was unable to attend the hearings in person—ironically, he was forced to remain at City Hall because of the possibility that Los Angeles would institute mandatory gasoline rationing—he delivered a lengthy written exposition of his city's disastrous experiences with the automobile. The Senate subcommittee's report observed that Bradley presented "a picture of Southern California crisscrossed with concrete and covered with gas-guzzling dinosaurs."

Asserting that 22 percent (65 percent in the central city) of Los Angeles' land use was devoted to the auto in 1974, Bradley recalled how only thirty-five years earlier, his city had been served by the world's largest interurban electric railway system. At the time Pacific Electric System spun off more than 1,160 miles of track from Los Angeles into more than fifty California communities. Were it still in existence in the seventies, the Pacific Electric would have been the answer to Los Angeles' pollution and commuter passenger prayers.

But the shiny rails had long been gone and Bradley, pointing an accusing finger at Detroit, lamented the rubber-tired "solution" as not only physically smelly but also sociologically damaging to his metropolis. "Freeways to accommodate our autos," said Bradley, "have 'divided and conquered' our city with ribbons of concrete—separating people from their jobs and from each other, destroying the integrity of neighborhoods and encouraging urban spread and the destruction of needed open space." The mayor of Los Angeles, no doubt recalling the Watts area rioting in the black community, suggested that racial tensions had been exacerbated by highways and more highways splitting neighborhoods.

"Those without automobiles," said Bradley, "and those who cannot drive in Los Angeles find their mobility and access to jobs—the doctor, shopping, schooling—seriously impaired." This, however, was not the case when Pacific Electric's "Big Red cars" traveled north to San Fernando, east to San Bernardino, and south to Santa Ana. Bradley then zeroed in on his culprits:

In 1938, General Motors and Standard Oil of California organized Pacific City Lines as an affiliate to the National City Lines to "motorize" West Coast electric railways. In 1940, PCL began to acquire and "scrap" portions of the $100 million Pacific Electric System, including rail lines from Los Angeles to Burbank, Glendale, Pasadena, and San Bernardino.

Subsequently, in December 1944, another NCL affiliate—American City Lines—was financed by GM and Standard Oil to "motorize downtown Los Angeles." American City Lines purchased the downtown electric system, "scrapped" its electric cars, tore down its power transmission lines, up-rooted the tracks, and placed GM diesel buses, fueled by Standard Oil, on Los Angeles City Streets. By this time, Los Angeles' three thousand quiet, pollution-free electric train system was totally destroyed.

At the conclusion of World War II, competition in the American bus industry included Mack, Twin Coach, and American Car and Foundry, as well as General Motors, but not for long. Eventually, the General Motors bus became so ubiquitous on American streets that it was considered an event when a vehicle manufactured by another company made an appearance. Mayor Bradley took due note of GM's virtual dominance of the omnibus industry. "Since 1952," he went on, "when the bus was limited to practically one manufacturer, city motor bus ridership had declined to 4.5 billion and intercity motor bus ridership had fallen to 125,000,000, or a combined loss of 3.8 billion passengers. Consequently, bus production and sales have declined from 8,480 in 1951 to only 3,700 in 1972 or about 56 percent."

Bradley, like Alioto, minced no words when it was time to affix the blame. "As you can see," he concluded, "from these series of historical events, the destruction of a system in Los Angeles with over one thousand miles of tracks took place in a very calculated fashion. The fact that a handful of giant corporations determined the form of ground transportation for the country's three largest cities—and for a hundred other cities—should not be easily forgotten. . . ."

To the casual commuter, unaccustomed to the machinations of moguls in multinational corporations and their lobbies, the revelations were, to say the least, enlightening and, for electric traction boosters, thoroughly depressing. But the counterattack had just begun and the General Patton of the trolley bloc turned out to be Bradford C. Snell, assistant counsel of the Senate Antitrust Subcommittee. A year earlier, Snell, following a grant supplied by the Stern Fund of New York, completed a report, "American Ground Transport," which did more to expose the alleged duplicity of the trolley killers than any document. Snell's report supplied the background for his dramatic arguments against Detroit at the subcommittee hearings. Among other things, Snell asserted that once GM set up its bus business, it deliberately refrained from improving the design. As a result, Snell charged, the "noisy, foul-smelling buses turned earlier patrons of the high-speed rail system away from public transit and, in effect, sold millions of private automobiles."

In his report Snell tied together many of the loose ends of years of transportation transition to present a picture of public policy goals influenced by private business considerations. Ultimately, the report was submitted (February 1974) to the Senate Subcommittee on Antitrust and Monopoly. Trying to be fair, Snell insisted that his report was "not a study of malevolent or rapacious executives . . ." and that many of the corporate actions portrayed in the report could be viewed as reasonable from the point of view of the interests of stockholders.

Tracing the events that led to GM's involvement, Snell observed that when in the 1920s America's auto market appeared to be saturated, GM moved into the mass transit sector but, significantly, not in the manufacture of trolleys. Instead, the conglomerate began manufacturing city and intercity buses.

After its successful experience with intercity buses [wrote Snell] General Motors diversified into city bus and rail operations. At first, its procedure consisted of directly acquiring and scrapping local electric transit systems in favor of GM buses. In this fashion it created a market for its city buses. . . .

On June 29, 1932, the GM-bus executive committee formally resolved that "to develop motorized transportation, our company should initiate a program of this nature and authorize the incorporation of a holding company with a capital of $300,000." Thus was formed United Cities Motor Transit (UCMT) as a subsidiary of GM's bus division. Its sole function was to acquire electric streetcar companies, convert them to GM motorbus operation, and then resell the properties to local concerns which agreed to purchase GM bus replacements . . .

"In each case," GM General Counsel Hogan stated, "GM successfully motorized the city, turned the management over to other interests and liquidated its investment." The program ceased, however, in 1935 when GM was censured by the American Transit Association (ATA) for its self-serving role as a bus manufacturer, in apparently attempting to motorize Portland's electric streetcar system.

Starting with the smaller companies, GM moved into major municipalities, including the biggest of them all—New York City, which then was interwoven with one of the grandest streetcar systems in the entire world. In his report. Snell asserted: "The massive conversion within a period of only eighteen months of the New York system, then the world's largest streetcar network, has been recognized subsequently as the turning point in the electric railway industry."

In 1936 General Motors organized National City Lines (NCL), according to Snell, who went on:

During the following fourteen years General Motors, together with Standard Oil of California, Firestone Tire, and two other suppliers of bus-related products, contributed more than $9 million to this holding company for the purpose of converting electric transit systems in sixteen states to GM bus operations. The method of operation was basically the same as that which GM employed successfully in its United Cities Motor Transit program: acquisition, motorization, resale. By having NCL resell the properties after conversion was completed, GM and its allied companies were assured that this capital was continuously reinvested in the motorization of additional systems. . . . By 1949, General Motors had been involved in the replacement of more than one hundred electric transit systems with GM buses in forty-five cities including New York, Philadelphia, Baltimore, St. Louis, Oakland, Salt Lake City, and Los Angeles. In April of that year, a Chicago federal jury convicted GM of having criminally conspired with Standard Oil of California, Firestone Tire and others to replace electric transportation with gas- or diesel-powered buses and to monopolize the sale of buses and related products to local transportation companies throughout the country.

The court imposed a sanction of $5,000 on GM. In addition, the jury convicted H. C. Grossman, who was then treasurer of General Motors. Grossman had played a key role in the motorization campaigns and had served as a director of Pacific City Lines when that company undertook the dismantlement of the $100,000,000 Pacific Electric system. The court fined Grossman the magnanimous sum of $1.

Although punished, General Motors was able to escape with what could be construed as only a slap-on-the-wrist fine. Certainly, a $5,000 fine is less than the cost of a truckload of new Chevrolets. Snell took due note of the fact that

General Motors plunged ever forward in, what he believed to be, its campaign to wipe out the electric traction systems.

Despite its criminal conviction [wrote Snell] General Motors continued to acquire and dieselize electric transit properties through September of 1955. By then, approximately 88 percent of the nation's streetcar network had been eliminated. In 1936 when GM organized National City Lines, 40,000 streetcars were operating in the United States; at the end of 1955, only 5,000 remained. In December of that year, GM bus chief Roger M. Kyes correctly observed: "The gas motor coach supplanted the interurban systems and has for all practical purposes eliminated the trolley.". . .
Electric street railways and electric trolley buses were eliminated without regard to their relative merit as a mode of transport. Their displacement by oil-powered buses maximized the earnings of GM stockholders; but it deprived the riding public of a competing method of travel.

To fortify his case, Snell obtained the testimony of such urban transit experts as George M. Smerk, who fired additional salvos at the alleged GM scheme. "Street railways," said Smerk, quoted in the Snell report, "and trolley bus operations, even if better suited to traffic needs and the public interest, were doomed in favor of vehicles and material produced by the conspirators. . . ."
One of the most stunning charges delivered by Snell centered upon the quality of the GM bus. According to Snell's postulation, General Motors deliberately designed a bus with only the most modest assets. By so doing, GM, if Snell is to be believed, put out a vehicle that did nothing to woo riders to mass transit unless they absolutely were compelled to take a bus for economic (not having a car) or other possible reasons. Snell, on this subject, elaborated as follows:

General Motors' gross revenues are ten times greater if it sells cars rather than buses. In theory, therefore, GM has every economic incentive to discourage bus ridership. In fact, its bus dieselization program may have generated that effect. Engineering studies strongly suggest that conversion from electric transit to diesel buses results in higher operating costs, loss of patronage, and eventual bankruptcy. The studies demonstrate, for example, that diesel buses have 28 percent shorter economic lives, 40 percent higher operating costs, and 9 percent lower productivity than electric buses. They also conclude that the diesel's foul smoke, ear-splitting noise, and slow acceleration may discourage ridership. In short, by increasing the costs, reducing the revenues, and contributing to the collapse of hundreds of transit systems, GM's dieselization program may have had the long-term effect of selling GM cars, in Snell's estimation.

Such publications as *The Third Rail* found the facts in the Snell report distressing in terms of the demonstrated ability of industrial power brokers to possibly alter the course of transit planning.
As Snell elaborated:

[The auto industry] has used [its revenues from auto sales] to finance political activities which, in the absence of effective countervailing activities by competing ground transport industries, induced government bodies to promote their product (automobiles) over other alternatives, particularly rail rapid transit. . . .
On June 28, 1932, Alfred P. Sloan, Jr., president of General Motors, organized the Na-

tional Highway Users Conference [whose] announced objectives were dedication of highway taxes solely to highway purposes, and development of a continuing program of
highway construction.

During the succeeding 40 years, the National Highway Users Conference (now Highway Users Federation for Safety and Mobility—HUFSAM) has compiled an impressive
record of accomplishments. Its effect, if not its purpose, has been to direct public funds
away from rail construction and into highway building. At the state level, its 2,800 lobbying groups have been instrumental in persuading forty-four of the nation's fifty legis-
latures to adopt and preserve measures which dedicated state and local gasoline tax revenues exclusively to highway construction. By promoting these highway "trust funds," it
has discouraged governors and mayors from attempting to build anything other than
highways for urban transportation. Subways and rail transit proposals have had to compete with hospitals, schools and other governmental responsibilities for funding. . . .
From 1945 through 1970, states and localities spent more than $156 billion constructing
hundreds of thousands of miles of roads. During that same period, only sixteen miles of
subway were constructed in the entire country.

Furthermore, Snell pointed out that transit organizations cannot compete
with the highway lobby because they are

financially weak and torn by the conflicting interests of their membership. The American Transit Association, the largest element of the transit lobby, operates on an annual
budget of about $700,000, which must be apportioned between the conflicting political
needs of its bus and rail transit manufacturing members. . . . The third and smallest element of the transit body, the Institute for Rapid Transit, operates on a meager budget of
about $200,000 a year. In short, HUFSAM and the Motor Vehicle Manufacturers Associ-
ation alone outspend the three principal transit organizations by more than 10 to 1.

Unfortunately, the GM influence was felt even by the groups that support
transit:

Due to its position as the nation's largest producer of bus and rail vehicles [Snell pointed
out], it is a major financial contributor to both the American Transit Association and the
Railway Progress Institute. It is also an influential member of the Institute for Rapid
Transit.

Snell's predictions for the future involvement of the auto industry in the development of mass transit were grim.

General Motors is engaged in a continuing effort to divert government funds from rapid
rail transit, which seriously threatens the use of cars in metropolitan areas, to GM buses,
which fail consistently to persuade people to abandon their autos. In place of regional
electric rail systems, for instance, it promotes diesel-powered "bus trains" of as many as
1,400 units, each spaced 80 feet apart. Instead of urban electric rail, it advocates the use
of dual-mode gas/electric vehicles which would be adapted from GM's minimotor
homes. In sum, the automakers embrace transit in order to prevent it from competing
effectively with their sales of automobiles.

One of the most horrendous charges—although a peripheral concern—made
by Snell in this 1974 report was that General Motors, while systematically wip-

ing out the electric traction industry, also was arming Hitler's Nazi war machine. (See Appendix A.)

Snell's allegations of the GM-Nazi link, for reasons best known to the media, received precious little attention in terms of the potential newsworthiness of the story. However, the Snell attack on the conglomerate's antitransit schemes did receive considerable ink. Snell charged that General Motors had both the power and economic incentive to maximize profits by suppressing rail and bus transportation.

The economics are obvious [Snell explained]: one bus can eliminate 35 automobiles; one streetcar, subway or rail transit vehicle can supplant 50 passenger cars; one train can displace 1,000 cars or a fleet of 150 cargo-laden trucks. The result was inevitable: a drive by GM to sell cars and trucks by displacing rail and bus systems. This section describes that process. It discloses, for example, GM's role in the destruction of more than one hundred electric surface rail systems in forty-five cities including New York, Philadelphia, Baltimore, St. Louis, Oakland, Salt Lake City, and Los Angeles. More specifically, it describes the devastating impact of this widescale operation on the quality of life in America's cities.

Nowhere was the ruin from GM's motorization program more apparent than in Southern California. Thirty-five years ago Los Angeles was a beautiful city of lush palm trees, fragrant orange groves and ocean-clean air. It was served then by the world's largest electric railway network. In the late 1930s General Motors and allied highway interests acquired the local transit companies, scrapped their pollution-free electric trains, tore down their power transmission lines, ripped up their tracks, and placed GM buses on already congested Los Angeles streets. The noisy, foul-smelling buses turned earlier patrons of the high-speed rail system away from public transit and, in effect, sold millions of private automobiles. Largely as a result, this city is today an ecological wasteland: the palm trees are dying of petrochemical smog; the orange groves have been paved over by 300 miles of freeways; the air is a septic tank into which four million cars, half of them built by General Motors, pump 13,000 tons of pollutants daily. Furthermore, a shortage of motor vehicle fuel and an absence of adequate public transport now threaten to disrupt the entire auto-dependent region.

Part II also suggests that General Motors' common control of auto, truck, and locomotive production may have contributed to the decline of America's railroads. Beginning in the mid-1930s, this firm used its leverage as the nation's largest shipper of freight to coerce railroads into scrapping their equipment, including pollution-free electric locomotives, in favor of more expensive, less durable, and less efficient GM diesel units. As a consequence, dieselization seriously impaired the ability of railroads to compete with the cars and trucks GM was fundamentally interested in selling.

In this regard, GM's dieselization of the New Haven Railroad is illustrative. During fifty years of electrified operation, this road had never failed to show an operating profit. In 1955, the year before GM dieselized its operation, the New Haven earned $5.7 million carrying 45 million passengers and 814,000 carloads of freight. Then, in 1956, GM persuaded it to tear down its electric lines and scrap its powerful, high-speed electric locomotives. By 1959, three years after dieselization, it lost $9.2 million hauling 10 million fewer passengers and 130,000 fewer carloads of freight. In 1961, it was declared bankrupt; by 1968, when it was acquired by the Penn Central, it had accumulated a capital deficit of nearly $300 million.

In sum, GM's dieselization program may have eliminated a technological alternative, electric trains, which could have helped the railroads compete more effectively for passengers and freight with highway transport. Today, when virtually every other industrialized nation has electrified its railroads, America and what is left of America's railroads are locked in to GM diesel locomotives.

The motorization of Los Angeles and dieselization of the New Haven are two of the most appalling episodes in the history of American transportation. These and other shocking incidents, however, were the inevitable outgrowth of concentrated economic power. Whether General Motors' executives actually intended to construct a society wholly dependent on motor vehicles is unlikely and, in any case, irrelevant. That such a society developed in part as a result of that firm's control of competing forms of ground transportation is both relevant and apparent.

Assuming, for the sake of argument, that Snell's arguments and facts are sound, how were General Motors and other competitors of the trolley industry able to persuade Mr. and Mrs. America that they were traveling in the wrong vehicles? One answer was supplied by editors of *The Third Rail*, who argued in 1974 that Madison Avenue hype and high-pressure press agentry paved the way for conversion from rail to macadam. "No force," commented *The Third Rail*, "captured and guided the American imagination in the Twentieth Century so powerfully as the concept of 'progress.'

" 'Progress' implied the steady and natural advance of a nation moving forward toward a future goal, even as our predecessors in the last century pursued 'manifest destiny' until our national borders stretched from ocean to ocean. This same 'progress' demanded that we put aside all which the forces of change decreed as 'obsolete'—and that we never look back."

Even today, support for that statement is as fervent in many quarters as it was in 1974. The facts speak for themselves: the United States now has half of all the motor vehicles in the world. And our reliance on automobiles and trucks continues.

Consider this awesome fact: *Annually, more than five million people are killed or injured in automobiles!*

Now if five million citizens died or were maimed each year as a result of accidents in, say, the food or toy or mining industry, the government would call a national emergency, shut down the industry, and see to it that changes were immediately implemented to eliminate the carnage. Yet, somehow, the auto product kills more and more Americans, and Washington merely adds up the statistics. A Department of Transportation study released March 17, 1977, revealed that "motor vehicle accidents cost American society nearly $38 billion annually, in terms of deaths, injuries, lost income and property damage" (DOT news release).

If that isn't a terrifying case against the auto in favor of mass transit, nothing ever will be.

13

General Motors Fires Back

Bradford Curie Snell's unremitting broadsides were not accepted by General Motors without a mighty counterattack. Snell told this writer that he was told that the conglomerate had organized "a truth squad," designed to detail GM's side of the story and destroy the credibility of "American Ground Transport," which was the foundation of Snell's assault against the company. "I was informed via telephone by several mayoral assistants that GM's representatives had visited mayors and newspaper editors in all the cities which carried any publicity about the hearings," Snell told this writer, "to dissuade them of its revelations."

A General Motors spokesman, in response to this writer's query, denied Snell's allegation about a GM "truth squad." James Smidebush, GM's public relations director, replied:

"We stand firmly on what we said in our official reply. I don't understand what he means by a 'truth squad.' We put all the facts forth in that document and we will stand pat on what we said at that time."

In addition General Motors delivered an extensive rebuttal to the Snell report for use in the Senate. Whereas Snell detailed General Motors' activities to destroy rail transit in America, GM elaborately defended its actions and submitted its position to the Subcommittee on Antitrust and Monopoly of the Committee on the Judiciary of the Senate in April 1974. (See Appendix B for details of General Motors' rebuttal.) It was comprehensive, effective, and convincing.

Reviewing Snell's charges paragraph by paragraph, GM asserted that they contained "wholly unfounded accusations" and argued that "the record must be set straight." This allegedly was accomplished by means of the rebuttal paper, called "A Reply by General Motors." In this four-part rebuttal, the conglomerate proceeded to zero in on what were the two most sensitive and widely publicized charges—that General Motors aided the Nazi government during World War II and that General Motors deliberately sabotaged the rail transportation capability of the United States.

Partial details of General Motors' emphatic denial of the above accusations, among others, follow:

PART I. GENERAL MOTORS DID NOT ASSIST THE NAZIS DURING WORLD WAR II

The Snell document asserted that GM (and Ford) actively assisted the Nazi war effort, specifically naming Adam Opel, a GM subsidiary beginning in 1929.

GM replies that in the years prior to 1939, Adam Opel had produced only its traditional products—cars, trucks, and spare parts. After the German invasion of Poland in 1939, the American personnel resigned from management positions rather than participate in the production of war materials, even though at this time the United States was neutral. The General Motors *Annual Report* for that year supports GM's assertion that they withdrew their personnel, though it temporarily retained "nominal representation" on the board. The last of GM's American employees departed from Germany in early March 1941. The company argues that Opel, while under GM control, possessed no special aircraft product technology. The product development and engineering know-how required to manufacture aircraft parts was brought to Opel by the German government. GM, therefore, claims that it had nothing whatsoever to do with the aircrafts and engines pictured in Snell's document.

In view of these facts, the rebuttal states, the charge in "American Ground Transport" that GM became "an integral part of the Nazi war effort" is totally false. Not only were these claims irrelevant to the subcommittee proceedings, they are illustrated only with photographs.

Further charges, the rebuttal continues, that GM and other firms "were able to shape the conflict to their own private corporate advantage," and that it served their "best interests to cooperate in the Axis war effort," and, finally, that if the Germans had won the war GM "would have appeared impeccably Nazi," have no foundation in fact and are totally irresponsible.

PART II. GENERAL MOTORS DID NOT SUPPRESS RAIL TRANSPORTATION WITH THE DIESEL LOCOMOTIVE; IT ADVANCED IT

According to the GM reply, the argument that GM repressed railroad transportation was introduced by and was entirely dependent upon the following unqualified assertion:

"As the Nation's largest shipper of freight GM was able to exert considerable influence over the locomotive purchasing policies of the Nation's railroads. It used this powerful form of leverage to sell its diesel locomotives."

This statement, the company insists, was the cornerstone of the claim that GM foisted inferior mass transportation equipment on the unwilling carriers, to the detriment of America's entire transportation system.

The U.S. Department of Justice had conducted an exhaustive investigation of this very matter and the prosecutors concluded—not once but twice—that they had no case. GM claimed that Snell ignored the Justice Department findings, basing his case against GM on five unsubstantiated references. GM elucidates that the reference to the Gulf, Mobile & Ohio Railroad, for instance, was supported only by unproven allegations in the indictment in the government criminal case which was voluntarily abandoned. The case of the Baltimore & Ohio Railroad, which allegedly was falsely presented as a quotation from a letter, was supported only by one of the author's ubiquitous confidential interviews. GM charges that had the quotation been genuine, it would still not establish that GM sold locomotives through reciprocity, only that a railroad president tried to obtain freight business that way.

The fifth reference was the most misleading of all, GM fires back. Snell, according to GM, removed a sentence from a privileged memorandum entitled "Reciprocity as Proof of the Offense of Monopolization Under Section 2 of the Sherman Act." This single sentence, it continues, was totally distorted by its removal from context. Reproduced below was the sentence and the *very next sentence* (italicized for emphasis) in the same memorandum showing, as GM suggests, how deceiving the statement could appear by itself.

"GM, could, in all probability, have successfully capitalized upon the railroads' sensitivity to reciprocity by frequently reminding them of GM's considerable traffic, and could have done so without ever interfering substantially with the economical routing of traffic. *The fact that GM did not do so, while EMD's competitors did engage extensively in reciprocity, appears to be a tribute to the strength of GM's policy against reciprocity.*"

GM's positive contribution to the welfare of the railroads goes further than their honest policies, the company goes on. Their pioneering development of the diesel locomotive is cited by GM as a great success story in American competitive enterprise. Fred Gurley, former chairman of the Santa Fe Railroad, testified on the initial diesel freight locomotive, saying, ". . . here we had the ultimate. Here was an engine that in my judgment outperformed anything in the country. I just made up my mind to two things right now: That the day of the steam engine was history; that I owe a debt of gratitude to the fellows that made it all possible, and that was your company . . . General Motors."

PART III. GENERAL MOTORS DID NOT DESTROY STREET RAILWAY SYSTEMS; THEY FAILED EVERYWHERE BECAUSE THEY WERE NO LONGER ABLE TO GIVE ADEQUATE SERVICE

General Motors takes Snell to task as follows: "American Ground Transport," it points out, set up General Motors as the scapegoat who caused the "destruction of more than 100 surface rail systems" which had a "devastating impact . . . on the quality of life in American cities." The simple cure: Force GM out of the mass transportation business, presumably to clear the way for the return of the streetcar.

General Motors devoted its counterattack in this area to points that supposedly prove the street railway systems in this country were not the thriving and effective enterprises that Snell claims and that their demise cannot be blamed on GM, and their return can hardly be the panacea for the future.

Snell's case against GM centers, the firm argues, on a modest investment in National City Lines (without any managerial control) and their subsequent conversion from streetcars to buses. GM made the investment in 1939, and went on to invest in American City Lines (a National subsidiary), in 1943, and Pacific City Lines (beginning in 1938 when that company was also a National subsidiary), at the request of those companies when they had trouble raising money from other sources. GM spent a total of $2,900,000 on the three companies, it says. Similarly, partial requirements contracts for GM buses were only negotiated after the customers themselves had requested them, the firm concludes.

Although these investments and contracts were found to be an antitrust violation, they had nothing at all to do with the replacement of cars by buses, GM rebuts. There is not one word in either the government indictment in the criminal case or civil case which charges GM with unlawfully scrapping or eliminating street railway systems.

GM cites an opinion which supposedly points out the flaw in the accusations against General Motors:

"In 1938, National conceived the idea of purchasing transportation systems in cities *where streetcars were no longer practicable* and supplanting the latter with passenger buses."

Equally false, charges the company, were statements that "GM extracted" contracts from transit companies requiring the purchase of gasoline-fueled equipment. The diesel buses that GM was trying to sell do not run on gasoline. Moreover, the supply contract used in the report did not apply to any cities in California, which the author cites as his prime examples of the ruin wrought by GM, the company concludes.

LOS ANGELES

GM zeroes in on Snell's charge that in 1936 GM organized National City Lines to convert the remainder of America's electric transportation systems to GM buses. A prime target was the "quiet" and "efficient" Pacific Electric interurban system and the Los Angeles Railway. He claimed that National City Lines, in 1940, began to acquire and scrap portions of the Pacific Electric, including links to the Los Angeles system. Having severed those links, he reported, "GM and its auto industrial allies motorized its downtown heart," by converting the Los Angeles Railway from streetcars to buses.

To that GM counterattacks that National City Lines was not around in 1917 when the Pacific Electric began the progressive abandonment of its own rail passenger service. In a 1958 *Pacific Railway Journal*, it was reported: "The establishment of bus lines as a substitution for unprofitable rail service began in 1917. . . . Times were changing in Southern California and since PE could not provide proper rapid transit, it had no alternative but to change with the times."

GM points out that in 1940, the California Railroad Commission gave their approval for the conversion of the Pacific Electric Railway to buses: "... Collapse of the financial structure of Pacific Electric is inevitable without outside financial assistance if operations are continued on the basis as experienced during past years. . . . One of the logical sources of reduced costs is substitution of motor coach service for rail lines. . . ." GM adds that by 1950, the California Railroad Commission had authorized the conversion to bus service for nine major lines in outlying communities. The substitution continued into the 1950s and 1960s when the system was run by Metropolitan Coach Lines, no connection to GM, and later by the Los Angeles Metropolitan Transit Authority, a public agency.

GM alleges that Snell ignored the fact that Pacific Electric itself and its successors converted from rail service to bus service for a period of four decades. Similarly, the conversion of Los Angeles Railway from streetcars to buses was well under way, for sound economic reasons, before National City Lines or American City Lines were even organized.

The rail transit systems of Los Angeles were singled out by Snell as the showcase examples of successful enterprises which he claimed were eliminated by the machinations of GM. But the company insists that they were eliminated by economics; that their demise was caused by the same economic problems that affected their counterparts across the country and had nothing whatever to do with a plot hatched by General Motors.

New York and Oakland were also high on the list of cities that Snell said GM had victimized. Their cases were similarly detailed and came to much the same conclusion as the city of Los Angeles. General Motors pointed out repeatedly that they did *not* generate the winds of change that doomed the streetcar systems; it did, however, through its buses, help to alleviate the disruption left in their wake. GM was able to help with technology, with enterprise, and in some cases, with capital. If GM had really been interested in destroying mass transportation and creating complete dependence on the automobile, it would hardly have put forth such energetic efforts to develop and promote the sale of buses. GM, the company says, never conferred anything but a positive benefit on the entire community.

PART IV. THE PAPER ON "AMERICAN GROUND TRANSPORT" IS REPLETE WITH ADDITIONAL FALSE AND DECEPTIVE STATEMENTS

GM charges that Snell delivers other untrue allegations including a statement revealing that the U.S. Department of Justice, in January 1973, documented charges that the chairmen of GM and Ford routinely held "summit meetings" to fix prices on automobiles. The company replies that not only is there no mention of the defendant's acquittal in Snell's document, but the "summit meet-

ings" described in the bill of particulars were for the discussion of "future negotiations for labor contracts." At no time did the government ever contend that
the labor meetings were illegal; it argued only that they could have provided
"opportunity" for improper price discussions.

The subcommittee, says GM, was not exposed to an innocent mistake here; it
has been victimized by a deliberate effort to mislead.

Other statements made by Snell, argues GM, were deliberately worded to
give the reader false impressions. For example: ". . . there are some indications
that the Federal Government has sought to protect American automakers from
competition with imports by imposing 'voluntary' automobile quotas on foreign
governments. . . ."

GM suggests that the auto industry has historically been a staunch advocate
of free trade and that no quotas on imported cars have ever been imposed.

GM further disputes Snell's claim that: "By 1972, in a move which possibly
signified the passing of bus transportation in this country, General Motors had
begun converting its bus plants to motor home production."

GM countercharges that Snell neglected to find out that no "transit coaches"
had been built in the GM plant re-equipped for motor homes for at least twenty-five years. Moreover, the implicit assumption that GM is the only company
that sells buses in this country is, of course, totally incorrect.

14

Postscript on Snell and General Motors

Bradford Snell's strong, well-documented case that General Motors engaged in what one author described as "exceedingly questionable tactics" to force trolley companies to eliminate trolleys and to buy General Motors' buses received an elaborate rebuttal from Detroit. As seen, the conglomerate tried to mitigate Snell's report, "American Ground Transport," with a mighty rationale, claiming that trolleys were already in decline when General Motors bought and started retiring the lines. One critic charged that the logic is tantamount to a doctor bleeding a patient to death because "the patient already is ill with the measles."

In fact a few critics who have analyzed the General Motors' response with care have discovered what they regard as enough inaccuracies to make the corporation's response unconvincing—albeit lengthy—in the extreme. In the view of some critics the GM arguments collapsed on impact in the manner of a Cadillac grille ramming a brick wall at 55 miles per hour.

One who blew the whistle in print on General Motors was author Alec Dubro, who examined Snell's report and the automaker's response. Writing in the monthly magazine *Mother Jones*, Dubro analyzed GM's rebuttal and opined: "Few people familiar with monopoly tactics have been willing to accept that answer and contend that GM went after the successful lines, those that did survive, and brought them down one by one. It's difficult to believe that an entire mode of transportation could be wiped out by the actions of a single company, but then GM is not just any company."

Dubro was not impressed by the auto company's suggestion that trolleys had been oversold to America. "GM," snapped Dubro, "through treachery or aggressive marketing (which, in this case, is only a semantic difference) eliminated the trolleys where they were doing a perfectly admirable job."

Syndicated columnist Nicholas von Hoffman questioned the General Motors' alibi, and frankly asserted that the GM "conspiracy" was "much more serious than Watergate in its effects on our lives."

Other serious observers, such as the publication *Fifth Estate*, recoiled in horror at allegations of the GM-Nazi ties, described by Snell. In its March 16–19, 1974 issue, Volume 8, No. 24, *Fifth Estate* perceived the catch-22 nature of the GM both-sides-of-the-fence operation. Stated *Fifth Estate*:

"Although the charges [that General Motors simultaneously supplied weapons for the Allies and Nazis] are of the most serious magnitude, GM saw fit to issue only a three-sentence denial."

A story that under contemporary journalistic standards should have been a headline grabber far in excess of Watergate was, somehow, virtually ignored by the nation's dailies. "The Detroit papers," commented the *Fifth Estate*, "buried the whole story." (The *Free Press* put it on page 16–F.)

Unlike the Pablum treatment given GM's war role, the *Fifth Estate* published an excerpt from Snell's copyrighted statement documenting GM alleged cooperation with the Nazis.

To nearly every American, comprehending this dual role was like explaining the inexplicable. How could a family who sent its sons off to war—and death—deal with the fact that its children allegedly were being slaughtered by weapons made in former GM plants in Nazi Germany? What effect did these disclosures (buried though they were) have on children who grew up in World War II days, singing such patriotic songs as "Comin' In on a Wing and a Prayer"? Explanations would test the mettle of the most cynical of those among us. "Patriotic members of the Veterans of Foreign Wars might feel complete bewilderment at the paradox of General Motors, that ultimate institution, aiding a wartime enemy," commented the *Fifth Estate*. "But all these paradoxes are easily sorted out by the cost-accounting minds of America's business leaders, like GM's Chairman of the Board, Richard Gerstenberg. For as long as GM is assured of a friendly investment atmosphere, it can just as easily invest in fascist countries as in bourgeois democracies. The investment dollar crosses national boundaries as easily as the wind."

Snell's charges were picked up by some major newspapers. The Washington *Post*, for example, assigned Morton Mintz to the story and he noted both the GM World War II role and the allegation that the conglomerate attempted to ruin city rail systems. Jack Thomas, covering the story for the Boston *Globe*, did examine the demise of the trolley in favor of the automobile. Thomas spoke at length with Fred Salvucci, Boston's transportation advisor at the time.

Said Salvucci, "That kind of policy definitely hurts us in Boston. Even though we've retained our transit system, it's extremely difficult to purchase equipment because the manufacturers of trains and trolleys have driven us out of business.

"We're purchasing streetcars," Salvucci was quoted in the Boston *Globe*, "but it takes six years to get them. World War II was won in four years.

"It's also damaging to us because it results in a complete distortion of the role of the automobile in our culture," he added, "and it's also expensive.

"In the past two years, we've had to spend $5 million repairing streetcars that are obsolete. It's a losing proposition."

By the time the Senate hearings had been concluded, it had become apparent that only a small minority of the press had latched on to what could have been one of the biggest stories of the half-century and an even smaller minority, including columnist Nicholas von Hoffman, cared to put the GM position in relation to mass transit under scrutiny. "Half our population," wrote von Hoffman, "is marooned and held for ransom in the suburbs by the car, tire, and oil companies. That we are in this fix is not accidental . . . General Motors took our money, our health and our sanity. . . ."

Another authority on transportation who lashed at General Motors for its refutation of charges that GM conspired to kill trolleys was Commander E. J. Quinby of Summit, New Jersey. In May 1974 Quinby asserted: "It is incredible that GM would have the nerve to claim such total innocence and adopt such an injured air in the face of the cold fact that we got them indicted, tried, and convicted (by a jury of twelve good women and true) back in 1949 and that the executives of each of the corporations participating in the conspiracy were given the choice of a $5,000 fine or one year in the Federal penitentiary!" (*Railroad* magazine, July 1949, columnist Stephen D. Maguire). Quinby added: "Bradford C. Snell, accused by GM of idiocies and 'cheap shots,' is quoting historic facts such as those revealed in my 36-page brochure which I distributed back in 1946, and which provided information on which the Department of Justice based their action that brought about the convictions. Included in that brochure were the statistics of how GM financed and participated in the campaign to wreck the whole goddam electric railway industry. The area in which each electric railway operated was considered by GM as a 'saturated market' which had to be eliminated so as to make way for their own transportation equipment and supplies. The [present] campaign by GM to cover up their past and present misdeeds should be exposed as just another 'Watergate' accelerating the present trend toward breakdown in the moral fiber of our large institutions, if any exists."

Obviously, the revelations of General Motors' alleged role in stifling mass transit and operating plants in Nazi Germany had little impact on the general public and less impact on the automaker. It was business as usual in Detroit. The battle against electric traction had, for all intents and purposes, been won.

The plants in Russelsheim and Cologne, which once cranked out war matériel for Adolf Hitler, had retooled and once again were in the profitable auto-making business. According to Bradford Snell, those two plants captured more than two-thirds of the German motor vehicle market.

For the average reader, General Motors' elaborate denial of these charges was, at least superficially, convincing. The *Fifth Estate* described the denial as "curious." It amplified: ". . . Although the German government could have confiscated the GM holdings, there was actually no reason to do so, since GM was cooperating completely in the German war effort. During this entire period, GM facilities in the Allied countries were in communication with facilities in the Axis countries. Information and material were exchanged. GM's stockholders continued as usual to derive profit from its German facilities."

General Motors has vigorously denied involvement with Hitler's Nazis. (See Appendix B).

Unquestionably the most perceptive and rational analysis of the traumatic testimony was provided by the newspaper *Fifth Estate*. It concluded: "Were it not a question of fascism and big business versus human progress, one might re-

call the absurdity of Milo Minderbinder of *Catch-22* and his fantastic speculation schemes to sell arms, information, food and clothing to generals on both
sides. As it turns out, Joseph Heller's fictional imagination in *Catch-22* had real
historical reference. As Milo (or GM's German executives) would tell you, war is
first of all big business."

While the General Motors' defense of its motives, operations, and policies was
elaborate, formidable, and convincing to many observers, a small but significant
number of critics refused to accept GM's seemingly logical arguments. Clint
Page, associate editor of *Nation's Cities Weekly,* a publication of the National
League of Cities, is one who dismantled the GM defense as easily as GM could
dismantle a Chevrolet. In an article which appeared in the October 1977 issue
of *Nation's Cities* (then a monthly), Page supports, point by point, the Bradford
Snell assault against GM. One of the most telling points concerns the GM assertion that in 1936 New York's mayor Fiorello La Guardia testified to the superiority of bus transit. In his article Page reinforces Snell's charge that the facts did
not support any assertion by the mayor that New Yorkers favored buses over
trolleys. "And," wrote Page, "apparently the widespread support for bus transit
was not as widespread as GM suggests: a 1936 survey of the riders of one Brooklyn transit line showed that of 1,350 respondents, 1,258 people preferred the
latest model streetcars, 54 preferred trackless trolley and 38 people preferred
the bus."

Page as well as transit critic and author Don O'Hanley of Middletown, Rhode
Island, correctly argue that GM's argument against trolleys (or light rail vehicles) is erased by living proof in Europe. "It amazes me," says O'Hanley, "that
transit planners in this country don't take a longer look at developments in Europe where they have wonderful light rail systems and excellent PCC-type
equipment which is less complicated and easier to service than the Boeing version of the LRV."

The value of trolleys has been further emphasized in a study done for the Urban Mass Transit Administration in which it was pointed out that in 1975 there
were 310 light rail systems in operation—100 of them in the Soviet Union
alone, another 80 in Western Europe and North America. "Streetcar lines,"
writes Clint Page, "remained an important part of mass transit throughout Europe."

This, however, cannot obviate the fact that trolley genocide virtually exterminated systems in all but seven cities—Boston, Cleveland, New Orleans, Newark,
Philadelphia, Pittsburgh, and San Francisco—in the United States. General Motors says it wasn't the company's fault that trolleys were abandoned everywhere
from Los Angeles to Albany. "They [trolleys] failed," says GM, "because they
were no longer able to give adequate service." The rebuttal (see Appendix B)
was slick, smoothly done but not persuasive to all; least of all Bradford Snell.
"They [GM] pay guys $150 an hour to write that kind of stuff," Snell concludes.

He says the GM rebuttal really doesn't answer the facts and can't change
them. GM was convicted and fined in 1949. Justice Department material and
the evidence in the case, he says, make it clear that GM did intend to take over

trolley lines and replace them with buses. "There isn't any law against doing that," notes Clint Page, "so there could be no criminal charge on those grounds." However, Snell notes that the charges were implicit in the monopoly charge: in order to monopolize the sale of buses GM would have had to create a sizable market for its buses, and taking over trolley lines was a logical step along that road.

In conclusion, Snell emphasizes that the monopoly charge (against GM) was proven. "GM," he says, "has the right to say the courts are wrong, but that doesn't change the facts!"

Nor could GM critics be silenced in the public prints. In a letter published in the January 1979 issue of the magazine *Mother Jones*, Fredrick S. Gram of St. Paul, Minnesota, alluded to the Snell report:

Your readers should also know about the activities of the federal bureaucracy to suppress this report.

I first learned of the Snell study at the Twin Cities Metropolitan Transit Commission. Somebody had a photocopy of it, having been unable to get an original. I took the name, date, official Government Printing Office number, and wrote to the Superintendent of Documents asking for a copy. In due course, I received a printed notice that the office was unable to fill the request because it was unable to identify the document.

I brought this to the attention of my senators and Congress members, as an example of bureaucratic insolence. In a few days I received a phone call from the office of the Superintendent of Documents, informing me that they were now able to identify the Snell report and would send me a copy forthwith.

When it arrived, I found two supplements: General Motors' rebuttal and an order from General Motors to the United States Senate that no further copies of the report are to be circulated that did not contain their rebuttal.

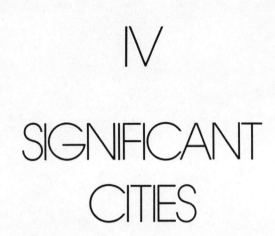

IV

SIGNIFICANT
CITIES

15

Toronto–From Trolleys to Utopia

If the more than two million citizens of Metropolitan Toronto had suffered any doubts about the quality of transportation in their growing metropolis, they were put to rest on January 21, 1978, with the arrival of the day's Toronto *Star* on local newsstands. In red type, blazing across nine columns on page one, shouted the headline: STOP GRIPING, METRO'S TRANSIT IS THE TOPS. In its way, the story by Alan Christie was the classic example of the hoary bromide: "I'm the best; and if you don't believe it, ask me!" Yet there is substantive evidence that, by North American standards, Toronto offers a quasi-utopian example of metropolitan people-moving.

The *Star* merely confirmed what others have suggested for a number of years. In 1975 *The New York Times* reported that Toronto is "widely recognized as a transportation showcase." Experts from Toledo to Timbuktu cite the Ontario capital as *the* place to go when it comes to running a street railway, electric bus service, diesel bus, or subway. For more than a decade, transit leaders from several continents had beaten a path to Toronto to obtain urban transit know-how. The Toronto Transit Commission (TTC) proudly and freely dispensed its expertise until, finally, in 1975 it realized that the time had come to charge for the expert advice. Nobody in the people-moving business seemed to mind because Toronto's eminence had clearly been established among professionals in the field. "It [Toronto] is certainly one of the outstanding systems in the world in the facilities it provides for all kinds of users," said Herbert Scheuer, director of administrative services of the American Public Transit Association.

Representing three hundred transit systems in North America, the American Public Transit Association admired the manner in which the TTC was attacking its problems. "They have a very practical approach," said Scheuer, "using present-day technology."

Translated into workingman's language, it meant that the TTC had been able to mold the best of its transit heritage dating back to the nineteenth century with the concepts of the late twentieth century. Thus, Toronto boasts the largest streetcar network in North America (in some cases operating on lines that existed in 1900), a comprehensive diesel bus system, a relatively small but nonetheless noteworthy electric bus unit, and the fastest-growing subway on the continent.

Although the parent Toronto Transportation Commission was born on September 1, 1921, the TTC was unable to spread its roots and blossom until after World War II. Until then, Toronto—known as the Queen City of Canada—was a metropolis to be sure but nevertheless regarded as a rather dowdy, conservative, white Anglo-Saxon stronghold. But war's end spurred a new immigration, fresh thinking, and insightful blueprints for an even bigger and better Toronto.

The heady formulas for expansion finally crystallized on April 15, 1953, when regional government was imposed on the Metropolitan Toronto area. The twelve surrounding suburban communities, which heretofore had battled Toronto on transit issues, were unified into a single municipality of Metropolitan Toronto, often called Metro. The Ontario Provincial Government, which has more authority than an American state in these cases, supervised the fusion which saw Toronto burgeon from a 35-square-mile city to a 240-square-mile metropolitan region.

From the viewpoint of transit growth, the creation of Metro Toronto was a bonanza. *New York Times* transit writer Ralph Blumenthal observed that the development "permitted far more comprehensive planning decisions including those involving transportation. Toronto's transit success is usually traced to one momentous development: the imposition of regional government."

Now that it embraced such far-flung and rapidly growing suburban communities, Toronto could decide whether it was prudent to unify them with subway, bus, or streetcar and, with considerably less red tape, turn their dreams into reality.

The most tangible result was a subterranean spread of subway roots which have continued growing from its opening in 1954 to twenty-six miles of track by 1975. The cost in that period—$670,000,000—was relatively low in terms of the short- and long-range benefits. For example, between 1952 and 1962 property values along transit lines increased 38 percent, against a rise of 25 percent elsewhere. More important, by 1975 the TTC had managed to put public transport within two thousand feet of the homes of 95 percent of the Metro population.

Unification also permitted the veining of streetcar, bus, and trolley bus lines into the subway system, enabling riders to transfer freely from one route to another. The TTC had, by 1975, neatly arranged a commutation web in which 95 of the city's 111 surface routes made 131 connections with the subway system. The transit connective tissues were further enhanced by other amenities, such as underground bus loops at subway-bus stations to eliminate the need for congesting left-hand bus turns into traffic, not to mention a "kiss-and-ride" station, where motorists are able to drop off or pick up spouses at a round glass terminal and circle until a space opens up.

"We have the best integrated system between surface transit and the subways of any major system in the world," said the TTC's chief general manager Michael Warren in 1978. By that time Warren was able to boast that 119 of the 131 connections between buses and subways enabled the commuter to walk into the station protected from the weather, all for one ticket or token.

Robert Johnson, general manager of New Jersey's Port Authority Transit

Commission (PATCO), underlined Warren's point. "The TTC should be highly commended," said Johnson. "Its system is comprehensive to the point of being a shining light to the rest of the industry. Coordination between bus, streetcar, and subway is outstanding." To which Robert Coultas, executive vice-president of the Washington, D.C.–based Institute of Rapid Transit, added: "Toronto has the best combination of public transit facilities of any city in the western hemisphere."

But the combination was hardly equitable. In 1974, the TTC fielded a roster that included 1,097 petroleum-burning buses as compared with 410 subway cars, 397 streetcars, and 152 trolley coaches.

Perhaps most astonishing of all is the fact that not only did the TTC operate streetcars, but they actually had more than 300 in use. Toronto, in 1978, was the only system in all of Canada to retain streetcars and only one of a handful in North America to offer trolley service. "Our streetcars are the least flexible but they have many other advantages," said TTC spokesman William Hayward. "They last a long time and they carry a lot of people—many more than buses. Besides, the public likes them."

Torontonians' affection for trolleys is unique in North America. In 1973 a bride and groom elected to hold their wedding party on a fifty-year-old Peter Witt model tram that had plied Toronto's streets since the Roarin' Twenties. Not only would Torontonians refuse to phase out trolleys but on November 20, 1973, the TTC did the unthinkable and actually voted to reintroduce the Bloor-to-King tram service which had been abandoned in 1948. Vice-chairman Gordon Hurlburt called it "a historic" decision—"the first time Metro has approved a new streetcar route."

Not only were Toronto's trolleys glorified in magazines, news columns, and books, but they became the first system in North America to be immortalized on a long-playing record. During the month of September 1962 HRN Productions of Toronto placed its sound-recording systems on a 1922 Peter Witt TTC car and another system on a more modern 1938 PCC car. The result was an album called "The Sound of Streetcars."

One might reasonably wonder why anyone would choose to purchase an album with three bands to each side with nothing but the sounds of trolleys. The producers themselves offered a prosaic answer. "The purpose," they said, "is to reproduce in condensed form a day's operation of two streetcars on a large and busy railway system."

The liner notes offer a further insight into the attraction of rail, hiss, clang, and assorted other trolley trivia which, nonetheless, titillated Torontonians: "The day's work begins in the storage yard as the motorman releases the hand brake and pumps up the air. We note the change in sound as the pressure builds up in the tank. Then after the traditional two bells the car makes its way through the complex trackwork in the large yard, stops to set a track switch . . . and so out onto the street. Here the distinctive gear whine is heard clearly. . . ."

That "distinctive gear whine" has been heard in Toronto longer than in most cities. As Mike Filey, Richard Howard, and Helmut Weyerstrahs proudly noted in *Passengers Must Not Ride on Fenders*, Toronto was the first city of any size in North America to make a comprehensive attempt at laying out an electric tram network. "Beginning in 1883," they wrote, "a group of entrepreneurs led by one Van Depoele rigged up a couple of small wooden cars with electric motors to shuttle passengers from Strachan Avenue into the grounds of the Toronto Industrial Exhibition. They charged five cents apiece. Torontonians were skeptical but enchanted, and the ride became a regular feature."

At the time dobbin was the king of mass transit and had been since 1861, when horsecars plied Yonge Street—Toronto's main north-south artery—and continued to rule until the last decade of the nineteenth century, when the Toronto Railway Company began replacing the oat burners with newfangled electricity eaters. William Mackenzie, a successful Canadian rail and mine promoter, galvanized Toronto's trolley growth and the last horse-drawn car clip-clopped along McCaul Street in 1894. "The average Torontonian," wrote Filey, Howard, and Weyerstrahs, "earning perhaps ten dollars a week, could look to such a system with hope as well as pride. It meant mobility, a cure for his predicament." Not long after the carbarn door was closed behind the last Toronto horsecar the Toronto Railway Company had ninety miles of track and carried more than 23,000,000 fares.

As Toronto expanded, the TRC seemed to slacken its growth. This was particularly evident early in the twentieth century when suburbs burgeoned so rapidly that city fathers insisted that the TRC extend its tracks and buy more rolling stock. When Mackenzie's TRC refused, the city rushed in with cars from its own Toronto Civic Railway.

The first publicly owned transit system in Toronto, the TCR purchased Birney Safety Cars, four-wheeled cuties that inspired Fontaine Fox to draw his legendary "Toonerville Folks" comic strip. Unlike Fox's Toonerville, both the TRC and TCR were competing with what appeared to be an overpopulation of automobiles and trucks. By 1911 the twenty thousand trucks and cars were enough to cause a Civic Improvement Committee to recommend construction of a Toronto subway. (The suggestion was fulfilled after World War II.)

Despite its obvious foresight, the subway plan was rejected amid applause from assorted sectors. One daily, the *Globe*, ridiculed the subway proposal as "an ill-digested scheme put out by the boomsters, who had laid their plans for a renewal of land speculation on a large scale." All of which meant that the future of Toronto transit remained on the surface as World War I came and went. Unfortunately, coordination between the TRC and the TCR was like placing a square peg in a circle. Even worse, TRC equipment had deteriorated and trolleys were rarely repaired. Several rationales were offered, including a persistent rumor that, sooner or later, the city would buy out Mackenzie and make him even richer than he was.

Torontonians knew what they wanted in mass transit, and they weren't getting it from the TRC. Pressure mounted for some remedial action, and it finally took place in a referendum held on January 1, 1920. The result was voter approval for the city's purchase of the TRC as well as the Toronto & York Radial Railway for more than $11,000,000. Given the green light, the Toronto City Council promptly analyzed Toronto's situation in relation to other successful transit systems on the continent and ultimately opted for a "commission" form of operation. The Province of Ontario offered its blessing with the establishment of the Toronto Transportation Commission (the original TTC), armed with three commissioners.

Compensating for all the physical and psychological damage inflicted by the TRC's deteriorating service would be a Promethean task for the new TTC and the manner in which it coped with these dilemmas would go a long way in determining the future of Toronto transit. As it happened, the citizens of Canada's Queen City were most fortunate; the TTC realized that it had to revise the physical plant while putting on a new public relations face. Without hesitation, the TTC promised a brave new world for riders—and then surprised many by delivering on the promises.

"The TTC ordered tens of thousands of tons of new rail and specialwork to implement the most comprehensive track replacement program ever undertaken by a transit operator," wrote John F. Bromley and Jack May in *Fifty Years of Progressive Transit*. They added: "Excitement on the part of the local citizenry grew strongly as the TTC carried on a large public relations and advertising campaign, announcing more and more plans for improvement."

Everything about the TTC's campaign came up roses, from its new bright red livery to the superb Peter Witt–model trams. One of the most fortuitous events was the emergence of the Peter Witt car onto the transit scene at the start of the twenties. The all-steel car, which already was becoming a staple on systems from Brooklyn to Cleveland, had been ordered prior to creation of the TTC. Thus, the TTC was only a month old when the sleek Witt cars invaded Toronto and captured the hearts of its citizens. The TTC was off to a rip-roaring start! It annexed local tracks and built more of its own; by the end of 1922, it had produced fifty-seven more miles of single track.

In its quest for excellence, the TTC constantly probed the public tastes. Questionnaires were distributed to riders in 1922 and, as a result of replies, a complete revision in major routes was approved. New lines were added, others were altered, and a few were cut altogether. As fifty years later when a hallmark of the TTC was its integration of different vehicles into the system, in the early twenties the TTC began experimenting with ways to link other modes of transport with the streetcars. Its first bus route was launched in September 1921 and a year later the city's first electric trolley bus began rolling on the Mount Pleasant line, replacing a gasoline bus line. This presented an interesting confrontation between competitive vehicles. Both the gasoline-powered bus and the trolley coach were relatively small, conspicuously ugly vehicles compared with the large, sleek Peter Witt trolleys. Both buses lumbered on thick (nontube) rubber tires, whereas the trolleys now were cruising on smooth tracks, freshly laid throughout the city. Even the appearance of double-deck buses in 1923 failed to distract from the fact that the Peter Witt cars were *the* modus operandi. Nor could one deny their acceptance: in 1929 patronage on the TTC reached a record high.

More important, perhaps, is that the Witt cars were durable. Although the Witt-style car was introduced in 1921, not a single car was taken off the TTC roster until an accident involving a gasoline truck and a Witt car roasted the trolley to the ground. From time to time cosmetic improvements were made. In 1936 dash lights were added to the two sides of the headlight and a bluish-green bullet-type light was installed on the brow of the Witts to alert passengers several blocks away that a streetcar was en route.

Unfortunately, more and more motorists were crowding the trolley lanes, making it conspicuously more difficult to propel a tram along its tracks without incessant clanging and a herky-jerk stop and go. It was not uncommon at intersections such as Yonge and Queen streets for taxicabs or regular passenger cars to block the trolley's movement by edging onto or close to the tracks. The automobile and the Great Depression combined to siphon riders away from the TTC, and in 1933 the total number of riders had plummeted to less than three-quarters of what it had been in 1929. Competition wasn't on the horizon—it was there for the TTC to see; and soon substantive moves were being made to find a cure.

Although the Witt car was an attractive hunk of rolling stock that had done its job well and could never be faulted for its durability or serviceability, the public virtually demanded that a new, more streamlined, more comfortable tram be developed. This was not merely perceived by TTC bosses, but was also expressed by streetcar operators on both sides of the border. Aware of dwindling ridership, owners of several streetcar systems united in the early thirties and hammered out a program to develop the ultimate in trolley transportation, the streamlined PCC car.

Once the PCC cars had proven themselves in Brooklyn, the TTC ordered 140 pieces of the rolling stock. When the first two rolled off the assembly line, they were rushed to the 1938 Canadian National Exhibition grounds and put on display prominently at the entrance. Torontonians loved them at first sight. Nevertheless, the TTC was true to the grandes dames of the system. Not only did the Peter Witts remain in service but the Toonerville Birneys continued to roll until December 1940, when the last Birney car groaned over Toronto streets.

Just how much the PCC car did to boost patronage is a moot question because other factors were at work. The onset of World War II and gasoline rationing inspired drivers to garage their Fords and Chevys and take the trolley. In 1940, for example, a total of 168,000,000 riders were counted but in 1946 the number had leaped to 310,000,000.

What would be more significant to the TTC's future in the years immediately after World War II was the new affluence of the late forties and the availability once more of automobiles and gasoline. The trolley, which reigned supreme throughout the war, was now being threatened. Spanking new autos rolling off the assembly line proved strong competition for the doughty fleet of

Montreal was a mass transit pioneer in Canada. The horse-drawn omnibus above (1861) and the Montreal Street Railway tram and trailer (1894) typified rolling stock in the bilingual city.

(*Top*) Relatively late with subways, New York City experimented with an elevated railway (1867) demonstrated by Charles Harvey. (*Left*) An inclined track was used to haul rolling stock from street level to the tracks of New York City's Gilbert Elevated Railroad.

(*Top*) In 1878, the Third Avenue Elevated Railroad sported a spanking-new look. (*Above*) Teeming traffic at the juncture of Broadway and Fifth Avenue (Madison Square) in 1893 was a compelling reason to build a subway at the turn of the twentieth century.

(*Left*) A late-nineteenth-century tableau in front of New York's old Grand Central Station. (*Middle*) A rarity among rapid transit vehicles was the private car of IRT subway baron August Belmont. (*Bottom*) The Montreal streetcar system boasted open-air "Golden Chariots" which climbed the city's scenic Mount Royal.

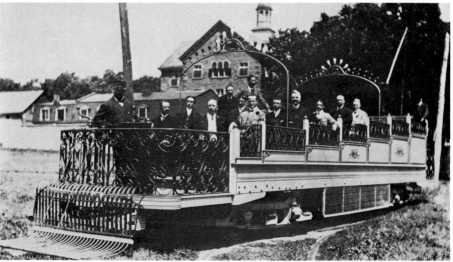

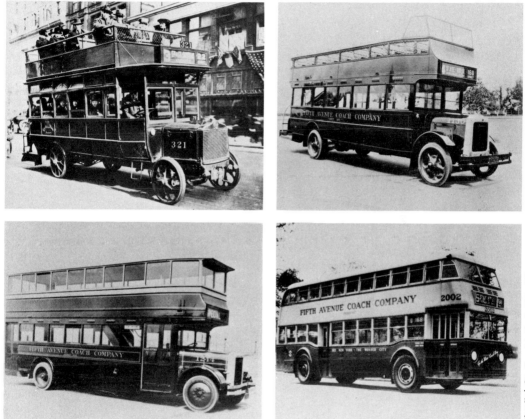

(*Top left*) The double-decker bus flowered in New York City early in the twentieth century. (*Top right and bottom left and right*) No company in North America popularized variations on the double-decker more than The Fifth Avenue Coach Company.

Early mass transit in the suburbs: (*Top*) The Montreal, St. Laurent, Cartierville interurban trolley; and the Delaware, Lackawanna, & Western's commuter lines (*middle*) proliferated through New Jersey. (*Above*) New York's original subway (1904) featured mosaics and bas reliefs such as this Fulton Street station.

(*Top*) The heyday of the electric streetcar preceded World War II. Passengers jam a Montreal tram at Bonaventure Station in 1907. Brooklyn trolleys: the semiconvertible (*middle*) and the Peter Witt streetcar (*bottom*), which continued running after World War II. (This trolley actually gave the Brooklyn Dodgers their nickname; Brooklynites became known as Trolley Dodgers.)

(*Top*) Accidents are inevitable in rapid transit. The worst, by far, took place in Brooklyn on November 1, 1918, at the Malbone Street Station, when an inexperienced motorman lost control of his train as it approached a dangerous curve at the tunnel portal. The resultant crash cost ninety-seven lives. (*Above*) Despite the Malbone Street crash, wooden cars continued to operate for many years on the tracks of New York, such as these pieces of Third Avenue Elevated Rapid Transit cars.

Peter Witts and PCC cars that had been worn to a frazzle by wartime service. More important, perhaps, was that the Toronto city government failed to grant the trolleys an exclusive lane on the streets. Not that Toronto was overlooking its transit responsibilities. In 1944, a year before the war's end, city fathers anticipated a grandiose postwar growth and developed a master plan to accommodate the expansion. The Toronto Planning Board was looking thirty years ahead and it opened new vistas in transit. The blockbuster was a blueprint for building the first subway line in Canada, under Yonge Street.

Yonge Street is to Metro Toronto what Broadway is to New York City—*the* main drag, from which other main routes radiate. Yonge Street begins at the lip of Lake Ontario and then bisects Toronto's business district in its northward meander toward the suburbs. It was an ideal thoroughfare under which to build the first subway, just as Broadway provided the original route in Manhattan in 1904. The difference was that in 1904 the New York City planners displayed infinitely more foresight than Toronto engineers forty years later. For one thing, the Torontonians underestimated the size of the subway (two-track local instead of four-track express and local, as it is in New York City) needed in relation to passenger requirements. The Toronto planners were also willing to do something that New Yorkers, wisely, in 1904 considered heretical: eliminate streetcars. Instead of concentrating on the mass transit (subway, tram, electric bus, and diesel bus) complex, the Toronto Planning Board elected to spend considerable time and money investigating creation of superhighways which would funnel the vehicles into the already congested inner city.

Had the Ontario planners possessed 20–20 foresight and ample courage to go with it, they would have legislated bans on vehicular passenger traffic in the core of Toronto (providing fields of auto parking facilities on the perimeter and adjacent to proposed subway and commuter railroad stations) and reserved downtown transit for commercial trucks, a limited number of taxicabs, emergency vehicles, streetcars, buses, and assorted necessary municipal vehicles only. But this was not to be and, instead, the Toronto Planning Board blueprinted several superhighways which would ultimately doom the streetcar system.

This lapse on the part of the "visionaries" would take place in 1946 when the TTC discontinued several carlines. Meanwhile, the city's Rapid Transit Department (created in 1944) began developing plans for the subway-to-be.

As the postwar years unfolded, Toronto city planners seemed to be manic-depressive in their attitude toward trams. While erasing lines at an alarming clip, the TTC nevertheless displayed strong affection for the rolling stock by doing what precious few municipalities in North America considered at the time: the TTC invested in new PCC cars. Thus, on December 22, 1947, at a time when showrooms were displaying Studebakers, Pontiacs, and Packards, the TTC rolled out its first all-electric PCC car with such dazzling extras as standee windows and, ultimately (on later models), fluorescent lighting and forced-air ventilation. More PCC cars were ordered in May 1948, some of the doughtier Peter Witt cars were renovated—new electric blast heaters were installed—and the TTC even looked elsewhere to purchase equipment. In later years when the cities of Kansas City (Kansas), Birmingham, Cleveland, and Cincinnati trimmed their trolley systems, the TTC bought their rolling stock.

When New York City's Third Avenue Railway System put four used double-truck sweepers up for sale, the TTC grabbed them up and the Commission kept an Argus eye out for whatever suitable surplus equipment might be available. It was apparent, as the frantic forties ended, that Toronto would doggedly retain its trolleys and thereby establish itself as the only city on the continent with a truly diversified people-moving system. As the TTC's general manager of operations, J. H. Kearns, once put it: "Pound for pound the streetcar is still the best transit vehicle we've produced."

Nevertheless, the incursion of the auto was forcing Toronto to seek alternate means of transit and, apart from the planned subway, rubber-tired vehicles were on the offensive.

After World War II, Torontonians, consumed with postwar euphoria, ignored the fact that their beloved streetcars—like their counterparts in Brooklyn, Los Angeles, and Chicago—could become an endangered species. There were, of course, more "important" things to worry about. Would the Toronto Maple Leafs win the Stanley Cup? Could the city support its first big-league basketball team? And, for those interested in municipal affairs, would the much discussed subway ever be built? The prevailing thinking about trams was simple enough: the trolleys had been with Toronto almost from the beginning of its cityhood, so why shouldn't they be around forever? The answer, of course, lay in the highly competitive transit marketplace where numerous modes of transport were vying for the Toronto dollar.

One of the strangest contraptions to challenge the supremacy of the streetcar was an experimental omnibus that offered a few virtues of a traditional bus and one of the essential assets of the tram, electric power. Known as the trackless trolley, it was a combination trolley and bus developed early in the twentieth century. Taking its power from two trolley poles that linked with a pair of overhead wires, the vehicle was rubber-tired and allowed a flexibility unavailable from traditional streetcars. Unencumbered by tracks, the trolley bus could wander as far as the twin poles would allow.

By the start of the twenties, the new TTC decided to test four of the vehicles on its Mount Pleasant line. A chassis was built by Packard, Westinghouse supplied the electrical equipment, and the Canadian firm of Brill-Preston assembled the vehicles. Service commenced in June 1922 and within a very short time proved attractive; in fact, so attractive that the trolley coach's success proved its very doom.

Business was so good on the Mount Pleasant line that the TTC elected in 1925 to replace the trolley coaches with regular trolleys, which could carry substantially more passengers per vehicle. It was deemed more efficient to extend the St. Clair streetcar line than to buy more trolley coaches. Following World War II, however, a new breed of trackless trolley appeared and, once more, the TTC expressed interest in the curious vehicle.

This time the electric bus showed considerably more staying power than the first time around and, in fact, routed the trams from a number of lines, starting with the Lansdowne trolley, on June 19, 1947. Less than five months later a second trackless trolley route was established, and by the end of the year another streetcar line was declared *finis* and in its place a new trolley coach run was established. Clearly pleased with the results, the TTC opened a fourth trolley bus line in 1948, when the Weston line's streetcars were replaced. Sufficient engineering and aesthetic improvements had been made in trolley coach construction for the vehicles to prove appealing.

Unlike the ugly electric duckling of 1922, the 1948 trolley coach manufactured by CCF-Brill was a relatively roomy vehicle that generated almost no noticeable noise or pollution. It was soon successful. Whereas its predecessor was scrapped after only two years, the post–World War II trolley coaches became a long-running hit. After more than twenty years of service, the TTC in 1969 approved a $4,000,000 contract for new bodies and an additional $1,000,000 for in-house reconditioning and installation of electrical equipment.

Proud of its trolley buses and equally exhilarated over its decision to continue their lives, the TTC embarked on a commendable ad campaign with a poster featuring a beat-up 1948-vintage trolley coach dreaming of what beauty it will offer after its face-lifting. "Please Pardon My Appearance," shouts the caption. "I Will Soon Be Rebuilt, Modernized, and Pepped Up in the TTC's $5 Million Trolley Bus Rehabilitation Program." The Toronto trolley bus revival program drew the interest of transit experts everywhere.

"It is interesting to note," wrote John F. Bromley and Jack May in *Fifty Years of Progressive Transit*, "that the TTC discovered a new trolley bus with reconditioned electrical equipment which cost $4,000 less than a new diesel bus, and it also was found that electric buses are still less costly to operate and maintain than diesels."

With all the success enjoyed by the trackless trolleys, their renaissance in the forties and again in the seventies was still not enough to wipe out the regular tram fleet.

If the trackless trolley provided only a mild threat to the life of TTC's tram system, the gasoline diesel bus was a considerably more ominous presence. As far back as 1908, when French-built double-deckers appeared on New York's fashionable Fifth Avenue, the gasoline-powered bus loomed as the ultimate successor to the trolley. Throughout North America, bus ridership climbed in the twenties, and by 1932 more than fifteen thousand buses were operating on the continent, moving more than a billion passengers.

In this regard, Toronto remained an anomaly. Yes, the TTC recognized the gasoline and later the diesel coach but, no, they would not push the trams out of business. Thus, while San Diego, Minneapolis, St. Paul, Detroit, and Vancouver systems, among others, were junking their trolleys in favor of diesel buses, the TTC, wisely, failed to capitulate completely to the brand of omnibuses so ubiquitous in other North American cities.

While the diesels appeared mighty in numbers, they could muster little public appeal compared with the trolley, which by 1972 even had an unofficial lobby fighting its cause. The Streetcars for Toronto Committee was organized in 1972 as a direct result of a TTC decision to eliminate the St. Clair tram line. Devoted to their trolleys, a number of Torontonians wrote letters of complaint to their local elected officials, who promptly called a meeting to discuss appropriate action to forestall the TTC's move. "The result," said Toronto *Star* City Hall columnist Michael Best, "was to bring men like Steve Munro, a computer programmer, Howard Levine, an urban planner, and Andrew Biemiller, a professor of child psychology, together. Many of them were in their twenties and the more they looked into it, the greater their conviction that the streetcars had a huge potential when adapted to a rapid transit role."

Determined to prevent any further incursion of diesel buses at the expense of their beloved trams, the Streetcars for Toronto Committee launched a serious, low-profile campaign. Instead of raising petitions or forming placard-waving picket-lines, they put together a facts-and-figures case.

Programmer Steve Munro was named chairman of the tram group, which soon brought its mountain of statistics and rhetoric before the TTC. The proposal was clear: Reverse the policy of streetcar abandonment. The TTC liked what it saw, and so the Streetcars for Toronto Committee came back again and again whenever a valid transit issue emerged. "We have never yet made a presentation where we were told we were full of hot air," said Munro.

The committee's track record was excellent. It got the policy of streetcar abandonment reversed, and later, it persuaded the TTC to restore trolley operations on Spadina Avenue and to back a study of streetcars as an alternative to an elaborate, glamorous but little-tested German-designed system of transit into the suburbs. "Nostalgia," said Michael Best, "has nothing to do with the Committee's aims. It is a matter of stern practicality."

Soon a chain reaction of developments indicated that a trolley renaissance was, in fact, occurring in Toronto. On May 1, 1974, a Canadian firm announced that it would build an ultramodern streetcar that could do for Toronto in the eighties what the Peter Witt trolley did in the twenties. Kirk Foley, president of the Ontario Transportation Development Corp., unveiled a new streetcar design that induced the TTC to order two hundred of the vehicles at $250,000 each.

The trolleys—saddled with the Madison Avenue euphemism "Light Rail Vehicles"—would be larger, faster, and quieter than the PCC models then in use and could accommodate at least 150 passengers, compared with the PCC's capacity of 130 riders.

There were, to be sure, sufficient foes of the trams to make it clear to members of the Streetcars for Toronto Committee and their bloc that perpetual vigilance would be necessary. But supporters were in abundance, such as Mike Filey, Richard Howard, and Helmut Weyerstrahs, authors of *Passengers Must Not Ride on Fenders: A Fond Look at Toronto—Its People, Its Places, Its Streetcars*. The authors recalled how, when they were asked to append a defense of the streetcar in their book, they suffered second thoughts.

It soon became evident [they wrote] from researching various articles prepared in the early seventies, at a time when it looked as if the streetcar in Toronto was to be phased out of existence, that the idea of moving people on electrically operated steel-wheeled vehicles in a safe, economical way did not require defending. . . . Not only were the cars operationally sound, with the best passenger capacity available and free of pollution, but it turned out the people of Toronto actually liked their streetcars.

An armistice of sorts between trams, diesel buses, trackless trolleys, and subways appeared to be tacitly worked out in the seventies with some notable exceptions. In an area called North Jarvis, for example, the residents complained in 1976 about pollution delivered from the exhausts of TTC diesel buses. On September 5, 1976, the TTC responded to the complaints by introducing trackless trolley service on the Bay Street line which serviced the area. To a rider, the commuters saluted the diesel's exit and commended the quieter ride of the trolley buses.

Wrote Jack May in *Fifty Years of Progressive Transit*:

The TTC's decision to retain streetcars was a bold one; it takes great fortitude not only to stand up to an automobile lobby, which wishes to clear the streets of high-capacity vehicles, but to demand additional space for transit vehicles and get it! Another example is the retention of the trolley bus. While most cities in North America were busily abandoning this pollution-free form of transportation, Toronto developed a new, attractive trolley coach, and breathed new life into this dying form of transportation.

Whether or not Toronto can maintain its healthy attitude toward mass transit while minimizing the use of the automobile in the eighties remains an open question. One of the best barometers remains the issue of the Spadina expressway—more particularly, whether or not it will ever be built as planned. In a landmark decision on June 3, 1971, the cabinet of the Province of Ontario voted to discontinue construction of the automobile route known as the Spadina, which was blueprinted to link with downtown Toronto. "The city does not belong to the automobile," said Ontario Premier William Davis in defense of the decision. And throughout the early and mid-seventies the unfinished motor route remained a monument to those who believe that trams, buses, and subways are better for a city than cars.

Discontinuance of the Spadina construction in 1971 coincided with the fiftieth anniversary of the TTC and suggested to some dreamers that expressway planning would be put on the back burner. This, however, was not completely the case as Spadina proponents maintained a relentless pressure to complete the expressway. While the battle raged, the TTC's attention was riveted on another threat to the trolley, but this one from a more desirable source: expansion of Toronto's relatively new and fascinating subway system.

One night in September 1953 Torontonians were treated to an unusually symbolic—and, to some, sorrowful—sight. A venerable Peter Witt streetcar, which had plied the Yonge Street route for several decades, was seen towing a spanking-new red *subway* car along Yonge Street toward the Davisville yard.

The old order was about to changeth. A subway was being built; a trolley fleet was about to be dismantled, in part.

Toronto's decision to build a subway originated in the late 1930s, when it was fast becoming apparent that the metropolis, like its counterpart in the Province of Quebec, Montreal, was growing faster than its mass transit facilities. Not until 1942 did Toronto planners actually detail an answer: Move the electric coaches underground; that is, build a subway.

Of course, this might never have been necessary had a total ban on pleasure automobiles been placed in effect and the trolleys given a right-of-way priority in downtown Toronto. But this was much too much to expect from city planners in the late thirties and early forties. The TTC knew that roads shared with private motor vehicles would never be as efficient as trolleys with their own right-of-way.

Although there had been talk of building a Toronto subway as early as 1910, the first serious discussions were held in 1942, when the TTC confronted the Toronto City Council with a plan to run trams underground along two major subway routes which ultimately would emerge from the tunnels and run at surface level. The City Council greeted the proposals with a resounding rejection and then came up with a countersuggestion: Give us another subway plan but make it simpler! This time the TTC hired the same firm that had designed the just-finished Chicago subway under State Street. The Chicago planners joined forces with a Toronto consulting engineer, and in 1946 they produced a basic subway plan running under Yonge Street, connecting Eglinton Avenue on the north with Union Station to the south near the waterfront.

A secondary proposal for an east-west subway also was submitted, but this was a more modest plan—along the lines of the Boston underground, which placed trolleys in the tunnels. This second tram-subway proposal was priced considerably cheaper ($19,300,000) than estimates on the standard rapid transit subway ($28,000,000). All costs would be borne by the TTC. Now the question was: How would the electorate react to a subway referendum? On January 1, 1946, Torontonians flashed a big green signal to the idea with a resounding nine-to-one vote in favor of subways.

Ground breaking for the initial Union Station–to–Queen Street section took place with appropriate fanfare on September 8, 1949. Although the natives greeted the event with enthusiasm, a precious few transit analysts realized that the TTC, while doing right in building the subway, was consummately wrong in its planning. The principal mistake was in underestimating Toronto's growth and the concomitant increase in ridership on the Yonge Street line within two decades of its completion date. The egregious error was a decision to build a two-track local line covering the twelve stations from Eglinton to Union Station, rather than a four-track express and local facility.

The decision not to go express was inexcusable and would have disastrous ramifications. There was sufficient precedent for such a facility. In New York, for instance, the original Interborough Rapid Transit subway (IRT) featured an elaborate four-track local-express system as early as 1904. Subsequent subway construction in New York City on the Interborough as well as the Brooklyn Rapid Transit and later Brooklyn Manhattan Transit lines, not to mention the municipally operated Independent Subway system, featured high-speed express runs to complement the locals. Yet forty-five years after the IRT began rolling, the TTC broke ground on a system that would be obsolete before it opened. Why did Toronto settle for a mere minor-league local operation when a big-time express-local tandem unit was an alternative?

Apologists for the TTC argue that engineering and economics were the two key factors. They assert that since Yonge is a relatively narrow (sixty-six-foot) roadway, it would have been difficult, if not impossible, to construct a four-track-across subway like the one that runs under Broadway in Manhattan. The second consideration militating against the four-track express-local was the fear among TTC executives that it would be too expensive and might be rejected by the electorate.

Neither rationale makes much sense. Although the express-local, side-by-side track plan might not have been feasible for a street such as Yonge, which is not very wide, the TTC could easily have resorted to the alternative employed in New York City when the Interborough Rapid Transit was begun under Lexington Avenue, a thoroughfare as narrow as Yonge. New York City engineers placed the pair of express tracks on one level and the pair of local tracks above them. As for the expense, the TTC later spent great amounts of money on additional subways. An express certainly was in order at the time.

Naively, the TTC proceeded with construction of the two-track subway amid the inaugural festivities and the stirring "Road to the Isles" march played by the 48th Highlanders Band as the first trench was dug along Yonge Street. The TTC elected to employ the cut-and-cover method of subway construction along Yonge Street, which meant that extensive excavations were made along the busy thoroughfare. Because of this technique the Yonge tram tracks had to be ripped out of their beds. This might have been an excellent excuse to scrap the Yonge trolleys altogether but, as Bromley and May pointed out: "During the next four years, subway construction was to result in no less than 28 major streetcar diversions. The TTC refused to downgrade the line by the simpler, if less desirable, expedient of bus conversion."

The TTC was still sticking by the streetcars in 1949; subway construction was still in progress when the TTC decided to buy a new fleet of PCC trams. But to the commissioners' dismay, they learned that streetcar manufacture was fast becoming a lost art and, as a result, the price of trolleys had skyrocketed. So, instead of the original order for one hundred trams, the TTC sliced it down to fifty.

All subsequent streetcar purchases in the fifties would be made from municipalities such as Cincinnati, Birmingham, and Cleveland. Although the cars were used rolling stock, TTC inspectors checked them out in advance and discovered that they were eminently usable. No such buy-used-merchandise policy was operative when it came to stocking the new subway with passenger cars. In 1951 the TTC bestowed the lavish contract for 104 subway cars on an English firm, the Gloucester Wagon and Carriage Company. The first two pieces of rolling stock left the factory in 1953 and were shipped to Toronto for a formal display at the Canadian National Exhibition.

In a bitter-sweet touch of irony, the new subway cars were unloaded at Hillcrest, a good distance from the Exhibition grounds. To facilitate the transfer, the TTC temporarily suspended service on the Bathurst trolley—diesel buses were used instead—and ran the Gloucester rolling stock over the tram tracks to the Exhibition grounds. When "The Ex" concluded its annual run, the sparkling red subway vehicles were attached to a Peter Witt L-1 model trolley and pulled by night to the TTC's hitherto unused subway yards in Davisville. The delicate operation was not without incident; upon arrival at the Davisville portal the first Gloucester car mounted a temporary track connection and while its wheels screeched around the curve a flange lost its grip and the car derailed.

The same year that the first two subway cars arrived Toronto became Metro Toronto, with the switch to regional government. The Toronto Transportation Commission, for more than euphemistic purposes, became the Toronto *Transit* Commission. Since Metro Toronto would embrace suburbs, it was only fair that the TTC give representation to the "outer" city residents. The TTC board was therefore puffed from three to five members, and the TTC was given jurisdiction over the 240 square miles of Metro. "The TTC," wrote Bromley and May, "was granted a public transportation monopoly within the Metropolitan area, except for taxis and railways. The Commission immediately set about the task of purchasing the local bus lines in the region and began planning their integration into an enlarged TTC system."

The annexation of the TTC by Toronto's Metro Council was a godsend for the transit system. In the twenty years between 1954 and 1974 the TTC spent $130,000,000 to add 1,744 vehicles to its fleet. Unfortunately, about 70 percent of them were buses. Early in 1954, however, Torontonians turned their attention on the almost completed four-and-a-half-mile-long Yonge Street subway. Section One of the Toronto subway officially opened on March 30, 1954.

Although there was much to commend in the facility, its drawbacks were obvious to serious subway students. Those who had experienced the New York City system were appalled to discover that the TTC planned to close down its subway every night at 1:30 A.M., reopening again at 6 A.M. By contrast each of New York City's three subway divisions (IRT, BMT, IND) operates twenty-four hours a day, no matter how light the ridership on some lines. Another mistake was the notion that because the subway was running underground, the Yonge Street tram line could be scrapped. Yet, the TTC greeted its new subway with a March 1954 massacre of trolley lines. In addition to the Yonge Street wipeout, the TTC made numerous other alterations that suggested that streetcars had to go when subways arrived.

Despite these shortcomings, the TTC's new subway left much for Torontonians to be proud of.

One who realized the TTC subway potential was G. Warren Heenan, president of the Toronto Real Estate Board. "If an urban rapid transit system never earned a dime," said Heenan, "it would pay for itself many times over through its beneficial impact on real estate values and increased assessments."

Few argued Heenan's point and, in time, the TTC amassed overwhelming evidence to prove the value of subway construction. "To the vital downtown business core," said TTC Chairman Ralph C. Day, "the subway has proved to be the anchor that brought a feeling of permanence and stability. It has created a climate for growth. Toronto has not experienced the flight of commercial and retail business from the downtown area that has occurred in some cities. On the contrary, it is in the midst of a downtown building boom that is the envy of many larger cities."

The University Avenue subway was opened on February 28, 1963, while work continued on a completely new line running east-west along Danforth Avenue and Bloor Street. With commendable foresight, the TTC planners arranged bilevel station connections with the existing line. And with equally laudable daring in the realm of engineering, Toronto subway builders decided to try several forms of construction techniques to burrow under the streets. The successful results were made evident on February 26, 1966.

Its shortcomings notwithstanding, Toronto's gradually expanding subway was becoming the talk of the continent and an inspiration to many cities that previously had waffled on the issue of subway construction. One of them was Montreal, Toronto's archrival in the areas of culture, sports, and not surprisingly, construction.

Montreal's decision to build a subway of its own (called *Le Métro*) was influenced no doubt by the splendid results of the Yonge Street line. In 1962, for example, Toronto construction analysts predicted that their new subway would inspire more than $2 billion in new construction by 1977. So Montreal responded by completing its first subway in 1966. It differed from Toronto's in many ways (not the least of which was that the cars ran on rubber tires) but it could not possibly catch Toronto in terms of size and future growth. (In 1976 Montreal's transit system carried only about one-tenth the number on the TTC.) Toronto, for the first time, extended its subway beyond the city line and into the suburbs when, on May 11, 1968, it opened extensions of the Bloor-Danforth line.

This new construction did detract, however, from Toronto's superbly maintained and efficient streetcar fleet. It was not inevitable that the trolley suffer at the expense of the subway; we can thank both the subway mania and the planners' failure to guarantee traffic-free tram lanes. By 1968 there was ample evidence that the subway had replaced the trolley as *the* way to get around Toronto.

The TTC chopped up the ten-mile-long Bloor-Danforth trolley line and erased other trolley routes outright. The curious theory proffered by the TTC was that a subway line automatically rendered the streetcar line irrelevant. Actually, the trams should have been saved and the automobile restricted. But the subway was king and now the TTC looked ahead to another arresting project: the $212,000,000, 6.17-mile Spadina line.

If Torontonians were becoming blasé about their burgeoning underground transit system, the Spadina line would cure them of that malady. Taking a cue from the lavishly appointed Montreal stations, TTC planners commissioned $300,000 in new subway art to grace each of the stations.

Approved by the Ontario Provincial Government on January 18, 1973, the Spadina line was more than just another subway with frills. It was a statement of purpose: the province two years earlier had rejected the Metro Toronto Expressway and put the kibosh on the controversial and pollution-inducing Spadina Expressway.

Now the Province was reinforcing its philosophy that "cities are for people, not cars," with a subway in the shadow of the aborted motor route. So proud was the TTC of its new Spadina subway that on January 25, 1978, just three days before its opening, full-page ads were taken in all three of Metro's dailies heralding the event and inviting the public to ride free. The TTC had engineered a superb gambit, providing, of course, that its subway could then follow through with the grand service that its press releases promised.

At 6 A.M. on Saturday, January 28, the Spadina line was launched in grand style. Toronto transit leaders were convinced that the dazzling array of new features would woo potential motorists away from their cars and into the three-hundred-passenger Hawker-Siddeley subway cars manufactured in Canada. One of the outstanding features was the conspicuous absence of noise on the Spadina route.

The quiet ride is due to rubber pads, thirteen inches in diameter and three inches thick, on which the steel tracks sit. The rubber pads reduce the vibration and deaden the sound. But, within weeks, there were sounds that TTC officials could not deaden: the shouts of anger coming from disillusioned passengers who discovered that the new subway was conspicuously imperfect. On February 12, 1978, a headline blared in the Toronto *Star:* SPADINA SUBWAY SHUNNED AMID BREAKDOWNS, DELAYS.

As February 1978 unfolded so did the ever growing list of problems: a broken air hose closed the line for 13 minutes; switch heaters malfunctioned, causing a 6-minute delay; a train lost air pressure, forcing a 14-minute shutdown.

Like an effective commanding general, TTC Chairman Gordon Hurlburt counterattacked before his commission was overwhelmed with invective. Hurlburt insisted that it would have been unwise to delay opening the Spadina line, arguing that the difficulties were increased by inclement weather.

The long-awaited spring thaw not only melted away many of the TTC's Spadina line problems, but a small yet perceptible increase in ridership was recorded. By June 1978 the TTC's turnstiles were ringing up eight thousand passengers an hour on the new subway, and it was freely predicted that the goal of fourteen thousand per hour would be reached no later than 1980. Michael Warren, the TTC's chief general manager, insisted that the Spadina route was significantly different in ridership potential from the TTC subway lines and, therefore, the TTC necessarily had to be more patient with its new baby.

By the summer of 1978 complaints against the Spadina had dropped and ridership increased. Many of the early mechanical difficulties—flat wheels, stuck switches—were remedied, but the TTC conceded that the Spadina right-of-way was more exposed than the other subway lines and would present weather problems in years to come.

With the Spadina line rolling, the TTC now boasted 710 miles of subway, streetcar, bus, and trolley bus lines. The lines of subway described a basic cross shape, with an additional loop in the south and the Spadina route snaking first along the Bloor line and then north vaguely parallel to the Yonge Street line.

In many ways Toronto could rightfully brag that it had the cleanest, most efficient subway on the continent, if not the biggest. Those in San Francisco–Oakland, Chicago, Philadelphia, Cleveland, Boston, Montreal, and Washington, D.C., could not match the TTC's operation, and nobody knew this better than the TTC high command.

Although through 1978 the TTC received the award for the safest and most efficient rapid transit system in North America for seven successive years, it remained a system beset with problems and virtually overwhelmed by criticism within the Metropolitan Toronto area.

From late 1978 through March 1979, when the TTC raised its fare (from seven tickets for $3 to six) riders expressed their displeasure with the system. Excerpts from an assortment of letters to the Toronto *Star* reveal what low esteem some Torontonians held for their supposedly superb system.

"If the TTC plans to gain the money that it apparently direly needs, it is going about it in the wrong way," wrote one concerned reader.

"A raise in fares would result in the loss of a considerable number of riders, putting the commission no further ahead than it is now."

"TTC officials are aware that increased fares, cutbacks in routes, poor schedules, etc., reduce the ridership which in turn decreases income," wrote another.

"Obviously, the solution is to attract riders. To do this, comfort and minimum travel time cannot be overemphasized."

Complaints notwithstanding, Toronto's subway had reached the big time by 1979. It had become runner-up to New York City, the North American champion, in number of passengers carried each year.

Not bad for a local.

16

Boston–A Pioneer in American Transit

New York City fancies itself the "Big Apple," where trends are launched. But every so often Gotham misses the boat—or train, as the case may be—and finds itself upstaged. Such was the case when the subway phenomenon crossed the Atlantic Ocean and reached the New World. After the underground was built in London, the Métro in Paris, and a rapid transit tube in Glasgow, it was Boston, not New York, that took the lead in North American subway construction. The project had symbolic value, for it would keep Boston at the forefront of progressive transit thinking through the seventies, when planners in America's Hub City chose to put their faith in trolley cars—known in the trade as LRVs—while rejecting federal attempts to push a superhighway through the Massachusetts metropolis.

Before Boston ever dreamed of burrowing underground to transport its citizens, the Hub was crisscrossed with streetcars. At the peak of streetcar transit in the nineteenth century, some two hundred trolleys rumbled along Tremont Street in each direction every hour to what historian-author Brian J. Cudahy described as "hopeless confusion and the ruination of schedules."

So thick was congestion along Tremont Street opposite the Old Granary Burying Grounds that pedestrians found the thoroughfare virtually impassable in midafternoon on any workday in 1895 or thereafter until the subway was built. Clearly, relieving the flow of street traffic on Tremont Street was a major order of business for Boston planners. Finding the ideal method was the mystery perplexing transportation experts in the Hub. For precedent there were the subways of Europe, the elevated railroads of New York City, and even some experimental rapid transit work in Boston itself. As far back as 1886, a steam-operated, supported monorail ran over Bridge Street and the filled-in bed of the Miller River. "It was a full-size working model," noted Electric Railroaders Association historian Tony Fitzherbert, "consisting of three cylindrical-shaped cars, a steam dummy, a tender, and open-platform coach."

Built by the Meigs Company, the Boston project was the third monorail built in the United States and won the approval of the Boston Railroad Commission for construction between Bowdoin Square and Cambridge. Despite the official green light on the blueprints, it remained more theoretical than practical and never got off the drawing board in its fullest form.

A traditional elevated line would have appeared to be the most likely successor to the Meigs Elevated Railway Company, except that construction of an overhead line carried with it certain drawbacks. Like the Wall Street area of Manhattan, roads in the Hub were an intricate maze apparently worked out by cows in their spare time. You'll see this in the narrow, winding streets that comprise Boston's central business district. To place an elevated line in such a maze would not only erase the available sunlight but also deface the historic area. It fell to the Boston Transit Commission to make the final decision. The commission was compelled to consider the trolley boom that had consumed Boston to an enormous extent. At the intersection of Park and Tremont streets on one Saturday in 1894 exactly 2,613 northbound trolleys rolled by and 2,219 southbound streetcars.

Since there had been no precedent for full-scale subway construction in the United States, Boston officials were open to several possibilities. They could look to Europe for inspiration or produce their own unique proposal. The result was a subway that utilized not traditional railway carriages but trolleys, the same trolleys that had been the bane of pedestrians through the 1890s.

For Bostonians, the decision to fill a subway with streetcars was not greeted with dismay. Ever since January 1889, when Boston introduced its first electric trolleys, they were treated with a fondness matched only by Toronto among North American cities.

While the general public welcomed the concept of inserting trolleys in tunnels, some proper Bostonians as well as merchants took a dim view of the idea. Brian J. Cudahy, writing about Boston's subways in *Change at Park Street Under*, recalled the concern among Hub bluebloods. "Certain old-line residents," wrote Cudahy, "viewed the notion of a subway with slightly less alarm, say, than a report of Attila the Hun marching east through Dedham. Some downtown property owners were convinced that their Tremont Street buildings would be undermined by the construction, and eventually collapse."

A significant bit of political chicanery was necessary to push through a bill to set the rapid transit proposal in motion. This was accomplished by the Massachusetts legislature (General Court) in July 1894 when many antisubway members were vacationing. The subway proposal then went to a general referendum which the pro-underground adherents won. The design specifics now were left to Chief Engineer Howard A. Carsen, who believed that the most expeditious plan was to take the streetcars into the downtown area via three channels: one from the north and two from the south. Trolleys would enter the tunnels through ramps, or inclines, as the Boston Transit Commission chose to call them. Special underground turnabouts would reverse the trolleys. The total length of the tunnel was to be two and two-thirds miles for a cost placed at $5,000,000.

Foes of the project tried desperately to derail it in the courts but they were unsuccessful, and the way was clear for construction to begin. The first spade was put to the ground on March 28, 1895, in the Public Gardens opposite the Providence Railway station. For Bostonians it was a moment of great triumph. Hub citizens could boast that they not only had gotten the jump on their rivals in New York City but were ahead of every other city in North America.

Because it was a first, the project was fraught with anxiety. Physicians, obsessed with the fear of pulmonary disease which was prevalent at the time, wondered whether subway air would be too polluted for the human lung. Others were concerned about cave-ins, too-low temperatures in the summer, and assorted other bugaboos.

Unlike the London subway, which featured raised platforms to accommodate the railroad-style coaches, the Boston Transit Commission opted for track-level entrances as if the trolleys were operating on streets of the Hub. For safety's sake, however, a one-foot-high platform was constructed at the original stations.

Boston's subway planners could not avoid disaster. Nine workers were killed as a result of an explosion that occurred during excavation at Boylston and Tremont streets. "Beds of quicksand gave trouble," wrote Cudahy. "A further macabre duty was the reinterment of the remains of 910 bodies exhumed as the excavators worked their way through colonial burial grounds."

Despite these and other obstacles, opening day (September 1, 1897) arrived less than three years after ground breaking had taken place. It was, by any standard, a momentous occasion, viewed critically by correspondents from various parts of the United States, Canada, and Europe. Would it work? Would the public approve? Would the press commend?

The answers began filtering through as motorman James Reed and conductor Gilman Trufant guided streetcar 1752 into the portal at Tremont Street. According to the Boston *Globe*, "The trolley hissed along like a brood of vipers." But it negotiated the incline and pulled into the new Park Street station, making history and winning raves.

Since New York City was cleanly beaten out in the subway derby by its New England rival, it was not surprising that *The New York Times* obliquely needled its own City Hall with these editorial lines: "That so conservative an American town should happen to be the pioneer in adopting this is viewed as remarkable."

No understatement, that. Boston's subway, the first in America and the fifth in the world, handled more than 50,000,000 passengers during its first year of operation, five times the first year's total of the London underground. "It permitted an increase from 200 to 400 cars an hour in each direction in the peak period of the day," said John Anderson Miller in his definitive transit analysis, *Fares, Please!* The subway also reduced the running time in the center city and, as predicted, relieved traffic congestion.

In short, the Boston subway worked; and since it did prove practical and not overly expensive, it fired the public imagination and still another major Boston subway project was proposed. Once again the transit barons had to agree on a modus operandi. Would it be the same trolley-underground system? Would it be a rapid transit, using railway rolling stock? Would it be an elevated line? Or something in between?

Because a maneuverable streetcar that could snake through narrow Boston streets had to be relatively thin and they were rather fragile in appearance, the "dinky" trolleys were not regarded as the wave of the future. The Transit Commission believed that Bostonians were ready for something bigger and better. So, a year after the debut of the Tremont Street trolley tunnel, the commission gave the go-ahead for the second landmark project, a combination elevated-subway line which would be the forerunner for still further rapid transit expansion in the Hub.

No longer were there doubts about the practicality of electric-powered vehicles underground. Banished were the fears of frigid subway air or disease. One magazine critic gave the subway high marks for its air and temperature. In a somewhat partisan but nonetheless understandable editorial, the Boston *Journal* waxed ecstatic about how its subway "opened the eyes of the country to the fact that this city is more than a centre of literary and historic associations, and that it has an eye on the future as well as to the past."

In a sense the Transit Commission's eye was on the past—New York City's past—as much as it was on the future and, therein, the Hub was forever victimized by shortsightedness at a time when more daring long-range thinking was in order. Progress came in the form of a decision to eschew the underground trolleys in future construction in favor of rapid transit rolling stock. The Boston Transit Commission's shortsighted decision was to build an elevated railway while snaking only some of the tracks underground, rather than a full underground subway.

What Bostonians learned this time was that the commission favored a mostly elevated railway reaching Charlestown on the north, and Dudley Street on the south. In the heart of the city it would run through the trolley subway. This bizarre arrangement of streetcar and rail car side by side would remain a part of Boston's curious transit fabric to the present. More than a century ago, the elevated plan was scorched by a number of critics as a poor compromise and a retrogressive plan copying the nineteenth-century New York City elevated railways which guaranteed the defacement of an attractive, historic metropolis. Nevertheless, the plan was approved and work begun on the uglification of Boston.

Built upon steel columns supported on a concrete foundation, with heavy cross girders spanning the street, the elevated structure despite its aesthetic deficiencies would add immeasurably to the mobility of Bostonians. Instead of the "dinky" streetcars, the Boston el would be graced with major league rolling stock. Three separate builders—Wason Manufacturing Company, the Osgood Bradley Car Company, and the St. Louis Car Company—constructed the first elevated cars. They had wooden bodies, open platforms, and steel underframes, with seats for 48 passengers and a maximum seating-standee capacity of 162 riders each. One truck of each car carried two 150-horsepower motors.

Having been bitten by the building bug, the commission continued to plan

more lines, including a rapid transit subway under Washington Street. Meanwhile, roars of protest were heard over the meshing of the original elevated line
and the trolley tunnel. "The use of the Tremont Street Subway for the el trains
proved to be very unpopular, inconvenient, and expensive," commented one
transit critic. "Even before the elevated opened, there was public demand for a
separate tunnel in downtown Boston for high-platform rapid transit."

Boston's efforts, no matter how unpopular they may have been in some quarters—while popular in others, as proven by the turnstile counts—did cause continent-wide reverberations. Nowhere was the awe more noticeable than just
down the Atlantic coast in New York City, where subway talk had been bruited
about for several decades without result. The moment Boston's Tremont Street
tunnel had its premiere, New Yorkers got jealous. The success of Boston's first
subway encouraged advocates of a subway in New York. And this resulted in a
blueprint for a fifteen-mile all-underground line that was considerably more
elaborate than the Tremont Street subway.

But years before New York's Interborough Rapid Transit line made its debut,
Boston's Main Line El was trundling along in impressive, though noisy, fashion.
Attempts to pacify the public were made in various ways. Elaborate Victorian-
style stations were built overhead and other amenities provided. More than
200,000 fares were recorded on opening day, a total that more than pleased
promoters. What proved disturbing for the future, however, was the prospect of
future delays caused by the intricate subway construction techniques.

Boston's Transit Commission employed the traditional cut-and-cover technique of excavation. First, the street was opened, then the digging done, the
subway superstructure built, and then the pavement (cover) restored. But street
traffic was thoroughly disrupted as little attempt was made at the turn of the
century to provide a temporary pavement while work was in progress. This, of
course, inspired a hail of protest from merchants whose businesses were interrupted. Protests notwithstanding, a 1902 Rapid Transit Act won voter approval
for a subway tunnel serving the entire business center. The tunnel under Washington Street opened for business on November 30, 1908. From incline to incline, the tunnel measured 1.23 miles. To accommodate the narrow streets
above, engineers on the project designed tunnels so that tracks could be built on
separate levels. Wherever possible—such as Union-Friend Station—designers
cleverly provided passageways between elevated platforms and trolley platforms.

The building boom continued unabated with the Washington Street Elevated
extended by two stations to Forest Hills in 1909. While all the aboveground
work was taking place, commission members remained acutely tuned in to public opinion, which had been against the el concept in the first place. Two cos-
metic-engineering efforts were made to soothe the populace. Solid, more mod-
ern-looking plate girders were used to support the tracks on the Washington
Street elevated extension rather than the geometrically appealing but old-fashioned lattice girders.

At Forest Hills, the line's new terminal, the commission pulled out all stops in eschewing the Victorian station concept and, instead, designed a most modern-appearing edifice clothed in poured concrete. Located opposite the New Haven Railroad station, the Forest Hills terminal linked with several Boston trolley lines and, according to Boston subway historian Brian J. Cudahy, was the *"chef d'oeuvre* of rapid transit development in Boston down to this time." The concrete design, incidentally, was used more extensively on New York City's Flushing Line of the Interborough Rapid Transit system in the Long Island City and Sunnyside sections of Queens. For its time the Forest Hills terminal was attractive and practical, while stifling what few critics remained to lambast the Transit Commission. The Hub was committed to more and more rapid transit, encouraging ridership in 1907 with the introduction of steel cars (although wooden rolling stock remained in use through 1928).

Boston continued to upgrade both its streetcar and subway equipment. The original trolleys were single- and double-truck open cars, as well as box cars with open platforms and Brill-built semiconvertibles. The state of the art in Boston streetcars progressed to the cumbersome Type 4s, followed by center entrance cars and lightweight T5s. Ultimately, the Hub was graced with streamlined streetcars and, most recently, stocked its lines with the ultramodern LRVs. Subways enjoyed a similar progression, from open-end platform el-subway trains to 1951-built East Boston cars that bear a striking resemblance to New York City IRT cars in roof design.

Boston's subway-el rolling stock achieved worldwide eminence when the Cambridge subway opened on March 23, 1912, connecting Park Street Under and Main Street, Cambridge. The forty original cars, constructed by Standard Steel Company, were almost seventy feet long, then the largest subway cars in the world. (Even now few cars—Toronto's 74-footers, Barcelona's 72-footers— are longer.) The Cambridge-Dorchester line had an especially appealing feature in summer months: the end doors of the trains were left open, protected by a wire screen, and cool breezes wafted through the cars.

Those familiar with the Boston system have found much to commend despite many shortcomings. Peter Blake, an architect and chairman of the School of Architecture at the Boston Architectural Center, rated the Boston system with high honors for its efforts at the start and in the seventies. "Boston's subway system," said Blake, "is the oldest in the United States—and still one of the best. The subway is not uniformly or even predominantly gorgeous; some of its stations continue to remind one of those sewers under the city of Vienna so dramatically filmed by Orson Welles in *The Third Man*."

Unlike its New York counterpart, the Boston elevated has escaped major disaster. In November 1918, a derailment of a Brooklyn elevated train entering a tunnel portal took ninety-seven lives. The worst el wreck in the Hub occurred on July 22, 1928, when a four-car train, moving at a speed considerably over the limit, derailed at the sharp curve at Harrison Avenue and Beach Street. Three passengers were killed.

But Boston's rapid transit suffers conspicuously in comparison with the New York system in other ways. Whereas New York concentrated on placing its trains underground, Boston, by 1978, acknowledged that half of its subway-streetcar mileage is overground. However, when it came to the handling of its surface operation, Boston provided the ultimate practical and philosophical triumph over the New York thinkers. Hub transit planners consistently saw the value of retaining trolleys and realized that judicious use of trackless trolleys (electric buses) could deliver a well-rounded system. It would make the most of the limitations imposed by an ancient subway, capitalize on the innumerable assets of streetcar operation, and meld them into a contemporary system that also utilizes diesel buses with trackless trolleys.

The melding of these clearly suggests Toronto's superb transportation system—with one notable exception. Boston did what Toronto failed to do when streetcar lines began proliferating early in the twentieth century. In the Hub, extensive private right-of-way was provided for the trolleys. Rolling along the center strip of such boulevards as Huntington Avenue, Beacon Street, and Commonwealth Avenue, the trolley was given the space that it deserves in an urban setting, free to speed at semirapid transit rates without interference from auto or truck traffic.

Such streetcar exclusivity was carried to the zenith as far as the Mattapan-Ashmont Line was concerned. Running a total of two and a half miles, the high-speed streetcar is unique among North American transit lines as the only operating trolley line that traverses a cemetery. Opened in 1928, simultaneously with the debut of the Dorchester Tunnel extension, the Mattapan-Ashmont Line rolled over the right-of-way of a New Haven Railroad branch. This again typified the delightful knack Boston transit designers had for capitalizing on railroad abandonment for trolley use. When, for example, the Boston and Albany Railroad terminated commuter passenger and freight services over its Newton-Highlands Branch between Riverside and South stations in 1958, the Massachusetts Bay Transportation Authority moved in and reconstructed the obsolete railroad into an efficiently operated tramline. When it made its debut on July 4, 1959, the speedy, quiet, nonpolluting service marked the appearance of the nation's newest trolley route and proved beyond any doubt that Boston transit chiefs knew what they were doing when they placed their faith in the future of the streetcar.

The passenger use of the Riverside line so rapidly exceeded all expectations that it produced an equipment shortage that lasted for years. Precisely because of that shortage and the government's realization that, yes, there was a need for trolley transportation in many parts of the country, a movement began once again to manufacture a mass-produced tram. As it had in the past, Boston was at the forefront of this noble but often ignominious experiment.

One of the fastest and most unusual costume changes in transit history developed on an April weekend in 1924 when Boston transportation officials ordered a major alteration for the East Boston line. On Friday, April 18, the line wore the dress of a streetcar route. On Monday, April 21, gleaming new multiple-unit subway cars were click-clacking along the very same East Boston run.

This was a remarkable accomplishment by more than 1,500 workers who executed a complicated changeover from trolley tracks to the heavier subway matériel, including third rail. The near-impossible changeover—many experts said it couldn't be done—inspired el general manager Edward Dana to take pen in hand and eulogize the project:

> Listen good friends and you shall read
> Of an all night toil on an urgent need.
> On the eighteenth of April in twenty-four
> Hardly a soul heard the hammer's roar—
> Or thought of the men who accomplished the deed.

It was neither the first nor the last time Bostonians boasted about their system. Oliver Wendell Holmes did so in the nineteenth century, and in the middle of the twentieth century tunesmiths Bess Hawes and Jacqueline Steiner wrote a ditty about "Charlie," a character who found himself penniless on the MTA because of a fare increase. Day after day, night after night, Charlie rides the Boston subway, receiving food from his wife, who hands him sandwiches through the car window as the train passes Scollay Square. Pressed on a Capitol record, another tune, "The MTA," was recorded by the Kingston Trio, a popular musical group in the fifties, and became a smash hit.

Many transit critics believed that Boston deserved the acclaim. The MTA, later the MBTA (Massachusetts Bay Transportation Authority), was not only trying hard to run a good railway; it seemed to be trying harder. But, try as it might, neither the MTA nor the MBTA could claim that the Hub system was good enough. To understand the failure of mass transit in North America, it is worth noting how well Boston has done and where it has missed the station.

Boston has always been looked to by other cities for inspiration and advice. San Francisco, Cleveland, and even so highly commended a transit commission as Toronto's have kept an Argus eye on Boston for help.

What intrigued the TTC and other systems was the MBTA's decision to sell monthly passes in advance for use on the mass transit lines. The MBTA launched the program in 1974 and, within four years, fourteen other North American cities jumped on the bandwagon. And for good reason—riders save money and gain convenience.

The MBTA even persuaded a growing number of employers to pay part of the cost of transit passes. "Other employees," said one transit critic, "like the chap with a parking space, get 'perks,' so why not the subway rider? It sweetens relations and is a lot cheaper than building parking lots."

By March 1978 the MBTA confirmed that every month twenty new firms had signed up for the pass program and, in one year, ten thousand new pass-users had signed on, a 60 percent increase. They buy their passes on payroll deduction plans through 558 employers, including Polaroid, Gillette, and the State of Massachusetts.

MBTA riders can choose from six plans, depending on the kind of transit used. The most expensive general pass enables the holder to use anything in the transit system for $34.20 a month. In return, the sponsoring employer obtains goodwill. "We found," said Ernest Parsons, coordinator of commuter services for the John Hancock firm, "it was something we could do for our people."

Several years will be required to determine just how successful the MBTA monthly pass plan is. So promising were its early results that Toronto's TTC began a study in 1978 on whether to use monthly passes in Toronto. In Chicago, the monthly pass plan also showed promising returns. A survey in the Windy City showed that 85 percent of passholders thought better of the Chicago Transit Authority than they had before the pass program.

Likewise, passholders in the Boston area thought better of their system for other reasons, not the least of which was a milestone development on August 25, 1977. On that day a colorful one-car train pulled into Norwood Central station, fifteen miles south of Boston, and disgorged a spate of politicians and reporters. Tom Nelligan of *Passenger Train Journal* was awed by the scene:

> When the acting governor of the Commonwealth of Massachusetts, Thomas P. O'Neill III, proceeded to bang away at a silver spike in a nearby crosstie, the passerby probably would have concluded he was watching an inexplicable reenactment of Promontory Point [the meeting of the Union Pacific and Central Pacific for America's first transcontinental railroad] in deepest suburbia.

Officials had sped out to Norwood to celebrate the opening of a $13,600,000 program of track upgrading for Boston's commuter rail network, servicing fourteen thousand passengers who rode to work on the combined MBTA–Boston & Maine commuter trains. Rather than dismantling the venerable B&M tracks as other American communities have done to their abandoned passenger lines, the MBTA played ball with the B&M and the result was a magnificent marriage of the units. In 1975 the MBTA purchased 269 miles of B&M track and eighty-four pieces of passenger rolling stock for $39,500,000. Under a five-year contract signed with the MBTA, the B&M operates the trains on schedules set by the Authority and obtains reimbursement for all operating deficits as well as a ten-cent-per-passenger incentive payment. "At five million riders per year," noted Nelligan, "that brings in a $500,000 profit that the financially troubled B&M put to good use."

By the start of 1978 Boston's suburban rail system comprised two physically separate divisions. On the North Side, seven routes, totaling 118 route miles, unfold with 247 weekday trains and 16,000 passengers. From North Station, the trains link with Rockport (35 miles), Ipswich, and other Atlantic coast localities. On the South Side, former Penn Central tracks (the MBTA purchased 145 miles of Penn Central track in January 1973 for $19.5 million) snake along five routes, totaling 95 route miles with 75 weekday trains and 12,000 weekday passenger trips, all emanating from Boston's venerable South Station, not to mention a vital stop at Back Bay.

The result of offering the carrot of rail transit was happily reflected in the numbers; by November 1977 it was reported that Boston suburban ridership had been increasing by about 5 percent a year. "To keep business on the upswing," Nelligan wrote in the November 1977 edition of *Passenger Train Journal*, "the MBTA has a number of physical plant improvements in store." New ties, welded rail, and improved signaling would all be added to further boost ridership. Added Nelligan: "The combination of a well-funded transit authority, a cooperative local railroad, and a public willing to support rail service foretells a healthy future."

Tangible evidence that the future was bright was as plentiful as rail joints on the Boston subway. Apart from increased ridership, the public responded in other ways. Author Marylyn Donahue, for example, took pen in hand and wrote a testimonial to Hub rail travel in the Boston *Herald-American* magazine in April 1977 called "Subways and Suburbs." Author Donahue, in her enthusiasm, pointed out that riding the MBTA "can be exciting—and even enlightening."

She rhapsodized over the Red Line but saved her most wondrous words for the Blue Line:

Like Ishmael in *Moby Dick*, whenever "my hypos" get the better of me, I feel the need to pay a visit to what Melville refers to as the "watery places of the world." Trying to satisfy such an urge any place else would probably be a problem, especially if you are short of cash and have little time to spare. But not so in Boston, thanks to the Blue Line. Why, even its very name bespeaks the sea and, indeed, for only twenty-five cents, it will carry you to shore's edge within a matter of minutes

Nevertheless, even the most ardent admirers of the system found cause for complaint. Peter Blake, for one, was dismayed by the unavailability of so simple a staple as a subway map. "To obtain a subway map," Blake wrote in the Cooper-Hewitt Museum's publication, *Subways*, "it is usually necessary to buy a T-shirt with a map imprint at the Harvard Co-op, since routine subway maps are hardly ever available at MBTA stations."

Early in 1978 the MBTA's image suffered a few more bruises in odd places. During January 1978, the MBTA suffered two subway crashes, one on January 20 at the height of a snowstorm. More than fifteen persons were injured and hundreds of riders, stranded by the crash, had to be sheltered for the day in a subway car shop while city officials tried to find food for them. And when the winter snows had melted, problems remained. On April 24, 1978, the Boston *Globe* socked it to the MBTA with an "exclusive," asserting that the most expensive painting job ever done by the Authority—a $2,500,000 contract to preserve the Forest Hills line's elevated steel structure for the next ten years—"already deteriorated extensively a few months after the work was completed. . . ."

The MBTA wasted no time in counterattacking. It suggested that the *Globe* waited too long in its forty-five-paragraph story to make mention that the MBTA had refused to accept the job because of the peeling. In a detailed rebuttal, the Authority concluded: "The fact that 17 percent of the top coat is peeling is unacceptable to the T. The job will be corrected at no public cost and within environmental procedures which present law and society demand."

True, there were bugs, but the gremlins were not fused irrevocably with the machines. If nothing else, the new Boston trolleys (light rail vehicles) demonstrated that Boston was willing to be innovative and delightfully old-fashioned in a practical way. The Hub valued its clean air, or what the diesels and trucks and autos left of it, and was trying to improve. From time to time even the LRVs got a good press. TO BE SPECIFIC, T CARS TERRIFIC lauded a headline in the Boston *Herald-American*.

Those with an affectionate interest in the MBTA appreciate the mistakes—a modest local subway like Toronto's, abandonment of many efficient trolley-bus lines—but also laud the creativity and daring in spite of trends in other directions. There is much to be said for the simple description of Boston's MBTA atop Peter Blake's story in *Subways:* "The Oldest Subway System in the Land Is Rapidly Creaking Its Way into the Future."

That Boston should be a leader in the development of electric surface transportation in the 1970s is hardly surprising considering the city's heritage as a leader in urban transportation.

Errors were made, to be sure, but innovation was also a feature of the Boston system. The subway arrived before the turn of the century and, along with the streetcar, dominated the Boston public transportation scene until the early 1920s, when the Boston Elevated Railway Company decided to replace several streetcar lines with gasoline-powered buses. Between 1922, when the first conversion took place, and 1935, more than forty streetcar–to–gas bus changes had been made. In time the company would realize how seriously it had erred. Bradley H. Clarke, author of *The Trackless Trolleys of Boston*, explained the errors. "The program," said Clarke, "had a number of drawbacks. The gasoline bus was reasonably cheap to operate, but it demanded constant maintenance. And as the number of bus lines grew, the Elevated found itself with power generation and supply facilities which far exceeded its needs. A further problem was that bus passenger-carrying capacity was less than that of a streetcar."

By the mid-thirties the gasoline buses produced enough headaches for Boston Elevated officials to seek relief in an alternate mode of transport. Their remedy was the trolley bus, which, ironically, had been demonstrated in 1887 in a vacant lot on Harrison Avenue. Another demonstration was conducted in Boston fourteen years later, but the city was not yet ready for the machine. When the first practical trolley bus was introduced in the summer of 1913 by E. S. King, manager of the Merrill (Wisconsin) Railway and Lighting Company, Bostonians couldn't have cared less. However, other transit experts found the trolley bus appealing in several respects.

Equipped with two overhead trolley poles so that it could obtain central station power (two wires were needed since there were no rails to act as a return circuit), the electric bus was relatively lightweight and so flexible it could swivel several feet on each side of the overhead wires. Maintenance requirements were low, yet the trolley bus had a larger passenger capacity than the gasoline-power counterpart. "Small wonder," commented Clarke, "that the Boston Elevated turned to the trolley coach to ease its difficulties." The date was 1936, following four years of promotion by builders (J. G. Brill Company) and trackless trolley proponents of various stripes.

"In its reincarnation," observed transit expert John Anderson Miller, "the trolley bus had many desirable qualities. Its operating cost was relatively low. It was quiet and comfortable to ride in. It was fast, but smooth in starting and stopping."

Bostonians were enthusiastic following the debut on April 11, 1936, of trackless trolleys on the Lechmere line. Boston Elevated moguls responded by adding thirteen more electric bus lines. Impetus to the growth of a trackless trolley network was provided in post–World War II years by Edward Dana, who served as general manager of the Boston transit system through the late fifties. It was Dana who created the successful system and, naturally, took an avuncular interest in the vehicles until his retirement in 1959.

That turned out to be a pivotal year for the future of the electric buses as well as the development of transit in Greater Boston; for it was then that Boston (along with Brooklyn in New York) failed to see the value of the trackless trolleys as progressive Toronto had. Whereas Toronto sensed the value—ecologically, aesthetically, and economically—of electric buses, Boston (and Brooklyn) capitulated to forces whose thinking on the subject was, at best, fuzzy.

Dana's successor, Thomas J. McLernon, came to Boston by way of the New York City Transit Authority. His tenure in the Hub was stormy and between 1961 and 1963 several electric bus routes were replaced by diesel bus operation. McLernon, himself, was replaced in 1965 by General Rush B. Lincoln, but by that time the Boston trackless trolley fleet had been ravaged to the point of near extinction.

To those familiar with the virtues of trackless trolleys, the MTA's extermination program bordered on tragic. This is especially true when one considers that in 1955 Boston boasted the third largest trolley coach fleet in the United States (behind Chicago and Atlanta) and owned the largest collection of electric buses built by the renowned Pullman Company in America. But most vexing of all were the fatuous alibis offered by the MTA for eliminating the superb piece of transportation.

As was the case in Brooklyn, where a similarly large post–World War II electric bus armada was destroyed, justification for the annihilation was weaker than a thirty-year-old gasoline bus. One rationale had it that the electric bus "presented an antiquated image of the Authority." (Gasoline buses had been around as long.) It also was alleged that the trackless trolleys functioned poorly in frigid weather, a charge that was actually refuted by the Authority itself in its 1947 annual report. On page 36 of the report a photo depicting electric buses is accompanied by a caption reading: "Trackless trolleys operating despite Winter conditions."

If that wasn't embarrassing enough, the Authority charged that the electric buses were noisy and rough-riding. Yet the Boston Elevated Railway annual report for 1944 stated: "Because of quietness and smoothness of operation, modern trackless trolleys have earned popular approval wherever used." But the fleet was abruptly scuttled in the early fifties and replaced by diesel buses.

Fortunately, Boston never eschewed its nonpolluting streamlined trolleys.

Even though they had aged chronologically, the Hub's PCC cars were hand-somer in 1950, 1960, and 1970 than any diesel bus produced by General Motors, Flxible, or AM General. The MBTA maintained the sleek rolling stock and waited for the day when a trolley of the seventies would be produced. That day came in mid-June 1971, when the Boeing-Vertol Company was selected as systems manager for the U.S. Government's Urban Rapid Rail Vehicle and Systems Program; in short, a belated bid by Washington to revive interest in trolleys as a mass transit vehicle of the late seventies, eighties, and nineties.

The Authority felt its *coup de résistance* was its argument that there were no manufacturers in the United States who built electric buses. "While this was true at the time [early sixties]," pointed out Clarke, "the Toronto Transit Commission had disproven this by having its trackless trolleys rebuilt to thoroughly modern standards by a domestic manufacturer. Apart from this, however, the bulk of the Boston fleet was in fairly good condition and with proper maintenance and selective line removal, the trackless trolley system could have served the area many more years. And with the current public outcry against air pollution, the MTC would have made a substantial contribution to its control had such a policy been considered."

But it wasn't, and Boston has since suffered for its sin. By comparison, Toronto has enjoyed nothing but success with its trolley coach renaissance. On the other hand, the Boston experience was not unique. Following World War II, New York City's Board of Transportation replaced traditional streetcars on several Brooklyn routes with an excellent St. Louis Car Company trolley coach. These electric buses were, as always, quiet, efficient, and nonpolluting.

Administered by the U.S. Department of Transportation's Urban Mass Transportation Administration (UMTA), the make-the-trolley-respectable program was aimed at the two cities that had kept the faith with streetcars, Boston and San Francisco. Mostly, though, it was geared to Boston. On May 1, 1973, Boeing Vertol Company received a contract from the MBTA and San Francisco's Municipal Railway Improvement Corporation (MUNI) for production of 230 of the light rail vehicles (LRVs). Taking the lead, Boston ordered 150 of the sleek streetcars while San Francisco's bid came to 80 vehicles. It marked the first time streetcars would be built in the United States since 1951.

The first shipment of LRVs arrived in Boston in 1975 and were put through an eleven-week series of tests on the MBTA's Green Line, which appropriately was the nation's first subway, served initially by single-truck "dinkys." By contrast, the new rolling stock was seventy-three feet long, featured air suspension and air conditioning, and included an articulated joint in the center to permit negotiation of tight curves on city streets.

On August 13, 1975, the LRVs completed their tests on the Green Line and, supposedly, equaled or bettered "all specified performance requirements, i.e., speed, acceleration, braking, energy consumption, ride quality, and noise level." Boeing Vertol officials were so proud of their product they seemed to be busting vests every time the LRV was mentioned. A communiqué released by Boeing Vertol's propaganda ministry in Philadelphia sounded as if the LRV was, in fact, a major answer to the transit problems of medium-sized cities such as Boston.

The trolley of the future was tested on the surface line from Riverside to Fenway Park and in the tunnel from Kenmore Square to Park Street. "The response," said Boeing Vertol representatives in a moment of rare modesty, "was enthusiastic."

Equally jubilant was the reaction of the U.S. Department of Transportation's Pueblo, Colorado, test plant, where the LRVs were being examined by the Urban Mass Transportation Administration. "A particularly strong contender," a transportation agency report said of the LRV as a solution to medium-city transit problems. The LRV was touted for urban areas that wanted fixed-line economical transit but could not "justify the high cost, long lead times and disruption associated with the construction of heavy rail rapid transit."

Now all that mattered was whether the LRV could get similar rave notices under regular revenue conditions. The answer was so obviously negative that it appeared the MBTA would have egg on its face for a decade at least.

As unmitigated disasters go, the Boston LRV experiment ranked right near the top. After the first thirty-two ultramodern trolleys were delivered, MBTA Chairman Robert Kiley ordered a freeze on the delivery of future cars. The reason? The trams, despite the supposedly exhaustive testing, could not all hold the rails. The LRVs, according to *The New York Times*, "had a bad habit of jumping tracks on tight curves, among other things."

Kiley had a quick answer, explaining that the cars were rushed into service after minimal testing. He asserted that breakdowns of the old PCC cars on the Green Line had been so numerous because of a harsh winter that the LRVs were needed sooner than anticipated.

The unexpected failure of the LRVs stunned the MBTA to the core; especially Chairman Kiley, to whom the enormous quantity of questions were directed. Kiley wasted no time arming himself with answers. He described the LRVs as a product of "space age technology," on the assumption that that was automatically a valid explanation.

An autopsy of the LRV lemon revealed a mechanical defect in the truck section that contained the vehicle's wheels. The inflexibility of this part apparently forced the wheels to leave the tracks on slow curves, Kiley explained. Sadly, the trucks were not the only LRV parts giving the MBTA moguls migraines. Boeing Vertol engineers also were checking out complaints that the overly complex door mechanism—originally it contained an absurd, Univac-oriented 1,300 parts—functioned improperly. Despite the defeats, Chairman Kiley put on a happy face and insisted that he was "guardedly optimistic" about the LRV, which had already been dubbed "The Little Engine That Couldn't."

Kiley frequently relied on the "too new to tell" argument and suggested that time might be the best healer for the wounded LRV. "We expected it would take about two years to work out all the bugs," Kiley said in defense of the experiment. "The vehicle itself is a superb, smooth-running vehicle, and it is obviously pleasing from the users' point of view."

MBTA and Boeing Vertol officials convened around the drawing boards and, following a large infusion of new money and several modifications—the number of parts on the door was drastically reduced, for instance—the trolleys were returned to service. By now Boeing had made more than sixty-five modifications to the LRV's body. Boeing also lashed back at the MBTA, suggesting that the tracks on the Green Line were in poor condition. "It's not unusual for any new car to have problems," said Arthur Hitsman, general manager for surface transportation of Boeing Vertol. "There are a lot of things you find out only through usage."

And usage was just what the LRVs needed to gain the missing kudos. Following Boeing Vertol's intensive reworking of the trolley, it returned to Boston tracks and, this time, captured the imagination of many critics who previously were quick to stamp it a has-been before it even got rolling. On March 20, 1978, *The New York Times* rhapsodized over the LRV. BOSTON'S TROLLEYS NOW SEEM ON THE RIGHT TRACK, cooed the *Times*'s headline. Reporter Grace Lichtenstein noted that the MBTA had set new, tough rush-hour performance standards for the new trolleys and that "those standards have been reached."

MBTA officials appeared less tense about their trolleys than they had been in 1977. David Gunn, the MBTA director of operations, believed that the LRV would ultimately prove its worth. "They [trolleys] are extremely popular," said Gunn, "and we expect to have 175 of them operating by 1982. We'll supplement them with at least 50 completely rebuilt streetcars. The net result will be a 35 percent seating capacity increase. And we're finally training a set of new, highly skilled mechanics to handle even the most complex problems quickly." Nevertheless, the LRV gremlins continued to surface through 1979.

The MBTA virtually exhausted its patience with the Boeing Vertol Light Rail Vehicle early in 1979. One of the most destructive (to the Boeing Vertol image) episodes occurred on December 5, 1978, when the MBTA announced that it was returning thirty-five of the LRV cars to Boeing Vertol because the trolleys simply didn't work.

"The LRVs," said the Boston *Globe*, "have been plagued with breakdowns of doors, air conditioning, electronics, propulsion systems, and many other components." In a turnabout from his earlier optimistic stance, Gunn said that he had had a team of twenty-five men working on the cars since they began arriving in 1976 but that even with modifications, paid for by the contractor, they have provided "unacceptable" service.

In 1973 the MBTA ordered 175 of the long, sleek cars, which bend in the middle, and had taken delivery on a total of 150 by early 1979, including the thirty-five that were sent back. Gunn said that another six LRVs, which had been damaged in service and had parts "borrowed" from them, were being stored temporarily in an unused MBTA tunnel until they could be repaired. The MBTA, he said, was refusing to take delivery of the other forty cars in the original order until LRV performance is generally more reliable.

Gunn asserted that it takes more MBTA personnel to keep fifty-odd LRVs going on the Green Line than it does to maintain 220 rapid transit cars on the Red, Blue, and Orange lines.

Sold to the MBTA for $300,000 apiece, LRV parts "have failed at an extremely rapid rate," Gunn said, and the car's performance "has been miles off criteria." Gunn added that out of a pool of ninety to ninety-three LRVs on a given day, "we've been lucky if we have fifty-five going."

"Everybody was taken by surprise by the LRVs' rate of failure," Gunn said. "They were supposed to be reliable, but it just wasn't true."

A new LRV would cost more than $900,000 today, according to Gunn. San Francisco's Bay Area Transit Authority has put in the only other order for the Boeing Vertol LRVs, which were designed to U.S. Department of Transportation specifications.

"They only had four so far and they just operated them experimentally with sandbags instead of passengers," Gunn said. "Ours worked fine with sandbags."

Problems were no less complex in the underground and on the elevated lines traveled by the heavy rapid transit nontram lines. For one thing, the rolling stock had in the post–World War II years become what subway critic Peter Blake described as "clearly antediluvian." Since it was the original subway in America, the stations, not surprisingly, had become equally antique in their appearance. "Some of the lighting," commented Blake, "appeared to be pre-Edisonian, and some of the essental signage is missing."

Creeping obsolescence was a concern, but Boston also pushed ahead with additional rapid transit. In 1952, thanks to legislative approval of use of the old Boston, Revere Beach, and Lynn line, service was pushed ahead to Revere Beach and Orient Heights. Bostonians now could crow that they had the first American transit line to link with a major international airport (Logan). The line was graced with spanking new rolling stock from the St. Louis Car Company that rivaled the best subway trains operating in New York City, Philadelphia, Chicago, or Toronto at the time. Just five years later another addition was hailed when the New York Central Railroad sold the MTA a nine-mile right-of-way that bisected the communities of Newton and Brookline and, happily, was a grade-free route. Dubbed the Riverside Line, the limited-stop route utilized PCC cars and made stops at handsome old Boston and Albany Railroad stations such as Newton Centre. "Riverside," wrote Brian J. Cudahy, "was built cheaply, at a time when few cities were investing in any transport facilities other than highways . . . the longest transit route ever put into service all at one time in Boston."

Meanwhile, the Main Line El was prettied up with spiffy new Pullman-Standard cars and there were clear signs that the creaky old system would be ready for a renaissance.

The decisive turnabout occurred in the early sixties, when an unequivocal decision was made to refurbish the system, top to bottom. This demonstration of faith in rapid transit was as characteristic of Boston as was its first experiment with underground trolleys in 1897. This time, however, the Hub was faced with

the Promethean project of reversing what had been an overwhelming movement of the middle class to the innumerable suburbs sprinkled around Bean-
town. A massive urban renewal program focused around Government Center
promised to revitalize downtown Boston. But it could succeed only if people
could get to the new downtown Boston rapidly and conveniently.

To help them do so, MBTA launched a campaign in 1964: "There'll Be Some
Changes Made." Responsibility for this was placed on the shoulders of the
MBTA, which ruled not merely the Boston subway system but the entire Massachusetts Bay area as well. General James McCormack, chairman of the then
newly formed MBTA, promised to modernize the rapid transit network. The
general said his unit would put on a new and happy face and, in time, it did.

For starters, the MBTA got itself a slogan—"Transportation Begins with a
'T'"—and contracted with a high-class architectural and design firm to do
more than put lipstick and rouge on the system. The outfit was Cambridge Sev-
en Associates, and they took the assignment with relish.

"They decided to use very simple devices," said Peter Blake. "Color to identify the four principal lines of the system; uniform typography to convey essential information; pictorial images to relate the subway platforms below to the
scenes or landmarks above; and good subway car design to make the ride comfortable and attractive."

And so the beat went on; the MBTA drew up a master plan which the Electric Railroaders' Association described as moving the "transportation facilities of
New England's most important city to the forefront of the industry."

The beautification part of the renaissance did not go without notice in other
regions. *Time* magazine enthused over the repainting and refitting of the ancient Arlington Street station and noted that it made most New York City subway stations appear maudlin by comparison.

Partially funded by the United States Department of Housing and Urban Development, the Arlington Station face-lifting was completed on August 17,
1967. The philosophy of the Arlington project was articulated as trying to make
stations become "places . . . where the passenger must at all times be oriented."
To do so, visual matter was used extensively, and to good advantage. For example, the station features no fewer than twelve five-by-twelve-foot floodlit porce-
lain enamel photo murals along the platform walls depicting the swan boats in
the Public Garden, the quaint Newbury Street shops, and other notable sites in
the vicinity.

Complementing the new station design were new subway cars. In 1969 the
Pullman-Standard Company delivered a fleet of fully air-conditioned cars that
strongly resembled the Pullman-built rolling stock that has been running on the
Main Line Elevated since 1957. Initial complaints turned to compliments as
new lines grew from the inner city all the way to distant suburbs.

Peter Blake was a smidgen more cautious, yet enthusiastic. "The MBTA's
subway is not uniformly or even predominantly gorgeous," he wrote in *Subways,* a special publication of the Smithsonian Institution. "Still the MBTA is
clearly getting there."

More stations were pegged for renovation and, by 1979, it was evident that the exodus to the suburbs had been halted and downtown Boston was alive, well, and getting better—thanks, in part, to the MBTA's efforts. As for the future, Peter Blake was optimistic. "The lights will be brighter," he wrote in *Subways*, "the stations cheerier and safer, the cars more silent, and the graphics more informative."

Boston, which had reached a milestone in 1897 when the four-wheel, open-bench car #1792 plied the route through America's first subway, had now achieved another milestone. It had developed a neatly meshed transportation system, including subways, els, trolleys, electric buses, and diesel buses, for the eighties.

17

Seattle—From Tracks to Trackless

Nothing says it more for the failure of mass transit in the northwest metropolis of Seattle, Washington, than a series of episodes in 1978. Early in February of that year City Councilman George Benson arrived at the offices of the Melbourne, Australia, Tramways office to purchase a pair of trolley cars for $5,000. At the time of purchase the cars were *fifty-two years old*.

In 1978 Seattleites were being told by Seattle Metro Transit that they had a superior operation, when the facts suggested otherwise. Seattle's diesel buses had proven less than ideal. Experiments with "exclusive bus lanes" in downtown areas met stiff resistance. A program for the replacement of diesels with trackless trolleys forced the closure of all trolley routes to permit reconstruction of overhead wiring. A three-bus crash triggered a probe that revealed flaws in Metro's maintenance operation as well as questionable practices in the replacement of bus tires. By the summer of 1978 it appeared that the only cause for jubilation was official word that, yes, Seattle *had* obtained a pair of immaculate 1926 W-2 Class, fifty-two-seat, fifty-three-foot Australian trolleys. The cars' cost of $5,000 was augmented by a $55,000 shipping fee. MELBOURNE'S FINEST HAS ARRIVED, a headline in the Seattle *Times* trumpeted when the first jade-and-cream tram was hoisted down to the Seattle waterfront.

"Mint condition," Benson said, beaming at the warm Victorian interior accented by varnished wood-slat benches, carved wooden scrolls and hand holds, and slatted floorboards. "Look," said the councilman, "even the wood screws are all set so the slots go with the grain of the wood."

Benson examined the polished chrome handrails, immaculate leatherlike seats, wood-slat shutters, sliding wooden doors with graceful windows, as if he were an antique collector studying a prize find. What made the vignette so bizzare was that the 1926 Melbourne cars were not purchased to be still-life antiques; Seattle wanted them because the trolleys were a better-made product than the buses; more beautiful and, as Benson knew all along, more utilitarian. "It will not be a tourist thing," the councilman asserted. "The trolley will replace the waterfront buses. We're expecting great crowds. The streetcars will be our transit system along there."

Benson's "discovery" that trolleys could be a viable means of mass transportation in the 1980s was not a lonely voice of an electric railroad fanatic in the wind. The Seattle councilman was merely echoing a question that had been troubling Washingtonians for years. It was best articulated in a column by Dick

Moody in the Seattle *Times*, where the headline succinctly told the story: DID
SEATTLE MISS THE BUS ON STREETCARS?

The answer, when one considers that the trolley era in Seattle spanned six
decades, is an unequivocal yes. When Councilman Benson proudly coos over a
mile-long trolley line costing $1,200,000, he is automatically indicting his politi-
cal predecessors, who allowed a superb street railway system to go to rot. Here
is how the long-term disaster unfolded:

Following the introduction of horsecars in Seattle by a young man named
Frank Osgood in 1884, the Seattle Street Railway proved both practical and
welcome in this burgeoning northwest frontier town built on seven hills. It was
inevitable that if horsecars could work, so could an electric tram system. On
March 30, 1889, the first car of the Seattle Electric Railway and Power Company ran over the completed system. The true test, as far as skeptical Seattleites
were concerned, would be the tram's ability—or inability, as many believed—
to climb the 11 percent grade between First and Second avenues.

Ironically, in 1978 the Seattle *Times* would complain that General Motors
diesel buses "are forced to struggle up and down hills which trolleys handled
easily." But exactly eighty-nine years earlier, a huge crowd gathered at the foot
of James Street, watching with a mixture of curiosity and awe as the motorman
pulled the controller and the four-wheeled tram attempted to negotiate the hill.
The trolley conquered the incline, as one newspaper report put it, "with the
evenness of a running stream." It was a symbolic start for the Seattle Electric
Railway, which operated with astonishing efficiency. Not even the menacing
great Seattle fire of June 6–7, 1889, could keep the streetcars from running. Service continued uninterrupted all through that conflagration.

Only a small minority of Washingtonians took issue with Osgood's operation.
One was a Seattle woman who took the trolley company to court. She charged
that as she was reclining in bed, electricity escaped from the trolley wire below
her window, sputtered into her room, and attacked her from the ceiling. The
woman asserted that she received a shock that rendered her a nervous wreck.

"It was proved," noted Leslie Blanchard in his chronicle *The Street Railway
Era in Seattle*, "that what she had seen was a reflection in the ceiling of her
room of the arcing of a trolley as it passed under a connection, and the court
found in favor of the company."

Like San Francisco, another metropolis built on seven hills, Seattle was
graced by both traditional electric trolleys and cable cars. It is a tribute to the
insightful thinking of San Francisco city fathers that the Golden Gaters still
boast a cable car system, while Seattle now has only memories of a halcyon era
in which cable-operated streetcars were as ubiquitous as the traditional overhead trolleys. The Front Street Cable Railway and the South Seattle Cable Railway entered the decade of the 1890s along with the Lake Washington Cable
Railway in a mood of optimism. Although the city had a population under fifty
thousand, its potential was impressive and was underlined by a report in February 1892 by Acting Mayor George W. Hill.

The steady and enterprising extension of our streetcar system is one of the best assurances that increased traffic will find adequate facilities [wrote Mayor Hill]. Prior to 1888 there existed hardly five miles of horsecar line in Seattle; today [1892] nearly every portion of the city is accessible by one car line and in many parts by two.

Even those who are familiar with the system hardly realize what exceptional advantages the city possesses. . . . Seattle's car line system extends over 48 miles by electricity and 22 miles by cable, altogether 70 miles, a record unparalleled by any other city in the United States.

By the turn of the century suburbia had become a meaningful term in outlying areas of Seattle and, as a result, an impressive system of interurban trolleys began snaking around the area of Puget Sound. One of the most spectacular operations belonged to the Seattle, Renton and Southern line. In 1909 that company introduced the first modern interurban cars, a pair of McGuire-Cummings goliaths 55 feet long that weighed 35 tons and were dubbed Bull Moose. The rolling stock commanded considerable attention. There was, for instance, the undeniable problem that they stood a full 12 feet 10 inches above the rails, which rendered the Bull Moose too tall to clear the Yesler Way overpass across Fourth Avenue. Ultimately the Moose was equipped with an arched roof so it could negotiate the overpass.

Seattle, Renton and Southern continued expanding and in 1910 let a contract to Moran Shipyards of Seattle for construction of fifty-foot interurbans that could hit speeds of 50 miles per hour on the straight track between the southern city limits of Seattle and Renton. They proved an instant hit, luring so many passengers that more cars were ordered immediately. Meanwhile, the Seattle-Everett Traction Company operated a fleet of Niles interurbans. The Seattle-Everett firm was a branch of Boston's Stone and Webster Engineering Company, which had become a dominant force in electric interurban development in the Washington region. Its first major route was the Puget Sound Electric Railway, which opened in 1902 between Seattle and Tacoma.

In 1908, Stone and Webster outlined a network of trolley lines that would have erased traffic congestion and growing pollution. Fingers of tracks appeared between Seattle and Everett and Mount Vernon and Bellingham, among many other routes emanating from Washington's ever growing city. The grand plan was to link Seattle by interurban with Vancouver, British Columbia, but World War I intervened, construction was halted and never resumed. The glorious project would have stretched tracks south to the state capital in Olympia and, possibly, fifty miles west to the community of Grays Harbor on the Pacific. Again, wartime construction delayed the projects and little more than a few short branches were laid south of Tacoma.

What was most significant for the future of Seattle's transportation system in the twenties, thirties, and forties was the misunderstanding or negligence on the part of city planners when it came to establishing rights-of-way. It became apparent in the twenties and thirties that the private automobile was receiving preferential treatment at the expense of trolleys. Although Boston was sensibly creating special rights-of-way for its trolleys, without paving for automobile crossings, Seattle's open tracks would become the bête noire of the Seattle Municipal Railway. As historian Leslie Blanchard noted, "This issue finally sealed the doom of the [interurban] Seattle and Rainier Valley Railway Company."

The battle between automotive interests and the street railway companies continued into the thirties, but the handwriting was already on the wall for the Washington interurbans. Undoubtedly, the most telling blow was delivered in December 1934, when the Seattle and Rainier Valley Railway Company petitioned the Seattle City Council for a new franchise. One would imagine that an enlightened group of elected officials would have relished the idea of perpetuating the mass transit facility (after all, Seattle was still growing) and encouraged the company. Instead, the Council refused to renew the franchise.

Stubbornly, almost as if the Council's action were nothing more than a nightmare that would pass in the morning mist, the interurban line continued running. However, the Council then fortified its decision by ordering the company to suspend operations by the end of 1936. The Council boasted that the city had received a $45,000 federal grant to widen and pave Rainier Avenue (on which the interurbans rolled), which was delightful for motorists but doom for the trolleys. It no doubt never dawned upon the politicians that the grant could have been used both to widen the street and to provide an exclusive lane for the trolleys.

That the petroleum industry was the ultimate beneficiary of the Council's decision was underscored in 1937 when gasoline buses began plying the Rainier Avenue route and another bus company, Lake Shore Lines, took over business on the Renton-Seattle run. "Most deleterious of all," wrote Leslie Blanchard, "was an unsympathetic absentee management which deliberately played up a competing bus service at the expense of the electric cars. . . . Stone and Webster had already gone into the highway transportation business on a large scale; and from this time (1930) forward it embarked on a deliberate and persistent policy of downgrading its railway service."

Robert S. Wilson, another who was intimately acquainted with the annihilation procedure against the Seattle trolleys, detailed his analysis in 1945 in an article, "The Rise and Fall of PNT," which appeared in *Interurbans Special Number 7*:

The management had embarked on bus operation, paralleling its own rail lines with highway routes and providing these latter in many instances with more frequent service and new equipment. Moreover, all publicity of these companies favored the buses. Rail schedules, in some cases, were not even posted in terminal waiting rooms. Inquiry at ticket windows brought grudging admission that "we *do* have a train for Everett (or Seattle) at such and such a time," coupled immediately with a suggestion that the traveler would find the company's bus schedules and service much more attractive. Within the cars themselves there appeared placards proclaiming, "Highways are pleasant ways— Travel by bus." Needless to say, the buses carried no reciprocal ads for the rail service.

Ironically, the safety record of the Seattle-Tacoma area cars was never a factor in the demise of the trolley system. Major mishaps were few and far between, although in 1900 a trolley filled to capacity with Fourth of July celebrants lost its brakes on the Delin Street hill. While the motorman attempted frantically to slow the runaway car, it picked up speed, jumped the track at the curve at the bottom of the hill and landed upside down in a deep gully after plunging seventy-five feet. Passengers were crushed by the car trucks and motors, which crashed through the trolley's floor. The result was a death toll of forty-one and more than fifty injured.

Fearful of a similar disaster occurring on its perilous hills, the Seattle Municipal Railway developed extraordinary precautions against the hazard of runaway cars. Of particular concern was its Lake Burien line, which included a 4.5 percent grade with a sharp curve at its base. To insure against mishap, the Seattle Municipal Railway installed a safety siding that had a 15 percent reverse grade to halt runaway cars. The hope, of course, was that the device would never be used. Not long after the siding's installation a descending car lost its brakes and rampaged out of control at speeds in excess of 58 miles per hour. The eight passengers and the motorman crouched on the floor in abject fear, but the conductor jumped from the speeding car before it reached the safety siding. As the car hit 60 miles per hour it was diverted smoothly to the siding and slowed to a safe halt. Apart from a few headaches suffered by the traumatized riders, all escaped injury except the conductor, who was hurt upon his impetuous descent.

More perilous, in the long run, was the feat of keeping the Seattle trolley lines from sinking into a sea of red ink. Some critics believe that a major cause for the city's street railway woes was municipal ownership, which began on March 31, 1919, when D. W. Henderson took over the operation of Seattle's trolleys on behalf of the city. There were many advantages for the commuters with municipal ownership, not the least of which was unlimited transfer privileges between all of the city's lines. But the disadvantages seemed to match the pluses. "Wrecks, financial deficits, labor disputes, jitney competition—such was the succession of events which soured the hopes and expectations of those who had only a few months before held up municipal ownership as a cure-all for the city's transportation ills," commented a Seattle transit critic.

A number of transit physicians examined the patient and questioned whether municipal ownership should be blamed for Seattle's trolley troubles. In 1929 H. L. Purdy of the University of Washington in Seattle published a study of the financial and economic aspects of the Seattle Municipal Street Railway operation. Titled *The Cost of Municipal Operation of the Seattle Street Railway,* the survey indicated that the financial difficulties were the result of causes other than municipal management.

The Purdy report concluded as follows:

The only inherent weakness of municipal operation that appears among the causes of the financial straits in which the street railway finds itself is the interference of political forces . . . and possibly in delayed execution of needed operational economies. However, this study has shown that the two major causes are heavy capital payments and private automobile competition, neither of which can be laid at the door of municipal operation.

Superintendent of Public Utilities Clark R. Jackson in 1926 cogently analyzed the role the automobile was playing in destroying the trolley business—forever. Wrote Jackson in a report:

The automobile owner should be very appreciative of the street car. We furnish him with "ready-to-serve" transportation for 18 hours a day and 365 days a year. When his automobile breaks down or the snow and ice prevent its use he gets his usual opportunity of giving our transportation system a few sledge-hammer blows, because he does not arrive home as early as he would had he driven his car. . . .

He never stops to realize that it is this same automobile which contributes to a large degree to his delay. Next day he will proceed to double park his machine while he buys a cigar, perhaps delaying 200 people for a period of one minute while a line of cars passes around his parked machine.

The auto, to be sure, was the fair-haired child of Seattleites but there remained those who cottoned to the streetcars both for utilitarian and humorous purposes. Surely, anyone who rode the Ray Street Shuttle *had* to have a special sense of humor, because this was a rare stretch of municipal transportation.

Operating in the early twenties (it closed in 1928), the shuttle spanned a quarter of a mile between Ray and McGraw Streets on Queen Anne Avenue. One solitary car, a Birney trolley, bounced and clacked its way by appointment only! If a Seattleite found himself at one end of the short line he simply pressed a button on a pole alongside the terminal point and the Ray Street Shuttle would head back. On a good day the shuttle would carry a grand total of 125 riders, usually less. Seattle seemed to have an inordinate penchant for similar short trolley lines, each in its own way more unique than the next.

One such line was recalled in a letter written by John A. Lee to Lawton Gowey on May 30, 1961. To wit:

I . . . particularly recall with fond memories the Birney car that ran on 20th NW and on to 85th. In its waning days (around I believe the early thirties) it was a lonesome-looking little vehicle stopping sedately to cross Market Street with nobody aboard but a dignified-looking motorman of huge proportions who—it seemed at the time—might any moment cause the car to topple its unbalanced front end to the pavement. My dad was undoubtedly among neighborhood community-minded souls who helped discourage the continuance of the Sixth Ave. NW car line in favor of the new one on 8th Ave. NW. I recall riding on the big cars on this line. . . . Survey experts pointed out to the city the disadvantages of these cars on such routes as this particular one. It always appeared that we would go crashing right into someone's living room where the car made two violent jogs following the narrow street at Market and one just a few blocks before Market.

Prior to . . . 1927 we lived in a log and shingle house in the woods right off the Fauntleroy Endolyne tracks about a half mile before the loop itself, and although this was 1924–25 and I was only a baby, I remember vividly the car crashing and banging against the overhead boughs as it raced down to the avenue out of the woods.

The "crashing and banging" of Seattle's trolleys would not last much longer.

The Municipal Railway staggered into the thirties with a surplus of headaches, mostly financial. Out of this the city fathers created still more chaos. In 1932 a five-man nonpartisan transportation commission was organized; or, at least, it was *supposed* to be, but the recommendation never became reality.

The outcome of this election [wrote Leslie Blanchard in his Seattle trolley chronicle] was farcical enough to have done credit to Gilbert and Sullivan. The voters turned down the commission and manager proposals, but *approved* the amendment abolishing the Public Utility Superintendent's position. Since this had only been put on the ballot to clear the ground for what was expected to be a new regime of street railway management, the result was utter confusion; the system being left without a manager until the new mayor took office.

For Seattle's trolleys the end of the line was in sight. With each year the ditty, originally in the *Sante Fe Railroad Magazine*, regarding the perils of trolley travel seemed more and more pertinent to Seattle's riders:

> Any girl can be gay in a classy coupe,
> In a taxicab all can be jolly,
> But the girl worth while is the one who can smile
> When you're taking her home in the trolley.

Unfortunately, the trolley didn't survive in Seattle, but where cities such as New York and Los Angeles chose the polluting diesel omnibus (usually a General Motors product) as the replacement for trolleys, Seattle surprised many transit critics by selecting electric buses for the 1980s.

It was a decision that did not come easy for the citizens of the city on Puget Sound. For most of the thirties, while the streetcar system wobbled and groaned, politicians and professionals had debated whether to scrap the trams and switch to other means of transportation. Ever since 1929 the Seattle Transit System, which had taken over operations of the Seattle Municipal Railway, had been falling behind on its debts. A federal loan of $10,500,000 was required to settle the Municipal Railway debts at about forty-five cents on the dollar. The rolling stock and physical plant of the railway were in very poor condition since little maintenance had been done for ten years.

What to do?

"A large investment of public funds had to be made," said Ruth Hertz, who had once been public information supervisor for Seattle's Metro Transit, "either to rehabilitate the rail system or to install a new system."

Apart from its obvious superficial problems, the street railway had the odds stacked heavily against it. As Leslie Blanchard analyzed the situation in the mid-thirties:

The forces and tendencies working against the street railway were legion: the appeal of the novel and chic as against the staid and old-fashioned, the obvious convenience and comfort of the automobile in those days as yet innocent of traffic jams, strangulated streets, and polluted air; and, above all, by the silent revolution that the motor car was effecting in almost every aspect of American life, custom, habit, and thought.

The trolley car, and the world associated with it, once full of glamour and luster and adventure symbolized by the gay electric park and the open breezes of warm and nostalgic summer evening memory, had long since faded into the grubbily utilitarian light of common day. Both social and cultural influences were working against it.

All of which brought out several opposing forces for the ultimate battle. In one corner sat the battered but proud trolley forces; in another were those determined to foist the gasoline (and later diesel) bus on Seattle; and, finally, there emerged an underdog but surprisingly vocal bloc in favor of the bastard child of mass transit, the trackless trolley.

At first the gasoline-powered omnibus appeared to have the inside track. Several streetcar routes were already being pushed out of existence by the buses. Sometimes known as the Tin Lizzie, the gasoline bus was described by one observer as "an early contributor to Seattle's air pollution problem."

By 1937 the streetcar system had fallen into such a miserable state of disrepair—a rock slide permanently put the Lake Burien line out of service in 1933—that an eleventh-hour decision about saving mass transit in Seattle had to be made. The hoped-for panacea was delivered by a New York engineering consultant outfit, the John C. Beeler organization. A firm that had specialized in the operation, financing, engineering, and management of city transport systems, the Beeler group produced a detailed blueprint for rejuvenating the Seattle system, financed mostly with federal funds—at the expense of the trolleys.

In time it was proposed that Seattle's three cable railways be abandoned, that trams be retained only on heavily traveled downtown routes, and that gasoline buses and trackless trolleys replace the streetcars on the lightly traveled runs. It was said that Seattle commuters would best be served by the acquisition of 240 trackless trolleys and 135 gasoline buses, with the best of the existing streetcars to be continued in operation or rehabilitated where necessary. Not long afterward a second reorganization plan surfaced, setting the stage for a bitter verbal free-for-all among the various transit power brokers.

Right off the bat, streetcar proponents suffered a blow when in January 1937 a runaway West Seattle streetcar jumped the tracks on a sharp turn at West Spokane Street and 30th Avenue Southwest. By the time the car had pitched off the tracks, plunged into a heavy concrete pillar, and rolled on its side, a twisted mass of steel and wood, two passengers were dead and sixty injured. A frail railing just barely retained the wreck, preventing it from hurtling fifteen feet farther down to the railroad tracks crossing under the streetcar grade. It was one of the worst streetcar disaster in Seattle's history; and a terrible setback for the protrolley bloc.

Undaunted, the Amalgamated Association of Street, Electric Railway and Motor Coach Employees of America, Local 687, which spoke for a thousand of the fifteen hundred municipal railway employees, unveiled a plan that would revitalize the Seattle transit system with an order of ultramodern PCC streetcars, a number of which already had made a big hit in Brooklyn, New York, and other communities. Other Seattle civic groups, such as the Meridian Improvement Club, endorsed the PCC plan, but the banking syndicate that was underwriting the bond issue for the revised Beeler plan turned thumbs down on this proposal.

Now the battle was reaching fever pitch. Pro-bus advocates argued that Portland, Oregon, had switched to trackless trolleys and found them acceptable. Trolley fans shot back that Portland was a city without Seattle's steep hills, which could better be negotiated by electric trolleys. Other trolley buffs asserted that the buses' life span—five to eight years—was significantly shorter than that of streetcars. On January 28, 1937, the Seattle *Times* quoted Mayor John F. Dore on the trolley coach issue: "From the operating standpoint," said Mayor Dore, "there isn't a city in the country that ever put trackless trolleys on main business streets. The first report Beeler made said the trackless trolley bus was absolutely impracticable for Seattle. He also said it would be financially unsound. . . . Then he gets hired by these people and so now he says the trackless trolley is the only thing for Seattle. That throws doubt on the value of any of his deductions."

Others, such as mass transit expert and consulting naval architect Carl J. Nordstrom, in an interview with the Seattle *Times,* lent his support to the plan for buying PCC streetcars.

Nordstrom fortified his position with these facts: the PCC cars were capable of carrying twice as many passengers as the largest bus and provided a more comfortable ride. In addition, Nordstrom reiterated an oft-mentioned point, that the streetcars cost significantly less to operate than buses.

The trolley coach bloc then produced a coup of sorts by organizing a "demonstration" run of brand-new Twin Coach electric buses. On February 27, 1937, the sleek vehicles bobbed and weaved their way, starting at Fourth Avenue and Union Street and running to Fifth, Union, Fourth, Dilling Way, Third, James, and then back to the starting point.

Many riders were enthused about the vehicles but the experiment was basically unfair. The same Seattleites were never allowed to ride on a demonstration PCC car, as proposed by the carmen's union, which had demanded "equal time." The plan, offered to voters on a ballot, was assailed right down to the wire by Mayor Dore. "If officials carry out their plan to burn the city's 450 streetcars," snapped the mayor, "and tear up its 232 miles of track, selling the metals for junk, Seattle will look like Rome did when Nero was fiddling. I'll not stand aside." Voters supported Dore by rejecting the plan 53,500 to 39,000.

It was, however, a pyrrhic victory for the tram tribe. In almost no time at all, the municipal railway had gone bottoms-up in bankruptcy and on April 18, 1938, the trolley's big booster, Mayor Dore, died. The new mayor was Arthur B. Langley. He and the Council soon named a new transit commission and hired Lloyd Graber as general manager. The group was renamed the Seattle Transit System and, once again, in another case of *déjà vu,* a consultant was asked to produce a renaissance plan for the city's transit. In August 1939 the report was ready and it was strikingly similar to earlier analyses.

By now the pro-streetcar lobby had been cracking at the seams, and the new consultants' plan was adopted by the commission on August 31, 1939. "The public announcement that Seattle was to have its electric railway network replaced by a rubber-tired transit system aroused little opposition," said Leslie Blanchard, "save from a minority of bitter-end trolley enthusiasts." Writing in the Seattle *Times*, James W. Wood observed: "Today the change is complete; the last decrepit streetcar has made its last run. We even doubt the desirability of keeping one of them as a relic in a city park. It will stir no pleasant memories. It will never be a shrine to anybody."

The powerful influence of the antitram faction would further cripple Seattle's potential as a tourist attraction as well as a sensibly thinking transportation city for the remainder of this century. This, of course, centered around the battle to save the city's venerable and highly cherished cable cars.

Little sensitivity was shown to Seattle's prized cable car system, even though Seattle and San Francisco were the last two cities in North America operating cable car routes. On July 31, 1938, Seattle's Board of Public Works announced that the city's three cable lines would be eliminated and replaced by omnibuses. Politicians who had been lulled into false security when opposition was tame over the streetcar elimination were startled by the outcry from the pro-cable car bloc. They jammed a special hearing on August 4, 1938, and raised so high a decibel count that the administration conducted an orderly retreat and agreed to operate the cable cars, at least for the moment.

It was a phony ploy. Like their cousins, the electric streetcars, the cable cars had been suffering for years from benign neglect. Just as a new fleet of PCC streamliners would have lured passengers back to the Seattle surface electric fleet, so a refurbished cable car system would have induced the public to ride the cable cars in 1938. Unfortunately, the last major overhaul of the cable railway had been in 1913, a quarter-century earlier! It was incomprehensible that these prized possessions should have been allowed to fall into such a dismal state of disrepair. But they had been, and the final surrender of the venerable Yesler cable car took place on August 10, 1940. Henry MacLeod, writing in the Seattle *Times*, described the last run of his city's prized piece of transportation:

Like a prehistoric bug lying in wait for its prey, Old No. 2 crouches on the wooden trestle at the foot of Yesler Way. It is Old No. 2's last day, for in a few hours the Yesler Cable will fold its doors like the Arabs, and a silence will steal its way over a street that has known no respite from the clanking cable line since the first car started September 29, 1888.

From the subterranean cavern beneath the car comes the eery whirr of the cables and the huge wheels that have made them turn on, and on, endlessly but to no destination—nowhere but in the tunnel under Yesler Way—year after year. . . . There is a clanging and Old No. 2 springs into action with a jerk and a shudder that rends her ancient orange frame. . . . At the top of the hill the car stops for a moment while an oiler prods the long spout of the can into the cable slot. A passenger says she has ridden on the cable cars 35 years. She remembers riding out to Leschi to dance when she was a girl. The car jerks and bounces her against an upright, but she seems to disregard this jolt from an old friend. She looks out of the window and says: "Maybe I'll be wearing crepe tomorrow. I hate to see the old cars go."

Her feelings, of course, were of no concern to those "experts" who had ruled that the cable cars had to be eschewed in favor of progress.

As the year 1940 unfolded, line after trolley line was eliminated and new buses or trackless trolleys appeared in their place. Before 1942 arrived Seattle's once proud streetcar system no longer existed. The new era of rubber-tired trackless transportation had begun.

Revenue service actually ended on April 13, 1941, fifty-seven years after Frank Osgood had launched Seattle's mass transit program with his Second Avenue horsecar line. "When the last car ended its last run," a Seattle *Times* reporter observed, "the last link between modern Seattle and the days of mud streets and gaslights, of timbered suburbs and bicycles built for two was severed."

Glowing tributes to the new era were due, in part, to a high-pressure selling job pushed for years by advocates of the gasoline bus and the trackless trolley. The fact that the venerable streetcars badly needed a paint job and a rewiring, and just plain looked like hell, was less their fault than the failure of their owners. Enthusiasm for the new vehicles was enhanced by their chrome, the shiny new paint job, and conveniences that supposedly marked them superior to the trolleys.

They weren't.

In 1943, for example, Seattle was bedeviled with a snowy winter. The new trolley buses were unable to negotiate the Queen Anne Hill. For almost a month service was suspended "in the interest of safety." Without its trolleys, Seattle began to suffer transit pains. "The rubber-tired transportation system found itself with a challenge that it just barely managed to survive," wrote Leslie Blanchard. "Citizens who had exulted in the rapidity and apparent success of the rehabilitation plan, and who had congratulated themselves over the disappearance of the 'noisy, ugly, and antiquated' streetcars from Seattle's thoroughfares suddenly began to have some second thoughts about the discarded railway system."

The editorial board of the Seattle *Times* agreed. In an editorial written after the last overhead wire had been torn down and all rolling stock had been carted off to the Northwest Steel Rolling Mills for scrap, the newspaper commented in an editorial: "One cannot resist the wistful thought that if some of that old equipment had been preserved, it might come in handy these days."

But 20–20 hindsight was useless in the waning years of the forties. Seattle now owned a fleet of gasoline-powered omnibuses and the trackless trolleys. In time the two breeds would stage a fight to the finish, and one that would surprise many railbirds in the transit industry.

Advocates of the gasoline and diesel buses insisted that their vehicles were inherently better than the trackless trolley because of flexibility. In the post–

World War II years the electric- and the petroleum-powered buses operated side by side. But in the sixties concern mounted over the hazards of air pollution generated by vehicles powered by gasoline. The stench emitted by Seattle's diesel buses was also a source of growing annoyance to air pollution experts such as Joseph P. Ruth and E. E. Van Ness.

In September 1963 Ruth completed a report on diesel exhaust and air pollution in Seattle. The questions raised were extremely pertinent to a decision between electric and diesel buses in Seattle's future: Does the diesel engine contribute poisonous air pollution? Is the amount of this contribution significant? Ruth's answers were in the affirmative. Slowly but relentlessly a campaign developed to eliminate as many diesel buses as possible and have them replaced with the nonpolluting electric coaches. One of the most effective polemics was delivered by E. E. Van Ness, a member of the Washington Society of Professional Engineers.

Van Ness's enthusiasm for electric buses was not isolated. For decades a significant number of commuters in the Northwest had become fans of the trackless trolley. In Portland, Oregon, for example, a large number of electric buses had been installed prior to World War II and had become immensely popular. In the spring of 1940 the city's newspaper, The *Oregonian*, conducted a poll to determine which mode of mass transit the citizens favored. According to the final results, four out of five Portland residents said they "would rather ride the trolley buses than either streetcars or gasoline buses."

The upsurge in popularity for the electric bus was in part due to improvements in design and, in the sixties and seventies, because of its pollution-free qualities. For this reason, Van Ness, chairman of the Civic Affairs Committee of the Seattle Chapter of the National Society of Professional Engineers, delivered an excellent comparison of the electric vehicle and its petroleum-fueled counterparts. The Van Ness arguments, which follow, were written in 1972:

... To determine the best vehicle for the job ... all we need to do is find which type most nearly meets a few of the more important parameters such as:

The motor must: 1) have *few* points of wear, 2) operate at *low* temperature, 3) be capable of its greatest *turning effort* at *zero* engine R.P.M.

The vehicle should also: 1) not carry its *fuel* on board, 2) not need a *transmission*, 3) travel the *farthest* per cost of fuel consumed.

The motors ... for the gasoline, LPG or diesel buses all share one thing in common: they have ... *hundreds* of points of wear! The 30-year-old D.C. traction motors in our newest trolleys have only 10 points of wear! (Count 'em.) The more points of wear, the higher the maintenance costs and the poorer the fuel (efficiency) so ... the trolley cannot possibly be as costly to operate as the I.C. bus ... and it doesn't take an engineer to recognize this fact! The internal combustion (I.C.) bus ... has very poor efficiency: only about *10%* at the wheels! This means ... that for every $10 spent on bus fuel, $9 goes out the tailpipe! Only about $1 goes toward moving people! The electric trackless trolley, on the other hand, has a wheel efficiency of about *83%* which means that ... for every $10 spent on kilowatt hours only about $1.70 is wasted: All the rest, $8.30, goes toward moving people!

This amazing difference in efficiency is due to more than just the number of points of wear! The I.C. engine not only has many more points of wear, but it must be turning at high speed before it can develop its rated torque! . . .

The D.C. traction (electric) motor develops highest torque at zero RPM. . . . This not only increases efficiency but, far more important, it means that the *I.C. bus* has to have a *transmission* whereas the electric does not! The importance of this difference cannot be overemphasized! Because any vehicle that must lose forward speed the more passengers it carries . . . or the more hills it encounters . . . can't possibly make a profit at acceptable *fares!* . . .

But poor acceleration, another "transmission related" fault of the motorbus, can better be used to illustrate why motorbuses lose money! . . . If Seattle transit had used trolleys in lieu of motorbuses in 1968 it would have saved more than $1.8 million! This is not just a rash statement! This would have been saved due to *acceleration alone*.

Why? Our findings show that a trolley's acceleration gives it a 17-second advantage per stop over the motorbus in accelerating to 30 mph and that the stops-per-mile in Seattle's operations average about seven. According to the 1968 Seattle Transit financial report the driver's wages averaged $4.66 per hr. and its motorbus fleet logged 11,974,696 miles. But 12 million miles × seven stops per mile × 17 seconds per stop is *396,000 manhours*. This, times $4.66 per hour, is $1,845,360 in driver's wasted wages! Remember, this waste is due to the difference in acceleration only. . . .

Let's now consider why a transit vehicle should *not* carry its fuel on board. The most obvious answer, of course, is . . . there's more room for passengers! . . . In the *nomenclature* of the *engineer* this is sometimes alluded to as the weight-to-horsepower ratio. But the main advantage to having no fuel on board is that it must then have its fuel brought to it from a central source. . . . At any point on its route it [the trolley] has available [to it] almost unlimited power with no increase in wt.-to-hp. ratio!

Van Ness and his supporters may not have realized it at the time, but they were about to help launch one of the most pivotal upsets in the century-long battle between oil- and electric-powered modes of mass transportation. The winner, in the end, would defeat the vast army of General Motors and others who propagandized the "value" of the diesel bus. Nothing reaffirmed the philosophy of the electric bus fans better than a story in the August 23, 1978, edition of the Seattle *Times* about the diesel buses and their failure on Seattle's many hills. The General Motors' coaches that operated on hills successfully plied previously by trackless trolleys, Bob Lane noted, had *doubled* their own breakdown rate.

Seattle had finally seen through the diesel smoke screen and would take a big gamble on electric buses, but not until a series of bizarre experiments in the sixties and mishaps in the next decade, including a highly-touted monorail.

As gimmicks go, Seattle's monorail has been more durable than practical and certainly nowhere near as popular a tourist attraction as cable cars might have been had the cable operation not been dismantled prior to World War II. But the cable car was gone when Seattle planners were devising blueprints for their World's Fair in the early sixties. It was decided that the monorail was "in," a mistake that has been made ever since the late nineteenth century.

Among the first tries at suspending a monorail from a steel superstructure was the one at South Park, Minnesota, in 1883. Less than twenty years later, designers in Elberfeld, Germany, devised an 8½-mile line with two running rails, one for each direction, suspended from steel arches spanning the streets. Part of the line, known as the Wuppertal Schwebebahn ("suspended railway"), ran above the Wupper River. At the time of its construction in 1901 the cost of the German monorail was $200,000.

Although the Schwebebahn operated successfully, only a handful of cities were interested in the concept and fewer actually moved a monorail project to the drawing board. Following World War II a resurgence in monorail interest was evident. Proponents suggested that it was considerably less costly than the traditional elevated railway and much cheaper to construct than a subway. In 1962 a mile-long monorail was built on the grounds of the Los Angeles County Fair at Pomona, California.

And then there was Seattle's entry into monorail country. Built on rather sleek concrete pillars, the Alweg Monorail described a 1¼-mile route from the downtown department-store area to the grounds of the Space Needle at Seattle's exhibition center. The Seattle project was mere gimmickry, as a spokesman for Seattle Metro privately admitted: "The Monorail never will be expanded beyond its present route because it's an impractical system."

A monorail is also contrary to the trend of city planning, which is to eliminate overhead obstructions.

The eminent rapid transit consultant Louis T. Klauder delivered the definitive kibosh on the monorail concept. "It is generally agreed," said Klauder in 1974, "that the monorail's greatest appeal is as a 'space age' novelty for the public. In reality, they are complex, expensive, slow, inflexible, and of limited capacity. This is not to imply that they are of no value but rather that they are more appropriate for short, simple point-to-point service."

Which is precisely the case in Seattle, where the monorail still operates. It's a modest tourist attraction but hardly as appealing or practical as cable cars would have been had they not been wiped out, as the San Francisco system has proven.

With the trolleys just a memory, the cable cars defunct, and the monorail not much more than a short ride to the exhibition grounds, Seattle in 1970 was left with a rubber-tired menagerie composed of diesel buses of assorted vintage, and trackless trolleys. The question that confounded experts was whether the balance would continue or whether a firm policy would be hammered out in favor of the electric coaches. Many argued that the diesel bus was a blight on the Seattle landscape.

For reasons that remain somewhat unclear, the offensive and contaminant qualities of diesel stench have never been explored by either the public or the media. Perhaps it was the legislative lobbying and good public relations by the bus builders and oil sellers that helped cloak the diesels in some ermine robes. Perhaps it was the limited competition for the buses in 1970—only trolleys and electric buses. Whatever the case, the diesel became ubiquitous but certainly not loved. In a bulletin about air pollution in the city, E. E. Van Ness put it well when he wrote:

As an engineer, I cannot understand the aura of sanctity which seems to enshroud the diesel vehicle, nor the blind worship it engenders in those who are charged with the responsibility of transit management. If calculations prove the diesel to be hopelessly costly in transporting people, yet extremely efficient in the production of toxic air pollution, then where is the justification for its use as an urban transportation vehicle?

It took a while but the message eventually sank in, and in the late seventies Seattle decided to rehabilitate and expand its electric bus system. "The result," said Ruth Hertz of the Seattle Metro Transit, "will be one of the largest and most modern trolley bus operations in the nation."

To facilitate the changeover Metro shut down the electric bus system early in 1978 to permit reconstruction of overhead wire. While work on the trackless trolley operation began in 1978, diesel buses were assigned to replace the electric coaches until the massive job was completed. Time and again diesels failed. Meanwhile, Seattle Metro tried a number of devices to keep the faith of their commuters, particularly in the light of criticism from such pillars of the media as the Seattle *Times*, which charged that the city "had one of the oldest bus fleets in operation in the country." A count made in August 1978 revealed that Seattle Metro operated 450 coaches which were built in 1968 or earlier. The system also operated 38 buses known as Jersey Junkers, 1950s models, acquired from a New Jersey transit system in 1974 and rebuilt by Seattle Metro at a cost of about $20,000 each.

Seattle Transit Director Charles Collins predicted that Metro will reach 1980 with 225 of the ancient buses still in operation. "I don't like that," Collins admitted.

A more positive note in the seventies was the Seattle Metro's apparent readiness to depart from tradition. Whereas General Motors coaches once appeared to dominate almost every major transit agency in the United States, Seattle was willing to buy buses from "minority" manufacturers. In 1976 and 1977, for instance, a fleet was bought from AM General. These comprised 215 buses. AM General also won a contract to build 109 electric buses, which were scheduled to begin operation some time in 1979 when the $37,000,000 rehabilitation program for the trackless trolley empire is completed. (Ironically, most of the new wire going up in the rejuvenation was installed on routes electrified by the city in 1940 and then converted to diesel bus service in the early 1960s.)

While Seattleites awaited the return of the electric buses (trolley bus service originally began in Seattle on April 28, 1940), a number of other innovations were taking place which caused a distillation of applause and anger, depending upon which side of the curb a Seattleite was occupying.

One of the more interesting experiments involved the use of another AM General product, the bending bus. A sixty-foot-long omnibus powered by diesel fuel, the bending bus was not exactly a new invention as buses go. In fact a large capacity motorbus with an articulated body was developed in 1938 but never achieved popularity, in part because of maneuverability problems on tight city streets. However, Seattle attempted to overcome that problem in 1978 when it launched the long-bus program by creating "exclusive" bus lanes.

The idea of creating a special corridor for buses was not a new one in North America, but the Seattle program, launched in August 1978, appeared to be a more determined effort—in terms of enforcement and publicity—than those attempted in other cities. Of particular interest was the reaction of motorists on Second and Fourth Avenues in downtown Seattle, where the right-hand lanes became "buses only" routes between 7 and 9 A.M. and 4 and 6 P.M. Cars were allowed in the lanes only to make right-hand turns. "We're asking people to make a major change in their driving habits and you have to expect that to take a while," said City Traffic Engineer Bill van Gelder. "We hope people will learn to jump on a bus and ride to a less congested area to be picked up there."

The concept looked better on paper than it did in action. For starters, the exclusive bus lane proponents immediately encountered surprisingly stiff opposition from a bloc of pedestrians and businessmen who organized a Downtown Traffic Planning Committee specifically geared to stop the exclusive lanes plan. "It is a system that is hostile to pedestrians," charged attorney Joseph Murphy, a member of the group opposed to the exclusive lanes. "It is a subjective thing, but if you're standing on the sidewalk with those buses racing past, you're going to feel uncomfortable."

Counterattacking, city transit officials argued that the exclusive lanes policy simply confirmed an existing situation—that there were so many buses in the right-hand lanes during rush hours that cars couldn't use them anyway. But this point was disputed by opponents. They insisted that with the exclusive lanes came additional buses on several routes. J. C. Baillargeon, president of Seattle Trust and Savings Bank, spoke for businessmen opposed to exclusivity. "The lanes," said Baillargeon, "won't be sufficient to contain the volume of buses actually traveling the street." He added that buses had already preempted the right lane, were spilling over into the second lane and filling it, then would spill over into a third lane until the thoroughfare was filled entirely with the bus fleet!

Some observers noted that bus drivers were less than scrupulous in their adherence to the new regulations. "Our bus driver just said 'This is crazy' and pulled out of the buses-only lane," said commuter Kim Nielsen of Seattle.

Likewise, the Seattle *Times* took issue with the errant bus drivers and questioned the exclusive lanes system itself. "Many of us applauded the idea of exclusive bus lanes," the editorial noted, "when it was first announced. One benefit of that concept was presumed to be that buses would stay in 'their' lanes, thus expediting the flow of auto traffic. One 'exclusive' lane ought to be sufficient."

The Seattle *Post-Intelligencer* worried about the effects on pedestrians. In a story on August 16, 1978, reporter Ruth Pumphrey commented: "Pedestrians are perhaps the most vulnerable to negative side effects of the exclusive lanes. A

stroll down Fourth Avenue during rush-hour traffic has never been very pleasant, and the new policy adds to what was already a bad situation."

Pedestrians, too, had their say. "It just kind of concentrates everything—
noise, fumes, the crowds—into one small area," said one harried pedestrian.

These complaints soon were drowned by a storm of outrage in an area in
which Seattle transit believed it was relatively immune to criticism: the realm
of bus safety. On August 22, 1978, while Seattleites were still glowing over their
fleet of fourteen bending buses, one of the city's worst transit accidents was taking place; a disaster that involved startling ramifications, involving driver com-
petence, maintenance, and the use of tires that failed both federal and state
safety requirements.

The collision occurred at 8:35 A.M. when three Seattle Metro Transit buses
were moving along a curving section of the Interstate 5 expressway in a southbound lane. Sixty-eight persons were injured in the pile-up which began when
the engine failed in the lead bus, a 1968 model General Motors. Passengers on
the bus reported that it began suffering engine problems as soon as it left on its
run. When the bus began slowing down, the driver steered the vehicle off to the
side of the freeway express lanes a half mile north of Stewart Street, pulling into
a narrow shoulder lane. However, the rear end of the bus protruded into the
traffic lane.

Within five minutes a two-year-old AM General coach, filled to standing
room capacity, plowed into the rear of the stalled General Motors bus. A third
Metro Transit bus, also a relatively new AM General product, struck the first
two vehicles, causing chaos on the highway. Still another collision in the chain
reaction was barely averted when a fourth Seattle Metro Transit bus was
brought to a stop a mere fifteen feet from the tangle of steel and rubber.

As the injured were removed to local hospitals, angry Seattleites questioned
the safety system of their Metro Transit. They noted that within a two-and-a-
half-year period no fewer than seven "life-threatening" accidents had befallen
the bus operation, five of them on a four-mile section of freeway. "We want to
know why the accident occurred," said Metro Transit Director Charles Collins.
"There may be more than one 'why.'"

At first, attention focused on the bus drivers who had piloted vehicles two
and three in the crash. Washington State Trooper John Lovick, investigating officer at the crash site, said that the driver of the second bus, which ran into the
stalled vehicle, was cited for "failure to exercise due care and caution." The
third driver was cited for following too closely, according to Trooper Lovick.
He charged that the collisions stemmed from "driver error."

However, Collins later told newsmen that pressure to meet Metro Transit
schedules may lead to driver speeding, "but we tell the drivers the schedule
comes second." He reiterated that a complete probe would continue and the
public would be informed of all facts behind the crash.

A triple set of scandal-tinged news tidbits soon emerged from the probe. Metro Transit officials revealed on August 24, 1978, that: the stalled bus had appar-

ently run out of fuel on the freeway; the same bus had run out of fuel the day before the crash, was taken to the maintenance shop, and was released for service on the day of the collision without being refueled; many buses in the Seattle fleet suffered tire trouble.

Trooper Lovick, the investigating officer, charged that one of the three buses involved in the crash had a bald tire and two other tires had the "bare minimum" amount of tread. Lovick added that the bald tire—on the second bus— might have had some effect on the bus's ability to brake because the highway was wet at the time of the accident.

Another question raised was the braking ability of the newer AM General buses. Transit Director Collins addressed himself to this problem and asserted that AM General coaches were involved in 42 percent fewer rear-end collisions than other kinds of Metro buses.

Collins said he believed that rear brakes on AM General buses wear out too fast. However, he did insist that they were safe. The Seattle transit czar concluded that AM General and brake suppliers had come to the city trying to solve the brake-wear problem, which Collins said had been noted by other cities owning AM General equipment.

More complicated and less satisfying was the explanation of the tire troubles. At a news conference Metro Transit officials admitted that as many as one third of the system's 650 buses might be running on tires that failed federal and state safety requirements. Collins said the tire dilemma was the responsibility of the manufacturer, which was under contract to supply, maintain, and repair tires used on Metro Transit buses. Collins pointed out that a probe showed that 12 to 13 percent of all tires, affecting up to one-third of Metro's fleet, do not have tread thickness of at least 2/32 of an inch as required by law. (It is not unusual for a transit operator to lease its tires from suppliers, who then assume responsibility for maintaining and replacing them.) "The tire company has a legal obligation to maintain fully legal tires," Collins asserted, "and they have not done that."

While the tire manufacturer absorbed potshots from Metro Transit, the Seattle agency itself bore the brunt of criticism and Collins was remarkably candid about Metro Transit's responsibility. He confirmed that one of the three buses had run out of fuel and that the supervisor responsible for fueling had been demoted. "It was," Collins admitted, "a serious supervisory error."

Also apparent was the frightening fact that a bus operation such as the one on the Seattle freeway relies on driver vigilance and ability whereas a system involving trains on rails (New York City's subway system) is able to prevent such rear-end collisions by use of fail-safe devices including automatic brake trippers. Collins' attempt at increasing safety was to order Metro Transit buses to reduce their maximum speeds from 55 to 45 miles per hour on the Interstate 5 freeway. "It is conceivable," Collins added, "that we will have to remove our buses from the I-5 expressway."

If that decision were taken, however, it would be still another capitulation, and an unnecessary one, of municipal mass transit officialdom to the auto-mobile. Rather than curbing bus use Collins should have been thinking in terms of discouraging automobile use of the highway so that buses could operate more efficiently on the road. The arithmetic in 1978 certainly indicated that the free-way was not adequately moving people in the manner that once had been an-ticipated.

In a span of three years, between 1974 and 1977, commuter traffic on Seattle freeways increased as much as 44 percent. The busiest spot on the freeway sys-tem was Interstate 5 at the Mercer Street interchange just north of downtown Seattle, according to State Department of Transportation figures. In 1974 an average of 146,400 cars passed that spot daily. In 1977 a daily average of 182,600 passed there, an increase of about 25 percent in only three years. Clear-ly, Seattle had to formulate a program for getting people out of cars and onto public transportation before the freeway system became clogged beyond hope.

Tragically, the attempted solutions ranged from piddling to pathetic. In 1978, for example, Seattle conducted a trial program of placing bicycle racks on the rear of buses (a similar program was working and expanding in San Diego, California) that crossed a bridge over Lake Washington from which bikes had been banned. A loading station was established at each side of the span. The fare was fifty cents and a temporary bicycle "hot line" was established to fun-nel information to potential riders.

The exclusive bus lane program also appeared more substantive in theory than in practice. Metro Transit officials themselves admitted in 1978 that the exclusive lanes were "a temporary solution." They hoped to complete a study of mass transit in the Puget Sound area some time by 1980, at which time Seattle Metro Transit would begin making long-range plans, which may or may not in-clude exclusive lanes.

Such promises did nothing but elicit sardonic laughs from cynical Seattle commuters, who had heard such optimistic bleats in the not-too-distant past. They recalled how Seattle had been told in the sixties that design work was un-der way for a proposed twenty-mile rapid transit system that would cost $111,000,000. What does the northwest metropolis have to show for it today? Nothing but a monorail that is a relic of Seattle's World's Fair—and memories of a splendid streetcar network and cable cars which today could rival the mov-ing pearls of the San Francisco hills.

There are two sides to Seattle's mass transit future; Seattle Metro's Larry Steele painted a rosy picture of a city where electric buses and diesels harmoni-ously coexist, while E. E. Van Ness, a member of the Seattle Chapter of the Washington Society of Professional Engineers, saw a future clouded by broken promises.

In 1972, Van Ness charged, the citizens of Seattle voted for the Metro to take over the existing transit systems with the promise that the electric bus lines would be brought back to life and that no more diesel buses would be ordered. Since that time, only 32 miles of the existing 110-mile electric bus route have been worked on and 28 miles of new line are being added.

"They took down all the overheads and started over again," Van Ness alleged, "and instead of letting the engineers who have been around for years and know the business work on them, they [Metro] have given the work to private contractors who don't know what they are doing."

The first of the 109 new AM General cars are not due to arrive until 1980, according to Steele, so Seattle Metro has decided to order new diesel buses to alleviate their transit problems. "The most significant thing right now is the growing ridership," said Steele. "Only one other city in the country is growing faster in commuter use than we are, and our ridership is outpacing our current [March 1979] supply of buses."

To handle Seattle's growing commuter population, Metro is relying on funds from UMTA to increase their bus fleet with 120 standard buses and 228 long "articulated" buses. A Seattle Metro spokesman added:

"The articulated buses are wonderful, excellent pieces of equipment. The framework, engine, and bodies were constructed by a German company and they did a really excellent job.

"There have been no problems at all with them. With their automatic steerable rear axle, they can make tight corners as well as standard buses."

Van Ness is concerned about the economic losses of Seattle Metro, some of them as a result of the long buses. "Bending buses can't make money," Van Ness said, "because their acceleration is so poor. What you save on having one driver to so many people, you lose on his time. It takes three times as long in acceleration as the trolley cars."

Van Ness charged that Metro's uneconomical policies have caused a leap in losses from when they took over in 1972 to 1979. Although Metro has extended their system by 70 percent, according to Van Ness, the losses are great.

The promises to restore Seattle's electric bus lines and discontinue the ordering of diesels remain just promises. "We're very concerned that we have been victims of a rip-off," said Van Ness. "After all, it has happened before."

In March 1979 Seattle was still dependent on its fleet of diesel buses. Metro still "anxiously" awaits the arrival of their electric buses so they can start operating along the completed lines by 1980. The steep hills of Seattle, Steele said, put the less powerful diesels out of commission before their time.

The monorail built for the 1962 World's Fair is Seattle's only nonbus public transportation. Plans are being discussed to integrate the monorail into a new major development called West Lake Mall, to be located at the southern terminus in downtown Seattle. Although various studies to expand the monorail into a continuous loop have been discussed, no plans have been made to change the existing system.

Seattle Metro is aiming for an advanced transit system that can provide the flexibility to meet the demands of urban and suburban commuters. Whether it can achieve this goal depends upon whom you choose to believe; the Van Ness bloc with its realistically cynical approach or the propagandists of Seattle Metro.

18

Los Angeles–Death of
a Supersystem

Only a sadistic mind with an urban bent could have conceived the Jekyll-Hyde conversion of Los Angeles from a glorious, clear-aired metropolis with a matchless electric railway network to a Marat-Sade municipality befouled with smog, bereft of rapid transit, and with no adequate, pollution-free people-moving plan a possibility before the twenty-first century. Yet the belle of Southern California not only has suffered the ignominy of a wasted golden age of transportation but it has also been so thoroughly outdistanced by its West Coast rival that Los Angeles has no hope of ever equaling the feats of San Francisco. Adding to the grim absurdity of the scenario is the indisputable fact that metropolitan Los Angeles boasted in 1910 all of the ingredients necessary to solve its rapid transit problems of 1980. Through the efforts of one Henry E. Huntington in the years just prior to World War I, Los Angeles could rightfully claim, as many transit historians have observed, "the world's greatest electric railway empire."

This was no modest accomplishment, considering that eastern cities such as Brooklyn (later to be incorporated into New York City), Boston, Philadelphia, and Baltimore had developed vast networks of streetcars and—in the case of Boston and New York—underground rapid transit facilities. Even more impressive was the manner in which Los Angeles transformed itself from an enormous desert formed by sandwiched layers of sand and clay (at a time when New York, Boston, and Philadelphia already were teeming metropolises) into a modest but promising community. In 1850 Los Angeles counted two thousand residents and was growing fast. With the arrival of the Southern Pacific Railroad from the north and the Santa Fe Railroad from the east, Los Angeles became a veritable boom town and that meant the time had come to develop ways and means of carrying the citizens about. Thus, in 1874 the groundwork was begun for what forty years later would correctly be labeled "The World's Greatest Interurban Railway."

It all began with a creaky little 2½-mile line called the Spring and West Sixth Street Railroad, organized by one Judge Robert W. Widney. Its rolling stock began and ended with one minuscule horsecar. Despite its modest beginnings, the Spring and West Sixth Street Railroad proved a portent of transportation to come; in a very short time, lines sprouted on Aliso Avenue, Second Street, and Main Street, to name a few.

In what was to be typical of streetcar give-and-take deals, the Main Street and Agricultural Park Railroad donated 308 lots to the University of Southern California in the late eighties "to ensure future patronage." The farebox figures indicated that patronage was ensured and horsecars proliferated into the 1880s throughout the ever growing community. Steven L. Easlon, writing in *The Los Angeles Railway Through the Years*, painted a vivid picture of the operation: "These primitive horsecars wound through fields, orchards, and handsome residential areas. They served new subdivisions, baseball parks, city parks and, most important of all, the old Los Angeles business interests centered south of the old plaza area."

The open horsecars—occasionally pulled by a pair of mules—plied a single track route, moving to a convenient siding when a horsecar approached from the opposite direction. Progress, in the form of cable cars powered by monstrous steam engines, pushed the horsecars into oblivion late in the nineteenth century, although they remained a part of the scene until the early 1900s. Cable cars proved more aesthetic than efficient. Floods bedeviled them in the winter of 1887, and two years later a tragicomedy on Christmas Eve underlined the need for an alternate mode of modern transit.

A Southern California squall drenched Los Angeles and flooded the city's cable railway system. The transit trauma proved too great a challenge to the Los Angeles Cable Railway high command to resist. A superintendent, more optimistic than realistic, boasted that the cable cars would be operating again by early afternoon on Christmas Day. At 1 P.M. on Christmas Day, as promised, the cables were turned on—unfortunately before the repair work had been completed. The resulting damage cost him his job, but he went around bragging about the cigar he had bet and won "that the cars would be operating."

Successful use of electric power to move streetcars in the East finally persuaded Californians that a change had to be made. Real estate promoter Charles H. Howland translated the plan into the Pico Street Line, which made its world premiere in 1887. The trolley comprised a bizarre combination of locomotive (which looked more like an oversized crate on wheels) pulling an old horsecar—without the horse, of course. The contraption worked, two more lines were laid out by the Los Angeles Electric Railway Company, and a bonanza appeared around the next corner, until an unpleasant boom was heard in the boiler room.

Someone at the Los Angeles Electric Railway Company's power plant should have been checking the power plant boiler because the resultant explosion not only rocked the community, it closed down the system. Meanwhile, operators of the Second Street Cable Railway Company could not obtain enough poultices for their many migraines, especially after still another flood crippled the cables in 1890. The dual disasters inadvertently paved the way for the grand entrance of General Moses H. Sherman, a latter-day Moses who would create a "miracle" of California transportation, along with his brother-in-law Eli P. Clark, a former schoolteacher who migrated to Los Angeles with Sherman from Phoenix, Arizona.

Sherman, whose "general's" epaulets were won in the Arizona state militia, proved to be the right man in the right place at the right time. The collection of cable failures inspired a committee of investors to guarantee $40,000 to anyone who could put the cable line back in business by July 30, 1891. Having arrived in Los Angeles during the summer of 1890—amid rampant newspaper speculation that he would pursue his streetcar interests in California—Sherman bought the Pico Street Line and bought the Second Street Cable Railway in December 1890. General Sherman was still confronted with the July 30 deadline and managed to complete track work to Westlake Park, as specified in the deal; the difference being that he had electrified the line and now had to persuade the committee that it should release the $40,000 cash on the trackhead.

Again, an *opera bouffe* scenario unfolded as Sherman discovered that the electric power plant, essential to operating the streetcars, was temporarily inoperable. What to do? In *The Los Angeles Railway Through the Years*, Easlon revealed how Sherman produced yet another miracle. "The resourceful company," Easlon wrote, "used a horse to pull an empty electric trolley car up to the top of a hill and let it coast down the long grade with the investors on board. The unsuspecting committee of investors were delightfully satisfied with their quiet streetcar ride and, thinking it was electric powered, gave Sherman his $40,000."

With his brother-in-law, Clark, operating as the front man while Sherman manipulated the money in the background, the invaders from Arizona soon had purchased all of Los Angeles' cable car lines and changed them to electric trolley operation. Employing the speed and dash of an earlier General Sherman marching through Georgia, Moses Sherman relentlessly pushed onward along trolley tracks. In April 1894 the General and his dynamic partner incorporated the Pasadena and Los Angeles Electric Railway Company. This marked a milestone in California transportation history because the company eventually became part of the first interurban electric trolley line in Southern California.

Later that year the swashbuckling Sherman-Clark team incorporated the Pasadena and Pacific Railroad Company, to link Los Angeles with Santa Monica on the Pacific Ocean. In their splendid history *Trolleys to the Surf*, William A. Myers and Ira L. Swett captured the élan generated by General Sherman. "Immediately," wrote Myers and Swett, "the newspapers were full of stories about 'Sherman's March to the Sea' as construction extended westward through the mustard fields toward the beach resort community."

But Sherman committed the egregious sin that has bedeviled generals through the years. In the euphoria of triumph and conquest, Sherman extended his lines until he was weak on every front. With his attention focused on the big interurban lines, he missed payments to bondholders of the Los Angeles Consolidated Railway, who, in turn, launched a reorganization of that company. "It all proved too much, too fast," observed Myers and Swett. "The extensions and reconstructions were having a disastrous effect on Sherman and Clark's fortunes." And another enemy was digging in: William S. Hook and his Los Angeles Traction Company had begun to expand with the city. The General, borrowing from a standard military text, executed what he hoped would be an orderly retreat. On the city traction front, he hammered out an armistice with bondholders of the Los Angeles Consolidated Electric Railway.

After the bondholders formed the Los Angeles Railway Company, Sherman and Clark turned the city lines over to the new firm and, in return, were given full control of the two interurban affiliates. In addition, Sherman and Clark won a clause in the contract that would enable them to repurchase the city lines in 1898 if the bondholders were unable to turn a profit.

With the dynamic duo removed from the inner-city operation, the new Los Angeles City Railway selected Fred W. Wood as its majordomo, whereupon a vigorous new program of renovation was begun. As galvanic as his predecessors, Wood promptly contacted the already renowned Pullman Standard Car Manufacturing Company and placed an order for a fleet of new four-wheel trolleys. For California, this was a significant change in rolling stock from the Toonerville cars that had for years been jouncing their way over the steel tracks. The Wood-era car offered a balance between open air (at each end) and an enclosed section in the center area to afford protection from the nasty elements. Thus, the first California streetcar made its debut. Impressive though they were, the cars couldn't overcome the bondholders' financial pains. The opportunity provided by contract to return the lines to Sherman and Clark arose, but the General and his brother-in-law were upstaged by a new and even more formidable protagonist.

The entrance of Henry E. Huntington onto the Southern California traction scene proved to be the most momentous development ever in Los Angeles' mass transit. In just a dozen years after his arrival in 1898, Huntington so thoroughly changed the face of surface transportation that even subdued, conservative viewers of the scene such as William D. Middleton were hard pressed to contain themselves. "Even in a region prone to generous superlatives and overstatement," wrote Middleton, "the title [World's Greatest Interurban Railway] was one that hardly could be disputed, for the Pacific Electric Railway simply encompassed more miles of track, operated more cars, and hauled more passengers and freight than any other interurban."

Plain arithmetic supported these claims. Not long after Henry E. Huntington had retired, his interurbans out of Los Angeles totaled 1,626 trains per day, comprising 3,262 cars over three distinct operating districts. Few municipalities in the world could make that statement; but, then again, few were ever graced with the likes of Henry E. Huntington. An obscure seventeen-year-old country-store clerk, Henry had the good fortune to be the nephew of one Collis P. Huntington, a railroad baron worthy of the name, who, along with his partners on the Central Pacific Railroad, had become a dominant figure in California politics and finance.

Writing in *Hear That Lonesome Whistle Blow*, historian Dee Brown described Collis Huntington and his three partners in less than glowing terms. "Eventually," wrote Brown, "they ruled California, buying up politicians and judges, forcing the public to pay interest on their own bonds, selling their land back to them at exorbitant prices, taxing them through higher and higher monopolistic freight rates."

The Big Four—Leland Stanford, Charles Crocker, and Mark Hopkins were the other three along with Collis Huntington—had ventured east for a high-level meeting when Uncle Collis stopped off for a reunion with nephew Henry. According to Steven Easlon, Uncle Collis sized up the young man and snapped: "Henry, I guess you had better come with me." To which the nonplussed Henry shot back: "How much will you pay me?"

Few would have dared address the imperious Collis P. Huntington with such impudence. The answer made an instant hit with the hard-headed Collis. Henry was quickly on his way up the organization ladder and by the 1890s was vice-president of the Southern Pacific. Henry's wealth and unquenchable thirst for new power and ventures proved a fortuitous blend for Los Angeles mass transit systems at the turn of the century.

Huntington's invasion of Los Angeles coincided with a death struggle between the Sherman-Clark interests and the rival Los Angeles Traction Company operated by William S. Hook, not to mention a nationwide business depression. After a series of byzantine deals in which corporations were organized, combined, and then concluded, Huntington gulped down both systems and promptly inaugurated a colossal building program that ultimately dwarfed anything conceived by his predecessors. In time it would lace all of Southern California together with a great electric railway network.

The Huntington rail grid embraced such locales as Los Angeles, Pasadena, Glendale, Santa Ana, San Fernando, Balboa, Arrowhead Springs, Redlands, Riverside, and Corona. Henry Huntington's dedication to the trolley was not enjoyed from the sanctity of his wood-paneled office. Henry ordered a trolley spur built right to his house. Following breakfast and coffee, Huntington would walk a few steps, climb aboard his private tram—adorned with such niceties as a wood-burning fireplace, galley, and bathroom—and ride to his office.

There was much business to conduct in Huntington's office. His Los Angeles Railway ruled trolley business in the rapidly growing city itself. The suburbs were linked to the metropolis by the Huntington-run Pacific Electric Railway, which also dominated the smaller municipalities where they connected. It was said with good reason that the closest distance between two points in Southern California was a Huntington trolley line; and if Henry wanted to go somewhere, and a line didn't exist, he would build one. Some of the Huntington routes were less than straight, and others were downright meandering, starting in Los Angeles, drifting to other communities before looping back to Los Angeles and the terminal again.

In almost no time at all Huntington became one of the most powerful trolley barons the world has known, owning the Los Angeles Railway Corporation, the Pacific Electric Railway Company, the Pacific Light and Power Company (he built the huge Big Creek hydroelectric plant in the High Sierras to bring in more electricity for the trolley lines), and innumerable real estate ventures. Henry's Pacific Electric Land Company worked hand-in-glove with the spreading traction lines as Southern California reveled in the biggest growth spurt in history. One vital item was missing, however: a first-rate streetcar to carry the potential passengers.

Huntington's battery of engineers plunged into this project with typical enthusiasm and in 1902 produced a superior streetcar that was the first of 747 similar pieces of rolling stock. Graceful and charming in its design, the vehicle offered an open-air design at each end and an enclosed portion in its center. Mounted on arch-bar trucks, the trolleys ordered by Henry soon became so ubiquitous they were dubbed Huntington Standards. Among their unique characteristics was a five-window front flanked by a pair of wrap-around glass windows. An especially classy feature was stained-glass ventilator windows in the clerestory roof.

The Huntington Standard achieved world renown, not so much because of its beauty and utility but rather thanks to Hollywood comedy film producer Hal Roach, who shot innumerable movies utilizing Los Angeles streets (and Huntington's trolleys) as the sets. For instance, a pair of Huntington Standards crush Laurel and Hardy's Model T Ford in their comedy *Hog Wild*. A broader view of the Standards is provided in Harold Lloyd's daredevil hanging-from-the-sky-scraper-clock sequences, high over streetcar-sprinkled downtown Los Angeles. The Keystone Kops, Charlie Chaplin, and Charley Chase were other comics who inadvertently popularized the Los Angeles trams.

Another prominent feature of the Huntington Standard was a Ubangi-lipped hunk of metal that jutted out in front of the trolley bumper to protect pedestrians from Henry's high-speed streetcars. The Eclipse "lifeguards" were designed both to catch and to protect any unfortunate Angeleno who jumped, fell, or was pushed into a passing tram. So useful were the lifeguards that they remained a part of the Standard's face until the vehicle finally was phased out of regular revenue service in the late forties.

Huntington himself was partially phased out of the Los Angeles traction scene in 1910, when Henry and the Southern Pacific split. The giant railroad bought out Huntington and eventually merged the Pacific Electric with other Southern California interurban routes. September 1, 1911, was a memorable date in American mass transit history, for it was then that all Los Angeles Pacific lines were acquired by the Pacific Electric Railway Company. This included 103.6 route miles, of which 77.97 miles were double track and 25.63 miles were single track. Pacific Electric was now the most comprehensive electric railway operation on the continent if not in the world—and was still growing. For four more years, until 1914, ribbons of steel wended their way through Los Angeles and out to the suburbs, in some cases even climbing the slopes of the Sierra Madre Mountains.

For convenience' sake, Pacific Electric was arranged in three distinct divisions—Northern District, Western District, and Southern District—each a meaningful commuter line in itself. The Northern District, largest of them all, covered the territory north and east from Los Angeles, embracing four hundred miles of track and thirty-three distinct routes. The variety of operations was breathtaking. One of the most popular was a narrow-gauge Alpine Division, which provided a pulsating open-car excursion over Echo Mountain and other nearby peaks. For speed there was the forty-eight-mile 1,200-volt San Bernardino line.

By contrast, the Western District contained much of the previously absorbed Los Angeles Pacific Company trackage (260 miles of track and twelve lines) and spread its rails to Hollywood, Burbank, Beverly Hills, Venice, Redondo, Santa Monica, and Glendale.

If the mountain run of the Northern District offered superb vistas, so, too, did the Southern District, which operated mighty trams at beachside in Long Beach on the way to such popular Pacific havens as Newport and Balboa, not to mention the orange groves of Santa Ana and the oil fields in El Segundo. It was a class operation and nothing epitomized it more than the rolling stock. Unlike the flimsy diesel buses plying Southern California routes today—vehicles that seem to disintegrate within months of arrival—the Pacific Electric operated trolleys that were not only handsome but durable. For example, the company's "1000" series, built by the Jewett Car Company in 1913, were still rolling virtually good as new thirty-five years later over the Long Beach Line.

Should an Angeleno suffer a death in the family, Pacific Electric offered a funeral car (originally built by the Los Angeles Railway Corporation) called the Descanso (translated from Spanish, "rest"), which stopped at the prescribed funeral parlor at a prearranged time. Mourners rode in a rear compartment while the casket was carried in a unique forward area. Following the ceremonies at the funeral parlor, the Descanso rolled out to any one of several cemeteries located at the end of the streetcar lines.

The need for gas-guzzling motor trucks was also lessened by a fleet of pollution-free freight-carrying trolleys, which were introduced by the Los Angeles Pacific to haul lemons from the groves in the Colegrove and Hollywood districts. Granite was carried by trolleys near Laurel Canyon and lumber delivered to Ocean Park. So successful was the freight-by-trolley business that a complete tram freight house was erected in Buena Vista in 1905.

The freight business by streetcar increased with the trackage, and in 1911 the Los Angeles Pacific could brag about freight trains heading from Los Angeles to such centers as Redondo, Venice, and Hollywood. Then there was the Pacific Electric freight operation—bigger by far than the Los Angeles Pacific—with a harbor served by the docks at Eighth and Hemlock.

Still another significant aspect of the Los Angeles–area trolley business was sightseeing; it has been said that Pacific Electric developed the tourist excursion business into a fine art. The Mount Lowe Line hauled visitors (and Los Angelenos) up Rubio Canyon and to the summit of Echo Mountain. The Alpine Division opened Mount Lowe Springs to excursionists on a roadbed carved out of solid rock. The Hollywood film boom, which coincided with the merger of the

Los Angeles Pacific and Pacific Electric, inspired a big spurt of ridership—both sightseers and film workers—for Pacific Electric, which enjoyed a monopoly in Hollywood for years.

By far the most popular tour was the "Balloon Route Trolley Trip," originated by the Los Angeles Pacific and further popularized by Pacific Electric after the former company had been absorbed in 1911. If today a visit to Disneyland is a high priority for any visitor to Greater Los Angeles, a similar must in the early part of the century was a ride on the Balloon Route cars, which touched such bases as Los Angeles, Melrose, Edgemont, Laurel Junction, Sherman, Rosedale, Rosemary, Sunny Slope, Morocco Junction, Sawtelle, and Santa Monica by the sea. An unusual crowd-pleaser for visitors was the "palatial observation cars" as well as the pitch "101 miles for 100 cents." Another Balloon Route flyer boasted: "We visit ten beaches, eight cities, Hollywood, the Soldiers' Home, with 28 miles along the Grand Old Pacific—making a 70-mile trip for $1.00. Be sure and get some moonstones from our famous Moonstone Beach!" Who could resist such a pitch?

Ruth Cavin, author of *Trolleys*, tells of another, more businesslike tour promoted by the Los Angeles transit interests:

> Trackage was laid to undeveloped areas; prospects would be taken out in the trolley to inspect the site, plied with free barbecue and sales pitches, entertained by bands and other gimmicks and, it was hoped, sold a lot.
>
> The community thus created would eventually swell the passenger traffic. Hollywood was developed this way, and so were other Los Angeles–area colonies.

Yet resistance to the trolley was apparent, if not intense, even in the halcyon days after the 1911 merger. During inclement weather the open sections of the Huntington Standard cars were susceptible to rain and winds that blew right through the enclosed portions. Despite the additional appointments in the handsome cars, heaters were absent, and on the occasional relatively cold day, protests were heated.

The Pacific Electric did muffle such complaints by producing bigger, better, and more comfortable rolling stock which was totally enclosed and provided protection from the elements. But there was another challenge from which the trolleys of Los Angeles could not obtain sufficient protection: the five-cent-fare autos, otherwise known as jitneys.

Starting in July 1914, more and more conventional passenger automobiles began plying Los Angeles' streets, offering citizens cheap transportation in what was still regarded as a novel mode of transit, the car. That the jitney could be a threat to the Pacific Electric streetcar empire was evident in an editorial carried by the Los Angeles *Record* in its October 1, 1914, edition:

> The Trolley Trust will not succeed in throttling the People's Five-Cent auto car service. The masses are aroused on this question and they will come to the front in such numbers and in such vigorous fashion in defense of the auto men that it will result in a greatly extended auto service in behalf of the public.

Operating on existing Los Angeles trolley routes, the jitneys took a significant

amount of business away from the trams and escaped without any form of regulation. The jitney ride was conspicuously less comfortable than the streetcar
counterpart, but trolley barons were hard pressed to combat the novelty of the
automobile. Edwin L. Lewis, once superintendent of the Los Angeles Railway,
estimated that jitneys cost the trolley system $3,000,000 annually in lost rev-
enue.

The jitney bus, born in Los Angeles in 1914, was to wreak havoc on trolley
barons across the nation. Taking their cue from the Los Angeles *Record*, other
editorialists began taking the jitney to their hearts. In Dallas, the *Dispatch* went
so far as to offer cash prizes for the best jitney jingles. One such winner rhymed
as follows:

> Hush, little Ford,
> Don't you cry,
> You'll be a jitney
> Bye and bye.

More to the point was a couplet that appeared in the Fort Worth *Telegram*.
To wit:

> If a streetcar meets a jitney
> Coming down the lane,
> And a streetcar hits the jitney,
> I wonder who's to blame.

As far as the trolley trust was concerned, the jitney was clearly the culprit. An
editorial in the *Electric Railway Journal* put it this way:

One feature of the jitney bus situation that stands out above all others is the need for
regulation. Primarily the new conveyance aims only at competition with the much-regu-
lated street-railway for the cream of its traffic—a fact borne out by the naive testimony
of a jitney operator in one of the western cities to the effect that he couldn't operate on
streets other than those occupied by railway tracks because he could keep his car full
only by picking up groups of people who were waiting for the streetcars.

From the standpoint of ethics it is manifestly impossible to enforce the principle of
regulation for the electric railway and to permit its competitor to go free of all restraint.
Unfortunately, however, ethics are frequently a poor basis for argument, and regulation
of the jitney, at least during its early stages, will probably come about not so much
through a spirit of fair play as through the realization by the affected cities that the advent of the unrestricted jitney involves more direct dangers to the community than
merely the abandonment of outlying and unprofitable electric railway lines. Already reports of extreme vehicular congestion are heard from the western towns where apprecia-
ble numbers of jitneys are operating, and fatalities to pedestrians struck by recklessly
driven vehicles have brought home generally the need for imposing responsibility by
means of indemnity bonds.

In 1917 Los Angeles finally responded and passed jitney laws. Restrictive li-
cense fees were ordered for use of the vehicles, but the wound inflicted on the
Los Angeles Railway was to leave a permanent scar.

Nevertheless, the trolley was very much a part of the Southern California scene at the start of the Roaring Twenties. The unanswered question at the time centered upon the effects of the internal combustion engine and its by-products—the car, the truck, the bus, and the taxi. For the next decade, at least, both the Los Angeles Railway and Pacific Electric would give the auto interests a hearty run for their money in what still was a smogless community bordering on megalopolis.

The life-and-death struggle between the trolley car and the gasoline bus was, in effect, as unpredictable as a battle between a cobra and a mongoose. In Los Angeles, trolley officials realized that bus technology was improving rapidly during the twenties and the built-for-the-purpose bus (as opposed to the built-over-a-truck-chassis bus) originated by Frank Fageol boasted enough assets even in its primitive state to become an instant threat.

One theory supported by some trolley people was the "if you can't beat 'em, join 'em" plan.

The Los Angeles Railway moved into the bus business (winning a case in court against William McAdoo's People's Motor Bus Company) in the mid-twenties. The vehicles were a great novelty but they soon proved what objective critics knew then as they did in the sixties and seventies: that a bus can never match a trolley for comfort and durability. The first Los Angeles buses, it was noted by Easlon, shook up their human cargo "like a nervous horse."

Meanwhile the trolley builders were not sitting on their laurels counting their profits. Responding to demands from the Los Angeles Railway and Pacific Electric, firms such as the St. Louis Car Company, Brill, and Pullman produced a series of unusually innovative designs, from the Sowbellies to the streamliners.

The St. Louis Car Company had the distinction of producing the Sowbelly trolley in response to feminist demands that a lower step be provided (to accommodate the day's fashions) for ease in entering. After studying a Los Angeles–built design, St. Louis Car Company produced a series of Sowbellies with low center doors. When the Los Angeles Railway requested a smaller, more economical tram, the answer was provided by Charles O. Birney, who developed the twenty-eight-foot Birney Safety streetcar.

In 1920 a fleet of seventy four-wheeled Birneys entered service in Los Angeles. Cute as they were, the Birneys proved to be a disaster in terms of comfort. Their single truck caused a bumpy, bouncy ride not at all pleasing to those who had become accustomed to the grand Huntington Standards. With this in mind, bigger and better vehicles were ordered and, once again, St. Louis Car Company came through with the proper product. Between 1921 and 1924, the redoubtable trolley maker delivered 250 steel "H" Type cars. Nicknamed California cars, the new rolling stock was equipped to run either singly or in multiple units. Pacific Electric also kept pace with the times and, just prior to the Great Crash of 1929, converted six cars from its Southern Pacific Oregon lines into reserved-seat parlor cars. For its service to Hollywood, Pacific Electric designed low-floor center-door cars in 1922, and for six years these popular and efficient trolleys were shipped to Los Angeles until the fleet of "Hollywood" cars totaled 160.

The rolling stock pouring out of J. G. Brill's factory, St. Louis Car Company, and other streetcar manufacturers was up-to-date and often innovative. St. Louis Car Company, for example, in 1925 built an experimental car for the Los Angeles Railway with a unique brake system which continually weighed the passenger load so that the proper amount of brake pressure was applied. Another interesting piece of equipment with low center doors and large motorman windows, also built by St. Louis Car Company, proved a hit when it arrived in 1930.

Yet trolley improvements alone were not enough to compensate for some of the failings inherent in the system. One mistake dated back to the early 1900s, when municipalities such as Boston and New York were doing what Los Angeles should have done: laid rails underground to avoid future surface congestion. It wasn't as if Los Angeles traction barons ignored or disdained the idea of building a subway. E. H. Harriman of the Southern Pacific, one of the most energetic railroad builders in the world, planned a four-track subway for Los Angeles in 1906. The blueprints called for a four-track subway on a private right-of-way that would link downtown Los Angeles with Vineyard. Harriman's scheme also called for a series of new connecting cutoff routes which, had they been completed, would have given Los Angeles, in the words of no less an authority than William D. Middleton, "the greatest rapid transit system west of Chicago." Today, more than seventy years later, one of the most pivotal tragedies in the development of transportation in Los Angeles is that Harriman's plans were short-circuited by the panic of 1907 and Los Angeles Pacific's subway remained a blueprint.

Another tragedy was the failure of the Los Angeles Railway to keep pace with the explosive growth of Greater Los Angeles between the years 1913 and 1925. Opportunities to extend the tentacles into valuable precincts such as the San Fernando Valley were missed. Instead of fully growing with the area, the Los Angeles Railway turned into a stunted local passenger system, although in 1925 it fielded an armada of no less than 1,243 trolleys out of a roster of 1,250.

But compared to Pacific Electric, the Los Angeles Railway was a piker. Historian Donald Duke pointed out in his book *PE—The Pacific Electric Railway* that the interurban giant operating in and out of Los Angeles was determined to keep up with if not ahead of the times. "New steel equipment was continually replacing wooden interurbans," wrote Duke, "faster schedules were introduced, everything possible to provide the best in services for the riding public."

Pacific Electric had gotten off on the right track back in 1905 when it opened a combined office building and terminal covering 400,000 square feet of floor space, the largest building in Los Angeles at the time. Located at Sixth and Main streets, the ground floor of the California version of a skyscraper housed the station, with double-through tracks at the south side. As the volume of trains increased, the Pacific Electric added an elevated terminal which took many of the interurbans off the street in the downtown area and allowed for longer trains.

So successful was the Sixth and Main depot and so bright was Pacific Electric's future at the start of the Roaring Twenties that exuberant plans were made to expand the system. This was accomplished with construction of the tall, sedate Subway Terminal Building at 423 South Hill Street, just a stone's throw from the older Pacific Electric Building.

The name—Subway Terminal Building—is deceptive in that it suggests that the structure at Hill Street was, in fact, the mecca for a grand underground system; of course, it was nothing of the kind. The original old Hill Street Station was the terminal for Pacific Electric's Western District and did a land-office business, with seven lines using the ground-level terminal as early as 1911. In addition the Balloon Route (so named because the two main lines—northwest via Hollywood and southwest via Vineyard—met at the ocean near Santa Monica and enclosed a balloonlike area with Hill Street as its nerve center) left Hill Street carrying hordes of customers. With congestion a problem in the foreseeable future, it was suggested that the four-track (Harriman) subway link Hill Street Station with Vineyard. As noted, the panic put an end to that and the subway plan was shelved until the early 1920s, when autos and trucks became ubiquitous and bothersome to the trolleys.

Considering the congestion as well as a shift in business potential from the southern perimeter to the northern one, officials of the Southern Pacific decided to relieve pressure on the northwestern lines by building a brand new terminal on the site of the old Hill Street Station. As noteworthy a decision as the terminal building was, its significance was dwarfed by the fact that Pacific Electric would also have, as part of the project, the very first subway on the West Coast. According to the plans, the subway would begin in a five-track stub-end in the new station's basement and run northwest to a point almost a mile away, emerging from the side of a steep hill and onto the street at the intersection of Beverly and Glendale boulevards. Here it would link with existing track of the hitherto separate Glendale and Edendale lines.

Cynics, who were still awaiting construction of the original Hill Street–Vineyard subway, scoffed at the new project but this time actual work began, on May 1, 1924. The project was widely hailed as an indication of Los Angeles' civic greatness. On December 1, 1925, the tunnel route was inaugurated. It proved an instant success and meshed neatly with the former surface terminal, which now was located just south of the subway building and continued to have five loading tracks of its own for heavy wooden trains. Gates led to it from the building and tickets were bought inside. All in all it was a neat arrangement.

That the subway worked was proven by Pacific Electric's revised timetable. The mile-long bore cut several minutes off the schedules of lines that used its underground tracks. The subway thrived on lines stolen from other terminals, such as Main Street Station and Hill Street. It was graced by a variety of equipment, including the first-rate steel "600" series cars, which were manufactured for Pacific Electric by the St. Louis Car Company. It also carried a number of wooden trains, not to mention the extremely popular Hollywood types, among others.

No piece of equipment was more closely linked with a mass transit line than the "Big Red" cars of Pacific Electric's "1200"-class fleet. At first they were designed as wooden cars but a calamitous wreck in 1913 at Vineyard involving a pair of wooden trains caused a switch from wood to steel. The Big Reds, according to Donald Duke, provided the "ultimate in comfort, speed and appearance—the finest 1,200-volt cars in the West." To satisfy the demand, fifty more steel cars—in the "1100" series—were added in 1924 to accommodate the traffic on Pacific Electric's Northern Division.

The advent of the great red trains marked the golden age of Pacific Electric mass transit operation. The system was short of perfection but superb nonetheless in many respects. The trackwork originally laid out by Henry E. Huntington and graced by the exceptionally effective rolling stock inspired rhapsodic prose. In his book *The Interurban Era*, William D. Middleton describes Southern California's best mass transit effort as follows:

Great trains of heavy steel interurbans, their air whistles shrieking hoarsely for road crossings, hurtled at mile-a-minute speeds down the inner rails of the Pacific Electric's four-track steel boulevards, overtaking mundane locals that skipped from stop to stop on the outer tracks. . . . In a time before Southern California became the world's most automobile-oriented society almost everyone rode Pacific Electric's "big red cars" to the beaches, mountains, race tracks, and other pleasure spots of the Southland, as well as to and from their daily work.

Sadly, the automobile transformation had already begun to take place, as well as a challenge to Pacific Electric ridership from buses. As early as 1917 a Pacific Electric line (San Bernardino–Highland–Patton) was replaced by a bus line because the interurban route was deemed unprofitable. In time local routes such as Long Beach, Pasadena, Santa Monica, Redlands, and San Pedro were eliminated. To combat competition from some bus lines, Pacific Electric simply purchased them. In 1930 the Motor Transit Company was partially absorbed by Pacific Electric and six years later Pacific Electric had bought all interests owned by Greyhound, merging them into the Pacific Electric bus system.

The handwriting began to appear on the wall for the center city–oriented Los Angeles Railway at about the same time. Conscious of the fact that neighboring San Diego boasted a fleet of trolleys that were not only fully enclosed but also sumptuously—by streetcar standards—appointed, Angelenos took a dimmer and dimmer view of their hard-seated, semienclosed trams. A further source of friction developed when the Los Angeles Railway boosted its fare from five to ten cents.

The company hoped to mollify critics with a minor cosmetic job, in which a few trolleys were graced with leather-upholstered seats, frosted interior lighting, and new, green-painted exteriors. It was a clever public relations move, except for one essential mistake: only a relative handful of the fleet was so embellished and to persuade riders that more such cars existed, the updated pieces of rolling stock were moved around the system (reminiscent of the Marx Brothers moving furniture from one room to another in a classic scene from A *Night at the Opera*) to give the impression that more "new" cars existed than were actually on the roster.

The Great Depression of the 1930s was a mixed blessing for the Los Angeles trolley network. One inescapable realization among the brass was that most of their trolleys had become outdated; some of them had been in service for more than twenty-five years and replacements were urgently needed. This called for a vast expenditure of cash which was not readily available. Rehabilitating old cars had also become an expensive proposition.

On the other hand the Wall Street stock market crash also meant that it had become considerably more difficult to purchase an automobile in 1932 than it had been in 1928 at the height of the economic boom. By the early thirties, the Los Angeles Railway had become an extremely important mode of transportation, which carried about 70 percent of all local passengers.

Estimates were that between 1912 and 1932, Los Angeles trolleys carried five and a quarter *billion* passengers over 660,000,000 miles. Given some insightful and sensitive management, attractive equipment, and cooperation from City Hall, the Los Angeles trolleys figured to ride out the Depression in reasonably healthy style. But support was sorely lacking, and competition from buses continued to cast a cloud over the tram's future.

Although the average life of a bus was only five years by the late twenties, engineers had been working assiduously on improvements, and in the early thirties the gas-electric design persuaded many municipal operators to switch to the gas guzzlers. One such operation, the Philadelphia Rapid Transit Company, ordered 125 double-deckers and 85 single-deckers with gas-electric drive. Los Angeles soon followed suit.

Next came the diesel-electric bus in the thirties, and the threat to trolleys became even more ominous. Still, the feeling among most transit pundits was that buses were merely supplementary "feeders" to the main streetcar lines and that trolleys should still be the major mode of surface transportation in cities with a population of more than a million, such as Los Angeles.

But streetcar companies, including the Los Angeles Railway, were less sanguine about the future of the contemporary early-thirties-model tram. When twenty-five of the major American streetcar companies convened early in the Depression, Los Angeles supported the convention's plank that a completely new, "revolutionary" trolley was needed to woo passengers back to the streetcar. The Electric Railway Presidents' Conference Committee poured more than a million dollars' worth of research into the project, and out of it came a truly revolutionary trolley: the PCC (Presidents' Conference Committee) car. The committee, organized in 1929, was not guilty of producing too little, but it was certainly too late. In 1932, while the PCC car still was on the drawing board, some fifteen thousand buses were plying the streets of America, carrying more than a billion passengers annually. In five years the number would double when, finally, the PCC car began rolling regularly off the production line.

When the PCC car won unanimous raves in Brooklyn, Chicago, and Balti-more, Los Angeles jumped on the bandwagon and, following a major refinanc-ing, ordered sixty PCC cars from the ever reliable St. Louis Car Company. It was a move in the grand style by a company that earlier in the decade had been widely criticized for weakness at the top. ("The fundamental problem," said one critic, "is poor management, not the railway. The railway is an excel-lent property with great potential.") When, on March 23, 1937, the first two of the marvelous PCC cars were delivered they received a Hollywood fanfare. With young movie superstar Shirley Temple in hand, Mayor Shaw unveiled the "million-dollar trolley" and ten thousand onlookers cheered the streamlined ve-hicle unlike anything that had previously been plying the streets of Los Angeles.

Placed into service on the Los Angeles Railway's heavily traveled "P" line, the PCC cars were as welcomed in the West as they were in the East and Mid-west. "The new cars," commented one newspaper report, "are to the old rattle-and-bang yellow cars what a supermodel streamlined automobile is to an origi-nal Model T."

Pacific Electric lagged behind the Los Angeles Railway in its pursuit of the PCCs but, finally, in November 1940 a fleet of thirty streamliners—the longest PCC cars yet built—began running on Pacific Electric tracks on the Glendale-Burbank run. Here again, the trolleys were lauded up and down the line for their speed, smoothness of ride, and snazzy good looks.

Sadly, Pacific Electric had lagged in its pursuit of ultramodern interurban transportation. Instead of immediately grabbing at the opportunity of running the delightful PCCs on its tracks, the company opted for an older group of Southern Pacific cars which had run in Oregon as well as a shipment of owl-faced former Southern Pacific Oakland–Berkeley–Alameda suburban cars. Slower than other Pacific Electric rolling stock, the émigrés from San Francisco Bay were dubbed "Blimps" because of their enormous passenger capacity. If nothing else, the Blimps had great staying power, eventually comprising the en-tire Pacific Electric interurban passenger fleet. Lacking the dash and dandy quality of the PCC car, the Blimps did benefit from a massive renovation pro-gram in 1946, when Pacific Electric spent $7,500 each on seventy-one such cars. Some of the changes included new foam rubber, two-and-two seating, bull's-eye interior lighting, new flooring, and a new paint scheme.

"With this nucleus of Blimps," commented transit writer Harry C. Oswald, "Pacific Electric had a first-rate interurban fleet."

The same could be said of the Los Angeles Railway, which, in 1943, received thirty more new PCC cars. Despite the intrusion of bus competition, the prolif-eration of automobiles, and the hostility of a powerful political segment, Los Angeles' streetcar and interurban empire had reached the forties not only alive but kicking. Following the entry of the United States into World War II in 1941, an unprecedented and totally unexpected demand for trolley use sent of-ficials of the Los Angeles Railway as well as the Pacific Electric rushing to the storage yard for additional equipment. Such obsolete and antique trolleys as the Huntington Standards, the Sowbellies, and Type "H"s had their mothballs dust-ed off and were paraded into use, side by side with the sleek PCC cars. Similarly, all available passenger interurbans were pressed back into service on the Pacific Electric to service regular commuters as well as those now employed in the many war industries sprinkled around the Los Angeles community. In one year, 1945, more than 109,000,000 passengers were carried on the Pacific Electric.

Under the circumstances, one might have assumed that as World War II wound down in 1945, both Pacific Electric and the Los Angeles Railway could enjoy only good fortune in the postwar years. But the omissions of 1907 were to have fatal reverberations forty years later when Los Angelenos needed the subway that never was built by Harriman.

Few objective observers of mass transit could quibble with the superior riding qualities of the Los Angeles PCC streamliners or the aesthetic assets of the modern trolleys. But it was an indisputable problem that they were confined to tracks, and many of those tracks were *not* located near the new suburban centers sprouting throughout Greater Los Angeles. Suddenly, Fords, Chryslers, Hudsons, and Nashes, which had been conspicuous by their absence during World War II, were not only available again but could reach these communities a lot easier than any PCC car. Besides, gas was still cheap, and the new cars had a special freshness appeal because of their absence during wartime. Certainly, a spanking new Pontiac could take on an ancient Huntington Standard in any 1947 popularity contest. In fact, it did, and not surprisingly, the Pontiac and its Detroit-made cousins won, hands down.

Sure, the glittering chrome of the new cars wooed riders away from the rails, but a mass exodus was not an inevitable result of peacetime USA. The problem here was a pathetic ignorance of the need to preserve the potential of Los Angeles' mass transit resources, even if it meant their annexation by the city itself. In addition, the inherent right of a streetcar to maintain an exclusive right-of-way should have become an imperative plank of any sensible people-minded politician in the Southern California community.

By depriving the PCCs and their interurban cousins of support, Los Angeles in effect pulled the plug on its vast body of mass transit. It should have developed a set of enforceable laws to protect its treasured transit resource while limiting the poisoning effect of unbridled auto growth. The abject failure of this omission eventually placed Los Angeles in the unenviable position of becoming the smog capital of the United States. By 1977 it was estimated by pollution officials in California that automobiles were the source of 90 percent of the smog.

It was no secret in 1945, at war's end, that Los Angeles was an area of 9,200 square miles with frequent weather inversions that trap pollutants. Nor was it a secret then—at a time when planning could have saved the city's air from being poisoned—that it would soon be necessary to reduce the amount of hydrocarbons which produce corrosive oxidants when they react with nitrogen oxides in strong sunlight. Considering the very predictable growth of auto sales during 1946–1956 and its effect on the air in the Los Angeles Basin, the fact that municipal officials did not address the oxidant problem with vigor, vigilance, and attention goes down as one of the most lamentable urban oversights of the half-century. Even in the mid-1970s, after considerable hullabaloo over pollution and belated restrictions imposed by government regulators, the state of air in Southern California's hub was, at best, deplorable. Writing for the Newhouse News Service in March 1977, Peter J. Bernstein suggested that Los Angeles had made little to no progress in licking the smog syndrome:

> Autos are still considered responsible for most of the pollution in the Los Angeles Basin, since state statistics show that the number of cars and vehicle-miles traveled has steadily increased and has largely offset the gains in air quality from smog control devices on new cars. Assembly-line cars have not been meeting design specifications, deteriorating over the years and undercutting clean air forecasts that overestimated the life-spans of emission control devices.

Stupidly, a number of naive federal and local officials had assured one and all that by 1985 the Los Angeles Basin would meet federal standards designed to protect public health against carbon monoxide, nitrogen dioxide, and hydrocarbons. But a careful look at the record and a closer look at the air indicated otherwise.

"The chances of Los Angeles or any neighboring county meeting the federal oxidant standard by 1985 or 1990 are zero," said Eric Lemke, assistant director of the Southern California Air Pollution Control District, in March 1977. "In fact, we don't think we'll ever meet the standard on photochemical oxidant unless we artificially introduce a chemical into the atmosphere. The natural oxidant levels alone make compliance impossible."

Other authorities were skeptical of Los Angeles' bid to clean its air. One was Dr. Arie Haagen-smit, the Caltech scientist who in 1949 discovered the chemical recipe for smog. Haagen-smit said the public repeatedly underestimated the sacrifices necessary to attain the clean-air goals. "The public wants clean air," said Dr. Haagen-smit, "if they don't have to go to too much trouble."

There, of course, was the rub. The public would have had to suffer little trouble if officials had capitalized on the available clean-air assets in the early postwar years. One suffers a painful sense of déjà-vu listening to Peter J. Bernstein capsulize the Los Angeles transportation trauma in 1977. "There is a widespread feeling," Bernstein concluded, "that the most urgent need for Los Angeles is a comprehensive rapid transit system that would save gasoline and help clean up the air."

Which is precisely what Los Angeles could brag about to the world in 1946 when the combined services of Pacific Electric and the Los Angeles Railway were serving the public in a reasonably efficient and inexpensive manner despite the burdens of antiquated equipment (hauled out of storage for wartime use) and the inevitable delays in obtaining new replacements.

The comprehensive mass transit system—rapid in many sections—was there. Millions upon millions were about to be poured into the construction of highways that would ultimately drive the mass transit system to ruin. But Pacific Electric and the Los Angeles Railway received hardly a crumb.

This was the pivotal point. Help was needed. Pacific Electric was faced with declining patronage as well as the need for new equipment and track rehabilitation. It was imperative that Pacific Electric and the Los Angeles Railway be annexed by a municipal government, an insight that apparently eluded officials. Considering their declining revenues (only the freight business was then profitable for Pacific Electric), both lines could have been bought for a relative song and the value of the rails and roadbed today would be in the billions. Instead, Pacific Electric tacitly conceded defeat as a passenger-carrying electric interurban line and pursued a policy of benign neglect. In 1947 the wooden "Tens" cars were removed from the Long Beach line, followed by the "Twelves" in 1950. By then none of Pacific Electric's own interurban rolling stock remained. All that remained were the acquired Blimps (rather than new PCC cars), which, despite cosmetic improvements, still suggested antique rolling stock rather than the modern machines demanded by Californians in the always redesigning era of the late forties and early fifties.

Pacific Electric's days as a passenger-carrying line were over. On October 1, 1953, Pacific Electric passenger service, including both rail and bus, was sold to Metropolitan Coach Lines. Curiously, new green paint schemes were applied to the buses but not to the venerable Blimps. There still remained a flicker of hope that the valuable interurban system of the once-proud Pacific Electric would somehow survive as a result of municipal insight and foresight. This, tragically, was not the case. "Metro made no secret of the fact that it desired the end of rail service," noted Harry C. Oswald, a historian with the Electric Railroaders' Association.

At first the coach operator refused to affix "Metropolitan Coach Lines" to the interurban cars but finally was compelled to by the demands of Pacific Electric, which, by now, was reaping profits in the freight business. It is perhaps apocryphal, but a story went the rounds that one official of the bus company suffered apoplexy the first time he saw an interurban roll by with his bus company's name painted on the side of the car.

The erstwhile glory of Pacific Electric passenger transit was wiped out as, one by one, the Western District routes became a thing of the past. Occasionally, the bus line was temporarily rebuffed in its attempts at dismembering the interurban giant. "Repeated efforts to divest themselves of rail cars on the Long Beach, San Pedro, Catalina Dock, and Bellflower (plus the Watts Suburban) lines met with failure," wrote Harry C. Oswald. "They did, however, permit the cars to literally fall apart on the rails, resulting in frequent, ever increasing interruptions of service, probably in the hope that public demand for better service would result in permission for bus substitution. It has also been suspected that Pacific Electric cooperated by making switching movements of freights at 'convenient' times to further delay service."

Extermination of the mass transit facility appeared to be averted in March 1958 when the newly created Los Angeles Metropolitan Transit Authority bought out private operators (Metropolitan Coach and Los Angeles Transit lines) in the Los Angeles area. Increased maintenance was the mirage that promised a glorious future at the end of the track but, actually, the new Authority merely lopped off a large number of old cars and when the dust had cleared the MTA had only one standard-gauge line: the Long Beach route.

The MTA did, however, attempt to gain a long-term lease over the Pacific Electric rails and wanted a lease of at least five years so that it could justify rehabilitation of the line. This reprieve did offer some hope as negotiations continued without result. In the meantime, MTA displayed at least a token interest in future rail service, although how serious their intent was remains debatable in retrospect. "Regardless of objections," Harry C. Oswald observed in *Headlights*, "the Metropolitan Transit Authority did show some inclination to attempt an upgrading of the line's equipment, and this should be credited to them. It was all in vain, though."

One obstacle was the refusal of the Southern Pacific to grant a suitable lease to the MTA. Theorists who believe that there was a conspiracy to destroy the line point to an egregious contradiction betrayed by the suddenly stubborn Southern Pacific–Pacific Electric interests in their refusal to negotiate a lease with the MTA. "At one point," noted Oswald, "they even claimed the electric overhead to be dangerous to freight train crews—this after nearly six decades of such operation!"

Looming like a black cloud on the horizon was a fleet of General Motors diesel buses, which were scheduled to replace the proud interurbans. Again, it appeared that a last-minute pardon might be at hand for the trains. In a rare (for California) burst of transportation foresight, the municipalities of Long Beach and Compton sought injunctions to prevent the conversion from rail transport to diesel buses. The judiciary ignored the pleas, but the California Public Utilities Commission was in a favorable position to strike a strong blow for rail transit in the decades ahead. The commission moved with a close-but-no-cigar action. It restrained Pacific Electric from making the line unsuitable for continued interurban operation, but failed to do the one thing needed—establish a five-year lease at an equitable figure with the MTA.

Having delayed the changeover to buses ostensibly to perpetuate the commuter rail lines, the MTA made it clear to Southern California that the end for interurbans was close at hand. The news hit the local populace like a delayed-action bomb. Suddenly those who had been aloof to the fate of the historic trains became not only interested but riders once more. One Californian who rode the line a week before it died recalled with astonishment the response of his neighbors. "Throngs filled the cars. It was so crowded that passengers had to stand; everyone seemed to realize that the end of an era was approaching." Never more would they glide majestically from the elevated train shed at Sixth and Main onto the viaduct, descending to San Pedro Street, crossing the narrow-gauge rails of the J and R lines on Seventh Street, traversing the dual-gauge rails shared for several blocks with the S line.

On April 8, 1961, at a time when progressive cities such as Toronto, Boston, and Montreal were expanding their rail service from the inner city to the suburbs, Los Angelenos watched their metropolis end service officially on the Pacific Electric's tracks. After nearly six decades of generally superb interurban service, the Pacific Electric was put to rest.

"It might well be," commented Donald Duke, "had the dreams of Pacific Electric come true, the 'Big Red Cars' might yet be seen racing down the middle of the Santa Ana or Hollywood freeways. Los Angeles and Southern California just grew and spread too fast. The silver rails which developed and built the suburbs became unwanted. The citizens wanted the ugly tracks removed for more streets and highways."

One of the more telling eulogies was provided by William D. Middleton, who wrote:

> In retrospect it is all too easy to write off the interurban railways as ill-conceived ventures for clearly they failed to achieve the lasting position and universal application that was once so freely predicted for them, and only rarely did they reap the promised financial returns that once made them so popular with investors. But in their time the electric cars served well the transportation needs of a growing nation, and this essential contribution can never be overlooked.

More important, however, was Middleton's review of the interurban and the vehicle that helped wipe it off the tracks, the private automobile:

> It is worth noting that the interurban railways were rendered obsolete not by a transportation development of superior technology but by one that provided only a greater mobility. As a mass transportation vehicle, the electric railway possessed many of the same virtues in 1965 that it had in 1900. For it could still transport large numbers of people far more economically, and quite often more rapidly, than its petroleum-fueled successors.

As the automobile began overpopulating the California countryside it became apparent that a mistake *had* been made. The freeways befouled the atmosphere as never before. The price of fuel continued to spiral upward in proportion to decreasing room on the highways. Motorists were soon discovering that the car was less than the ideal means of getting to and from business. But all Los Angeles could do as Pacific Electric became nothing more than a piece of transit trivia was look in awe—and later jealousy—at the progress being made by cities elsewhere. San Francisco built a masterful rapid transit system; Cleveland extended its subway all the way to its International Airport; and Chicago did what Los Angeles should have done—placed a rapid transit line in the middle of its freeway. Even worse, Los Angeles also allowed its inner-city mass transit system, the trolley lines, to die as well.

Officially, the Los Angeles Railway capitulated on January 10, 1945, when it was taken over by the Los Angeles Transit Lines, whose holding company, National City Lines, was owned by Standard Oil of California, Firestone Tire and Rubber Company, Phillips Petroleum, General Motors, and Mack Truck. National City Lines had been purchasing trolley lines throughout the nation and converting the systems to buses. But cynics in the streetcar industry were astonished when the company instead ordered the latest and most advanced form of PCC streamliner—the all-electric trolley—for Los Angeles streets. A fleet of forty PCC cars soon rolled off the assembly lines and, for a change, the immediate future appeared bright. Vintage trams were wiped off the roster and new yellow, green, and cream paint was put on whatever rolling stock needed a new face. The new PCC cars had a formal premiere—embellished by the appearance of movie starlet Janis Paige—on September 24, 1948, and they were warmly received.

Earlier, Los Angeles Transit Lines had eliminated many shorter routes and replaced them with diesel bus lines. In two other cases, trackless trolleys (electric buses) replaced the streetcars. Would trolleys survive? The advent of the Los Angeles Metropolitan Transit Authority in 1958 offered streetcar riders faint hope. Within two years (1960) only PCC cars were plying the streets of Los Angeles.

Not only were the PCCs rolling smartly but they were doing a good business on five lines as late as 1962. But the MTA seemed unimpressed with the arithmetic and Los Angeles MTA General Chairman C. M. Gilless sounded the death knell with a simple statement: "The streetcar is no longer a practical public transportation vehicle, except in peculiar circumstances."

Early in 1962 Gilless announced that all Los Angeles trolley lines would be motorized within three years. "Every major city in the country," Gilless asserted, "has already abandoned, or is planning to abandon, its streetcars and trolley coaches." Gilless was wrong on several counts; even today several municipalities are operating trolleys and electric buses. But it is irrelevant. The Los Angeles MTA had capitulated to the auto industry.

A number of fatuous rationales were paraded before the public to persuade riders that, no, they really didn't need those neat trolleys after all. Expensive maintenance, difficulty in obtaining parts, and inflexibility—all charges successfully refuted in Toronto and in countless European cities where trolleys continue to flourish—were cited as excellent reasons for dispatching the last remaining 162 PCC cars to the scrap heap.

Twenty years earlier the Los Angeles Railway had operated twenty-five streetcar lines, utilizing more than a thousand cars; in 1963 the city's trams were declared null and void. The fateful day was March 31, 1963, when the last PCCs gracefully rolled into the carbarns, never to be seen again in revenue service. Los Angeles became the largest all-bus city in the United States. The scenario was similar to that enjoyed by the interurbans as they rolled to their death in 1961. A transit commentator who covered the tragedy for *Headlights* magazine wrote:

"During their last weeks [Los Angeles] streetcars received more public attention than they had enjoyed in many years. Hardly a day passed without one or more items on the subject in the newspapers or on television."

As the curtain fell, a rare touch of irony was evoked by the MTA. PCC car 3002, the oldest car in service, had a face painted on the front end with huge tears dripping from its eyes. The "Teardrop Trolley" also had large, colorful letters painted on its sides with the message: "Goodby Forever, Old Sweetheart and Pals!"

On March 30, 1963, the Greater Los Angeles Press Club held a trolley "wake" on PCC 3002, returning on a new bus. As the newsmen walked away from the rear of 3002 they read the message painted on its back: "So Long." By nightfall crowds lined the streets where the last trolleys would roll. "Along with the sadness," noted one observer, "excitement was also evident as streetcars ran over fireworks and noise torpedoes like in the good old days."

Motormen, their wives, and children also attended the wake. One trolley driver, noticing a motorman friend coming in the opposite direction, mournfully cried out: "Oh, no! Not you, too!"

The power on the Los Angeles trolley lines was finally turned off at 5:04 P.M. on March 31, 1963, just a few days after the twenty-sixth anniversary of delivery of the first PCC streamliners to the Los Angeles Railway Company. As the diesels began smelling up the streets of Southern California, the princely PCCs were shunted to the used (trolley) car lot and put up for sale. The magnificent all-electrics purchased after World War II in the days when it appeared that Los Angeles transit planners really believed in streetcars went for a mere $2,000 each, while the older models sold for $1,500. One sentimental trolley buff brought a bugle along and sounded taps while a motorman leaned over and kissed tram 3081 good-by.

Nobody captured the irony of the trolley-to-bus changing-of-the-guard better than CBS newsman Robert Trout, who told a nationwide audience about the death of the Los Angeles streetcar system. "It was a natural move for the city to make," Trout wryly observed, "considering that *the streetcars were faster, smoother, quieter, and did not produce as much smog.*"

Others, such as motorman Earl Miller ("I had a lump in my throat"), shared Trout's sentiments. As the streamliners were sold off to companies in such diverse precincts as Egypt and Chile, more and more citizens realized that Los Angeles had committed a colossal blunder. "One of the nation's longest and most interesting local street railway systems is gone permanently," said a Californian who watched two PCC cars loaded on a freighter en route to Chile.

No sooner had Los Angeles' trolleys been exiled than the politicians, planners, and all those people who come so well armed with 20–20 hindsight, began clamoring for what had been lost. Pollution was bad and getting worse, the number of automobiles was increasing, and the General Motors fleet was hardly inspiring dancing at the bus stops. So, the ironies went into the transit fire and out of it came a proposal by the Los Angeles Metropolitan Transit Authority for (wonder of wonders!) construction of a sixty-four-mile, two-rail rapid transit system. According to the MTA blueprints, it would extend from Van Nuys in the San Fernando Valley to Long Beach and from West Los Angeles to El Monte. In November 1963 the cost of the project was put at $669,000,000. Streetcar supporters enjoyed a sardonic laugh when MTA General Chairman Gilless said, "The bus system cannot be considered an adequate answer to the transportation needs of Los Angeles because the buses are the victim of the same congestion that faces the automobile."

Almost annually, it seemed, Los Angelenos were fed rapid transit carrots which produced nothing but hot air. In 1964 the Southern California Rapid Transit District (SCRTD) replaced the Los Angeles Metropolitan Transit Authority under a law passed by the California legislature. According to the widely ballyhooed legislation, the SCRTD would have "sufficient power and authority to solve the transportation problems in the area and to provide the needed mass rapid transit system."

The expectation was that SCRTD would develop a general regional plan for a rapid transit system in the manner of the San Francisco Bay Area Rapid Transit District (BART). On paper it looked good, but the track record of Los Angeles was so deplorable only an optimist could see any light at the end of the tunnel. Transit critic Jeffrey Moreau was not that optimist. Viewing Los Angeles' attempts at developing such a rapid transit plan a year later (1965), Moreau minced no words. "*Incompetence, apathy,* and *disagreement;* three words that come to mind in reviewing the events that have transpired in attempting to establish a workable rapid transit plan for Los Angeles."

Writing in the July 1965 edition of *Headlights*, Moreau lashed out at those who had promoted diesel buses over interurbans and PCC streetcars. "Today," wrote Moreau, "as a monument to the folly of mass transit in Los Angeles, the mile-long (Pacific Electric Railway subway) tube sits unused, while thousands of motorists sit fuming amid automobile strangulation."

Zeroing in on the duplicity of the Los Angeles Metropolitan Transit Authority, Moreau pointed out how the MTA had been created with the express purpose of coordinating existing transit facilities in the many cities surrounding Los Angeles and developing a rapid transit system for the area. The MTA not only failed in its obligation to the public but also missed the boat when it came to hiring responsible officials to mastermind the master plan. "The first event that cast gloom upon the project," said Moreau, "was the retention of the bus-minded and bus-oriented management of the former Los Angeles Transit Lines, for the new LAMTA system. Next, instead of incorporating any of the existing standard gauge suburban electric services into the proposed rapid transit network, LAMTA, at its earliest possible opportunity, converted these services to motor coach operations."

Two less-than-modest attempts to upgrade service on the Long Beach interurban line had been used by LAMTA to "prove" that the Authority still was being fair to rail transit. Hard-nosed critics, such as Moreau, were not impressed. "Those two feeble attempts," said Moreau, "could have been merely a smoke screen tactic designed to cover up the plans for motor coach conversion on this heavily used commuter line."

One might also label the avid debate among Los Angeles' politicians and transit planners over a future rapid transit line a "smoke screen," so many decibels were produced, so much smoke was created—and so little tangible progress came of it.

The one crusader for a return to sensible, pollution-free rail service was State Senator Tom Rees, who proposed two major bills: the first would have provided authority for the SCRTD to impose a half-cent tax on auto registrations for a one-year period, in order to raise money for payment of engineering costs on the suggested system. A second bill would have placed on the ballot for public approval a one percent tax to be imposed for approximately forty years to finance the system of duo-rail trains, operating in major transit corridors throughout the Los Angeles area.

Under reasonable conditions, the bills might have had a better than 50–50 chance of passing; but this was Southern California, and the oil-freeway-auto lobby was mightier than mighty. On May 11, 1965, the bills collided with the Senate Transportation Committee and lost. In his analysis of the defeat, Moreau explained: "Senator Randolph Collier's (committee chairman Collier is the 'father' of the California freeway system) objections to motorists being taxed to support a rapid transit system were a major factor in the slowdown. Collier, himself, was under pressure from the Automobile Club of Southern California, mobile home organizations, and the Motor Dealers Association to keep the gas tax at its present level." Six days later the Los Angeles City Council rejected support of the Rees bills. The bills never reached the floor of the California legislature; they were wiped out in the Transportation Committee.

"We might as well write off Los Angeles rapid transit," said Senator Rees in his postmortem. "The system will become a bus company, and a mediocre bus company."

But nothing said it better for the motor-car, motor-bus machinations than a headline in the Los Angeles *Examiner* on May 27, 1965, less than three weeks after the rapid transit plan was put to rest: TWO-DECK FREEWAYS—PLAN TO END JAMS IN LA.

It was the ultimate in absurd proposals; but not the least surprising, considering California's record on rapid transit since 1946. Senator Collier asserted in May 1965 that "preliminary engineering studies have been conducted [for two-deck freeways] and have confirmed that the plan is feasible."

To which Jeffrey Moreau added a postscript: "Further comment on the rapid transit plans for Los Angeles would be superfluous. Or is it ridiculous?"

Sublime might best describe what followed. In January 1972, more than six years after the grandiose rail project was erased, construction began on exclusive bus lanes along the San Bernardino Freeway from Los Angeles to El Monte. Ironically, this marked the first high-speed mass transit in this direction since the Pacific Electric interurbans vacated the same right-of-way in 1950. Adding further absurdity to it all was the tab: $27,800,000. And this for a mere eleven miles of busway! Is it a wonder that Los Angeles had become in twenty years the laughingstock of the transit world?

Some indefatigable warriors still believed that a rail system could be laid out in Southern California. In fact, a subway-elevated proposal was suggested that would link Union Station in Los Angeles with Watts. Another proposal suggested utilization of existing railroad trackage for rapid transit. But by 1973, it had finally become apparent to the so-called sentinels of the electorate—the press—that something was very wrong with the manner in which Los Angeles transit planners were doing their job. Newsmen, among others, looked back and realized that in 1964 the Southern California Rapid Transit District was created *to design and build a rapid transit system for the Los Angeles area*. It suddenly dawned upon editorialists that the SCRTD had done virtually nothing for rapid transit. And on February 5, 1973, when the SCRTD decided to temporarily defer extensive work toward rapid transit, it finally provoked an editorial response from the Los Angeles *Times*, which branded the decision a "Reverse Gear Transit Plan." Still another editorial comment put it equally harshly:

The SCRTD has shown the public that it has no interest in anything but buses, a condition long surmised but previously unsupported. A statewide sales tax on gasoline had been invoked which was supposed to be used for rapid transit. Yet, the SCRTD noted that the $32,000,000 received in 1972 from the tax would *not* be used for rapid transit but instead be used to continue operations of the bus system. So much for taxing gasoline to improve rail rapid transit!

A day after the announcement, California Senate President Pro Tem James R. Mills, the man who had drafted the legislation for the gasoline sales tax, charged SCRTD officials with misusing public funds. Mills charged that the sales tax was intended to be applied 75 percent to rapid transit capital improvements and 25 percent for operating costs. Mills demanded that a new agency replace SCRTD and told reporters: "I am satisfied you are never going to have a rapid transit system if it is left up to SCRTD. The SCRTD is in the bus business and that is where its attention is directed." The SCRTD was also withered with criticism over its shabby job of "separating" the bus lanes on the El Monte busway. (The lanes were separated from other freeway lanes only by an emergency parking strip.) It was speculated that the cynical plan was eventually to open the bus lanes to motor car use.

As the seventies approached mid-decade, there was evidence that Los Angelenos were beginning to realize that the area's problem was not moving vehicles from one place to another but rather moving people. The tangential dilemma was cleaning the air. "From an air pollution standpoint," commented one expert, "Southern California has been informed that drastic steps must be taken toward mass transit." Further impetus to this line of thinking was given following the Arab oil boycott of 1974 when cities such as Los Angeles and Houston learned how devastating a prolonged fuel drought would be to them as compared to cities with comprehensive rapid transit lines such as New York.

In November 1974 voters in Los Angeles were given a rare opportunity when Proposition A was placed on the ballot on Election Day. The proposition gave voters of Los Angeles County the opportunity to spend $4.7 billion on 145 miles of fixed-guideway rapid transit and on improvements to the existing Southern California Rapid Transit District bus system. According to the plan, the network of new routes would link almost every portion of the county with any other area. Target date for completion was placed at 1982.

A visitor from another planet, unfamiliar with the Southern California mentality, would have assumed that Proposition A would win overwhelming approval. For one thing, it made sense economically, ecologically, and energy-wise. For another thing the campaign for rapid transit was led by Los Angeles' mayor, Tom Bradley. And there was the matter of simple arithmetic. San Francisco voters were paying $212 per family a year to support their magnificent BART rapid transit line; Los Angelenos were told that the average family would pay $70 a year to support their Rapid Transit District.

Final results showed 832,423 voters in favor, 963,861 against.

Excuses for the defeat were almost as plentiful as cars on the freeways. Respected transit critic William D. Middleton offered several reasons:

The pro-rapid transit drive led by Mayor Bradley never really seemed to get off the ground; the opposition drive—led by seventeen area mayors and eighteen chambers of commerce—seemed to do much better; there was opposition to the "regressive" nature of a sales tax financing measure; there was opposition to more taxes of any kind.

Also it was a reaction against RTD [Rapid Transit District] because of the strike of over two months' duration (immediately preceding the election); people didn't like the lack of specifics (i.e., mode, priorities) of the RTD proposals; people were afraid of the eventual cost, since there was no firm federal commitment; and, finally, I'm sure there are plenty down there who still think freeways and nothing else are just fine.

So, after more than twenty attempts and three area-wide referendums in a decade, Los Angeles looked to the 1980s without any genuine hope of achieving status as a rapid transit major leaguer in a class with its rivals in New York, Chicago, Boston, and Philadelphia.

Surely, there are those in Southern California who realize the absurdity of the situation. Newspapers in Los Angeles actively supported mass transit plans through the seventies, and from time to time, the average citizen showed more than a passing interest in curing the area's people-moving ills. But history has shown that there is little cause for optimism when rapid transit proposals are discussed in Greater Los Angeles. So, pollution worsens, freeway jams thicken, and motorists more and more consider the "degrading ignominy," as one transit critic put it, of forsaking personal mobility for a faster trip to work on a train.

If the soul of Los Angeles could speak today, one can just hear the words: "PCCs, Blimp cars, Pacific Electric tracks. Where are you now that I need you today?"

19

Growth of Mass Transit in Other Major Cities— San Francisco, Chicago, Baltimore, and Philadelphia

No city in the world is more synonymous with mass transit than San Francisco and its cable cars. Paeans of praise for the remarkable little vehicles are heard from transit experts to tunesmiths such as Tony Bennett, who warbled about ". . . the little cable cars . . . go half-way to the stars. . . ." Certainly, the Golden Gate has much to be proud of in terms of its well-balanced combination—subway, trolley, bus—of equipage and the cable cars which pioneered the switch from horsecars to modern transit.

Long before Gottlieb Daimler began tinkering with the internal combustion engine, Andrew Hallidie had designed and built the first of his cable cars, and they proved instantly that they could negotiate the city's perilous hills. Hallidie, like a true Scot, built his cable cars to last. And it is a tribute to Hallidie's remarkable ingenuity that this system is still running today.

Likewise, it is a tribute to San Francisco, a municipality that has retained its cable car system when other cities such as Seattle, Chicago, St. Louis, and Denver abandoned it for more traditional means of transport. It's even more remarkable that San Francisco still operates three lines—California, Powell-Mason, Powell-Hyde—when you consider that the traumatic San Francisco earthquake of 1906 wasted the city's vast cable system. So extensive was the damage that it was considered more economical to switch from cable car operation to electric traction rather than invest heavily in a totally new cable car project. More than two hundred new electric streetcars were ordered and the cable cars became secondary to trolleys in the San Francisco transit scheme but certainly not out of the picture.

Although some cost-conscious modern planners urged the abolition of the San Francisco cable cars, they continued to zig and zag around Clay Street, California Street, and four other steep hills right up to the outbreak of World War II, when the San Francisco transit system was tested to the limits. The lines remained operable and, despite their age, seemed to inspire more interest than ever in postwar years. One of the most surprising testimonials was delivered by the automobile-oriented *Road and Track Magazine*, which assigned writer Tony Hogg to give the San Francisco cable car a "road test." Hogg was amazed by his experience and said of the cable car: ". . . its superlative performance and unsurpassed beauty of line stands head and shoulders above all other machines."

Hogg went on to extol the vehicle as the ultimate town car, with instant acceleration, fantastic wear, all-weather traction, phenomenal passenger capacity, and an unmatched degree of customer loyalty. He wrote in his review:

As a basic package, the Powell car, due mainly to the purity of its original design, has remained unchanged since its conception. The total lack of model changes, or even recognition changes, is most refreshing, and we were pleased to note that the factory has steadfastly refused over the years to introduce the almost inevitable Gran Turismo model . . . we confidently predict that it will continue to withstand the test of time.

How right he was! In the early 1970s San Francisco saluted the hundredth anniversary of its cable cars with a gala centennial shindig and even considered spending more than $2,000,000 for an extension of the Mason-Powell line.

In 1979, $10,000,000 of San Francisco Municipal Railway Company's $300,000,000 modernization program went to renovating cable cars, according to Director of Public Services Robert Rockwell.

Plans include restoring the cable cars themselves, as well as gutting and rebuilding the storage building where cars are stored, repaired, and inspected. Rockwell said the entire cable car system will shut down from May to October 1980, while a new motive power system will be installed and the motors that run the cable itself will be replaced. The renovation process was suggested in a study completed by Chinn-Hensolt, Inc., an engineering firm hired to look into functions of the cable car system. The San Francisco cable car had not only become a national landmark but a transportation institution and, despite the high cost of operation, promised to live forever.

Nevertheless, the great San Francisco earthquake did change the city's transit industry. When the Municipal Railway was created in 1909 it was evident that the trolley would be king not merely for a day but for at least decades along the Bay. The Municipal Railway (or MUNI) competed with the Market Street Railway Company, which continued to operate independently until 1944, when it was bought and annexed by MUNI. During the height of electric traction service each line operated a pair of tracks, side by side, on Market Street in downtown San Francisco. Market Street Railway trolleys rolled on the inner two tracks while MUNI's trams ran on the outer rails. Market remained a four-track trolley boulevard until 1945, when the trackage was cut in half.

In addition to its sprawling trolley network, San Francisco luxuriated in a vast system of interurban feeder lines from assorted outposts in the California countryside. The "Key Route," for example, founded by Francis Marion "Borax" Smith (of 20 Mule Team Borax fame), got its start at the turn of the century when Smith founded the San Francisco, Oakland, and San Jose Railway. "Its trans-Bay ferry service," commented interurban historian Jim Walker, "and fast electric trains wrought great change to the communities along its routes, and prompted rival Southern Pacific to electrify, at great expense, its own suburban service."

Smith's empire became known as the Key Route because, viewed from above, its long trestle from shore to the mid-Bay pier suggested an old hotel door key. The company soon adoped the key as its symbol. On the left side the pier was depicted and on the right were three circles—Berkeley, Piedmont, and Oakland.

By any standards the Key Route was impressive. Its rolling stock, beginning with the wooden, railroad-roofed electric cars with pantograph current-collectors, remained formidable to the end. In addition, multimillionaire Borax Smith never omitted an amenity, no matter what the cost, which explains construction of the massive, handsome Key Route Inn at 22d and Broadway in Oakland, among other nonrailway projects. Smith also built the Claremont Hotel at the end of the 55th Street line, developed Piedmont Park for the 40th Street line, and Idora Park in North Oakland.

The halcyon years of electric traction on the Key Line spanned the twenties even though buses were soon to intrude upon and pollute the then glorious interurban picture. In 1930 the Key Line operated twenty streetcar and sixteen bus lines. Nevertheless, the interurban picture was brightened when, on January 14, 1939, East Bay Terminal, the bridge railway's major station at 1st and Mission, served as base for the dedication of the trans-Bay rail line. No fewer than five trans-Bay trains rolled over the San Francisco–Oakland Bay Bridge. At this point the Bay Area was in a superb position to develop a massive rail transit link throughout the area. The Key Line was not only strategically located but it also owned first-rate rolling stock, having purchased smart-looking, sturdy articulated trains from the St. Louis Car Company.

Tragically, the Key System and its numerous subsidiaries were hard hit by the Great Depression. A number of trolley lines were abandoned, and in 1946, the corporations were sold to National City Lines. This proved to be the death knell for the Key Route. National City Lines owned many other transit operations and was noted for its pro-bus policies. Thus, on April 20, 1958, the last five trans-Bay rail lines were converted to bus operation. The bridge rails were removed and the Bay bridge was made one-way on each deck to accommodate automobiles. In one of the sadder and more expensive ironies of American transit history, Bay Area residents apparently realized their colossal faux pas in allowing the cars to roll where trains once did. They voted to create the Bay Area Rapid Transit District (BART), which would ultimately build a subway costing billions where the Key System once operated.

Fortunately, San Francisco's cable cars and trolleys were never quite wiped out. Diesel and electric buses did intrude, to be sure, but streamlined PCC-type streetcars survived World War II and continued to attract a significant clientele. San Francisco has one of the highest per capita transit riderships of any city in the United States. . . . "One reason why the PCC has survived in San Francisco while it met a premature death in dozens of other United States cities," said Alan R. Lind, "is the heavy riding habit of citizens of San Francisco, and the many short trips which they make via streetcar, trolley bus, gas bus, and cable car. Another factor in the retention of both trolley buses and streetcars is the municipal hydroelectric power supply, which feeds electricity to the streetcars and trolley buses of San Francisco as well as supplying other municipal needs."

The trolleys have survived mainly because San Franciscans appreciate them and because they have been given extensive private rights-of-way. They have even survived the growth of the BART subway and the problem of age, wear, and tear on the venerable PCC streamliners.

Keeping the trolleys in good shape should be solved by the first shipment of futuristic trolleys (LRVs) which MUNI began testing late in 1978. However, chronic problems with the Boeing Vertol–manufactured trams left a pall over the prospects for the LRV, so the durable and lovable PCC cars continue to ply the streets of San Francisco more than thirty years after the original cars were delivered by the St. Louis Car Company.

San Francisco's commendable blend of all forms of surface and underground transport could have been matched by Chicago had the Windy City chosen to retain some vestiges of its once extensive cable car operation and equally notable trolley network. This, however, was not to be, although Chicago's contemporary transit operation has its roots dating back to 1882, when the Chicago City Railway opened its first cable car to revenue service. Running from Madison Street to 21st Street along State Street, the premiere was hailed by 300,000 spectators and an enthusiastic review in the Chicago *Tribune*. To wit: "The cars were covered with flags and banners, and in spite of the general prediction that they would jump off the track, it was agreed universally that they were the airiest and most graceful vehicles of the sort ever seen in Chicago or anywhere else."

The rave notices were not short-lived. Chicagoans loved their cable railways and promoters responded by building miles and miles of cable car track until the Windy City boasted one of the most impressive systems in the world. Unlike San Francisco, Chicago is burdened with fierce winter storms and these were regarded as a threat to the success of the Chicago cable lines. But the cable cars were more than a match for the blizzards. They were actually excellent snow fighters. On more than one occasion when all the steam railroads entering Chicago were tied up by a heavy snowfall, the cable cars ran as usual, and they plowed the only clear paths pedestrians and horses could find. It has been said, in fact, that the Chicago City Railway never lost a single trip because of snow, frost, or ice.

Nevertheless, the cable cars were to enjoy only a relatively brief career in Chicago. Trolleys became the rage not long after the turn of the century, and by 1906, when the State Street cable line folded, the efficient little vehicles were virtually extinct. What followed was a spate of grand growth by both the

Chicago City Railway and the Chicago Railways Company, which two merged into Chicago Surface Lines in 1913. In the early 1920s its operation entailed 3,500 trams, 1,070 track miles, and 1½ billion passengers annually.

Its impressive capacity was not enough to handle all of Chicago's commuters. An alternative to surface transit was inaugurated late in the nineteenth century when the South Side Elevated Railroad went into service on June 6, 1892. This was followed in 1895 by the Metropolitan West Side Elevated Railroad. At first the Chicago els, like their New York City counterparts, employed a tiny steam locomotive to pull the passenger coaches, but eventually the ubiquitous Frank J. Sprague, the father of modern electric railway transportation, was imported to install his multiple-unit system on the electrified els. After a couple of minor mishaps, the Sprague system was set in motion, and Chicago's els became permanently and successfully electrified.

The elevated lines in the Windy City became renowned not merely for their successful adaptation of Sprague's multiple-unit cars, nor for the high density of traffic, but also for the design of the elevated structure in the downtown section. Horseshoe-shaped when viewed from above, the el came to be known as the Loop and Chicago's shopping area soon received a similar appellation. Completed in 1897, during rush hour the Loop appeared to be bearing an endless necklace of el cars. What's most important, the Chicago els worked, and by the early 1900s they accounted for ninety-one miles of track. Unfortunately, Chicagoans were so infatuated with their el and its Loop that they completely neglected to build necessary subways for several decades.

While New York City, Boston, and Philadelphia were developing underground transit systems early in the twentieth century, Chicago seemed content with its elevated lines and surface transportation, with special emphasis on trolley cars. Not until 1938 (by which time New York City had three full-blown systems, the IRT, BMT, and IND) did Chicago begin to build its first subway under State Street. The five-mile line did not utilize the cut-and-cover technique, long employed in New York City and other metropolises. Instead, the Chicago engineers chose to construct twin tubes forty-four feet below street level and excavate by tunneling.

When it came time to burrow under the Chicago River, a double steel tube was constructed as long as the river's width, covered with concrete and sealed at both ends. It was placed in position above the proposed subway route and then lowered into a trench which had been dug. Later the ends were connected with the existing land portions of the subway. In 1943, some five years after digging had begun, Chicago's subway opened, linking the North Side and South Side els. Realizing that the subway was virtually a must for the city, Chicago set about the business of building more underground lines, completing the four-mile Milwaukee-Dearborn-Congress route in 1951; this under the aegis of the Chicago Transit Authority (CTA), which was organized in 1947.

While Chicago invested heavily in electric rail transportation in the first quarter of the twentieth century, it also managed to build one of the most impressive trolley fleets the world has known. By 1929 Chicago Surface Lines operated more than 1,000 single-track miles of line and carried more than 1.6 billion passengers each year. Until 1930, Chicago's fleet comprised 3,639 trolleys and eight motor buses.

In 1930, however, policy changed when Chicago Surface Lines ordered six forty-passenger trolley buses from the St. Louis Car Company. Soon Chicago was going for trackless trolleys in a big way. Four lines were opened in 1930 and a fifth in 1931. Almost overnight Chicago became the largest trolley bus operator in the United States, with forty-one vehicles servicing seventeen miles of route, and was still growing.

Nevertheless, Chicago Surface Lines maintained an interest in trolleys, and in the early 1930s ordered an experimental streamliner (preceding the PCC cars which were ordered in 1936) from both Pullman and the Brill Company. Only one such car was built—#4001—and it made its debut in July 1934. After a short career it was shunted off to the storage yards and Chicago concentrated on the already widely touted PCC cars. Chicago Surface Lines placed large orders for the PCC cars and, at one time, intended to outfit its roster with no fewer than 1,036 of the speedy, quiet, stylish vehicles. But in 1947 the Chicago Surface Lines ceased to exist; the private company was succeeded by the publicly owned Chicago Transit Authority.

The new Chicago Transit Authority (CTA) would completely reverse what had been a firm policy of continuing to use trolleys, although on a more limited basis than in pre–World War II years.

"Even though the PCC car was undoubtedly to be the backbone of the CSL's postwar system," Alan R. Lind told this author, "had CSL survived long into the postwar era, it might have been used on a maximum of fifteen to twenty lines out of one hundred or so streetcar lines in Chicago. Thus, eighty or so lines would have been converted to motor bus or trolley bus even under the most optimistic CSL plans. Even if CSL had purchased 1,036 PCC cars, this would have replaced less than one-third of its older cars, which numbered 3,517 in 1943. The balance of the equipment needed for full modernization would have had to be rubber-tired."

The CTA wasted precious little time reversing that philosophy. One of its first official acts was to cancel a contract with the St. Louis Car Company for the PCC trolleys. Construction of the streamliners was so far advanced, however, that the Authority had no choice but to accept the order. More troubles were in store for the trolley system: the CTA was suffering labor problems. The unions demanded and won hefty raises, which the CTA, in turn, passed on to passengers by boosting fares. Finding itself in a financial pickle, the CTA began searching for ways to save money and, not surprisingly, turned on the trolleys once more.

The CTA "solution" was a curious plan. It hoped to modernize both surface and rapid transit lines simultaneously. To begin with, the Authority offered the St. Louis Car Company and Pullman-Standard a deal whereby the car builders would buy back the PCC cars they were finishing. The builders, in turn, would scrap the car bodies but salvage the motors, trucks, control systems, seats, and other items.

From the salvaged items, the St. Louis Car Company would build an equivalent number of PCC-type rapid transit (subway-el) cars. It was estimated that the salvage value of the PCC trolley car components, most of which had been in service for several years, according to Alan R. Lind, came to $16,000 per car, which was enough to purchase a new diesel bus. The net effect for the CTA was that it was getting a rapid transit car and a bus by turning in its postwar PCC cars.

Clearly, the CTA did not do the right thing. The diesel buses that replaced the sleek, attractive trolleys contributed a noxious odor to the streets of the Windy City, and not surprisingly, the buses were by their very nature short-lived, built for replacement. Where San Francisco succeeded, Chicago failed.

Plans to move Chicago's trains underground and scrap the old elevated commuter-train tracks have been kept in their infant stages by conservationists and historical groups fighting to save the famous el that has served the Loop—the heart of downtown Chicago—since 1897.

A proposal to join Cleveland and Washington, D.C., the only two American cities with direct rapid transit access to their airports, by building an extension to O'Hare Airport is also a possible change to look for in Chicago's rapid transit future.

An experimental change that began in 1965 brought in so much revenue and patronage that it is now a permanent part of the Chicago rapid transit scene. The Skokie Swift, a five-mile high-speed line between Howard Street, Chicago, and Dempster Street, Skokie, was made a fixture of the CTA the following year.

All of the improvements to Chicago's transit system are still in the planning stages, leaving them a long way to go to catch up to cities like San Francisco, where mass transit is varied and efficient.

Not unlike Chicago, Baltimore is a municipality that once showed great promise in terms of transit flexibility. It began with horsecars, progressed to cable cars, and even had a downtown elevated structure on which trolleys from the Lake Roland Elevated Railway rolled. Some four thousand feet long, the elevated was double-tracked for its entire length. As originally built, the steelwork of the el followed the contour of the land, resulting in a series of dips and rises.

Baltimore's flimsy elevated was, nonetheless, historically significant because its trial on May 3, 1893, marked the first time in the United States that a car had been operated on an elevated line with electric power. At the time, els in both New York City and Sioux City, Iowa, employed steam engines.

As the city grew, so did the traction system, and in 1899 the street railways of Baltimore were consolidated into a single system. One newspaper report estimated that the street railways of Baltimore were worth $70,000,000. Whatever the actual value, United Railways entered the twentieth century with optimism that soon would be tempered by disaster.

On Sunday, February 7, 1904, a fire erupted in downtown Baltimore that would ultimately waste a good portion of the city's business district. The conflagration raged all day and into the night, coming perilously close to the company's offices in the Continental Building. Fearful officials summoned flat cars and ordered that all valuable documents be evacuated from the office. Everything from cash to records was transferred to the company's Madison Avenue carhouse. Still, the fire went on into the next morning, when, undaunted, the company's dispatcher gave the cue for the trolleys to begin their runs. It was, however, a futile gesture, since the fire was about to gut the trolley firm's main powerhouse and, soon, juice for nearly all thirty-four lines had ceased being transmitted over the wires. The fire wasn't brought under control until Tuesday, by which time more than one hundred blocks of the inner city had been involved in the blaze, causing damage totaling $125,000,000. The trolley operation suffered as much as any, with eight miles of overhead wire felled, the powerhouse ruined, the company office wiped out, and more than 110 cars stranded throughout the system. Most remarkable of all, a day later the company actually began operating streetcars again—only 10 percent of normal service—and by March had everything status quo ante.

Under the United banner the trolleys of Baltimore were expected to thrive. This, however, was not to be the case. Streetcars were almost constantly teetering on the brink of disaster. Traction interests were especially foolish in their failure to battle their chief competitor, the automobile, for a place in the sun. The streetcar companies continually permitted their private rights-of-way to be violated by other traffic. This, more than anything else the companies did, contained the seeds of self-destruction.

Not the least of a number of other egregious blunders United made was the purchase of a fleet of tiny Birney cars whose lack of speed caused rush hour delays. Experimental cars, which were subsequently tried, also failed. Finally, a series of versatile vehicles were put on the track in the late 1920s. But the battle for breathing room with the car was being lost.

Michael R. Farrell, in his book *Who Made All Our Streetcars Go*, wrote:

> Probably the most compelling reason for the demise of the streetcars in Baltimore was that they came to be regarded as intruders on the very roadways which in many cases had originally been their own private domain. Time after time the companies agreed to sacrifice their private rights-of-way so as to enable the roadbeds to be widened, thus surrendering the advantages of operating on an unobstructed pathway.
>
> As time went on, the manner in which many of the broad highways had originated was forgotten, and the motorists began to resent the curse of slippery rails, safety pylons, and ponderous articulated units. With the rise of the expressway syndrome during the 1950s, this type of roadway was hailed as the salvation of the city from its traffic problems.

Trolley supporters had hoped that the salvation of the streetcar network would be the advent of the PCC cars. When the streamliners began to proliferate on Baltimore tracks in the late 1930s, the public reacted with enthusiasm. When war came, more people were riding the Baltimore trams than had been the case for years. The street railways were still the most important factor in the public transportation picture.

Yet, less than two decades after the end of World War II, the streetcar system, which once boasted more than four hundred miles of track, was only a memory. Inept public officials showed astigmatic vision when it came to developing a sensible, balanced transit plan for one of the nation's most important cities. "The real culprits in the strangulation of downtown Baltimore," said Farrell, "were the city administrations, which, from the days of Thomas Swann on, looked upon the street railways as a means of filling the municipal coffers, rather than as arteries to Baltimore's heart, whose deterioration would threaten the existence of the entire city."

The threat became a reality when alleged traffic expert Henry "Barnes Dance" Barnes (later to become New York City's traffic commissioner) was imported from Denver and National City Lines obtained control of the Baltimore Transit Company. "Under the combined onslaught of Barnes and National City Lines," Farrell asserted, "the streetcar tracks which still connected all areas of Metropolitan Baltimore were, in the period between June 1947 and September 1958 (save only the #8 and #15 lines), covered under a blanket of black asphalt. . . ."

By November 1963 the last trolley line in Baltimore had been buried. The streets were covered with autos and more autos, diesel buses and trucks. A city that had erred was now paying for its sins. "Here we are today," Farrell concluded, "like the lemming, about to be swallowed up in a sea of traffic congestion unless pollution gets us first."

Baltimore would have been better served if it had looked to its neighbor not very far to the north, Philadelphia, for hints about melding trolleys, electric buses, and diesel buses, not to mention subways and elevated lines, into a comprehensive if not perfect transportation unit. While Baltimore never built a subway and had only the tiniest of elevated structures, it did once have numerous streetcar, trolley bus, and traditional gas or diesel bus lines. While Baltimore lopped off most of its nonpolluting vehicles, dispatching them to the scrap heap, Philadelphia has retained much of an admirable transportation tradition dating back to 1792 when turnpike toll roads were introduced. In 1831 the first horse omnibus line ran on Chestnut Street between Sixteenth and Second streets, providing an hourly service, and for a number of years thereafter omnibuses were the only regular means of local travel.

In 1858, Philadelphia's first horse railway was started by the Philadelphia and Delaware River Railroad on Fifth and Sixth streets from Kensington to Southwark. In time a number of other companies sprouted as Philadelphia's population soared beyond the 200,000 mark. Competition became so keen and haphazard that an organization called the Board of Presidents of Street Railway Companies was organized in 1859, remained active until 1895, and ultimately resulted in the United Traction Company.

While cities such as Boston and New York were experimenting with "newer" forms of transportation than horse-drawn vehicles, Philadelphia was also moving forward. In 1863 a steam dummy line was opened along Kensington Avenue between Kensington and Frankford. This was followed in 1877 by a steam line on Market Street between the Delaware River and the Permanent Exhibition Building in Fairmount Park. Neither system proved especially successful, compelling Philadelphians to take a crack at a cable car network. In April 1833 the first cable line was opened on Columbia Avenue from 23d Street to Fairmount Park by the Philadelphia Traction Company, which had been incorporated the same year. Three years later this line was extended to Market Street Ferry and subsequently in 1888 south from Market Street on 7th and 9th streets to McKean Street.

The limitations of cable car operations steered Philadelphia transit experts to look elsewhere for motive power late in the nineteenth century. In December 1892 the first electric cars were put on tracks in the City of Brotherly Love. So enthusiastic was the response to electric traction that horsecars were eliminated from the streets of Philadelphia by 1897 when the Callowhill Street Line was closed. Taking a cue from Boston and New York City, Philadelphia started work on a subway and elevated rapid transit line early in the twentieth century.

Construction of the first section of the Market Street Subway between 23d and 15th streets was started in 1903. The following year work on the elevated structure west of the Schuylkill River was started. A segment to 69th Street was completed in December 1906. Work on the subway east of 15th Street to 2d Street and on the Delaware Avenue section of the Market Street elevated was started in 1906, and the following year the subway-elevated service between 15th and 69th streets was opened for operation. The eastern end of the high-speed line under Market Street and over Delaware Avenue to South Street was opened on October 4, 1908, providing a subway-el line that now was 7.35 miles long.

In 1911 the Philadelphia Rapid Transit Company launched a program of rolling stock replacement which guaranteed a high standard of efficiency well into the 1920s. With few exceptions, Philadelphians rode modern, double-truck trolleys. Meanwhile, the demand for additional rapid transit brought about plans for the Frankford Elevated extension which was finally completed in November 1922, comprising 6½ miles of high-speed lines.

The flexibility of the Philadelphia Rapid Transit was evident in the early 1920s when its subsidiary, Philadelphia Rural Transit, began operating double-deck gasoline-powered buses over a route almost ten miles long. Another subsidiary, the Pennsylvania Rapid Transit Company, used electric buses over a six-mile route as a feeder to a number of intersecting crosstown trolleys.

Thanks to the astute operation of General Superintendent Thomas E. Mitten, the Philadelphia Rapid Transit became an operation that won nationwide acclaim both for its rolling stock and for its enlightened labor relations policies, which helped avert the strikes that plagued other streetcar companies. In 1923 Philadelphia's Rapid Transit unit owned more than three thousand cars, ran them over almost seven hundred miles of track, and carried more than 900,000,000 passengers annually. In 1928 another subway link opened—a new north-south Broad Street underground railway.

In addition to their excellent tram system as well as growing subway and el operations, Philadelphians were blessed with exceptionally useful interurban service. One such run was the Lehigh Valley Transit Company's Liberty Bell Route, between Philadelphia and Allentown, with a link to Norristown. The Philadelphia and Western interurbans, which touched such bases as Upper Darby and Strafford, achieved national renown in the 1930s when they introduced the then ultramodern Bullet cars to the system.

Not to be overlooked are the Philadelphia and West Chester Traction Company's Red Arrow trolleys. When the Chicago, North Shore and Milwaukee ceased operations in 1963, its two streamlined Electroliners were sold to the Red Arrow Lines. They were renamed Liberty Liners and put into rush hour service between Upper Darby and Norristown.

Where other cities capitulated to the fatuous Madison Avenue sloganeering that equated "progress" with a switch from electric traction to diesel bus, Philadelphia resisted the push and somehow maintained an excellent balance of rail to rubber through the World War II years and beyond. The Philadelphia Transportation Company, bucking the nationwide trend, proved what experts no longer believed possible, that a private organization could run a municipal transit system. Eventually, the Southeastern Pennsylvania Transportation Authority (SEPTA) took control of mass transit in the Philadelphia area but never eliminated entirely, as other cities did, the once great streetcar fleet. Philadelphia had some high-speed private right-of-way for some of its most important routes. The five subway-surface streetcar routes connecting Philadelphia's center city with west and southwest Philadelphia have a 2½-mile tunnel through the central business district. But even on the surface routes, streetcars seem better able to slip through the narrow streets than buses. More than 85 percent of SEPTA's tracks are on city streets, even in the downtown area.

Early in the 1970s SEPTA provided considerable hope to advocates of trolley transport. On paper at least, SEPTA took the position that the trolley cars "perform effectively as an alternative to the automobile." In practice, however, SEPTA's performance invited criticism. "Philadelphia's slovenly maintenance practices," wrote Lind, "extended beyond dilapidated car exteriors; the motors and control systems received equally poor attention. Compounding the problem was lack of adequate car barns and maintenance facilities."

The difficulties were further aggravated on October 23, 1975, when the venerable Woodland carbarn was totaled by fire. At a time when SEPTA was bragging that 180 PCC cars would be restored to peak operating condition, 60 PCC cars—including some that had just been rebuilt—were destroyed. The immediate problem was a serious car shortage at a time when no domestic firms were in the trolley-making business.

To plug some of the gaps on its trolley roster, SEPTA looked afield. Not long after the tragic fire, it obtained eleven all-electric St. Louis Car Company PCC trolleys from the Toronto Transportation Commission (which had purchased the cars from Kansas City in 1953), as well as nineteen all-electric PCC cars, built by Pullman-Standard. The latter fleet had originally been built in 1948 for the Birmingham, Alabama, tram system. Thus, Philadelphia had a PCC fleet of more than 300 cars, of which approximately 275 were operational at a given time. Without question, SEPTA still boasted the largest fleet of PCC cars in the United States.

Pessimists questioned whether Philadelphia could survive the carbarn fire and maintain its trolley fleet in reasonable condition; the evidence was that it could and would. By 1977 Philadelphia was being looked upon by transit critics such as Van Wilkins as one of the most remarkable urban-suburban areas on the continent in terms of traction. "Philadelphia," wrote Wilkins in the May 1977 edition of *Rail Classics* magazine, "probably provides more variety in electric operations than anywhere else in North America."

One of the most arresting aspects of the Philadelphia transit picture is its vast variety of rolling stock. Not only does SEPTA maintain a fleet of PCC streamliners but as late as 1977 was running the last Master Unit trolleys built by the J. G. Brill Company in the late 1920s, as well as the Brilliners, the closest thing to a PCC car built by the Brill factory. Add to that the Brill-designed Bullet cars, as well as conventional Brill third-rail commuter cars on the Norristown line. In addition there are the Electroliners, imported from the Chicago, North Shore, and Milwaukee; traditional Budd-built subway-elevated trains; PCC-type interurbans built by St. Louis Car Company in 1949 on the Red Arrow Division; and relatively new high-speed Budd cars serving the Lindenwold commuter line.

Philadelphia's mass transit operation has been vigorously aided by the Port Authority Transit Corporation (PATCO), one of the most successful rapid transit operations in North America. The Lindenwold Line, operated by the PATCO (a subsidiary of the Delaware River Port Authority), has won nationwide acclaim as an urban-suburban commuter train. Using as a nucleus a route connecting downtown Philadelphia with Camden, New Jersey, via the Benjamin Franklin Bridge, a line was built over former right-of-way of the Pennsylvania-Reading Seashore Lines, providing a total run of 14½ miles. As Van Wilkins reported:

New cars capable of 75 mph were built by Budd, large parking lots built at stations, and a system of financing developed which allows use of bridge tolls to pay costs not covered by fares. The result is a virtually automatic, high-speed transit line which is a resounding success. The parking lots are crowded, and motorists who choose not to use the train have an easier time because fewer cars crowd the bridge. Cars, stations, and right-of-way are immaculate, and the trains well patronized throughout the day.

PATCO opened five subway stations in Philadelphia and utilized a system whereby magnetic plastic tickets are dispensed from slot machines. The passenger inserts his ticket in a turnstile at the boarding station. It is returned to him for retention and insertion in another turnstile at his destination. Unfortunately, the beauty and efficiency of the Lindenwold Line is not shared by all of Philadelphia's rapid transit lines, especially the Broad Street subway.

Filthy to the point of unsightliness, the Broad Street subway runs the length of the city, north to south, with a short spur along Ridge Avenue to 8th and Market streets and a physical connection with PATCO. Despite its shortcomings, the Broad Street subway, as reviewed by Van Wilkins in *Rail Classics*, "is faster than transport on the surface, but otherwise has little to recommend it. . . . The Broad Street line does have one virtue. It connects with a number of surface trolley lines in the northern half of the city."

A pleasant surprise is the higher quality of the Frankford-Market subway-el. The line is cleaner, the service faster, although graffiti-defaced cars give a New York feel to the rolling stock.

Although SEPTA cannot match the Lindenwold Line in any respect, its Red Arrow rapid transit cars, operating to the suburbs of Norristown, Media, and Sharon Hill (as well as SEPTA's suburban bus lines), provide more than adequate transportation under the circumstances. Considering that the Bullet cars are almost fifty years old, they do a remarkable job of moving people, as do the Electroliners, and this provokes the question: Why doesn't Philadelphia operate the new LRVs manufactured in the Boeing Vertol plant right in the Philadelphia area itself?

The answer is a testimonial to the abject stupidity of mass transit planning in the United States. Although Philadelphia has the largest streetcar fleet in the nation it was overlooked in the design of the LRVs. The light rail vehicle built in the Boeing plant is an articulated car unsuitable for Philadelphia because of clearance problems. This, of course, was not an insurmountable problem; all the builders had to do in order to create a market right in their own backyard was to design and produce a *non*-articulated unit the size of the PCC cars operating on Philadelphia tracks. This, however, was not done, and SEPTA entered the 1980s proud of its trolleys even though they were PCC cars dating back to the era when Harry S Truman was President of the United States.

Philadelphia's loyalty to electric traction should not becloud the fact that, as in almost every municipality in the country, the diesel bus intruded upon the surface scene. Like Toronto, Philadelphia had its share of diesels, but in a one-on-one clash between trolley and bus, the trolley will inevitably emerge the winner where public opinion is concerned. In Philadelphia, fortunately, public opinion *was* heard when the Route 23 Trolley had to be abandoned in 1978 so that an extensive sewer pipe construction project could be built along portions of the trolley route. Traditionally in situations such as this, the trolley route not only is disrupted, it is discontinued—permanently. In this case there was good reason to expect the Route 23 run to become a diesel bus line forever. The PCC cars were relatively old and could not be replaced by new ones. The precedent set by transit companies in other cities suggested that the streetcar be shut down.

It was—but only for fifteen months. Philadelphians, who had grown to love their Route 23 Trolley, realized that the diesel bus could not match the performance of the streetcar, even if the tram was decades older than the buses. So, when the sewer construction was nearing completion, residents of North and South Philadelphia, center city, Tioga, Nicetown, Germantown, Mount Airy, Chestnut Hill and other neighborhoods where the twenty-five-mile Route 23 Trolley operated, demanded that it be restored to the tracks. And, lo and behold, it was! On October 28, 1978, the SEPTA PCC cars began rolling past skyscrapers and slums and mansions and malls. For a change, the diesel bus was defeated and a city administration admitted as much. "Buses," wrote Howard S. Shapiro in the Philadelphia *Inquirer,* "could not meet the challenge of Germantown Avenue. Their rubber tires jolted over the cobblestone surface and their engines strained to pull them up the street's steeper inclines. Passengers were constantly jostled." Not when the trolleys returned.

Where Philadelphia goes from here is a good question. One factor cannot be ignored: The city has maintained its streetcar service through extreme adversity and has proven that trolleys—in conjunction with subways, interurbans, and high-speed commuter lines—can work.

"Philadelphia," concluded transit critic Van Wilkins, "has an unusually complete and effective mass transit system. Those who use it daily, especially under Broad Street, may not see it in this light, but it is far superior to sitting in a cloud of carbon monoxide in a traffic jam as many of us from other cities are forced to do. . . . These [Philadelphia, Lindenwold, Norristown] routes show what can be done."

It is safe to assume that there will always be trolleys in Philadelphia. Of the twelve current trolley routes operating there, five are known as "subway routes," serving the West Philadelphia area. All five routes come to the same Central City terminus through a three-mile underground tunnel where a bus could not possibly operate. Those routes are in no danger of being converted.

Another sign that trolleys are in Philadelphia to stay is SEPTA's recent (1979) order of 140 new cars from a Japanese firm, Nissho-Iwai, a division of Kawasaki.

"There are no immediate plans to change the other seven routes," said Frank Friel, SEPTA's press officer, "although two of those have temporarily been converted to buses while we are in the process of rehabilitating the lines. The trolleys will probably return before 1980."

Friel said the trolleys are safe despite recent problems during the heavy snows in early February 1979. "Route 23, the largest trolley route in the world, runs from the heart of South Philadelphia up north to Chestnut Hill. During the snowstorms, automobiles were abandoned all over the tracks of South Philly. We were physically unable to run the trolleys down there until the cars were moved. It was five days before we resumed normal operations."

Although trolleys have their problems and bus maneuverability is often preferred in urban areas, SEPTA is convinced there are advantages to streetcars. "Trolleys run on electricity and don't pollute the way gasoline users do," said

Friel. "In the suburbs, where we have our own right-of-way and the lines are removed, for the most part, from other forms of traffic, the trolley is the most efficient form of transit."

An innovative and highly successful idea instituted on all forms of transit in the City Division on January 1, 1979, was the monthly and weekly pass. The so-called Gateway Transfer Program allows commuters to buy a pass card for the duration of a month or week for $22 and $6, respectively, and ride anywhere within the City Transit Division until the pass expires.

A Philadelphia market research group had predicted that sales of the passes would not exceed 15,000 until after April, but by the first week in February 20,000 copies of both passes were issued to customers. The Gateway program was a happy solution to commuters who were angered when fares rose from 45 to 50 cents in January.

"There are still limitations; the pass is good only in the city," Friel said. "But, hopefully, when we see how it works out, the program will spread to other divisions in the future."

Another improvement that SEPTA is proud of was introduced in response to complaints about passenger safety. In September 1978, SEPTA began paying the salaries of sixty-five policemen who were due to be laid off and added them to the Philadelphia Police Department's transit patrol. The action has resulted in an increased number of arrests and eased the minds of many commuters. "It is a program we hope to expand," said Friel.

Expansion is also on the minds of PACTO officials. The Board of Directors has approved the preliminary engineering tests necessary for the possible extension of the Lindenwold Line four miles eastward to Berlin, New Jersey. A new station, Woodcrest, was added to the line west of the existing Ashland Station and fifty new cars are under construction for delivery in 1979.

It appears that Philadelphians will continue to have their choice of new and varied mass transit systems in the future, all working side by side to meet the needs and desires of the city's commuters.

20

New York–How They Killed the Golden Subway

If New York City had continued to build subways at the same rate during the second three decades of this century as it did during the first thirty years, there would never have been a pollution problem in the metropolitan area, there would never be the chronic traffic congestion, and there would never have been thousands of lives lost. Had the presiding fathers of New York City not knuckled under to one man at several pivotal points during the late twenties, thirties, and forties, today Gotham would boast the most elaborate, efficient, safe, and practical transportation system per square mile in the world.

August Belmont's far-flung Interborough Rapid Transit System thrust New York ahead of its metropolitan rivals in the race for the best means of rapid transit. The IRT-BRT "Dual Contracts" provided another great leap forward, and finally, in the late twenties, the first segment of the "city's own" Eighth Avenue Independent subway was begun, linking remote areas of Brooklyn, the Bronx, and Queens with all points on Manhattan's West Side, from the financial district to the Cloisters at the very northerly tip of the island.

Were there a natural progression, completion of the IND would have immediately spurred a seriously needed spate of more subway construction. New lines would have fanned out from Manhattan, where a Second Avenue subway was a high priority. Brooklyn's rapidly developing shorefront areas such as Mill Basin, Sheepshead Bay, and Canarsie all figured in blueprints for extending the IRT's Flatbush Avenue Line all the way to the Atlantic Ocean. Completion of the George Washington Bridge to Fort Lee, New Jersey (opposite 188th Street in Washington Heights, Manhattan), was expected to be a boon to commuters. A branch of the IND's Eighth Avenue subway could easily be run over the proposed (later to be built) lower roadway of the span.

Extensions of already completed IRT lines in the Bronx would slink all the way to the Westchester County border while still untouched areas of Queens would benefit from additions to the IND's Queens Boulevard route as well as completely new routes and links to the city's airports. Even poor little Staten Island (Richmond), across the bay, figured in the planning.

Richmond, the city's black sheep borough, nearly obtained a transit link with the mainland (Brooklyn) in the early twenties. Work on a Narrows subway tube had begun in 1921 for a link between the BRT (soon to be BMT) Fourth Avenue Subway in Bay Ridge, Brooklyn, and the Staten Island Rapid Transit Line via an underwater tunnel. In fact more than $7,000,000 had been spent on digging four ninety-six-foot holes—two at the Staten Island shoreline and two at the Bay Ridge end—which were the shaft heads for the proposed subway tunnel. But Mayor John Hylan managed to block the project sufficiently to force its premature abandonment in 1923. Nevertheless, construction of the Verrazano Bridge over the Narrows in the late fifties could have guaranteed the Staten Island subway connection if space had been allotted on the span for trains.

There were several reasons why major subway construction came to a virtual halt once the IND completed its fingers of track into four of the city's five boroughs. Subway opponents such as Mayor Hylan always seemed to be about but none had the staying power, the clout, or the dynamic persistence of rapid transit's most awesome foe, Robert Moses.

Labeled "the power broker" in a best-selling book by Robert A. Caro, Moses dominated every New York mayor from Fiorello La Guardia to William O'Dwyer, Vincent Impellitteri, and finally, Robert Wagner. While it would be easy and convenient to attack these pillars of democracy as agents of the subway's downfall, the reality was that Moses and Moses alone was architect of policies that encouraged congestion, pollution, and the eventual destruction of what was almost the best rapid transit system in the world.

Moses worked his way into one of the mightiest positions of control in the United States. By the mid-fifties, he simultaneously held so many powerful commissionerships that he was boss of no fewer than ten other vital city and state agencies.

Moses was dedicated to the car. This was hardly surprising, considering his background. Moses was as removed from the average commuter's life as Egypt's King Farouk. "It was in transportation," wrote Caro, "the area in which Moses was most active after the war, that his isolation from reality was most complete; because he never participated in the activity for which he was creating his highways—driving—at all."

As Moses amassed more and more power, the city's vital transportation system suffered. By the late forties, Moses enjoyed nearly absolute power over public works construction in the New York area, and the tragic results for the air, for the city's poor (who couldn't afford automobiles), and for the subways were apparent.

In the years that Vincent Impellitteri ruled City Hall (with Moses, of course, looking over his shoulder), New York City spent $172,294,000 on highways—excluding federal and state expenditures—and built eighty-eight miles of new roads. During that span *not a single mile of new subways was constructed.*

Moses' inevitable response to demands that congestion be relieved along the city's arteries was to build more parkways. But each new road brought more polluting autos—and more congestion. Worse still, they were harmful to the citizens who most needed cheap, frequent transportation: the poor and lower-middle-class New Yorkers.

Apart from his obsession with building parkways for the sake of building parkways, there seemed to be no logic to Moses' preference for concrete over rail. A highway, at peak capacity, moves 1,500 cars an hour. *A single train track can carry between 40,000 and 50,000 persons per hour.* Equally important is the fact that the commuter trains would enable people to leave their cars at home, thereby creating thousands of parking spaces and cleaner air in the city.

From time to time a rare voice would be heard in opposition to Moses, who seemed to have the city's dailies in his hip pocket along with the politicians. After one of Moses' most egregious blunders was completed—construction of the Long Island Expressway, unaffectionately known as "the world's longest parking lot"—a few daring planners suggested that subway tracks be placed on the Expressway. Such an arrangement exists in Chicago and other metropolises, but Moses immediately rebuffed the request. Nevertheless the Metropolitan Rapid Transit Commission ordered a study to determine if, in fact, it was possible to place rapid transit on a seven-mile stretch of the Expressway.

The Philadelphia firm of Day & Zimmerman, Inc., consulting engineers, proved that Moses was dead wrong. In their carefully prepared study, Day & Zimmerman showed that a vital seven-mile stretch of train tracks could be built; and when all costs were in, including new rolling stock, etc., they would total only $20,830,000. Savings in the realm of human comfort were incalculable, but it was shown that such a link would significantly ease the motor traffic flow (not to mention poisoning of the air with carbon monoxide from automobiles), relieve bus traffic, and help the congested Long Island Rail Road. Instead, Moses talked about more highways.

"Moses," wrote Caro, "was planning to spend $500,000,000 for an expressway that would increase the one-way automobile-carrying capacity of Long Island by a maximum of 4,500 automobiles or buses per hour—during the two-hour peak period, by a total of 9,000 automobiles or buses. For $20,000,000—one twenty-fifth of that cost—he could reduce the automobile-carrying capacity *needed* by 6,500 automobiles and 400 buses. He could do as much for Long Island by spending $20,000,000 as by spending $500,000,000—if he spent it on rapid transit."

Moses feared the Day & Zimmerman report for very good reason; it exposed his weak underbelly. But the report's dangerous saber could be blunted by him if he could execute one of his traditionally effective ploys, the fait accompli. He knew that if rapid transit were to be included on the Expressway, heavier foundations would have to be sunk along the center mall. So, while the Day & Zimmerman study was being completed, Moses got the Expressway started. When the Day & Zimmerman report stated unequivocally that rapid transit should be included in the Expressway it was too late to do it. The lighter foundations already had been installed.

The Long Island Expressway was obsolete the day that it opened and has grown progressively worse ever since; and this despite the infusion of hundreds of millions of dollars to correct the original flaws. (One interchange that was poorly planned was reconstructed at a cost of $75,000,000—and that for only an interchange.) "If you eliminate one interchange problem," said Long Island planner Lee Koppelman, "all you're going to be doing is shifting the bottleneck east of the interchange, further out in Queens." Koppelman, of course, was right. Moses, again, was wrong but nothing could be done about it.

"Moses could not be fired," said August Heckscher, a former New York City Parks Commissioner, "because he had written the laws so as to insure his permanence. Nor could he be effectively criticized because he controlled access to the facts."

His critics rarely enjoyed Moses' access to the media. But everyone denounced the uncontrolled explosion in highway building. "A large part of the money we are spending on highways," said respected planner Lewis Mumford in 1946, "is wasted because we don't know whether we want people where the highways are going."

But Mumford was no dope. He realized that Moses was playing with a public relations man's dream. "Highways," Mumford added, "are impressive, flashy things to build. No one is against highways." Following World War II, Moses proved the point by building more than $2 *billion* worth of roads inside New York City alone.

Each ribbon of new Moses highway embellished the profits of General Motors, poisoned the already putrid air, and struck at the jugular of not only the efficient subways but the valuable commuter railroads as well. Such metropolitan-area-based railroads as the New Haven; Delaware, Lackawanna and Western; Erie; and Long Island were superbly clean passenger links between the suburbs and Manhattan when Moses began gathering power in the late twenties. By 1968, when Moses had reached the apex of his rule, most of the commuter rail lines were either dead or suffering arthritis of the tracks. But in 1968 the annual surplus of Moses' Triborough Bridge and Tunnel Authority was running more than $30,000,000 a year.

Among the most egregious sins of Moses' reign was the city's failure to extend the IND subway to Idlewild (now Kennedy) Airport in Queens. Such a Manhattan-Idlewild link was a transportation natural. Following World War II, plans were developed to build an expressway in Queens that would deliver automobiles to the new international airport. But it also was suggested that the superhighway—to be known as the Van Wyck Expressway—be built with rapid transit facilities.

Under the very best conditions three lanes of the Van Wyck Expressway can accommodate 2,630 vehicles per hour. But even one subway lane could have carried 40,000 persons per hour. Such a rail link could have connected Pennsylvania Station in Manhattan to Idlewild Airport in sixteen minutes. A number of other problems could have been solved by constructing the subway to the airport, each of which remains a problem today.

A relatively small subway construction job to the airport would have provided a long-needed connection between downtown Brooklyn and central and northern Queens, which are linked by automobile only. In addition, a branch of the IND's Fulton Street subway could also have been doubled with the Idlewild tracks, enabling Wall Street commuters to reach the airport with relative ease.

The Van Wyck Expressway was targeted with a $30,000,000 construction bill. A subway connection would have cost only $9,000,000. If logic had prevailed, today there would be subway trains rolling alongside the jammed autos on the long-obsolete Van Wyck Expressway.

A memorandum was, in fact, written for the airport "master plan" that stated rapid transit access should be provided for the international airport. But the memo infuriated the Moses brigade and was deleted before the airport master plan was approved. F. Dodd McHugh, the courageous author of the memo, found that his salary had been sliced in the next city budget and, eventually, he resigned, another insightful planner apparently defeated by Moses.

As for the Van Wyck Expressway, it was still another Moses disaster. "Traffic will flow freely," Moses bragged in a typical preopening hype. But it hardly flowed at all. Motorists soon learned that they could cover the four miles of Van Wyck on local streets in twenty minutes but covering the same distance on the highway required a half hour.

The solution—a subway directly to the airport—was never built.

Obviously, Moses was not alone in encouraging rubber over rails. He had effective accomplices as long as he held power. Mayor Fiorello La Guardia, one of the most likable and friendly city administrators, lacked vision when it came to rapid transit. La Guardia led the campaign to eliminate clean, comfortable street cars from Manhattan streets and replace them with diesel buses. His successor, William O'Dwyer, worked hand in glove with Moses, as did every mayor up to John Lindsay.

Their priorities seemed better suited for the wealthy than the citizens they served. For example, they campaigned for elimination of the Third Avenue elevated line at the end of World War II, without providing an adequate substitute. Workmen removed the last skeleton of the Third Avenue el in 1956 while city fathers promised to build a Second Avenue subway in its place. The subway, of course, was never built.

The men who have run the Transit Authority, from Charles Patterson through William Ronan and, more recently, David Yunich and Harold Fisher, have appeared more determined to turn people away from the subways than lure them to the underground. Since New York City has been poisoned with air pollution for the past decade, it stands to reason that administrators should promote the best nonpolluting means of transit. Yet the progressive deterioration of the system has been characterized by the elimination of trains, transit police cutbacks, and lengthened running times on many routes. The policy appears designed to ensure that more New Yorkers drive their own cars or take taxicabs.

Ronan's successor, David Yunich, was recruited to run the greatest railroad in the world because he had been an executive with Macy's department store. Yunich performed as one might expect a dry-goods specialist handling the most complex transportation system known to man. He resorted to Madison Avenue phraseology such as "dramatic progress," "welcome improvements," and "massive programs." But Joe Straphanger knew better because he rode the system. The trains got dirtier, the service got worse, and the riders stayed away in droves.

On December 29, 1975, Yunich surprised the citizens of New York City when he placed a signed, full-page ad in the *Daily News*. The MTA chairman dwelt at length (21 paragraphs) on the promises and the problems, the virtues and the vices of the transit facilities. The statement was so Pollyannaish that *News* columnist Peter Coutros replied a day later in a feature that was head-lined: REPLY TO YUNICH: PROSE DROWNS OUT LAUGHS.

Coutros demolished Yunich's essay. "Just get those windows washed once a month," he demanded. "Then, all of us can look out and see where we're at." Coutros, who had been riding the subways for thirty-five years, concluded that after reading the MTA ad, he was "wondering if Mr. Yunich had gone off his trolley."

Actually, Yunich was guilty of nothing other than being ill equipped to han-dle the job of running the subways. What the system needed was an insightful man with a love of the underground and one in touch with the very people who use it. This, of course, presumes that he will do what no subway commissioner, from Ronan to Yunich to Fisher, has ever done: ride the trains every day.

In 1977, New York governor Hugh Carey named his chief campaign advisor and close friend, Harold Fisher, to replace Yunich as MTA chairman. For the sixty-eight-year-old Fisher, it marked an emergence into the public eye after forty years of politicking for the Democratic machine.

Observers immediately questioned whether Fisher could fulfill his function since the MTA boss is charged with the safety, maintenance, and operations of metropolitan area subways. He also is assigned the duty of expanding and im-proving New York City's mass transportation.

"I just make policy," Fisher said. "I don't run the railroad, I don't run any-thing. I can't even drive a car, so how can I tell anyone how to operate a train?"

There were grave suspicions among transit critics of Fisher's qualifications, not to mention his support of mass transit. Fisher's support of the controversial billion-dollar Westway superhighway (at the expense of mass transit) cast fur-ther doubts on his motives in 1979.

Fisher's policies came under more criticism in 1979 as subway and bus break-downs, as well as a plague of menaced straphangers, found Fisher cast as the villain. To some riders, the system had reached an all-time low.

"Further complicating matters," wrote Richard Karp in *New York* magazine, "is the fact that Fisher got the job because of political savvy, not any special knowledge of mass transit. Indeed, Fisher talks about New York's transit system as if he had once read a pamphlet about it. 'Did you know we have a thousand engineers in the subway?' reports Fisher, like an attentive second-grader recit-ing a newly acquired fact."

Other criticism that came Fisher's way resulted from a large percentage of available funds going into the construction of three new subway lines—all of which were far from completion in 1979—while $350,000,000 in federal funds

Montreal Metro Photo File

Transit oddities: (*Above*) A one-of-a-kind eight-wheeled forty-seat Montreal gasoline-powered bus. (*Below*) A rare combination of a steampowered train load of just-built Independent line cars (New York City) being pulled from factory to the subway yards in the mid-thirties.

Stan Fischler's Collection

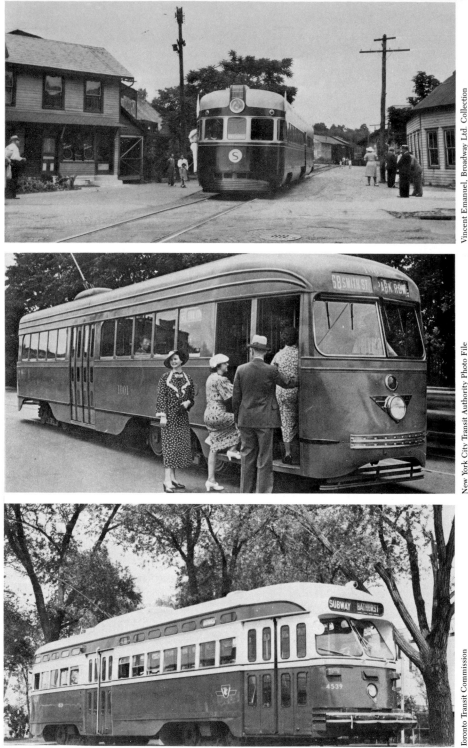

(*Top*) A New York, Susquehanna, and Western streamliner on a commuter run to its Jersey City terminal. (*Middle and bottom*) The trolley achieved its artistic pinnacle in the mid-thirties when the PCC (President's Conference Car) made its debut on the streets of Brooklyn. Note the rubber-water bumpers, still employed by the Toronto Transit Commission.

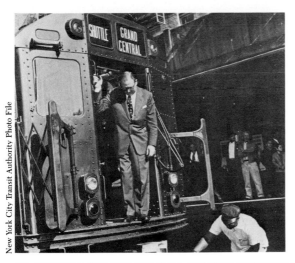

(*Left*) The TA experimented with an automated train in the early sixties. Evolution (though subtle) in subway car design: the musically immortalized "A" train (*middle*), circa 1947, and the famous World's Fair cars (*bottom*), 1964.

GMC Truck and Coach Division

GMC Truck and Coach Division

Grumman Flxible Corp.

(*Top*) The newest General Motors-RTS model began rolling off the production line in 1978, contrasting with its predecessor (*middle*), a ubiquitous fume-blower since 1959. (*Above*) Although General Motors has dominated the diesel bus field, other companies continued to compete with the Detroit giant, including Grumman Flxible.

GMC Truck and Coach Division

After years of lobbying for special equipment to service the handicapped, new devices such as the wheelchair-center door (*top*) have been incorporated into models for the 1980s.

Bay Area Rapid Transit Photo File

Metropolitan Atlanta Rapid Transit Authority

(*Middle*) A graphic example of rapid transit competing with the automobile as the San Francisco–Oakland BART system speeds along the freeway median. (*Above*) America's newest subway is being completed in stages by the Metropolitan Atlanta Rapid Transit Authority (MARTA), which, unlike other American lines, has purchased its rolling stock in Europe.

Mass transit, Japanese-style: (*Top*) A dapper electric line, the Keisei Railroad, and the "Bullet" (*middle*), considered the fastest train in the world (130 mph). (*Above*) Unique among North American subways, Montreal's Métro utilizes French-style rubber-tired trains.

(*Top*) Germany's 155-mph self-propelled Intercity train. (*Middle*) The first post-World War II subway in North America was built by the Toronto Transit Commission in 1954. (*Above*) London built the first subway and to this day operates one of the premier underground systems in Europe.

Boeing-Vertol, a division of the Boeing Co.

(*Above*) The trolley of the future has taken on several dimensions, including the "LRV" (Light Rail Vehicle) manufactured by the Boeing Vertol Company and now operating in Boston and San Francisco. (*Below*) A Department of Transportation experimental high-speed train being tested at the track in Pueblo, Colorado.

U.S. Department of Transportation

earmarked for rehabilitating subways remained idle because of political snags. Fisher defended his position by saying that no increase in passenger amenities will increase ridership, while in the past decade subway cars in service have dropped one thousand plus, meaning 50,000 fewer seats for New York City commuters.

Fisher, although he had not spent the allotted funds, announced an ambitious $17 billion ten-year capital-spending plan that has been attacked by City Council president Carol Bellamy as "a feeble effort . . . to develop and inform the public of long-term, transit capital needs. . . ."

If that weren't disturbing enough to riders, New Yorkers need only look at the state of the MTA under his arrogant baton to understand why mass transit was in a state of utter disarray and disrepair at the dawn of the 1980s. While Fisher tried to hail 1979 as the Diamond Jubilee (seventy-fifth anniversary of the first New York subway), passengers pointed to filthy rolling stock, mishandled maintenance, and an assortment of other minidisasters which unequivocally prove that New York has yet to find a man who knows how to run their railroad. Who, then, would be an ideal boss of the MTA?

What is needed is a subway lover with brains—a man such as Howard Samelson of the Electric Railroaders' Association and proprietor of Broadway Limited Antique Shop in New York City, who, unlike Fisher, knows every inch of the subway system, knows precisely what is wrong with the system and exactly what should be done to make it grand, glorious, and workable once more.

The formula is considerably simpler than that for devising a rocket to the moon: 1) The subways must be made safe. 2) Stations, rolling stock, and personnel should be clean and attractive. 3) The system should be made even more responsive to the public; hence prompt, regular service twenty-four hours a day. 4) The fare should be subsidized from car taxes or tolls on all city bridges that accommodate autos. 5) The system should be actively promoted the way General Motors touts a new car.

But will the municipal, state, and federal government grasp the necessity of renewing a multibillion-dollar asset? "What we are enduring," said columnist John Russell of *The New York Times*, "is not something intrinsically ignoble. It is the wreck—the foreseeable, avoidable, unforgivable wreck—of a system that was once the equal of any in the world."

It need not have happened and the continued decline need not happen. But the value of the system must be recognized in terms of both air purity and the need to move millions of passengers from one part of the city to another.

Obviously, this is predicated on a reorganization of values. The automobile has become a greater and greater burden upon society. But to lure people away from the car (and taxi) the alternative must be appetizing. The subway's dilemma is that nobody has taken the time to solve the problem. In fact, subway leaders appear to be more bent on sabotaging the system than salvaging it:

Exhibit A: Noise pollution underground has been a chronic problem since August Belmont built the IRT. In 1933 the IRT successfully built a noiseless train that was proven workable and could have been utilized throughout the system simply by rebuilding existing cars. Experiment proved the idea to be genuinely effective, but the IRT followed up by doing nothing.

Exhibit B: Noise pollution remains a problem today. The Toronto Transportation Commission showed that noise could be significantly lowered by inserting rubber mats between the steel rails and the wooden ties. In 1975 the Metropolitan Transit Authority replaced the rock-dirt ballast roadbed along sections of the Broadway IRT express and replaced it with a concrete roadbed. A significant *increase* in the decibel level was recorded along these replaced sections because the TA never got around to installing the rubber matting.

Exhibit C: Eye pollution has made the New York subways one of the most distasteful-looking pieces of "art" and engineering imaginable. One could excuse the MTA for operating a system less immaculate than August Belmont's spanking clean IRT. But the Authority has failed miserably in its token battle against graffiti. From the Bronx to Brooklyn subway cars and stations are covered with verbal filth. Perhaps it is impossible to wipe the system completely clean, but the MTA has done virtually nothing creative to wipe out the graffiti. The graffiti, in turn, along with stalled trains and subway crime, have diverted passengers out of the subway and into taxis and other transport.

Exhibit D: Ever since a millionaire rider had his diamond stickpin stolen on the IRT during the opening day celebration in 1904, crime has deterred citizens from riding the subways. But never have the subways been so crime-riddled as in the late seventies. One solution, of course, would be to post a policeman on every platform and every single train twenty-four hours a day.

The MTA's response to the surge of crime was a series of news conferences during which statistics were marshaled to prove that the system was, in fact, safe. About one-tenth of 1 percent of the riders believed one-tenth of 1 percent of those "safety" statistics, and in early 1979, the majority's worst fears were realized when a rash of violent crimes hit the New York City subways. Mayor Edward Koch responded by ordering cops on every train and every platform during the night hours.

Despite Mayor Koch's "war on subway fear," the level of violent crime inched upward in the second week of the campaign, according to a *Daily News* article of April 3, 1979. For the week of March 28, Transit Police Chief Sanford Garelik's office reported 165 felonies compared with 157 for the week of March 19, the first week of the campaign. However, 261 felonies were reported the week of March 12, just before Koch ordered the policemen onto the trains. That marked a 40 percent decline in violent crime since New York's cops began walking the train beat at usually peak hours for subway felons.

Exhibit E: There is, of course, safety in numbers. Subways suffer the fewest passengers during late morning, early afternoon, and late night hours. Safety would be ensured if more passengers rode the trains at these times, and if more trains were available at the off-hours. The cure is simplicity itself but has eluded the fuzzy-headed MTA planners: reduce the fare during off-hours. Have a "Dime-Time" from 11 A.M. to 3 P.M. and from 9 P.M. to 5 A.M. At ten cents a ride, passengers would flock to the subways during these off-hours. More trains could be provided, more people would ride the underground, and more safety would be assured.

Exhibit F: Operation of New York's enormously extensive subway, el, and surface transportation system was a Promethean enough job for the Transit Authority when it had complete jurisdiction over the system. But creation of the Metropolitan Transportation Authority (MTA) by Governor Nelson Rockefeller meant that it was now impossible to monitor the subway system effectively. In 1968 the MTA merged the TA, the city's bus system, the Long Island, Penn Central, New Haven, and Staten Island Rapid Transit systems under one supposedly coordinated unit. Its chairmen proved incapable of paying proper attention to the subway system. Ergo: many more problems than if the TA had remained an entity unto itself.

When confronted with problems ranging from crime to graffiti, the MTA propagandists instantly counter that "funds are simply not available" for such antidotes. In a sense they are right. Neither the federal government under the administrations of Richard Nixon, Gerald Ford, and Jimmy Carter, nor the state governments under Malcolm Wilson or Hugh Carey have recognized the essential value of the city's rapid transit system and the fact of life that revenue from passenger fares cannot maintain the lines in optimum condition.

What is required to provide the kind of transportation system the city needs and deserves is large infusions of cash from Washington and Albany; enough to guarantee a nominal fare—certainly not more than fifty cents—and assure that the system is able to maintain optimum service at all times with the most modern equipment and with a continued expansion to fulfill the requirements of communities without subway facilities. Finding such cash is rather easy.

The federal government could do it merely by scrapping approximately three wasteful Pentagon projects (how many billions already have been lost in cost overruns on obsolete military equipment?). That would produce a minimum of $2 billion. The state could do it merely by erasing for five years any future highway construction projects and diverting the monies to the transit systems of every metropolis from Buffalo to Brooklyn. The money produced from these sources would be enough to restore the dream of the early 1900s. It was then the manufacturers of Abbey's Effervescent Salt published a national portrait of a New York subway station and subtitled it *The Rapid Transit to Health*.

The decline and fall of the greatest railroad in the world need not continue. It is not as inevitable as death and taxes, nor should it be permitted to fail.

21

Sick Transit – What's Wrong with the World's Biggest System?

Few transit systems anywhere in the world can match New York City's network of subways, buses, and elevated railroads in the areas of safety, volume, and mileage. Yet the New York system has been rotting for more than thirty years, and not simply because of the politicians' less than benign neglect.

The New York Transit Authority was victimized as much as anything by the sheer weight of its incompetence at the highest levels. One era, 1955–68, serves as an appropriate example. It was during that time that I was covering the transit beat for the New York *Journal-American*.

One morning at a press conference in 1956, I suggested to Charles Patterson, then chairman of the Transit Authority, that the TA might increase business and better please its customers by washing its filthy subway cars, some of which were burdened by fifty years of grime. Patterson regarded me with the look of despair one might get after suggesting that the Bronx Zoo yak be taken to the barber for a crew cut.

"We don't wash the cars," Patterson tartly explained, "because the dirt and steel dust is good for them. *It protects the paint job underneath.*"

Too late the thought came to me that if the TA exuded the same concern for its riders as it does for its subway cars' paint jobs, New York's 3,000,000+ daily straphangers might find the life underground more tolerable. I mention Patterson's immortal retort as an example of transit logic. If you can understand that, you should be able to fathom the following paradoxes that have made life so miserable on the "safest railroad in the world."

- In 1951 voters approved a $500,000,000 bond issue for a Second Avenue subway to relieve congestion on the IRT East Side subway and to replace the demolished Second Avenue el. Instead, voters received such improvements on the IRT as longer platforms and improved signaling, but, significantly, no Second Avenue subway!
- In 1960 the TA removed the last of its 160 noiseless, odorless, speedy electric trolley coaches and replaced them with noisier, odor-spewing, and less speedy diesel buses, the likes of which recently have been condemned by air pollution experts.
- In 1966 the TA launched a poster campaign boasting "Nobody ever heard of

a batting average of .950. But the TA trains run 95 percent on time and we plan to do better." Soon after the signs went up, they were hauled down. A TA official explained: "When the poster campaign began, our Queens IND Division fell apart."

* In 1967, the TA found itself without a chairman and instead governed by two members, Daniel Scannell, a Democrat, and John Gilhooley, a Republican, who worked together as smoothly as fire and gasoline.

There are those experts in the transit business who consider these matters piddling compared with one of the TA's major projects of the fifties, which the Authority described as "one of the most significant rapid transit developments in the city since completion of the Independent subway in 1932."

That was what the TA euphemistically called the "Chrystie Street Connection," actually a three-part project involving the city's first new subway line since before World War II. One might expect a production of such magnitude to have been loudly trumpeted when it was finally finished but the Authority was discreetly silent on the matter, and for good reason.

For one thing the project, which included a new tunnel under Sixth Avenue in Greenwich Village, cost a whopping $129,000,000 for just 2.29 miles. For another, it took twelve years to complete. And the coup de grace: the new subway was obsolete by the time it was finally unveiled.

It could be argued that, obsolete or not, taxpayers were at least receiving a subway for their $129,000,000, which is more than they got for their $500,000,000 in 1951. But there are some citizens who prefer value for their money. They become annoyed when they consider that during the same period of time the city of Toronto built three brand-new subway lines, totaling fifteen miles, for only $266,000,000. They become even more rankled when they compare New York's 2.29-mile subway that required twelve years for completion with Toronto's 2.38-mile University Avenue branch that was built in less than 3½ years and cost $40,000,000, less than one-third of the TA's price.

For their money New Yorkers got reconstruction of the complex DeKalb Avenue junction in Brooklyn, a connection between the IND and BMT lines at Chrystie Street in the East Village, a new station at Grand Street, another at 57th Street, and a new express tunnel under Sixth Avenue in Manhattan.

"The grand plan," the TA said, "was for eliminating the chronic congestion of subway traffic at DeKalb Avenue, uniting the BMT and IND divisions, and increasing express train capacity under Sixth Avenue."

However, the grand plan inspired wrath years before it was finished, and then was described as "a fiasco" by the Committee for Better Transit, an organization of citizens dedicated to improving public transportation. In a detailed study of the TA plan, the CBT underlined two basic defects of the TA proposal: (1) Insufficient subway trains were provided per hour in each direction and (2) the headways on many services were long and irregular.

Such blundering inevitably infuriates the straphangers. But the riders' wrath is treated with disdain by transit officials. Riders, who for years demanded air-conditioned subway cars, were told "engineering difficulties" made such a project impossible. Then, when they discovered that Chicago's subways and the PATH Hudson Tubes had air-conditioned cars, they were told that such a system would be too expensive for New York. Years later the TA finally began buying air-cooled cars.

Wrath? How about the diesel buses contaminating the air with noxious fumes? The TA quickly retorts that bus fumes are not nearly as poisonous as those issuing from trucks and autos. No mention is made of the quality of smell generated by the TA's diesel monsters.

When critics point out that electric buses inflict the public with less noise and no poison, the TA counters that electric buses are less flexible in street routing, forgetting that drivers of the diesel buses have a fixation about stopping their vehicles in the middle of the streets instead of at curbside bus stops.

Much ado was made in 1967 about "new" stainless steel subway cars delivered to the TA. But the fact is they had fewer seats, were less comfortable, and despite a much-heralded ventilation system, were no more tolerable on hot days than the fifty-three-year-old cars still running on some of the lines. Of course, the "new" cars boasted better braking and accelerating mechanisms and improved lighting. That's fifty-three years of "progress."

What gains have been achieved by the New York transit officials have been mere tokens compared to what is really needed. Improvements for the most part have been more mechanical than personal and aesthetic. Commuters who are treated like cattle turn to auto transit wherever possible and the center of the city remains abysmally congested.

The depressed state of the New York City subway system reached its nadir in the winter of 1979. Under the leadership of Chairman Harold Fisher, the TA failed to cope with the growing problem of underground crime, and nothing said it more cogently than headlines in the local papers:

March 11: TWO MORE SUBWAY STABBINGS—New York *Daily News*
March 11: BROOKLYN 18-YEAR-OLD STABBED AND ROBBED AT MIDTOWN IND STOP—New York *Times*
March 12: A SUBTERRANEAN SUBHUMAN SUBJUGATES OUR SUBWAYS—New York *Daily News*
March 13: 2 SHOT IN LATEST SUBWAY VIOLENCE—New York *Post*
March 15: MAN SLAIN, WOMAN RAPED IN NEW SUBWAY VIOLENCE—New York *Post*
March 16: TEEN TERROR HITS SUBWAYS IN 4 BOROUGHS—New York *Post*

Perhaps the worst day of all occurred on March 17–18, when the following episodes took place:

- At the Burnside Avenue, Bronx, IRT station, three youths pushed a twenty-nine-year-old man to the platform floor and, at knifepoint, forced him to hand over $30 in cash. There were no arrests.
- At 3 A.M. at the Livonia Avenue station aboard the BMT LL train, a fifty-one-year-old man was rousted from his sleep by three men in their twenties. They emptied his pockets of $227 in cash. There were no arrests.
- A nineteen-year-old was accosted by a man with a knife at the Times Square

IRT complex at 3:30 A.M. Muttering obscenities, the knife wielder slashed the youth's hand and fled. There was no arrest.

- At 4:15 A.M., at the Jay Street Brooklyn IND stop, a youth attempted to snatch a woman's purse. She fought him off. There was no arrest.
- A woman was robbed of her purse containing $60 at 8 A.M. at the Broadway and 86th Street, Manhattan IRT station when a man with a gun confronted her in a stairwell. There was no arrest.

A massive "clean up crime on the subway" campaign began in late March and commuters breathed a little easier as blue police uniforms could be seen on every subway line at all hours. How long the police can maintain the new wave of patrols remains to be seen, as other regularly patrolled areas must go unguarded. Permanent change for the better on New York City subways has never been brought about with speed or ease.

Perhaps it is symbolic that one night a commuter consulted a map in the BMT station at 14th Street and Sixth Avenue. He noticed some unusual markings, looked closer, and realized it showed the route of the Third Avenue el and the Canarsie trolley car line, both long extinct.

The map was more than thirty years old.

V

THE FUTURE OF
MASS TRANSIT

22

Buses, Trolleys, Trains of the Future

For decades, slick public relations brochures have been cranked out portraying the diesel bus as the acme of surface transit. On paper, the diesel always has looked good. Paper doesn't smell. Diesels do. They also have suffered from more than cosmetic deficiencies. Unlike the trolleys, which ran on relatively smooth rails, the buses have been chronically wounded by irregularly paved streets.

In northern states, cold winters caused streets to be potholed and these surface pockmarks have for years been the bane of even the best-built bus (assuming such a creature exists). In New York City, for example, John de Roos, senior executive officer of the Metropolitan Transit Authority, complained in 1979 that "buses are not built to work under New York's [potholed] combat conditions."

Buses, though ubiquitous throughout the continent, have suffered endless critiques on other grounds (pollution, destructibility, etc.) but remained—for dubious reasons—*the* choice of a majority of municipal transit systems. With the virtual extermination of the trolley, the bus reigned supreme by default.

Nevertheless, it has been believed that a "better" city bus could be built if manufacturers put their minds to it. Using this theory, the government spawned a scheme to develop the bus of the 1980s—"Transbus."

When the Transbus program was launched in 1970, it seemed to many transit officials that their problems might soon be solved. Although the jitney-turned-omnibus may have proved a lethal competitor to the trolley during the early part of the twentieth century, by the 1970s transit commissioners in many American cities were beginning to wonder whether the diesel-powered buses were as practical a means of public transportation as they had at first suggested. Buses, even those manufactured by the top three manufacturing companies— General Motors, the Flxible Company, and AM General, a subsidiary of American Motors—were less than perfect. In some cases, they suggested other types of weaknesses. For example, most buses failed to serve the needs of the elderly and the handicapped rider. Despite the pressing demand for new buses in urban centers across the nation, bus companies in recent years have suffered severe financial losses which compelled them to order extensive layoffs.

In 1977, this paradoxical situation became magnified even though the Transbus program was supposed to encourage transportation development by financing the research efforts of the three principal manufacturers. A prototype bus for general use, as envisioned by the United States Urban Mass Transit Administration (UMTA), was not yet developed. Instead, "interim" buses of various designs were manufactured by the competing companies. AM General, a relative newcomer in the bus manufacturing industry, feuded with UMTA because the agency had agreed to finance a large bus order involving many cities and the order was won by General Motors.

The bus designed by General Motors met higher performance standards, according to some observers, than that developed by AM General, but the American Motors subsidiary still pressed a lawsuit that alleged the government had violated a congressional mandate forbidding "exclusionary" standards for the construction of new equipment that discriminated against some bidders. B. R. Stokes, executive director of the American Public Transit Association, refused to accept AM General's charges on the grounds that AM General's complaint would hinder the drive for bus improvement and allow the bus manufacturers to "be controlled by the least efficient, least innovative suppliers of mass transit equipment."

Essentially, AM General's complaint in 1977 was a statement of their frustration with a government that seemed consistently to side with the transportation giant, General Motors.

Later in 1977, AM General found itself back in the driver's seat when it sold an order of ten diesel buses to Seattle's Metro system and two hundred to the Los Angeles bus system. Government requirements and Transbus research combined to produce buses designed for easier and more comfortable transportation for the elderly and the handicapped. The ten buses developed for the Seattle system, costing a total of $863,000, were equipped with hydraulic lifts to hoist wheelchairs from the ground to the bus floor. Each bus contained space for two wheelchairs in the vicinity of the front door. To make boarding easier for the disabled and the elderly, these special buses were designed to "kneel" to remove the long step from the ground to the bus. The buses were also equipped with better lighting on doorways and visual passenger signals which up until this time had been used only in Europe—two lights that flash whenever a passenger pulls the cord for a stop. Despite their earlier difficulties in competing with the larger bus manufacturers, namely General Motors, AM General was the first company to build a large fleet of buses equipped with special aids for the handicapped, features soon to be required on all buses as announced by Transportation Secretary Brock Adams.

In April 1979, one of the nation's defense giants, the Grumman Corporation, which had previously taken over the Rohr-Flxible Company, won an $88,900,000 contract to add 837 new buses to the New York City surface transit system. Although no delivery date had been set, Grumman public relations director Peter Costiglio said that the buses should be ready by 1980.

The bus upon which Grumman pinned its hopes is the Flxible 870. Manufactured in Delaware, Ohio, the 870 went into service in Atlanta and Hartford.

Grumman officials endorse their bus as a product of the space-age research which put man on the moon. With a product such as the Flxible 870, Grumman hoped to establish greater diversification and more stable employment. Ironically, space purchases would, hopefully, be replaced by surface sales.

However, Grumman's bus had a powerful competitor in the General Motors Corporation's welded, stainless steel RTS model. GMC claimed that its bus would provide smoother rides because the RTS model supposedly was "pothole proof" (it is questionable whether any rational transit official believed all that hype). Potholes have long been a source of frustration to municipal transit officials, who regularly have complained that potholes have been a significant factor in bus breakdowns and resulting service delays. According to propaganda dispensed by the GMC Truck and Coach Division, the new vehicle is "an entirely new transit bus from the ground up."

The General Motors communiqué extolled it as follows:

It offers a completely new appearance and many advanced engineering concepts for greater passenger comfort, safety, and accessibility.

The RTS also contains many features for significant operating, maintenance, and repair economies. Passenger accessibility for all passengers, especially the handicapped and elderly, was a high RTS design priority. The RTS kneeling system reduces the floor height from its 32-inch stationary position to only 27 inches for easier boarding and exit. In addition, the wide rear door is designed to accommodate a hydraulic wheelchair lift.

The RTS's new independent front suspension system provides a smooth, stable ride and easier handling. Its stainless steel alloy body construction is strong, durable, and corrosion-resistant.

Acrylic-coated fiberglass lower body panels resist damage and minimize maintenance. If damaged, the panels can be quickly removed and replaced to save the hours of downtime required by conventional bus designs.

In addition, the new side panels are easily cleaned to frustrate graffiti writers. The half-inch thick acrylic RTS windows are more break-resistant than conventional laminated glass of equivalent thickness.

The engine, transmission, brakes, fuel, electrical, suspension, and heating and air-conditioning systems are all designed for easier maintenance.

A typical example is the new combination 12- and 24-volt electrical system for greater power where needed. Its design helps avoid connection mistakes and facilitates quick and easy repair. Heavy duty circuit breakers are easily accessible. They pop out to indicate malfunction and are reset with a touch of the finger.

Also designed for easier maintenance is the new RTS heating and air-conditioning system, which is fully automatic to maintain passenger- and driver-comfort levels.

RTS seats are mounted to the wall. Seat legs, which could cause tripping, are not required. If local transit systems want to relocate the seats to attain greater leg room, the seats are easily and quickly remounted to the wall.

Several unique bus manufacturing installations and processes are employed to produce the RTS. In a completely new manufacturing concept, the 40-foot-long RTS body is formed by welding together eight separate five-foot-long body modules in a huge, computerized, automatic welding installation.

Other new production techniques include ultrasonic testing of critical weld points, utilizing high frequency sound waves to penetrate metal, and precise front suspension and steering alignment by laser beam.

Robert W. Truxwell, a General Motors vice-president and general manager of GMC, commented, "In response to the stated needs of many transit system authorities, the RTS was developed to provide better service and attract new bus riders."

General Motors' attitude toward improving bus design has been questioned over the years by various sources. In his syndicated column of May 4, 1976, Jack Anderson attacked GM's motives with respect to the creation of a first-rate urban bus:

In 1971, the government began a $27 million project to develop a bus of the future. It was to have wide doors, special features for the handicapped, and other safety and efficiency improvements. But a federally funded report by Stanford University describes how the "Transbus" concept fell afoul of politics and corporate finagling.

In the beginning, the Urban Mass Transportation Administration provided funds to three firms to build a sample Transbus. The company with the winning model would win contracts that might eventually run into the billions. The three were General Motors, American General, and Rohr Industries. The two smaller firms, American and Rohr, were enthusiastic about trying to produce the new bus and expected continued federal funding.

"But," suggests the draft study, "General Motors, which is primarily an auto manufacturer, realized that the Transbus program had the potential of increasing mass transportation usage." This of course, "translates into a net reduction in auto sales" for General Motors. Then last year, for what the report describes as "technological, economic, and political" reasons, the White House stepped in and scrapped the laboriously prepared design specifications for Transbus. In their place, the White House invited the bus manufacturers themselves to come up with a bus design as long as it met certain performance standards.

This played right into the hands of General Motors. It permits the giant of the auto industry, which already controls 50 percent of all bus sales, to build the kind of bus it wants, as opposed to Transbus. The White House, meanwhile, has further aided General Motors by holding back future funding for the Transbus project. Since the two smaller companies cannot compete with General Motors unless they get the funding, the White House actions have effectively turned over future bus sales to General Motors—without "Transbus" reforms.

In rebuttal, the public relations director of the GMC Truck and Coach Division, Frank Cronin, said, "The allegations in the column were absolutely unfounded. Ten years ago, long before the federal government became involved in Transbus, we [GM], of our own volition and our own funds—not a nickel from the taxpayers—started a new bus, the RTX model with a significantly lower floor. And this was in 1968."

After a study of the RTX among government officials, transportation authorities, and the public, GM came up with the RTS. "It was the first new bus on the streets," according to Cronin, "with easier accessibility and new technology. Since that was all of our own volition, it should demonstrate we were not ignoring the accessibility question."

General Motors will have a chance to prove its sincerity now that the government has decided not to scrap the Transbus project. Seven years and $30,000,000 later, UMTA has developed a completed prototype with a precise list of specifications.

A consortium of Miami, Philadelphia, and Los Angeles has a combined order of 530 buses that meet the new specifications ready for bidding on by manufacturers. If terms and conditions are not contested by the bidding companies, the bidding will close, and the new specifications will become a must late in 1979.

Some of the new features for Transbus will be floors no higher than twenty-two inches, front doors at least twenty-four inches wide, four tires in the rear instead of the usual two, and a lift or ramp at the front entrance of the bus.

"We are engaged in an intensive study to find what it would take to meet the new specifications," said Cronin for General Motors. "We've been in the bus business for so long, I sure as heck hope we will be able to bid."

Meanwhile, new GMC buses were already rolling in revenue service in certain communities, such as Norwalk. Connecticut.

The Norwalk Transit District bought nineteen "ultramodern" buses with a passenger-carrying capacity of thirty-seven riders each from GM. The $88,000 buses operate along fifteen routes for thirteen hours a day, which makes Norwalk's bus fleet the largest municipally owned transit system in the state.

The green-and-white buses are engaged in a new travel pattern called the "radial pulse" system. Thirteen of the fifteen routes originate at the same "pulse point" and buses pull out simultaneously, "like the pictures of planes in war movies, where they roll off for the attack," said director of operations Bruce Carter. Buses leave at twenty-five and fifty-five minutes after every hour, and transfers at the pulse points are free.

"Public reaction to the new buses and system has been fantastic," said Louis Schulman, administrator of the Norwalk Transit District. "Norwalk is a special case because we have been essentially without bus service for years. Considering we went to this system all at once, response has been great. The level of transfers has been 38 percent in the first two months of operation, an important indicator for the radial pulse system, where transfers are a big part of the bus service."

Schulman was enthusiastic about the General Motors buses, despite some quirks. "Considering the fact that it is a new vehicle," he said, "it has performed nicely. There are some minor problems, but we are working with GM to alleviate them."

One problem is caused by the cold weather in the Northeast. The switch under the front step that controls the kneeling feature often becomes covered with ice in Connecticut's freezing temperatures and remains locked in the down position. If the bus cannot move up, it cannot move forward either. GM has developed a new magnetic switch to try to cope with the weather.

Such minor problems have not deterred commuters. "I'm dying to try this," exclaimed a passenger who hadn't ridden a bus in fifteen years.

The harshest criticism of the new General Motors product was delivered by

Westchester County (New York), which refused to authorize payments for the vehicles until corrections were made.

In a January 25, 1979, letter to G. M. Pegg of the GMC Truck and Coach Division, Westchester County Program Administrator Paul Tortolani cited the following unacceptable items discovered in the post-delivery inspection of the new coaches: leaking windows and front windshields, a stiff defroster switch, a speedometer starting at 13 mph, sensitive edges on wheelchair lifts not functioning, ill-fitted rear door seals, very slow-rising kneeling devices, excessive window rattling, excessive noise from a heating system, scratches and dents on radiator covers and seats, cracked front door trims, a loose rear stanchion, loose engine doors, interior and exterior panels out of line, an oil leak at the fan, irregular or incorrect decals and passenger numbers, missing washer fluid, wheelchair lifts that don't unlock, missing jumpseat knobs, rear doors that don't open fully, a 12-volt system not charging, loose air-conditioner belt shrouds, an auxiliary bus light out, missing driver's side mirror, cracked interior air-conditioner louver cover, an audible warning that didn't function correctly during bus operations, coolant leaking from radiator into a bus, "take-one" rack crooked or missing, water in a crankcase, short in a rear door exit buzzer, fluid missing from a steering box, transmission not shifting gears properly, a loose light cover, improperly aligned lift mechanisms, and a noisy steering system requiring adjustment.

Contacted by the author, Assistant Public Relations Director of the GMC Truck and Coach Division Keith Pitcher replied: "I assure you that we are in the process of correcting any inadequacies. You have to remember that this is an all-new bus and there are bound to be problems, but we will correct them as soon as possible."

Another old idea (1938) given a modern touch comes from the West German branch of AM General. Articulated buses, buses that bend in the middle, have made their debut on the Southern California Rapid Transit District's most heavily patronized lines, on Hollywood and Wilshire boulevards.

"It's one of the most promising modes of metropolitan area transit," said Allen Styffe, a Los Angeles transit official. "As ridership increases, you can still have fewer buses on the heavy lines."

Richard Diamond, communications manager of the Southern California Rapid Transit District, added, "They are, with the exception of a few minor bugs, getting a highly favorable reception. It will be six more months [from January 1979] before we gather data on maintenance problems—but they've all been minor—the air-conditioning and articulation mechanisms have occasionally needed minor adjustments. I shouldn't be surprised if we order more at the end of that time."

In addition to those already in service in the Los Angeles region, a total of 218 buses-that-bend (at a cost of $66,000,000) will be changing the look of commuter bus travel in the cities of Seattle, Minneapolis, Pittsburgh, Chicago, Atlanta, Washington, Oakland, San Diego, San Francisco, and Phoenix.

"We can get high-powered productivity out of them," said George Mc-Donald, manager of planning and marketing for Crown Coach Corporation, the transit agency that tested the articulated buses and declared them a success. "We get more passengers per driver. It's just that basic."

By the middle of the 1980s, the American landscape will be sprinkled with a mixture of General Motors, Grumman Flxible, and an assortment of foreign models such as the AM General long bus. It was clear that while General Motors had not been pushed to the background, Grumman Flxible was doing a fair amount of business.

In 1979, with the Grumman Flxible in service in Atlanta, Hartford, and, on a trial basis, in New York City, the underdog competitor also had bus orders from twenty-five cities including Los Angeles, Houston, Honolulu, San Francisco, and Dallas.

"With the production phase only a year old," said Joe Bargar, marketing administrator for Grumman Flxible, "we're very pleased. That's where we're at."

When asked how he viewed General Motors as a competitor, Bargar replied, "GM is the only one. They're the main competitor."

Although the diesel bus obviously had subdued its rivals—the trackless trolley, the light rail vehicle, and the battery-operated bus—its future was less than rosy. An inevitable fuel crunch, criticism of the diesel's polluting qualities, and its destructibility gave objective transit planners pause to reflect on other options.

Nothing said it better than a statement by the New York City Planning Commission in January 1979. In essence, the commission, headed by Robert F. Wagner, Jr., rejected the diesel bus as impractical for future use along one of Manhattan's main thoroughfares, 42d Street. After lengthy study, the commission concluded that the electric streetcar (i.e., the trolley or LRV) was the ideal surface vehicle of the future. Although streetcars have not been in service along 42d Street since 1946, the commission concluded that streetcars are cheaper, cleaner, and faster than buses. Twelve of the electric-powered vehicles provide the service of sixty-eight buses, and, furthermore, the streetcar cuts the time of the bus ride in half.

Said Robert Wagner, "Modern streetcars could be the answer to speed transit along one of the city's most heavily trafficked streets. Our outlook is positive."

Mayor Koch was equally enthusiastic about the project. "Streetcars may have the potential to fit in and reinforce the welcome changes taking place along 42d Street. They will serve to reinforce the city's continuing commitment to upgrade the area."

If streetcars do return to 42d Street, the federal government will pay four-fifths of construction cost, and New York State will pay one-half of the cost that the federal government does not. The operating cost of a streetcar line will be only 41 percent of the operating cost of buses. According to Wagner, the City Planning Commission is studying the possibility of constructing streetcar lines in other heavily trafficked areas of the city.

"Also under consideration," said Wagner, "is a spur of the line from 42d Street to the Convention Center site bounded by 34th and 39th Streets between Eleventh and Twelfth avenues."

The news that the diesel bus is not guaranteed endless longevity was greeted with jubilation by many transit critics. One of them, Rhode Island transit author Don O'Hanley, said he hoped that the commission's decision was a portent of things to come. "It would be truly wonderful," O'Hanley concluded, "if the second coming of the electrics marked the beginning of the end of big-city bus operations. Other municipalities would surely follow suit."

One of the most daring gambles by a municipality was taken by Edmonton (Alberta), Canada, which, in 1974, began construction of a light rapid transit system. When the line opened in 1978, Edmonton became the smallest city in North America to operate a rapid transit system.

The Edmonton line was championed by Gerry Wright, a professor in the University of Alberta's extension department, when in 1971 he and some of his cronies produced *The Immorality of the Automobile*. The little book argued that it did not make sense to spend $750,000,000 on expressways, ruining entire neighborhoods during construction, and still have the traffic problem that their statistics found inescapable.

Wright and his group, backed by anti-expressway citizens groups, found that European cities with populations as small as 200,000 were using light rapid transit systems, and produced a convincing argument that Edmonton should do likewise.

Edmonton decided to put one mile of its route and the two downtown stations underground. The other three stations and the rest of the route are aboveground. The cue for Edmonton's light rail line was also provided by experience in European cities where trams frequently are run down the middle of a street. It has been demonstrated that a single three-car train carries as many people as does a single lane of automobile traffic in an hour. "It's the flexibility of the system that makes it attractive," said Wright. Edmonton author Mary Kate Rowan observed that her city's experiment with light rail vehicles is "a big gamble for a small city." Whether it succeeds or not will not be fully determined for at least a decade but the experiment itself is significant—just as is the light rail experiment in Buffalo, New York—if only because it demonstrates that municipal planners are, more than ever, determined to find alternatives to the private automobile and the diesel bus.

One of the most pivotal boosts given to the mass transit business was provided in 1964 when the federal government agreed to provide financial aid to municipal governments that had bought private transit company assets and modernized their systems. The Urban Mass Transportation Act (1964) allowed the federal government to provide up to two-thirds of the funds needed for capital expenditures on transit projects.

UMTA funds continued to increase and by 1974 the government was providing up to 80 percent of the capital expenditures and 50 percent of the operating expenses subsidized by local governments. Typical of these grants was a $607,000,000 subsidy received in 1978 by the Massachusetts Bay Transportation Authority. This was the largest urban revitalization grant ever made by the federal government. It covers a five-mile strip originally bought for use in Interstate Highway 95. The highway scheme was abandoned a few years ago after intense pressure from ex-Governor Francis W. Sargent and incumbent Michael S. Dukakis. Both feel that mass transit is needed more than highways—which, of course, is true. The rail project will see the Orange rapid transit line relocated from its elevated structure over Washington Street. It will run from just south of Essex station through a new South Cove tunnel, now being built, to the railroad right-of-way, and this will be depressed 4.7 miles to Forest Hills.

Funds also have been spent by the U.S. Department of Transportation to determine the most effective means of luring travelers out of their cars and into mass transit vehicles. In an article written by Bonnie Potter for the United States Information Service, the suggestion that some cities might eliminate fares in the future was put forth. Potter explained it as follows:

> Several cities have already experimented with no-fare transportation in a limited area.
>
> Cities such as Seattle and Portland have instituted the system for certain zones usually in combination with a fare reduction for the rest of the system and improvement of the services. This combination actually produced a 12 percent increase in revenues in Portland, Oregon, where the 268-block no-fare transit zone served as a marketing device to attract and accustom new riders to public transportation.
>
> But the no-fare system in most cities would mean a huge increase in operating subsidies. When the city of Atlanta, Georgia, reduced its 40-cent fare to 15 cents, it increased ridership by 28 percent but at a cost to the city of $10 million a year. No-fare public transportation, which a congressional study estimates would boost ridership by 40 to 60 percent in most cities, would cost significantly more.

The U.S. Department of Transportation, which has conducted studies on the most effective methods to increase ridership, has concluded that the most effective means are to increase the speed, frequency, and quality of service. The second item influencing riders, they say, is how well the service adheres to its schedules. Next come fare reductions and lastly, the equipment. "Riders who have other transportation are willing to pay something for service," one expert says. "Lower income riders usually have no other form of transportation. They will pay high fares out of necessity. But for social and political reasons cities cannot allow these costs to rise too high." As for equipment, John Neff, a specialist at the American Public Transit Association, says that "transit riders seem willing to ride anything as long as it gets them where they want to go quickly and reliably."

The federal government has also intensified its development of fixed rail vehicles, from subway trains to trolley (light rail vehicles) cars. A major focal point for such testing has been the Department of Transportation's High Speed Ground Test Center in Pueblo, Colorado.

In 1971, the test center began to take shape as 9.1 miles of electrified track and a short trolley system appeared on the desert plain. About 275 persons are employed at the 30,000-acre test facility, which is close to 125 miles from Denver and subject to severe seasonal temperature changes.

"We intend to become a sort of consumers' digest for cities buying mass transit equipment," said an official of the Urban Mass Transportation Administration (UMTA), which supervises the transit research.

During the first years of the Nixon administration, the test center worked on a "linear induction motor" (LIM), which is designed to provide propulsion for new kinds of transit vehicles without wheels. Compressors in the vehicle will produce a thin cushion of air beneath it and on each side, so that wheels are not needed.

Despite the success of the LIM motor, most testing of advanced ground systems has been abandoned and the emphasis has shifted to what the Transportation Department calls "near term" problems, such as improving subway and commuter rail systems and working to reduce freight care derailments. The test center currently maintains one train specifically for testing new ideas—the Advanced Concept Train (ACT I).

ACT I waits on line these days while train and streetcars zoom up and down the testing track during their stopover in Colorado. The High Speed Ground Test Center's Public Affairs Director, Preston Lockridge, sees the day coming when all rail vehicles will come to Pueblo instead of directly from the manufacturer to the city mass transit system. "The advantage here is that you can run a car for twenty-four hours and send it right to the barn if there's a problem. If the doors jam or the engines fail you don't have thousands of people trapped here."

The test center most recently gave its passing grade to Boeing Vertol light rail vehicles now in use in Boston and San Francisco. Other cars headed for Boston's MBTA were being put through the center's Acceptance Test Program in March 1979. However, many of the Boston cars failed in revenue operation.

"We're expecting cars from Atlanta and several other cities soon," Lockridge said. "Now that UMTA has changed their policy and funds 80 percent of most urban systems, they'll want to be sure that cars are tested here first, before they go into service."

Colorado's test center, home of the desert's first subway and streetcar system, may soon serve as the way station for all of the nation's ground rapid transit vehicles. But if the cars pass muster in Pueblo, yet fail in regular use, the value of the test center must be questioned.

23

The Newest Subways
in America–San Francisco,
Washington, D.C., Atlanta

In a sense it was appropriate that San Francisco, the one city in North America that perceived the value of the nineteenth-century cable car (introduced in 1873), should have unveiled America's most modern rapid transit system since World War II in 1972, nearly one hundred years later. Graced with sleek 80-mph trains, the San Francisco Bay Area Rapid Transit System (BART) promised to be the very model of the mass transportation of the future.

That BART's rapid transit system came to be is an example of belated duplication, since a grand network of traction lines had previously existed. A splendid mass transit operation—the Key System—fanned out from San Francisco, serving much of the Bay Area in pre–World War II days. It was, in time, wiped out, only to be "replaced" decades later by BART, which has paralleled or duplicated many of the multimillion- (billion by today's standards) dollar rights-of-way that had served San Francisco with competent electric traction.

Strangely enough, by the time the last five trans-Bay rail lines, which had operated into San Francisco over the San Francisco–Oakland Bay Bridge, were converted to bus operation in 1958, a mountain of studies already had been made concerning the future of transport in the nine counties fronting on San Francisco Bay. In 1946 a joint Army-Navy report mentioned the possibility of constructing an underwater tube, which was the closest the bi-service study came to prophesying the future. While the Key System still was alive, another report was compiled by Parson, Brinckerhoff, Hall and MacDonald. It detailed a regional transit plan for nine counties. Harre W. Demoro, technical editor of *Mass Transit* magazine, lauded the thoroughness of the study. "The transit system," wrote Demoro, "was planned as part of the region along with the future use of land and other developments. It was a bold step for the Bay Area: creation of an integrated land and transportation plan."

Bay Area transit experts concluded that highways and rapid transit were needed. This was not unusual. Similar plans were being unfolded all over the

country; the difference in San Francisco is that the blueprints were not moth-
balled but, rather, were translated into action by the legislature. The result, in
1957, was the new San Francisco Bay Area Rapid Transit District.

Although a five-county rapid rail system was initially planned, the referendum put to the voters in 1962 called for a three-county operation featuring the
most modern rapid transit system in the Western Hemisphere. The electorate
supported the idea by more than 60 percent and approved a $994,000,000 fi-
nancing plan that included a $792,000,000 bond issue to be repaid by property
taxes. "At the time," said Harre W. Demoro, "it was considered the largest local
public works project ever financed. The cost ultimately was $1.6 billion."

How was it possible to win approval for such an expensive proposition less
than five years after the Key System was declared null and void in favor of the
automobile? The answer lies, in part, with the increasing realization by voters
that the automobile is doing considerably more harm than good to America.
Wrote Robert Lindsey of *The New York Times*:

The sooty haze of air pollution and the seemingly hopeless race to build more freeways
to keep up with wave after wave of more cars were causing increasing disenchantment
with the automobile. . . . Depicted as the ultimate weapon against the ailments of America, mass transportation was to be an urban I.C.B.M. that, in a single shot, would knock
out pollution, congestion, urban poverty, the exodus of city dwellers to the suburbs, inner
city decay, and wasteful consumption of energy.

Now that BART's subway was approved in theory, the time had come to
translate the available dollars into a realistic system; and here is where BART
failed. It opted for opulence and space-age technology when it should have followed the example of Toronto and chosen clean simplicity and tried and true
rapid transit. Standard, motorman-operated, third-rail subways had proven
themselves throughout the world but especially in New York City, Chicago, and
Toronto. BART and its planners decided to take on the automobile, and they
believed that an extremely sophisticated, technologically advanced, and artisti-
cally refined system was a must. Almost everything was to be different; instead
of standard 4-foot, 8½-inch track gauge, BART selected 5-foot, 6-inch gauge,
ostensibly to provide more stability for the trains. Whereas the average subway
uses 600 volts d.c., BART went for 1,000 volts d.c. for propulsion. Writing about
BART in the Smithsonian Institution's publication *Subways* in December 1977,
Harre W. Demoro delivered a superb analysis of BART and its development
from drawing board to trackside:

The boldest move [wrote Demoro] was the decision to put a complicated junction with
switches in the middle of the system at Oakland, and to control the entire railroad automatically. The junction allowed trains from any suburban route to duck through the
tube and take commuters directly into San Francisco, rather than requiring some of
them to transfer in Oakland. The automation was to allow fast running at close intervals
and with safety, and also make possible the almost split-second timing required to use
the junction, which required trains on two tracks to merge into one track.

Time would prove that the decision to install a computer-controlled network was highly questionable. Weeks after it opened, for instance, BART suffered a number of embarrassing breakdowns. Another decision that inspired considerable debate was the choice of car maker. Ordinarily, a subway city such as New York, Chicago, Philadelphia, or Boston would look to the old reliables, such as St. Louis Car Company, Budd, Pullman-Standard, or American Car and Foundry for its rolling stock. But times had changed and new companies were trying to get into the mass transit act. As Robert Lindsey of *The New York Times* wrote:

In cities such as Seattle, San Diego, and Bethpage, Long Island, many of the nation's aerospace companies and related industries could see that the missile boom and the moon boom, so profitable in the 1960s, were coming to an end. Searching for new markets, they began cranking out technical papers and fanciful art work proposing an armada of commuter systems using the know-how that was taking man to the moon.

One of the aerospace companies that jumped into the car-building business was Rohr Industries, Inc. In retrospect, it is astonishing to imagine that a relatively inexperienced car builder was designated to produce the vehicles. In 1964, for example, when the BART subway was in its formative stages, the St. Louis Car Company built a fleet of cars for New York City's IRT lines to serve the World's Fair. These St. Louis–built cars were the most maintenance-free of any recent New York City subway cars, averaging 61,000 miles between major failures, compared to the system average of 13,900 miles between failures. Yet Rohr Industries constructed the mostly aluminum cars.

"After three years," commented the January 12, 1976, issue of *Newsweek*, "BART still has its kinks. As many as half of the sleek cars are out of service at any given time, causing delays and standing room only for San Francisco commuters, who have dubbed it Bay Area Reckless Transit." In the Smithsonian Institution's issue of *Subways*, Harre W. Demoro looks back at the BART rolling stock and notes: "BART's cars have been troublesome with as many as 200 inoperative—out of a total of 450. In recent months, many more cars have been placed into service, and reliability is improving." However, one can only wonder how much better it would have been had BART employed a nonaerospace philosophy of technology, used standard cars, and given the car-building contract to a firm with more than sixty years' experience in the business, such as the St. Louis Car Company.

Was it a mistake to allow aerospace firms to build new subway and LRV-type trolley cars? Many observers believe this to be the case. In a cogent letter to *The New York Times* on June 2, 1974, Harry Rado and Greg Johnson of Syracuse, New York, put it superbly:

It is disturbing to watch Boeing, Rohr, and the rest of the aerospace cabal grapple ineffectively with the dilemma of urban mass transit.

They have spent millions of tax dollars trying to solve the problems of dispatching, signaling, car design, and motive power only to fail miserably in all departments.

Yet fully functioning mass transit systems were a reality in the United States between 1905 and 1930. The heavy interurbans and multiple-unit electric passenger railroads of 1925 were able to carry millions with an enviable record of safety and cost efficiency. Ninety-mile-per-hour speeds, five-minute headway, fail-safe signaling, and reliable operation were easily achieved with electro-mechanical technology of the World War I era.

Most of the world's largest cities built rapid transit systems at one time. These solvent and stable lines were demolished in the United States by a flight of capital to volatile growth areas.

The automotive industry, helped along by subsidized cheap gasoline and subsidized highway construction, was one such area. We are still paying a heavy price for this infatuation with the automobile.

We could meet the needs of today's gas-short and transit-hungry public by dusting off some fifty-year-old blueprints. However, the aerospace contractors are anxious to prove that their exotic technology is applicable to a new area of potential government contracting.

Extravagant solutions to justify excessive cost are a way of life for the aerospace industry, grown fat on the unquestioned consumption of Uncle Sam's billions.

How effective a solution can we expect from aerospace companies with business producing subsidiaries, and whose directors meanwhile also govern automobile manufacturing companies?

While engineers make plans to dynamite the ill-conceived Morgantown, West Virginia, people-mover, Muscovites are daily riding the best transit system in the world.

The same, unfortunately, could not be said for San Francisco–Oakland and its complicated BART. Glorious concepts such as automatically controlled ninety-minute headways were scrapped for the duration when the California Public Utilities Commission failed, at first, to provide full safety clearance for the intricate operation.

Apparently none of these gremlins had been anticipated in the euphoria of construction. When the first segment of BART's masterpiece of mass transit finally opened on September 11, 1972, the gloss of the aluminum cars and the beauty of the stations distracted viewers from the basic problem that the new rapid transit line was too sophisticated for its own good. In one instance, a train failed to slow down at the end of the line, barreled through a sand barrier, and did a nose dive into a nearby parking lot!

BART general manager Frank C. Herringer was hard pressed to defend a system that betrayed kinks three years after opening, but BART could blow its horn over a number of significant assets. Despite the inescapable problems, it proved to be one of the most modern subways in the world. When functioning, the comfortable, carpeted trains ran quietly and smoothly at a top speed of 80 miles per hour. Electronic signboards at each of the thirty-three spotless stations along the seventy-five-mile route flashed the impending arrivals and destinations of the trains. "Most San Franciscans agree," noted *Newsweek*, "that BART is great—when it runs." In January 1976 Herringer predicted that by 1978 the troubled transit system would be on the right track.

Unfortunately, many transit reviewers were not willing to wait that long to pass judgment. *The New York Times* critic Robert Lindsey allowed that the trains are fast, clean, quiet, and comfortable; the stations spacious, modern, and architecturally impressive; but he also took due note of its failings:

... the system that was designed to pay for itself is running heavily in debt and seems unable to get out of it; its record of reliability is atrocious; and it has hardly made a dent in the traffic jams it was designed to reduce substantially ... many of the commuters who continue to clog the freeways say that BART doesn't take them where they want to go.

BART, conceived as the best urban-transportation system that money could buy, was supposed to give the rest of the nation a look at its own future. But, so far, for a variety of reasons, the future hasn't quite worked.

Another critic was Professor Melvin W. Webber of the University of California at Berkeley. According to Professor Webber, the whole BART idea was a colossal mistake to begin with. The roots of his argument were found in a two-year study of urban transit. Professor Webber revealed that BART had attracted only 131,000 riders daily—half the original projection. Webber explained that the lack of patronage was due, in part, to the fact that BART simply isn't convenient.

The professor pointed out that in order to run its trains at high speed, BART built widely spaced stations. Most commuters thus have to take a bus or car to the nearest station—and many of them won't bother. "The paradox," said Webber, "is that potential passengers are not using it because it is too rapid."

Its critics notwithstanding, BART did get better with the passing of years. The trains proved that they could operate automatically without causing death-inducing collisions (an operator in the cab is able to prevent doors from closing on riders, and if the automatic equipment goes haywire, the monitor can halt the subway). More important, people who experienced the BART ride began to appreciate it if not actually love the new subway. Typical was a reaction of R. D. Soto, a former Californian who moved to the Seattle area after BART had been completed. In a letter to the Seattle *Times* on January 21, 1977, Soto remarked:

I anticipated that my commuting problems [in Seattle] would be greatly lessened. . . . What is not beautiful, however, is the "horror" I encounter every day trying to wend my way across the bridges into downtown Seattle. Bus service is not much better, since they must negotiate through the same mess. . . . Why is no one in Seattle/King County looking instead at a rapid transit system (i.e., BART in San Francisco)?

After its fifth birthday, during which BART's life was pockmarked with strikes, fires, and delays, there was evidence of meaningful progress. While motorists were regularly being killed on freeways, passengers on BART were enjoying a relatively safe ride. "There was not one passenger death," wrote Harre W. Demoro, "not even a serious injury. The subway and elevated stations retain a well-scrubbed appearance. The silvery trains are among the quietest and fastest in the world."

On January 17, 1979, BART experienced its first serious malfunction, resulting in a near catastrophe.

At 4:30 P.M., a BART train lost its "cover" (a line-switch box cover, constructed of aluminum, which is located under each car to protect the electrical wire system), which became lodged between the third rail and the rail hood. Trains subsequently passing through the track between Fremont and Daly City all struck the cover very slightly, not hard enough to be noticed, misaligning the third rail. Finally, the tenth train through hit the cover, causing a short circuit and sending sparks flying into the air, even setting some seats on fire. The fire sent forty-six commuters to the hospital with smoke inhalation and resulted in the death of one fireman.

A board of inquiry later declared that the cover had not been secured properly and the maintenance department inspectors would be held responsible for any future mishaps. Since the fire, the covers are checked every time a train is sent out, and there is a strict policy of signing in and out after each part of the machinery is inspected.

Clearly, BART had not nearly filled its potential. By the end of December 1977 the system still was operating only on weekdays. The thought of a subway closed on Saturdays and Sundays was anathema to a New York straphanger accustomed to seven-day-a-week service, twenty-four-hours-a-day.

Nevertheless, with seventy-one miles of electrified tracks, a 3.6-mile-long tunnel under San Francisco Bay, and thirty-four attractively appointed stations, BART has much to be proud of and a healthy future ahead. In the manner that Toronto's growing subways inspired new construction, BART is credited with stimulating more than $1 billion in new office buildings in the downtown areas of San Francisco, Oakland, and Berkeley, as well as subcenters such as Fremont, Hayward, and Walnut Creek. At least two decades of operation (September 1992) will be necessary before a thorough verdict can be delivered about the BART project. However, a meaningful interim report was delivered by Harre W. Demoro in *Subways*:

There is a growing platoon of riders who are discovering BART is a graffiti-free example of civilized urban travel. San Francisco was where the freeway revolt began. BART was the first major transit system built in the United States in fifty years. With the energy crisis approaching, some observers wonder if there is a lesson in BART.

If BART was, at least, a partial repayment to Bay Area commuters for the malevolent destruction of its Key System, Washington, D.C.'s Metro subway was a down payment to Capital District mass transit users for the irrational elimination in January 1962 of one of the finest transit systems in the nation, the D.C. Transit System, Inc., formerly the Capital Transit Company. For, in a city well-suited to their use, Washington employed streamlined PCC cars in the manner to which they were designed. The broad, tree-lined avenues of Washington, some of them with median strips reserved for the exclusive use of transit vehicles, enabled the nimble streamliners to demonstrate fully their rapid acceleration and smooth riding qualities. In the suburbs, lines such as Branchville and Cabin John furnished fast, comfortable rapid transit service on rights-of-way through the pleasant Maryland countryside.

Yet, as noted elsewhere in the book, the District commissioners rebuffed all attempts by the final streetcar owner, O. Roy Chalk (he had tried to get a bill through Congress preserving the car lines), to keep the streamlined trolleys on Washington's streets. After 99½ years of scheduled streetcar service, the last car ran early in the morning of Sunday, January 28, 1962. There were those who justifiably believed that they had seen the end, forever, of Washington mass transit rail service. But just three years later a startling turnabout occurred in the thinking of Washington's planners. President Lyndon Johnson signed a bill authorizing a twenty-five-mile, $431,000,000 rapid transit system for the Washington, D.C., metropolitan area, five years after the National Capital Transportation Agency was created.

According to blueprints laid out at the time, five lines would funnel into a subway under G Street, crossing the downtown section and connecting Capitol Hill, Union Station, and the White House areas. One branch was laid out to run under the Potomac River, serving the Rosslyn and Pentagon areas of Virginia. Another line would use the Baltimore and Ohio Railroad mainline right-of-way to Silver Spring and Woodside, Maryland. A third was targeted to head east past D.C. Stadium to serve Kenilworth. In its original proposal the agency called for thirteen miles of the twenty-five-mile system to run underground.

Not surprisingly, considerable changes were wrought before ground was actually broken for Washington's Metro. Instead of a twenty-five-mile subway, blueprints grew until a ninety-eight-mile network became the final plan. It was hoped that the first trains would run by 1970, but Metro didn't start operating until six years later.

Under the orchestration of the Washington Metropolitan Area Transit Authority (WMATA), ground was broken on December 9, 1969, at the site of the Judiciary Square Station. Immediately transit pundits turned their attention to Washington, and for very good reason. The capital's new system was viewed as a test case for the rest of the nation. In Washington itself, WMATA's role was regarded as that of the keystone to the solution of the area's commuter transit problem. WMATA itself took a singularly immodest view of the impending construction, calling it the world's largest public works project. In 1973 its cost was pegged at $2.98 billion and nobody believed that that would be the limit. Nor did anyone believe that WMATA would be free of problems since many aspects of the capital's system were being patterned after the San Francisco Bay Area's BART system. Similarities existed in the realm of automatic train operation as well as automatic fare collection. Each subway operates underground in downtown areas with much other construction at grade or on an elevated structure.

For answers to the question about making the system better than its predecessors, WMATA studied BART, Philadelphia's Lindenwold Line, and the Massachusetts Bay Transportation Authority's South Shore line. Despite the fact that Rohr-built cars had been plagued by numerous bugs on the BART subway, including sticking doors, erratic interior lights, excessive disc-brake wear, low brake system hydraulic pressure, short-circuits, and air-conditioning ventilation problems, WMATA gave Rohr a $91,600,000 contract to build three hundred transit cars. They were designed as seventy-five-foot units to operate as "married" pairs, with each piece of rolling stock to seat eighty-one passengers. Although the cars were built to travel up to 75 miles per hour, the average speed including stops is 35 miles per hour.

Unlike New York City's first subway, built almost seventy years earlier, and which was almost completely underground, Washington's Metro was placed in tubes for less than half its distance—47.2 miles of subway, 50.5 miles of surface and elevated lines. Because of the complex nature of the Capital District's rock and soil formation, several different techniques of subway tunneling were employed. For example, G Street, in the downtown shopping area, was excavated by the conventional cut-and-cover method, whereas rock conditions under Connecticut Avenue dictated the tunneling of several miles of deep hard-rock bore.

For the first time, "shotcrete" (a sprayed concrete) was applied in American subway construction. At first the rock tunnel—at points the twin twenty-one-foot semicircular tunnels are more than one hundred feet below street level—was strengthened by rock bolts. In addition steel ribs were placed every few feet along the bore. Then the "shotcrete" was used to seal the tunnel arch and cover the exposed steel.

In order to bite through the rock, contractors used both "drill and shoot" tunneling shields and newer tunneling machines called "moles," which cut the rock with giant slicing faces.

One of the major challenges was the reduction of noise and vibration, the twin plagues of many subways, especially older ones such as New York's IRT line. To reduce these problems, WMATA adopted the use of cushioned track on the entire system, putting floating track slabs in certain sensitive areas, such as under the D.C. Court Building complex in the vicinity of the Judiciary Square station. Here special pads support a concrete slab bearing the track and third rail. Welded track was installed to eliminate the clickety-clack and was cushioned by three-quarter-inch rubber or fiberglass pads.

Throughout its young life Metro was plagued with political problems and concomitant delays. Precise locations for stations and even station entrances were hotly contested. For example, the Alexandria (Virginia) City Council wanted the Springfield route moved into a subway that would pass under the downtown area rather than use the right-of-way of the Richard, Fredericksburg and Potomac Railroad several blocks to the west. Likewise, location of a station entrance at Silver Spring created a long-running dispute. "In this case," commented *Headlights*, the bulletin of the Electric Railroaders' Association, "WMATA engineers indicated that any of the three proposed locations was agreeable to the agency since all would serve the public about equally well. Local interests, however, kept the pot boiling several months while they argued it out among themselves. The total distance between the two most widely separated stair locations was about forty feet!"

The obstacles notwithstanding, Washington's Metro had its world premiere in March 1976 and then faced a series of skirmishes with the federal government, which sought to trim the system from a hundred-mile system of five lines serving the District of Columbia and nearby suburbs in Virginia and Maryland to an emaciated sixty-mile subway. After considerable bickering, the administration of President Jimmy Carter accepted the concept of the hundred-mile system. The new price tag was placed at upwards of $7 billion and the new target date was fixed at 1987.

Enthusiasm from the public paved the way for governmental acceptance of the grand plan. "Despite some occasional equipment malfunctions," commented *The New York Times*, "and a frequently balky automatic fare card system, Metro has generally won hearty acceptance. The number of incidents classified as criminal actions—harassment, assault, or theft, for example—has been extremely low. There is no graffiti problem. Trains and stations are clean. In two and a half years of operation there have been no passenger fatalities."

Unfortunately, there were numerous fatalities in the difficult construction process. By November 1978 fourteen workers on the subway project had died on the job, which is a rather high figure considering the alleged sophistication of construction work in the 1970s.

There were many parallels between Washington's Metro and the San Francisco BART development. The twelve-mile Blue Line sparked major commercial development at Rosslyn on the Potomac shore. Tall motels and office structures sprouted in the Virginia community and a twenty-two-story commercial center was built on top of the Metro station.

Until September 1978, however, the Metro was still regarded as a glorified commuter railroad because of its 6 A.M. to 8 P.M. service limits and the fact that the subway was shuttered all day and night on weekends. On September 25, 1978, Metro extended its operating hours to midnight on weekdays and five days later inaugurated Saturday service between 8 A.M. and midnight, thus bringing the then twenty-five miles of subway up to full operating status for six days a week. Sunday service was projected for the following year. Coincidentally with the expanded service in 1978, Metro opened a 7½-mile section of its new Orange Line to suburban Maryland. This segment extends to New Carrolton on the Washington Beltway and parallels Amtrak's main Washington–New York line.

In terms of its limited operation the Washington Metro was a success by 1978. More than 183,000 passengers were riding it on an average weekday and it had unquestionably provided a boost to downtown department store business. But it *was* limited. It still didn't go very far and was not open seven days a week, twenty-four hours a day, in the New York City tradition. These limitations, coupled with its ever-spiraling costs, gave pause to those who once unequivocally championed costly, long-term subway projects. So expensive had it become to build an underground railway in the late 1970s that New York City transit officials put the price at $100,000 a foot. Nevertheless, the dead end for subway construction had not yet arrived, thanks to the Metropolitan Atlanta Rapid Transit Authority (MARTA), which built a $2.1 billion fifty-three-mile rail system that opened in 1979.

BART's system was tarnished by mechanical failures and WMATA's mud-on-the-face was due to astronomically high costs, not to mention innumerable delays. It was the hope of MARTA officials to do something right, for a change, in the name of rail rapid transit. "Public transportation needs a winner," said Alan F. Klepper, general manager of MARTA, in May 1978. "Rail transit to a large extent rides on our success."

At least one fiscal innovation gave Atlanta a head start over its predecessors in San Francisco and Washington: for the first time the federal Urban Mass Transit Administration was paying the total cost of a subway. "That," said *The New York Times*, "gives federal officials a stake in the Atlanta program, since a failure could cause funds to dry up."

Congress was not viewing the Atlanta project with unabashed enthusiasm. For one thing most of its members had no particular stake in the new underground project and for another the potential cost sent shivers up the spine of fiscally conscious officials. "Every time the Urban Mass Transportation Administration goes to Congress for money," said Klepper, "they get San Francisco and Washington thrown at them." To combat the charges, Atlanta subway officials strained to keep the first phase of the project "on time and on budget." It was a noble, if unrealistic, target. The target date for opening was Christmas 1978, a hope that was soon erased and replaced by a 1979 expectation.

Another hope is that the MARTA rolling stock will be considerably more trouble-free than the gremlin-plagued San Francisco cars. Atlanta, rather than settle for an inexperienced domestic manufacturer, awarded a contract for manufacture of its first hundred cars to the veteran European firm Société Franco-Belge. The French firm had a track record of having built hundreds of cars for the French National Railroads as well as the Paris *Métro*. The first two cars that arrived in Atlanta were the first foreign cars to run through United States subway tunnels.

MARTA's list of innovations seems to stretch all the way from the Omni, Downtown, to the distant Avondale station. Instead of placing MARTA attendants at each station, the system has opted for fare boxes for exact change and monthly fare cards. Closed-circuit television monitors security, complemented by roving personnel. To obtain entrance to a one-stall toilet in a station, a commuter must buzz central headquarters.

Aesthetics was a prime consideration in Atlanta as it was in Washington and San Francisco. A different architect designed each station and MARTA insisted that elevated structures be a major design assignment. The els consist of a prestressed concrete roadbed deck, carried on a continuous steel box girder, supported by rectangular reinforced concrete columns.

It is the hope of subway advocates that, in time, MARTA will justify the faith of the federal Urban Mass Transportation Administration, which has funded the subway, not to mention the hope of Atlantans that their decision to promote rail rather than rubber—although buses will be funneled to the MARTA stations—proves as insightful as MARTA general manager Alan F. Klepper predicted it would in 1978.

"What we're doing is building for the future," Klepper asserted. "We can't justify a system for today or even ten years from now. When the energy crisis really hits, companies are going to be looking for cities with a good mass transit system. It's going to pay rich dividends."

24

Mass Transit in Europe, Asia, and Mexico

There has been a normal but somewhat unfortunate tendency on the part of chauvinistic Americans to assume that because Uncle Sam dispatched astronauts to the Moon, therefore he had already conquered the problems of people-moving on the Earth better than the inhabitants of South America, Europe, and Asia. This, of course, is not the case. Because of his addiction to the automobile, Uncle Sam has egregiously lagged in the realm of mass transit. The record speaks for itself; in the United States there are no more than a dozen subways in operation, or in the planning stages. Yet, Europe is blessed with excellent underground systems in Glasgow, London, Amsterdam, Rotterdam, Paris, Brussels, Barcelona, Lisbon, Madrid, Lyon, Milan, Nuremberg, Munich, Prague, Rome, Oslo, Stockholm, Leningrad, Moscow, Hamburg, East and West Berlin, Kiev, Budapest, Athens, and Vienna.

There are subways in such Japanese centers as Tokyo, Sapporo, Yokohama, Nagoya, and Osaka. Even Haifa, Israel, has an underground railway (climbing up a mountain in the center of town), not to mention Tbilisi, Baku, Tashkent, Pyongyang, Seoul, and Peking.

America still boasts the most extensive underground rail system—the New York Region, New York subway and three smaller lines, totaling 263 miles long. However, the next biggest are all overseas. London (260 miles), Paris (157 miles), Tokyo (122 miles), and Moscow (102 miles) head the list of biggest and best subways.

However, New York does not lead in actual numbers of people moved. Moscow holds that honor with more than 1.7 billion passengers annually, followed by Tokyo (1.5 billion), Paris (1.25 billion), New York (1.1 billion), and London (655 million).

Although most of the other subways are smaller by comparison, the proliferation of them overseas since 1960 is extremely significant. Transit expert Boris Pushkarev (author of *Man-Made America* and *Urban Space for Pedestrians*) cites reasons for this growth:

An obvious one is rapid urbanization in Asia, Latin America, and in the Soviet Union. A growing number of multimillion urban areas—from Yokohama and Seoul to São Paulo and Mexico City—have been faced with the need to move very large numbers of people over relatively long distances at a reasonable speed; and there simply is no other way to do that in a city except by predominantly underground trains.

That Europe should be the leader with more than 830 total miles of line (North America was only second with 580 miles in 1975) should come as no surprise. After all, London built the first subway, followed by Glasgow and ultimately Budapest, Paris, and Berlin. In pre–World War II years Parisians ranked among the most enthusiastic subway users on the Continent. The Paris Métro *(Chemin de fer Métropolitaine)* opened, ironically, with little fanfare on July 19, 1900, coincidental with the flamboyant *Exposition Universelle.* French author-editor Olivier Boissière observed that builders of the Métro were concerned about public reaction. "Afraid that this revolutionary means of transportation would be a flop," wrote Boissière, "the officials responsible for the project remained extremely diffident about its inauguration." Actually neither Fulgence Bienvenue, who designed the Métro, nor architect Hector Guimard had anything to be ashamed of, considering the grace and efficiency their talents lent to the first French underground.

Bienvenue held a firm baton over the Métro project from its development late in the nineteenth century to his death in 1932, by which time 116 kilometers were in use and most of the contemporary Paris subway operational. Guimard's legacy is the fancy filigree of Métro entrances, which, more than anything, suggests the trademark of the Paris underground, although "progress," in the form of more maintenance-free entranceways, inspired the demolition of much of this grand work.

In Spain, the entranceways proved extremely practical in a more serious vein. During the Spanish Civil War, residents of Barcelona and Madrid, where subways had been built, poured through these entranceways to find safety from the bombings that were taking place. While the Madrid subway was forced to stop for several months during the war, Barcelona's underground railway continued operating in spite of the bombs.

It is consistent with the Soviet socialist character that public urban transportation has always taken precedence over privately owned automobiles in the Soviet Union. Not surprisingly, Moscow's *Metropoliten* (or *Metro*, for short) is easily the most practical and rational way to travel in the city. A typical morning drive from the distant *Rechnoi Voksal* station in the suburbs to downtown Pushkin Square requires more than an hour, but the train does it in eighteen minutes. Moreover, rush-hour trains run every fifty seconds, so there is virtually no waiting, let alone catching one's breath.

The decision to establish Russia's first subway system in Moscow was made on June 15, 1931. Construction began in 1932. The rate of development was unprecedented: thirteen stations, covering 7.2 miles (11.6 km) of track were opened to the public in 1935. By 1976 the Moscow subway boasted 103 miles (165 km) of track and 103 stations, and in 1996 it is expected to cover 199 miles (320 km) of the city. Even World War II did not supersede the subway; construction continued during hostilities.

One of the more remarkable aspects of Moscow's Metro is that care was taken by its designers to make the riders forget they are traveling underground. Each station was separately designed by a well-known Soviet architect; each is revered for its majestic elegance. There are sculptures, mosaics, and stained-glass panels, and no advertisements of any kind to spoil the effect. There is an absence of litter and graffiti.

The train operator is also the conductor, and more often than not, it is a woman. There are no guards on duty, but women are employed to ensure that the doors are securely closed and that other safety measures are observed.

A ride costs five kopecks (less than seven cents) for a trip of any distance.

By New York City's standards, a major drawback of the Soviet Metro is that it is shuttered from 1 A.M. to 6 A.M., but a comrade in need of a ride can always take a taxi during these wee hours of the morning.

The decision to build a subway system in Stockholm, Sweden, was made in 1941. Originally, it was blueprinted to accommodate a maximum municipal population of 900,000. However, when construction finally began in 1945, there was an unexpectedly rapid increase in the city's population growth. The new count indicated a population of 1,100,000 to 1,300,000, and thus, it became necessary to implement several important changes in the subway's design, such as lengthening the subway platforms from 110 to 145 meters (from 360 feet to 474), and extending the length of trains from six to eight cars.

Today, Stockholm's subway—known as the T-Line—serves 360,000 passengers a day. The line runs sixty miles and has ninety-four stations. Bored through 2-billion-year-old granite, the T-Line often passes through water, since the city of Stockholm is built partly on islands. A major advantage of the T-Line is that it connects to the new shopping centers in the suburbs of Stockholm.

Like many other subway systems around the world, special attention was given to the beautification of the T-Line's tunnels and stations. In the 1950s, the stations were tiled, each one receiving a different color. The central station was more extensively decorated than the rest; the walls sport glass prisms, ceramics, and mosaics. The whole T-Line resembles an underground art gallery, with works by major Swedish artists from the 1950s through the 1970s. The early seventies saw the first of the "cave stations," in which the rock is in its bare, natural state or merely sprayed with cement. The art work on these walls suggests early man's primitive cave art.

Because there are no TV commercials in Sweden, much advertising is done through subway posters. Most anything can be advertised, with the exception of tobacco, pornography, liquor other than wine, and political or religious propaganda. These last items, however, find their way onto the walls in the form of graffiti, of which the T-Line has its fair share. One older station contains a large work, done graffiti-style, by a woman artist in the name of equal rights and world peace.

On a typical Friday night, it is not uncommon to see musicians and singers on the platforms, often playing accordions, guitars, or fiddles. But Friday is also the wildest night of the week. One night in 1976, it was reported that police had to intervene seventy-eight times to break up fights, prevent assaults, disturbances, and vandalism.

Admission to the train is gained by a single ticket, a book of tickets, or a monthly card that provides an unlimited number of trips.

Those who enter the Glasgow subway, or underground, discover a unique creation on the 6½-mile circuit that rings the city. More than a decade before New York City even began preparations for its underground rapid transit system, some thirty designers in Glasgow mapped out a system that provided for two-car trains to cruise around on circular parallel tracks encircling the business district. Because the cars ride continuously on a single set of track, the system needs no switching devices. For this same reason, only one side of the cars is ever exposed to the public view.

Curiously, when construction was begun in 1891, no allowance was made for Glasgow's subway cars to be switched off the track and into maintenance yards. Instead, an opening was provided in the tunnel for cars to be hoisted off the track by crane. This routine has remained virtually the same since the subway began operation. Today a car can be hoisted off the track and another one substituted in its place, all within six minutes.

Originally, the system was designed to use cable cars, as they had proven successful in other cities such as New York. But in 1934 the old cars were outfitted with 60-h.p. motors and an offset third rail was installed.

When engineers designed the Glasgow system they mistakenly believed they had accurately estimated the size of future rush hour crowds by providing for as many as two cars. Today, however, Glaswegians may be found lined up on the streets outside the busier stations during rush hour, waiting for a chance just to get in. Once inside a station the commuter may board a car that allows him only enough standing room if he positions himself in the middle of the car. Yet, in spite of its old age, the Glasgow subway system is far from obsolete. Indeed, the time-tested subway of Glasgow has earned the respect of those familiar with rail transportation. After riding on the Glasgow subway during one vacation, Herman Rinke, former president of the Electric Railroaders' Association, noted that "in a lot of things, they could give us lessons."

When the Vienna subway system is completed sometime during the 1980s, it will be a far cry from the horse-drawn coaches that once carried Vienna commuters to their destinations.

The most noticeable characteristic of the system will be its uniformity. All stations will be designed with red plastic and stainless steel enclosures covering reinforced concrete superstructures.

The system will be divided into two lines: the S-Bahn is scheduled to carry passengers from the suburbs to the city, where they will be able to ride the U-Bahn to their destination within the business district.

The completion of the subway system will mark the culmination of an effort that began as early as 1955. In 1968 construction was finally started; in 1970 the city held a competition to select the final design. Wilhelm Holzbauer and Heinz

Marschalek were both awarded second-place prizes for their plans, which were then combined to complete a final design for the project.

February 9, 1968, was a milestone for rapid transit in Holland, for it marked the opening of the first large-scale subway system in the Netherlands. Rotterdam's 3.65-mile system connects the north and south ends of the Maas River. The system, which contains seven stations (four underground and three elevated), runs beneath the world's largest harbor and serves a city of 731,000 people.

Because central Rotterdam is below sea level, engineers encountered several construction problems. For the 1.3-mile strip running through the center of the city, engineers had to abandon the conventional cut-and-cover method of subway construction. Instead, prefabricated tunnel sections were floated into place through a canal constructed along the route. Once the sections were floated to their proper locations, they were attached to pillars, then driven into the bottom of the canal.

The tunnel under the river was constructed in twelve sections. Each 295-foot section was built on a dock on Van Brienenoord island in the Maas River. When assembled, the tunnel sections were rested on piles as the wet sand at the river bottom was not stable enough to support the tunnel structure.

The elevated portion of the system was completed within two years, allowing track to be laid by the end of 1966. A cement factory designed for the sole purpose of turning out concrete for subway construction is still turning out prefabricated pillars and beams for future additions to the elevated.

Rotterdam's rolling stock consists of two-section cars measuring 95 feet long and 8 feet, 9½ inches wide. Each car contains 80 fiberglass seats and enough standing room for 196 more passengers, giving the standard four-unit train the potential to carry 1,104 people. The machinery on each car includes six motors, two under each of three trucks, capable of propelling the car at speeds of up to 50 miles per hour.

Fare collection on the Rotterdam subway is handled by turnstiles that accept magnetically coded tickets. Passengers may purchase their tickets from any one of at least eight vending machines in each subway station.

In many ways the subway of Mexico City—Metro de la Ciudad de México—suggests the Métro of Montreal; both are rubber-tired means of transportation as well as tourist attractions. Each station in Mexico City features its own unique design reflecting the cultural background of the country. Passengers who stop at the Pino Suarez station, for example, will find that the station is built around a genuine Aztec pyramid, uncovered during Metro construction. Likewise, the Artes station is adorned with Diego Rivera murals. Station walls are decorated in a two-tone color scheme, while each stop also has its own symbol for identification purposes. Pino Suarez, for example, has a pyramid for a symbol, while Zaragoza is identified by a rider on a horse. These distinct markings enable the commuter to recognize his destination even if he cannot read Spanish. An additional attraction is piped-in recorded music to soothe the weary nerves of the commuter or the tourist unable to find his direction.

The Mexico City Metro is only the fourth rubber-tired system in the world.

The others are in Paris, Montreal, and Buenos Aires. Serving a city located at 7,350 feet above sea level, the Mexico City Metro is also the highest subway system in the world. Most of the capital, as well as the technology, was supplied by the French. A $1.6 billion French loan at 6½ percent interest helped finance a major portion of the endeavor.

The system, which encompasses some 30.4 miles of track, is divided into three lines. Line 1, the first to open, in September 1969, took twenty-seven months to build, follows an east-west pattern, and connects Mexico City's airport with the famous Chapultepec Park. Pino Suarez, the station built around a pyramid, serves as a key transfer point on line 1.

Line 2, the longest of the three, runs through the center of the city, with La Taxquena in the southeast and Tacuba in the northwest as the end points.

Line 3, the shortest of the three lines, runs from north to south.

The rubber-tired cars of the Mexico City Metro were built in France, with a standard capacity for each car of 170 riders. An entire train can carry a maximum of 1,500 passengers. Cars can cruise along at a top speed of 48 miles per hour, while pneumatic tires support most of the weight. Steel-flanged wheels are also present, not only to guide trains through switches but also to avoid a catastrophe should one of the rubber tires deflate.

A few thousand miles south of Mexico City, Caracas, Venezuela, is utilizing some of its oil money to finance a subway system, which has been in the planning stages ever since a United Nations report suggested that Caracas, population 3,000,000, construct a subway before 1970. In the mid-sixties local engineers began their own studies, but it was not until the mid-seventies that the government provided the green light for the project.

Projections indicate that the total cost for the Caracas system will exceed $1.5 billion, or double the 1968 cost estimate. The first stretch of the 31¼-mile system will be a 12¼-mile trunk line, running from east to west, which is scheduled to open in 1983. The trunk line will encompass twenty-two passenger stations and employ fully air-conditioned steel-wheeled cars that will travel on steel rails and carry an estimated 1,000,000 commuters daily.

A city does not require a population of 3,000,000 people, like Caracas, to support a rapid transit system. Citizens of Edmonton, Alberta, Canada made this discovery when Edmonton became the smallest city in North America to own a rapid transit system. Edmonton, a city with a population of less than 1,000,000, is the proud owner of 4½ miles of track, which is served by fourteen German-made cars. These lightweight cars attain speeds of up to 40 mph, while one three-car train can carry as many people as a single lane of automobile traffic in an hour.

A major asset of the Edmonton system is its relatively low cost of construction and its use of low-cost, lightweight equipment. Because the lightweight trains are quiet, they can be run above ground and even down residential streets. This means that a lot of money is saved that would have been used to pay for tunnel work. Still, Edmonton chose to run its one mile of track downtown underground to avoid taking a car lane away from commuter traffic. Gerry Wright, a University of Alberta professor and one of the biggest proponents of the Alberta system, is convinced that the city could have saved even more money if it ran the entire system above ground.

It was Wright who got the ball rolling on the Alberta system when he produced a study showing that European cities with populations of only 200,000 were employing rapid transit systems. Wright's study persuaded the people of Edmonton to choose construction of a rapid transit system over the addition of five freeways, which would have cut across park land and bisected the city. In an earlier study, Wright had shown that freeways on the average are filled to capacity after only three months of operation. The $65,000,000 that the initial 4½-mile stretch cost is only a fraction of the $750,000,000 it would have cost to build the freeways.

Edmonton's lightweight system, which averages between 35 and 40 mph, is no match for the Japanese bullet train, the fastest in the world. A bullet train can attain speeds between 130 and 160 mph, and has recently been introduced in several countries around the world. In Zaire engineers from Japan National Railways are aiding in the construction of a 100-mile bullet train route from Banana, on the coast, to Matadi, the country's major port, at the mouth of the Zaire (formerly Congo) River. Japanese engineers in Brazil are also planning a bullet train line from Rio de Janeiro to São Paulo. In the United States Amtrak officials have been looking into the possibility of bullet train transportation for the future. At the moment, however, American bullet train operation offers several problems. The initial one is that a bullet train, which glides along seamless rails, cannot operate efficiently with snow on the tracks. A second problem is that the bullet train might raise some environmental uproar with its high noise and vibration levels.

Help is on the way, however, as the Japanese are working on a quieter version of the bullet train, the bullet train II. This modified version will attain speeds in excess of 300 mph with less noise and vibration. The train will float along the repulsion between the magnetic field in its own base and another magnetic field generated by current passing through the rails.

While Japan may own the fastest train in the world, Hong Kong will soon be the owner of the most heavily used rapid transit system in the world, when the city completes its thirty-eight miles of subway track in 1980. Hong Kong officials estimate that a record 7.5 million people will ride the subway daily, helping to alleviate traffic congestion in a city of 4.4 million people and 300 cars per mile of roadway.

Hong Kong is not the only city that is working on subway plans. Prague and Honolulu are either in the planning or building stages. After years of planning, Prague's subway system commenced operations in 1977. Two years later, the route was extended through the center of the city while additional branches were under construction throughout the ancient capital of Czechoslovakia.

Back in the United States, the city of Honolulu is considering plans for a twenty-three-mile rapid transit corridor which would run from Pearl City to Hawaii Kai. The proposal calls for an initial fourteen-mile stretch running from the Kohala shopping district to the sports stadium. The fate of Honolulu's rapid transit system now rests in the hands of politicians who are alternately considering a proposal to build more freeway lanes for buses.

On the mainland, Baltimore's MTA began heavy construction of an eight-mile underground and aerial train system that will stretch from Charles Center, the heart of downtown Baltimore, northwest to Reisters Town Plaza station. The target date for completion of the project is late 1982, when vehicles from the Budd Company should begin rolling.

On June 7, 1979, construction of an all-elevated heavy rail system for Miami, Florida was begun. The $870,000,000 el will run from south to north with a Hialeah branch, operating in part on existing right-of-way. Residents will be treated to special landscaping along the twenty station route, "a far cry from the ugly Third Avenue El," according to one Miami transit official. The new cars, to be supplied by the Budd Company, similar to the Baltimore cars are expected to begin running by July 1984.

Once a subway system is completed there is always room for improvement. Paris, for example, in 1977, completed a sixteen-year effort to improve its Métro service by opening up a new main station and adding a fast train that could cross the city in under ten minutes. Paris officials claim that the new station, named Chatelet–Les Halles, is the world's largest. The station is built on five levels and allows commuters a choice between taking express trains to the west, southeast, or east, or a fast train to the suburbs.

When the new additions to the Paris subway were unveiled on the weekend of December 10 and 11, 1977, Parisians were allowed free rides in honor of the occasion. The festivities also included underground concerts, art shows, and even a karate exhibition, all courtesy of the Paris Transport Authority.

Improvement also has been the hallmark of the London subway system, long hailed for its comfort and concern for riders. In April 1979, Londoners hailed still another amenity when a new subway line was opened through one of the busiest parts of the metropolis. Requiring seven years to build, the new addition links Baker Street and Charing Cross Station and runs for three miles under Oxford Street and the center of Mayfair. Dubbed "The Jubilee Line," the latest addition to London's Underground is the ninth intersecting line on this splendid people-moving system. At the new Baker Street station, for example, large posters depict scenes from the adventures of Sherlock Holmes. Like many of its European counterparts, the London subway is one whose standards should be the envy of those in North America.

VI

THE HIT PARADE
OF MASS TRANSIT

25

Which North American Cities Do It Best and Why

Is there a city in North America with a perfect, four-star (★★★★) system of municipal mass transit?

No, there is not; not by long shot.

Does any metropolis on the continent rate three and a half stars (★★★+) for its people-moving apparatus?

Again, sadly, the answer is negative. For the fact remains that because of ignorance, nearsightedness, bankruptcy, and conspiracy—sometimes acting in tandem, sometimes independently—every city has failed to fulfill its potential for transporting its citizens swiftly, dependably, and cheaply from one end of town to the other.

Of all the metropolises on the continent, only one qualifies for a good or three-star rating. Toronto has done what no other municipality in North America has accomplished: It has a relatively new network of subways, all constructed after World War II. It has a spate of streetcar lines, emphasizing that Toronto, like no other city from the Atlantic to the Pacific, has revered its trolleys, perceived their value, and resisted the bus industry con to convert the tram empire to diesel buses. The variety of Toronto's rolling stock is further underlined by its impressive fleet of electric buses and, of course, the traditional diesel bus. Nearly every critic questioned on the subject of which cities do it best, and why, selected Toronto at the very top or close to it.

One of the most perceptive evaluations was provided by Stephen D. Maguire of Belmar, New Jersey, a veteran transit critic who writes the column "Transit Topics" for *Rail Fan & Railroad* magazine:

Toronto [says Maguire] has the best mass transit system in North America. The service is excellent; equipment is kept in top shape and company officials have an interest in providing good service.

True enough, but Toronto's subways, as good as they are, remain far from perfect. For example, they all lack express lines, which means that the two-track TTC underground, spanking clean and relatively new, nevertheless is nothing more than one big local. In this regard, the vast, express-filled New York City subway puts Toronto to shame.

More than others, however, the TTC seems to be genuinely interested in luring passengers to its services. Regular huge newspaper ads promoting its assets and special features, (e.g., free rides on New Year's Eve) give the impression that Toronto is always trying harder.

Finding competitors for Toronto's position of eminence was not easy. Several key consultants were polled on the question. These include Howard Samelson, co-owner of the Broadway Limited Antique Company in New York City, who has ridden every major system in North America and is one of the most perceptive students of mass transit in the world; Joseph Spaulding, who worked for several years for the New York City Transit Authority and currently is president of his own transportation consulting firm in Albany, New York; and Dr. Ira J. Sheier of Miami Beach, Florida, a longtime transit buff, who has studied most of the systems on the continent.

THE MASS TRANSIT LEADERS IN NORTH AMERICA

1. Toronto
2. New York City Area
3. Boston
4. San Francisco–Oakland Bay Area
5. Philadelphia Area
6. Chicago
7. Atlanta
8. Washington, D.C.
9. Pittsburgh
10. Montreal
11. Cleveland
12. New Orleans
13. Seattle

NEW YORK CITY—THE BIGGEST BUT NOT QUITE THE BEST

George M. Cohan once said that any place outside of New York City "was Bridgeport" and, to a certain extent, that is true of public transportation. Gotham has the largest concentration of public transit in the United States: an incredible subway system, a staggering fleet of diesel buses, innumerable commuter lines, an inexpensive ferry that crosses New York Bay, and even (in nearby Newark) a small trolley system still utilizing PCC streamliners. For surface transit New York offers an elaborate fleet of diesel buses.

Fortunately, Gotham's elaborate subway system makes bus riding virtually unnecessary. Three divisions—IRT, BMT, and IND—operate a total of 6,674 cars on 26 routes carrying more than 3,000,000 people daily. With certain exceptions, the subway system runs efficiently and, in some cases, with excellent headways.

BOSTON—THE HUB HAS EVERYTHING, ALMOST

It is appropriate that Boston, which pioneered America's first subway, should continue to be a mass transit leader through the 1970s. While other cities talked about a return to high-speed, ultramodern trolley lines, Boston *did* something about it, operating the first fleet of American-built trolleys (LRVs) of futuristic design, built by the Boeing Vertol Company. Although the product itself—the LRV—has been flawed, Boston cannot be faulted for its endless attempts to promote mass transit over auto use. The continuous campaign is waged by the Massachusetts Bay Transportation Authority (MBTA), which provides a wholesome variety of services including trams, trackless trolleys, subway-el lines, commuter rail lines, diesel buses, and ferryboats. All that is missing is a cable car.

The surface transit system utilizes some 1,100 diesel buses, 50 trackless trolleys, and 300 trams on surface and subway-surface routes. The rapid transit system uses 400 cars on seven subway, elevated, and surface lines. Rail commuter service—one of Boston's special assets—is operated under contract by the Boston and Maine Railroad over eleven routes. Additional bus service is provided by private companies in the outlying areas.

SAN FRANCISCO—YOU NAME IT, WE'VE GOT IT!

A visitor to San Francisco has no trouble discovering why the city boasts a proud transportation heritage dating back to the middle of the nineteenth century. The Golden Gate's cable cars are one-of-a-kind on the continent, retained long after Seattle abandoned its cable fleet in the 1930s. In addition, the Municipal Railway of San Francisco (MUNI) has well utilized a fleet of 115 streamlined PCC trolleys, not to mention 333 electric buses. Further, some 1,760 buses are provided in the Bay Area, operated by several organizations. These, however, are small potatoes compared with the Bay Area Rapid Transit System's (BART) ultramodern subway-el, which links San Francisco with Oakland thanks to a tube system under the Bay. BART's subway-el earned the transit niche as the first new large-scale rapid traction system to be built in the United States after World War II.

Critics have correctly singled out numerous flaws in the BART subway—among other things, the rolling stock was built on too sophisticated a level by an inexperienced manufacturer; the system nevertheless is basically sound and promises to grow in value through the years.

Complementing BART is a commuter rail service provided to 8,000 daily riders on a forty-seven-mile route of the Southern Pacific Transportation Company, as well as a commuter ferry service to trans-Bay locations, thus giving the Bay Area one of the most comprehensive collections of transit modes in any metropolitan area.

PHILADELPHIA—W. C. FIELDS WOULD BE PROUD

In the film classic *If I Had a Million,* the humorist W. C. Fields portrayed a man whose lifetime ambition was to eliminate road hogs from the streets. In his native Philadelphia, this is being accomplished by use of a coordinated rapid transit and trolley system that is not thorough or perfect enough to get *everyone* out of a car, but is winning many erstwhile motorists nevertheless.

The Philadelphia transit story is one that now features two public authorities and several private operators utilizing five modes of service—subway-el, streetcar, trackless trolley, diesel bus, and commuter rail lines. While Philadelphia is to be criticized for eliminating many trolley lines in the past, it rates the highest raves for retaining others and, in one case, restoring tram operation after killing it in favor of diesel buses on one long line.

Like San Francisco, Boston, and Toronto, Philadelphia has managed to distill significant ingredients of electric traction (e.g., PCC trolleys), trolley coach, and subway-el into its transit stew, along with the ubiquitous though distasteful diesel bus. While the City of Brotherly Love has a major subway with roots going back to the turn of the century, its underground system isn't as worthy of civic bragging as the high-speed and relatively new Lindenwold Line, which links Philadelphia with suburbia.

CHICAGO—THE AGONY AND THE ECSTASY

Mass transit experts agonized over the decision by Chicago to eliminate its once vast and proud trolley fleet and replace it with diesel buses. The agony was not immediately followed by ecstasy for it required decades for Chicago to reshape its mass transit policies into a more balanced and sensible form. Yet in many ways this has been accomplished in the late 1970s under the administration of the Regional Transportation Authority (RTA). Yes, the trolleys are gone from the Windy City but electric traction still holds forth above, below, and on the ground. Approximately 1,150 transit cars serve 125 route miles on five major elevated and two subway lines. On some runs, the subway attains remarkably high speeds. One of the newest of the regional transportation organizations (1974), the RTA encompasses a large number of separate rail companies and has pursued an aggressive modernization program.

The result has been a relatively modern and attractive fleet of rolling stock with an exceptionally low average age. One of the most laudable aspects of the Windy City subway has been its use of median strips on interstate highways for rapid transit right-of-way. RTA also operates more than 2,800 buses covering 1,042 route miles. These act as effective feeders for rail transit and direct downtown conveyances. Even more important in some ways are the rail commuter lines operated by a number of companies under purchase-of-service contracts with the RTA. The busiest of these, the Chicago and Northwestern, serves

98,000 riders daily on four routes. (Less significant, it is the only commuter rail line outside the New York area with bar cars.) Additional commuter service for 135,000 daily riders is operated by the Burlington Northern, Milwaukee Road, Rock Island, Illinois Central Gulf, Norfolk and Western, and Conrail. Nearly all trains have new locomotives and cars.

ATLANTA—THE BEST IN DIXIE

Of all the major centers below the Mason-Dixon line, Atlanta is the runaway leader when it comes to progressive people-moving. The Georgia metropolis is far from perfect (it is egregiously lacking in electric traction on the surface), but the system has gone from fair to good and certainly is getting better and better.

Unlike other cities that inherited mediocre systems, Atlanta was the beneficiary of an exceptionally competent outfit, the Atlanta Transit System. In time it was absorbed into the Metropolitan Atlanta Rapid Transit Authority (MARTA) and then modernized.

MARTA was approved by a 1964 referendum and created by a 1971 plan passed by the city and some of the surrounding counties. The result was an organization that has progressively served the Atlanta area with a dense bus network as well as its *chef d'oeuvre*, a brand-new subway that is part of an ongoing rapid transit construction program.

Clearly, the jewel of Atlanta's mass transit necklace is its multi-billion-dollar rapid transit system, which opened seven miles of the 54-mile route from Avondale through Decatur to the downtown Atlanta, Georgia, State Station in 1979. In December, the trains should be able to continue for five miles through the Five Points main terminal to High Tower Station.

WASHINGTON, D.C.—GETTING THERE ON THE RAILS

The demise of electric traction on the streets of Washington, D.C., is regarded by many transit analysts as one of the sadder tales of people-moving mismanagement in the nation's long litany of failing to cope with municipal transportation needs. In this case Congress was to blame for allowing the nation's capital, with one of the best trolley systems in the country, to annihilate its fleet of well-kept, pollution-free PCC cars in favor of polluting diesels.

While the trolley's phoenix has not risen as it has in Boston and San Francisco, there has been a very positive compensating development in the form of Washington's brand-new subway, which will not be completed in its entirety for many years. The most modern, automated rapid transit system in the country, the Metro now has three operational lines of an eventual 100-mile complex. This subway-el is completely coordinated with bus and rail routes in the District of Columbia.

The Washington Metropolitan Area Transportation Authority (WMATA) handles 120,000,000 passengers annually with 2,000 buses on an unusually dense downtown system, which is, in turn, fed from suburban lines. Bus lines also feed the Metro from outlying areas, eliminating the necessity of continuing bus routes into the downtown center, as in pre-Metro days. Further, bus route structures are continually revised to serve each transit route as the new subway is extended and opened.

PITTSBURGH—TROLLEYS, YES!

Once the site of a flourishing electric traction system, Pittsburgh recently enjoyed a renaissance under the orchestration of the Port Authority of Allegheny County. Port Authority Transit (PAT) has rebuilt existing services, including the remnants of Pittsburgh's once glorious tram empire.

PAT evolved with 1,000 buses and 95 streamlined PCC trolleys operating on the surface in downtown and suburban areas. Although the PCC cars are chronologically aged, they have functioned well and, with a brazenly colorful decor, have retained, if not embellished, their appeal. To supplement the PCC cars eighty new LRVs will be purchased.

Pittsburgh, like San Francisco, earns a special transit niche because of one inimitable operation. While the Bay Area boasts the cable cars, Pittsburgh's claim to nineteenth-century fame is a pair of incline (funicular) rail routes giving access to the 400-foot escarpment on the south side of the Monongahela River. One of the two inclines is operated as part of PAT Transit and has the oldest transit vehicles in the country (1862 incline cars); the other is privately operated as a museum.

Another curio is Pittsburgh's rail commuter service, one of the smallest in the nation, provided by contract with the Chessie System to Versailles, carrying an estimated 1,500 riders daily. Additional private rail service is provided by the Pittsburgh and Lake Erie.

MONTREAL—THE GALLIC TOUCH

Among all the cities in North America, Montreal's Métro is unique and totally artistic. Like the predominantly French-speaking city itself, the Métro has a very Gallic touch, accentuated by the fact that Montreal's underground has subway cars with rubber-tired wheels, instead of the traditional steel wheels. This idea was put to practical use in Paris long before the Montreal subway was built and helped inspire the Québecois to take a leaf from Paris' transportation book. While critics have argued that the rubber-tired rolling stock has flaws, there is no denying that the Montreal Métro has one of the quietest operations of any big-league subway in the world. There is an unmistakable smell of rubber in the tunnels—but one can't have *everything* in the bargain.

If the rubbery odor is a liability, there are, on the other hand, innumerable assets to balance the ledger. Montreal's subway stations—each laid out by a different designer—are, to be conservative, exquisite—and clean. The cars themselves, though thinner and smaller than, say, Toronto's big, steel-wheeled rolling stock, are attractive and well appointed. Except for occasional crowded conditions, then, Montreal's subway is a pleasure to ride from both a practical and an aesthetic viewpoint.

CLEVELAND—A MIDTOWN-TO-AIRPORT RAPID

A city that was home not only to a superb streetcar empire but also to a formidable trolley maker (Kuhlman), Cleveland lost much of its traction riches to rubber-tired buses but nevertheless has retained and added several attributes. Diversity in the Ohio center is offered in the way of a combined bus, light rail, and rail rapid transit system, administered by the Greater Cleveland Regional Transit Authority (RTA). Surface operations handle some 67,000,000 riders annually on bus routes and an additional 3,600,000 on the surface light rail system.

The pride of Cleveland's rapid transit system is its midtown-to-airport rapid transit line. Thus, Cleveland offers inexpensive direct airport service with a new rail line and rolling stock—including luggage areas—built specifically for that service. Airport trains depart from the center of the city and roll directly into the airport terminal.

One of the few American cities to retain streamlined (though old) PCC trolleys, Cleveland is modernizing its fleet. In a surprise—and pleasant—move, the RTA leased two former Illinois Terminal interurbans from the Illinois Railroad Museum for revenue service. They represent the only museum-owned trolleys in daily passenger operation. New cars on order are expected to beef up Cleveland's light rail fleet.

NEW ORLEANS—STREETCARS NAMED DESIRE

New Orleans' trolleys inspired playwright Tennessee Williams to author *A Streetcar Named Desire*. Some of those same venerable trolleys are still plying the routes of the Louisiana metropolis, utilizing both city streets and verdant grass median strips that partially isolate the trams from vehicular traffic.

America's oldest trolleys, the trams are operated by New Orleans Public Service, Inc., and are complemented by a large bus system. In all, some 76,000,000 riders are handled annually by the 465 buses and 35 trolley cars. In addition to being the last major privately owned system, New Orleans Public Service is the only American operator still using a fleet of pre-PCC streamliner equipment for its streetcar line.

SEATTLE—HOME OF THE TROLLEY BUS

The tragedy of Seattle's transit saga is the city's loss of two superb modes of transit: cable cars and trams, both of which were part of the woof and warp of the city for fifty years and more, from the late nineteenth century to a period before the outbreak of World War II. City fathers in this Washington hub lacked the foresight to perceive the practicality of preserving cable cars and the usefulness of trolleys.

Nevertheless, Seattle in its own way has developed some interesting people-moving schemes, although one of them—the monorail—developed into more of a gimmick than a useful aspect of rapid transit. The major plus of the monorail is its uniqueness in the United States. After that, its value ends.

Also unique but infinitely more useful has been Seattle's comprehensive trackless trolley system, which has suffered a long and not always pleasant history.

The result of public opinion on the side of the electric coaches has been one of the largest conversions to trolley coaches of any municipality in the latter half of the twentieth century. By early 1979 the massive job of erecting trolley wires and stanchions had begun so that ten existing trolley coach lines and six diesel bus routes could be converted to trackless trolley operation for the remainder of the twentieth century. In addition two routes that never had trolley coaches received service. All new rolling stock has been built for the Seattle trolley bus network and power facilities have been upgraded.

26

Postscript on Progress

That the tracks of mass transit's future have been hammered with good intentions is an irrefutable fact. But the difference between good intentions and efficient transport is like the difference between a sloth and a rabbit. Time and again, in recent years, viewers of the business of moving millions have been appalled by the failure of so-called experts in private industry and government to produce a sensible program for mass transit.

No example of blundering tells it better than the decision by the government to support the return of trolleys (light rail vehicles) as a people-mover of the 1980s. It should have been a simple project since years of research and millions upon millions of dollars *had,* in fact, produced the perfect trolley: the Presidents' Conference Car (PCC car), which had been successfully built and refined throughout North America and Europe. In every way—from design to performance—the PCC model was capable of first-rate performance in the 1980s. It was designed by the streetcar industry for streetcar use. Its durability was there to see; PCC cars dating back to the 1940s are still operating successfully in Toronto.

But, no, taking the proven, sensible, less expensive, and easy method was eschewed instead for a difficult and expensive attempt to re-create a trolley technology; and worst of all, by technicians from the aerospace industry. Thus, Boeing Vertol won the bid for the first fleets of standard light rail vehicles that would ultimately be operated in Boston, San Francisco, and an entirely new light rapid transit system in Buffalo, New York.

Boeing, of course, could not be faulted for attempting to diversify but the Urban Mass Transit Administration deserves more than a spanking for overlooking the virtues of the PCC car and the ease with which it could be placed back in service, spanking new and improved.

At first, the new LRV received the usual Madison Avenue hype. It was described as a "modern, streamlined, high performance streetcar that includes every passenger amenity." But it proved a terribly complicated vehicle and painfully expensive. The average price for the Boeing Vertol LRV started at $300,000 per car. By 1977, when Cleveland opened bids for new cars, it discovered that prices ranged from $430,000 to $870,000 per car. By that time the first cars were being delivered to Boston and the first negative feedback was being heard. "New technology," notes Clint Page, associate editor of *Nation's*

Cities Weekly, "means bugs to be worked out and a whole new job of selling the public on what today would be a basic fact of city life had the old trolleys not gone back to the barn forever."

The "bugs," which likely would not have surfaced had the very practical PCC car been revived, began to torment riders and officials in Boston. Further, the standard LRV car—an articulated vehicle—proved too long to suit some transit systems which at first had appeared interested in reviving trolleys. By 1979, the LRV experiment appeared to be more a disaster than a delicious concept for people-moving. Boeing Vertol decided to get out of the business and Boston's Massachusetts Bay Transportation Authority, in turn, refused to comment on their problems with the new LRVs because they were involved in "a disagreement over a possible breach of guarantee by Boeing Vertol," according to one MBTA official.

Boeing public relations director Bruce Jay said that problems should be expected with an all-new vehicle, and although their LRV cars were given the okay by the test center in Colorado, there were bound to be problems in the real world of mass transit. "Out there [in Colorado], they just had to worry about running over rattlesnakes," Jay said. "There were skilled engineers pampering them at all times. In regular use in the real world, you have to worry about thousands of people cramming in these cars daily."

Buffalo, New York, will be taking a long look at Boston's problems as they seek to upgrade their mass transit system. A city where commuters are totally dependent on diesel buses, Buffalo will soon begin construction of a light rail vehicle line.

By early 1979, two construction contracts had been signed and the first ground-breaking took place in April of that year. Jack Bayer, construction administrator for Buffalo's transportation department, said he expects to see buses and electric cars serving Buffalo by 1984.

Buffalo's 6.4-mile light rail system will include a surface stretch downtown, a cut-and-cover subway, tunnel, and a fleet of forty-seven trolleys. Despite several setbacks, Torontonians remain hopeful that a similar 4.5-mile light rail line will be built from the Kennedy Road subway station at the eastern end of the Bloor Street subway to the suburban Scarborough Town Centre. Edmonton, Alberta, built a light rail system and even the New York City Planning Commission in 1979 suggested that LRVs replace buses along its heavily traveled 42d Street route.

If development of adequate rolling stock is—and no doubt will be—a problem, so, too, is the ticklish matter of financing municipal transit systems.

"In Toronto," says Alan Christie of the Toronto *Star,* "the philosophy is clear. The user pays with 70 percent of the Toronto Transit Commission's costs covered by the fare box. The province of Ontario and Metropolitan Toronto share the other 30 percent." In 1979 the TTC charged $3 for six tickets on its subway.

But Toronto's "user-pays" philosophy is not shared by all cities in North America. Such American metropolises as Boston, San Francisco, and Atlanta have been able to charge less for rides because of subsidies obtained in a variety of ways. In San Francisco, for example, the rapid transit system is largely funded by the property taxpayers of San Francisco as well as federal, state, and regional grants.

Likewise, the Metropolitan Atlanta Rapid Transit Authority has desperately attempted to keep fares as low as possible. In February 1979 MARTA was charging only 15 cents for rides on its system but then hiked the tariff to 25 cents on March 1, 1979. MARTA hopes to retain the 25-cent fare on its subway and buses well into the 1980s. This has been possible partially because of a one-half-cent sales tax in the two counties around Atlanta as well as a federal operating grant. Without such subsidies it would be impossible to keep the fares below one dollar. (In 1978 only 23 percent of MARTA's operating expenses came out of the fare box.)

Ken Gregor, special assistant to the general manager of MARTA, suggests that the government should rethink its ways and means of supporting municipal mass transit systems. "If public transit systems are to be considered public utilities," says Gregor, "there has to be more subsidies from the government either through the sales taxes or property taxes."

The Massachusetts Bay Transportation Authority reported that in 1978 fares covered only 25 percent of the cost of running Boston's rapid transit system. The federal government gave the MBTA a $26,500,000 operating grant and the state a $72,000,000 grant. About $74,000,000 was shared by the seventy-nine communities in the greater Boston area through property taxes.

One of the world's newest subways, the Metro in Washington, D.C., has been burdened with high costs. In 1978 costs on the Washington Metropolitan Area Transit Authority (WMATA) reached $59,800,000. Revenue was $30,300,000. The remaining $30,000,000 was shared among eight jurisdictions in Maryland, Virginia, and the District of Columbia through property taxes.

These subsidies, while hardly a balm to the motorists who also shell out property taxes, have been a balm to the low- and middle-income commuter. The subsidies also enable such municipalities as San Francisco and Atlanta to provide an assortment of special fares for senior citizens and schoolchildren. In 1979 in San Francisco, for example, it cost a senior citizen only a nickel to ride a bus; likewise in Atlanta children paid only 15 cents to board a bus. Boston allows students, the elderly, and the handicapped to ride at half fare.

As the worldwide fuel shortage inevitably worsens it will be incumbent upon the federal government to realize that across-the-board federal subsidies will be necessary for all mass transit systems in the country to keep fares down and induce motorists to stay out of their cars. Historically, it has been proven that as mass transit fares rise, ridership drops. Unfortunately, in most cases, the transit authorities refuse to fight the good fight. They raise fares. A few, such as the Montreal Urban Community Transit Commission, buck the tide. Guy Jeanotte of the Montreal Commission was one who realized in 1979 that it would be counterproductive to raise the fares—it is still 50 cents cash or 13 tickets for $5 as it has been since 1975—and lose the riders. "There was a lot of discussion," says Jeanotte. "Should we or shouldn't we raise the fares. But we realized that we lose 5 percent of our ridership with a fare increase, so we decided let's not have it."

Hopefully, this will be the signal for a new continent-wide change in the thinking about mass transit fares while there is still time to save the systems.

In conclusion one wishes to be optimistic about the ability of the Federal Urban Mass Transit Administration to sensibly interpret the people-moving needs of the nation but the reality can only inspire pessimism. While large amounts of money are spent on experimentation—the light rail vehicle, for example—little has been accomplished in terms of substantive accomplishments. Nothing symbolizes the big-talk, no-action syndrome more than a program commissioned by UMTA to create an ideal taxicab. The federal agency commissioned four manufacturers to create prototypes and they, in turn, received design aid from the New York City Museum of Modern Art.

The four manufacturers, Volvo, Volkswagen, American Machine and Foundary, and Steam Power Systems, each built an experimental vehicle. In June 1976 they were put on display at the Museum with appropriate fuss and fanfare. The taxis received rave notices and it was hoped that UMTA would pursue the program to a suitable conclusion. Stewart T. Johnson, the museum's curator of design, was one who has been disillusioned by the project's apparent demise. "My understanding," said Johnson, "was that all of the prototypes were returned to the manufacturers—and that's the end of them."

One could say that like the "trolley of tomorrow," the taxi of tomorrow, never made it into the world of today.

By mid-1979, the mass transit picture was more than grim. Upheaval in Iran, uncertainty in Saudi Arabia and confusion in Washington, D.C., produced an energy crisis, the likes of which the United States has never known. By the summer of 1979 the price of gasoline in some parts of the country had climbed to $1.25 per gallon, amid projections that it would reach $2 per gallon in the not-too-distant future. This fact of life appeared to have solid impact on an American public which *represents only 5 percent of the world's population yet consumes 30 percent of the world's energy.* The "gasoholic" American rider was in trouble, big trouble. It was obvious to Harold Fischer of New York's Metropolitan Transit Authority, who added more trains to meet the demand. And it was obvious to Henry Gay, editor and publisher of the Shelton-Mason County (Washington) *Journal.* In a cogent editorial, Gay noted: "In spite of rising prices and the knowledge that they are wasting a disappearing resource, Americans are gulping gasoline in record quantities. The pursuit of happiness now includes the luxury of driving to work in a pickup-camper that gets six miles to the gallon. Or, driving two hundred horses to the grocery store to pick up a loaf of bread."

State transportation planners in Los Angeles cautioned that unless car usage is reduced, peak-hour traffic will almost stop on the metropolitan area's 625 miles of major freeways.

Once the belle of the Rockies, Denver had become so locked into the grip of automobiles that state health officials rated air quality as "good" on only two days in the 1977–1979 time span, because of car pollution.

Houston's freeway congestion, it has been predicted, will double in five years. Linda Cherington, of the Metropolitan Transit Authority, suggested that a 5-mile drive, which now consumes 20 minutes, will take one hour and 37 minutes in some areas by 1984. And so it went *ad nauseum*.

Jack Gilstrap, general manager of the Southern California Rapid Transit district, indicated that Los Angeles blew its opportunity to alleviate the transit dilemma as far back as 1968. "The system we had planned," said Gilstrap, "would be operating now. We had built a lot of long-range capacity into it. If we had it today [1979] it would be a godsend."

Compounding the problem is the fact that, for the first time in the twentieth century, only one major American supplier of subway cars, commuter, and intercity rail coaches exists in the United States. With the decision in March 1979 of Pullman, Inc., to withdraw from the business after one hundred years of building rail passenger cars, only the German-owned Budd Company remains as the sole domestic supplier of such equipment, and industry leaders question how long Budd will remain. Thus, Pullman joins Boeing Vertol, General Electric, Rohr Industries, and the St. Louis Car division of General Steel Industries (formerly St. Louis Car Company) among those who have withdrawn from car building. This can only hurt mass transit operators, as John deRoos, senior executive officer of the New York City Transit Authority, pointed out. "Diminution of suppliers means decreased competition," said deRoos. "What you may wind up with is one bid and when you have that, you might as well have none at all."

An official of the American Public Transit Association explained that it has been difficult for car-building companies to stay in business, considering the state of the industry. "There simply hasn't been enough business for one manufacturer, let alone three or four."

If the transit industry's failure wasn't discouraging enough, there was the benign neglect of mass transit needs by the federal government in Washington. George Wilson of the Philadelphia *Inquirer* put it best when be wrote: "For all the rhetoric from the White House on energy problems and the urban crisis, there has not been the strong federal financial commitment to urban mass transit that would give motorists the real incentive to leave their automobiles at home and take the bus or trolley or subway or train. If transit fares went down as gasoline prices went up, there would be such incentive. A federal energy policy combined with a federal transportation policy, both designed to make energy-efficient mass transit more attractive in service and fare structure, would get people out of their automobiles a lot faster than exhortations at presidential press conferences."

Perhaps the most telling commentary on the sick state of mass transit was provided, again, by New York City in June 1979. It was then that 109 R-46 cars built by the Pullman Standard Company were withdrawn from service, on orders from Mayor Edward Koch, because of defects.

For five days the pages of the three New York dailies chronicled a Byzantine story of how in 1979 a fleet of relatively new subway cars apparently could not be produced any better than those manufactured seventy-five years earlier. The supposed "dream" car of the 1980s turned into a nightmare. And that, more than anything, tells what's wrong with mass transit in America.

Appendix A

Excerpts from Bradford C. Snell's charges regarding General Motors' involvement with the Nazi war machine, delivered in testimony before the Senate Subcommittee on Anti-Trust and Monopoly in February 1974

... GM's Chairman Sloan reportedly told a group of stockholders on the eve of Germany's invasion of Poland in 1939 that his corporation was "too big" to be affected by "petty international squabbles."

... In 1929, General Motors acquired Germany's largest automobile company, Adam Opel, A. G. By the mid-1930s, these three American companies (General Motors, Ford, and Chrysler) owned automotive subsidiaries throughout Europe and the Far East; many of their largest facilities were located in the politically sensitive nations of Germany, Poland, Rumania, Austria, Hungary, Latvia, and Japan. As the Axis Powers overtly prepared for war, General Motors, Ford, and, to a lesser extent, Chrysler found themselves involved in serious conflicts of interest and national loyalties. Due to their concentrated economic power over motor vehicle production in both Allied and Axis territories, the Big Three inevitably became major factors in the preparations and progress of the war. In Germany, for example, General Motors and Ford became an integral part of the Nazi war efforts. GM's plants in Germany built thousands of bomber and jet fighter propulsion systems for the Luftwaffe at the same time that its American plants produced aircraft engines for the U.S. Army Air Corps.

As owner of Germany's largest automobile factory, General Motors was quite naturally a more important factor in the Axis war effort than either Ford or Chrysler, whose investments were substantially less. GM's participation in Germany's preparation for war began as early as 1935. That year its Opel subsidiary cooperated with the Reich in locating a new heavy truck facility at Brandenburg, which military officials advised would be less vulnerable to enemy air attack. During the succeeding years, GM supplied the Wehrmacht with Opel "Blitz" trucks from the Brandenburg complex. For these and other contributions to wartime preparations, GM's chief executive for overseas operations in 1938 was awarded the Order of the German Eagle (first class) by Chancellor Adolf Hitler.

... Given the dominant structural positions of GM (and Ford) in the war economies of both America and Germany, these firms had the power to influence the course of World War II. They could determine, for example, which belligerent would benefit from their latest advances in war-related technology. Refusal to aid in prewar preparations, of course, was unthinkable. It would have resulted in confiscation and irreparable economic harm to GM and Ford stockholders. In any event, due to their concentrated economic power in both economies, they were able to shape the conflict to their own private corporate advantage. Whether in fact their profit-maximization determinations were also in the best interests of international peace or, more specifically, in accord with the national security objectives of the United States at that time is entirely unclear.

The outbreak of war in September 1939 resulted inevitably in the full conversion by GM and Ford of their Axis plants to the production of military aircraft and trucks. During the last quarter of 1939, for instance, GM converted its 432-acre Opel complex in Russelsheim to warplane production. From 1939 through 1945, the GM-owned Russelsheim facility alone assembled 50 percent of all the propulsion systems produced for the JU-88 medium range bomber. According to the authoritative work of Wagner and Nowarra, the JU-88 by 1940 "had become the Luftwaffe's most important bomber, and remained so for the rest of the war." The Russelsheim facility also assembled 10 percent of the jet engines for the ME-262, the world's first operational jet fighter. Wagner and Nowarra described this jet plane as perhaps "the most important military aircraft to come out of Germany." With a top speed of 540 miles per hour, it was more than 100 miles per hour faster than the American P-51 Mustang, the fastest piston-driven Allied fighter. Not until after World War II were the Allies able to develop pure jet aircraft. By producing ME-262 jet engines for the Luftwaffe, therefore, GM's Russelsheim plant made a significant contribution to the Axis' technological superiority in the air.

On the ground, GM and Ford subsidiaries built nearly 90 percent of the armored "mule" 3-ton half-tracks and more than 70 percent of the Reich's medium and heavy-duty trucks. These vehicles, according to American intelligence reports, served as "the backbone of the German Army transportation system." In addition, the factories of Ethyl G.m.b.H., a joint venture of I. G. Farben, General Motors and Exxon subsidiaries, provided the mechanized German armies with synthetic tetraethyl fuel. During 1935–36, at the urgent request of Nazi officials who realized that Germany's scarce petroleum reserves would not satisfy war demands, GM and Exxon joined with German chemical interests in the erection of the ethyl tetraethyl plants. According to captured German records, these facilities contributed substantially to the German war effort: "The fact that since the beginning of the war we could produce lead-tetraethyl is entirely due to the circumstances that shortly before the Americans had presented us with the production plant complete with experimental knowledge." "Without lead-tetraethyl," the wartime document added, "the present method of warfare would be unthinkable."

It was, of course, in the best interests of GM and Ford to cooperate in the Axis war effort. Although GM, for example, was in complete management control of its Russelsheim warplane factory for nearly a full year after Germany's declaration of war against the United States on December 11, 1941, its refusal to build warplanes at a time of negligible demand for automobiles would have brought about the economic collapse in its Opel plant. Moreover, it might have resulted in confiscation of the facility by the German Government. In fact, on November 25, 1942, the Reich did appoint an administrator for the Russelsheim plant who, although not permitted to interfere with the authority of the GM-appointed board of directors, was instructed to oversee operations. Nevertheless, communications as well as material reportedly continued to flow for the duration of the war between GM and Ford plants in Allied countries and those located in Axis territories.

After the cessation of hostilities, GM and Ford demanded reparations from the U.S. Government for wartime damages sustained by their Axis facilities as a result of Allied bombing. By 1967, GM had collected more than $33 million in reparations and Federal tax benefits for damages to its warplane and motor vehicle properties in formerly Axis territories, including Germany, Austria, Poland, Latvia, and China. Likewise, Ford received a little less than $1 million, primarily as a result of damages sustained by its military truck complex at Cologne. Since World War II, the rebuilt Russelsheim and Cologne plants have enabled GM and Ford, respectively, to capture more than two-thirds of the German motor vehicle market. Meanwhile, GM's truck plant in Brandenburg, East Germany, and Ford's facilities in Budapest, Hungary, have more than likely become substantial factors in these Communist economies.

Due to their multinational dominance of motor vehicle production, GM and Ford became suppliers for the forces of fascism as well as for the forces of democracy.

Appendix B

General Motors' reply to Bradford Snell's charges delivered in "American Ground Transport," made before the Senate Subcommittee on Antitrust and Monopoly, February 1974

At the initial round of Senate hearings on the automobile business, the Subcommittee on Antitrust and Monopoly received a document, prepared by a staff attorney, Bradford C. Snell, entitled *American Ground Transport: A Proposal for Restructuring the Automobile, Truck, Bus, and Rail Industries*. The following is a slightly condensed version of General Motors' detailed rebuttal of Snell's accusations concerning GM.

The two most widely publicized charges were that General Motors aided the Nazi government during the Second World War and that General Motors deliberately sabotaged the rail transportation capability of the United States. It is claimed further that this destruction was accomplished by a farsighted plot, extending over decades, under which GM first coerced rail carriers into abandoning electric vehicles for diesel locomotives and buses, and then cleverly made its diesel products as unattractive as possible so that people would have no choice but to buy cars.

We do not attempt to refute each and every statement contained in "American Ground Transport." This paper will focus on the facts with respect to those basic propositions upon which the whole argument turns. These are: (1) the claim that GM coerced railroads into buying unwanted diesel locomotives by capitalizing on its position as a large shipper and (2) the claim that GM was responsible for the destruction of thriving street railway systems. Since these basic propositions are shown to be untrue, the entire argument advanced in "American Ground Transport" fails.

This memorandum consists of four major parts. Part I refutes the claims that have been made about World War II. Part II deals with the long-refuted claim that GM "forced" the railroads to buy its diesel locomotives. Part III answers the erroneous charge that GM "destroyed" thriving street railway systems. Finally, Part IV refers to various additional misstatements contained in "American Ground Transport."

Although "American Ground Transport" has not been endorsed by this subcommittee or by any individual on it, the document has been widely publicized as the work of a subcommittee staff member and may be construed as bearing the imprimatur of the subcommittee. The false accusations, misleading inferences, and erroneous conclusions which it contains have been repeated across the country, to the damage of General Motors, in newspaper stories, in national television broadcasts, and in public statements by the mayors of two great cities.

We submit that this created an unfortunate situation whereby GM has in effect been indicted publicly without proper means of rebuttal. In an effort to remedy this unusual situation in a fair and equitable manner, we suggest that the subcommittee, upon due deliberation, take the following action—

First: that all further distribution of "American Ground Transport" be suspended at this time;

Second: that this reply by GM be printed in the same manner as "American Ground Transport" by the Government Printing Office;

Third: that this reply should follow "American Ground Transport" in the published record of these proceedings and should be bound with it if any further distribution by the subcommittee is undertaken.

PART I.—GENERAL MOTORS DID NOT ASSIST THE NAZIS DURING WORLD WAR II

Since it has no relevance at all to the Industrial Reorganization Act, it is hard to understand why the discussion of the Second World War in "American Ground Transport" was inserted. This document makes the extraordinary claim that GM (and Ford) actively assisted the Nazi war effort.

The former employees of General Motors who have been slandered by these statements are, for the most part, no longer here to defend themselves. Fortunately, they are adequately defended by the record.

In the years prior to 1939, Adam Opel (a GM subsidiary since 1929) had produced only its traditional products—cars, trucks, and spare parts. After the German invasion of Poland in 1939, the American personnel resigned from management position rather than participate in the production of war materials, even though at this time the United States was neutral. The General Motors Annual Report for 1939 states:

As a result of the declaration of war, and in line with the corporation's operating policies, with full recognition of the responsibility that the manufacturing facilities of Adam Opel A. G. must now assume under a war regime, the corporation has withdrawn the American personnel formerly in executive charge of this operation.

With these resignations, though it temporarily retained nominal representation on the board, GM relinquished effective control over the day-to-day operations of Opel. As early as October 1939, the German Government had prohibited the transmittal of financial or operational reports from Opel to General Motors.

The last of GM's American employees who had been assigned to Opel departed from Germany in early March 1941. A meticulous search has disclosed no communications whatsoever between Opel and General Motors Corp. after September 2, 1941.

Following the German declaration of war on the United States on December 11, 1941, the relationship with Opel was entirely severed. No Americans sat on the board of directors, even nominally, after that time. In 1942, a German custodian was formally appointed by the Reich Commissioner for Treatment of Enemy Property.

Opel, while under GM control, possessed no special aircraft product technology. The product development and engineering required for the production or assembly at Russelsheim of aircraft parts for the JU-88 medium range bomber, and, later, the jet engine of the ME-262 jet fighter, was supplied by German aircraft and aircraft components firms. The German Government brought this German aircraft technology, including know-how, into the Opel plant to build the products of war. GM has nothing whatever to do with the design and development of those aircraft and engines pictured in the document presented to this subcommittee (and in any event no complete aircraft were built at the Opel facilities).

As the war drew to a close, the Russian army occupied what remained of the Opel facility at Brandenburg. (Brandenburg happened to be in the Soviet Zone of occupation, later to become East Germany.) The Russians dismantled the plant and shipped all machinery and equipment by rail to Kutau in the Russian Caucasus. The dismantling even included removal of portions of the buildings. (It should be noted that the Potsdam Agreement of 1945 specifically provided that the Soviets could satisfy their claims against Germany by removing property from the Soviet Zone.)

In light of these facts, the claims that GM "became an integral part of the Nazi war efforts," that "GM . . . was in complete management control of its Russelsheim warplane [sic] factory for nearly a full year after Germany's declaration of war against the United States," and that GM American personnel served on the Opel board of directors "throughout the war" are totally false.

The unqualified statement that "GM's plants in Germany built thousands of bomber and jet fighter propulsion systems for the Luftwaffe" and that since the war, "GM's truck plant in Brandenburg, East Germany . . . [has] more than likely become [a] substantial" factor in the Communist economy without any mention of the fact that GM has or had nothing to do with these operations is totally misleading.

The further charges that GM and other firms "could determine . . . which belligerent would benefit from their latest advances in war-related technology," that they "were able to shape the conflict to their own private corporate advantage," that it served their "best interests . . . to cooperate in the Axis war effort," and that if the Germans had won the war GM "would have appeared impeccably Nazi" have no foundation in fact and are totally irresponsible.

These charges that General Motors assisted the Nazis in World War II are entirely irrelevant to the issues before the subcommittee. Yet, for some reason, they are illustrated with the only photographs in the entire document. If the purpose was to attract publicity, irrespective of the facts or their relevance, it succeeded—at the cost of assaulting the good name and memory of many former employees of General Motors whose patriotism and undivided loyalty to the United States is evidenced by the record.

PART II.—GENERAL MOTORS DID NOT SUPPRESS RAIL TRANSPORTATION WITH THE DIESEL LOCOMOTIVE; IT ADVANCED IT

The argument that GM repressed railroad transportation is introduced by and is entirely dependent upon the following unqualified assertion:

As the Nation's largest shipper of freight GM was able to exert considerable influence over the locomotive purchasing policies of the Nation's railroads. It used this powerful form of leverage to sell its diesel locomotives.

This statement is crucial because it is the cornerstone of the claim that GM foisted inferior mass transportation equipment on unwilling carriers, to the detriment of the Nation's entire transportation system.

The author must have known, because he refers to the fact elsewhere, that the U.S. Department of Justice has conducted an exhaustive investigation of this very matter. In fact, it did so for a period of over a decade in the administrations of three Presidents of both political parties. Hundreds of witnesses were interviewed and thousands of documents were examined; in the end the prosecutors concluded—not once, but twice—that they had no case. The charge that GM used freight to sell locomotives was (we thought) finally laid to rest when the Government moved to dismiss the sole remaining case, with the following statement which is a matter of public record:

Plaintiff recently completed an extensive review and re-evaluation of the available evidence. Based upon this re-evaluation it is plaintiff's view that the available evidence is insufficient to establish the violations alleged.

One would think that anyone who now disinters these abandoned charges would at least acknowledge this past history when he does so. Moreover, if he asserts them as truth in aid of crucial proposition, should he not also come forward with some convincing demonstration that the prosecutors made a mistake? What is offered instead are a grand total of five references which, even if substantiated, would hardly prove a nationwide course of conduct lasting for decades and which, in fact, cannot survive even cursory scrutiny.

The reference to the Gulf, Mobile & Ohio Railroad is supported only by unproven allegations in the indictment in the Government criminal case which was voluntarily abandoned! The reference to the Baltimore & Ohio Railroad, which is set forth to give the appearance of being a quotation from a letter, but isn't, is supported only by one of the author's ubiquitous confidential interviews! Note also that, even if the quotation were genuine, it would not establish that

GM sold locomotives through reciprocity—only that a railroad president tried to obtain freight business that way.

The charge that GM "reportedly used its freight leverage to coerce the [New Haven] railroad into scrapping all of its electric passenger and freight locomotives in favor of GM diesel passenger units" is again supported only by a confidential interview. Moreover, Harold L. Smith, currently general manager of the electromotive division, points out in his statement that the New Haven never scrapped all of its electric locomotives anyway—its successor operates them today. Finally, the charge is belied by the fact that the overwhelming majority of the diesels which were initially ordered by the New Haven were supplied by GM's competition. As of the end of 1956, the year in which the author claims GM induced the New Haven to switch to diesels, only 50 out of the road's 400-odd diesels were GM units—and these 50 diesels were all yard switchers and freight locomotives, which hardly could advance a plot to divert passenger traffic!

The fourth reference [in Snell's report] to "standing instructions" issued on freight shipments in 1935, when read in its entirety, makes it clear that routing is to be based on merit. This is entirely consistent with the instruction which GM's president, Alfred P. Sloan, Jr., issued earlier in the year that freight shall be routed and locomotives shall be sold solely on their separate and individual merits.

The fifth reference upon which the author seems to place great reliance because he mentions it first in the text is not specific, but nonetheless the most misleading of all. In some manner unknown he obtained a copy of a privileged memorandum from the files of GM's outside law firm in the locomotive litigation. This memorandum, entitled "Reciprocity as Proof of the Offense of Monopolization Under Section 2 of the Sherman Act" contains 73 pages. The author of these charges against GM has relied on a single speculative sentence from the memorandum and the significance of this single sentence is totally distorted by its removal from context. Reproduced below is the sentence quoted by the author and the *very next sentence* (italized for emphasis) in the same legal memorandum which makes it clear that the speculation had no basis in fact.

GM could, in all probability, have successfully capitalized upon the railroads' sensitivity to reciprocity by frequently reminding them of GM's considerable traffic, and could have done so without ever interfering substantially with the economical routing of traffic. *The fact that GM did not do so, while EMD's competitors did engage extensively in reciprocity, appears to be a tribute to the strength of GM's policy against reciprocity.*

The author's accusation that GM used its position as a large shipper of freight to sell locomotives has not been sustained. When it collapses, the author's thesis that GM has impeded the development of railroad transportation in the United States collapses as well. But, one can go further and demonstrate that GM has made a positive contribution to the welfare of the railroads.

The significant contribution which General Motors made through its pioneering development of the diesel locomotive is a story that has been often cited as one of the great success stories of American competitive enterprise. It is set forth at length in the booklet *The Locomotive Industry and General Motors*, which was supplied to the subcommittee a year ago and which is submitted for the record at this hearing. It is summarized in the statement of Harold L. Smith, also submitted at this hearing. It is perhaps best summed up in the 1956 staff report of this subcommittee which stated:

... The diesel locomotive revolutionized the railroad industry. General Motors can point to its entry into this field as an example of the operation of a progressive company at its best—entry into a new field, with a new product satisfying an economic need, and offering progressive reduction in the pricing of its product.

Or, as one railroad president put it:

The greatest single contribution to the economic and efficient operation of our railroads during my 40 years of association with the industry has been the development of the Diesel locomotive.

Another railroad president testified on the initial diesel freight locomotive as follows:

... here we had the ultimate. Here was an engine that in my judgement outperformed anything we had in the country. I just made up my mind to two things right now: That the day of the steam engine was history; that I owed a debt of gratitude to the fellows that made that all possible, and that was your company, my good fellow, General Motors.

As the Government knew when it decided to dismiss the *Locomotive* cases, chief executives of other railroads throughout the country were prepared to give similar testimony had the cases gone to trial.

PART III.—GENERAL MOTORS DID NOT DESTROY STREET RAILWAY SYSTEMS; THEY FAILED EVERYWHERE BECAUSE THEY WERE NO LONGER ABLE TO GIVE ADEQUATE SERVICE

For those who seek simple explanations for complicated urban problems, "American Ground Transport" provides a convenient scapegoat, General Motors, which is charged with the "destruction of more than 100 surface rail systems" which caused a "devastating impact ... on the quality of life in American cities." It also provides a simple cure, namely the forced ouster of General Motors from the mass transportation business, presumably to clear the way for the return of the street car.

Although the accusations against General Motors appear to be detailed and complex, their truth can be tested (as it was in locomotives) by examining the fundamental claim on which the whole argument turns. If the street railway systems in this country were not the thriving and effective enterprises that the author claims, then their demise can hardly be blamed on General Motors and their return can hardly be the panacea for the future.

We will set forth in this section the facts about the street railway systems in those cities which the author himself has selected as the prime exhibits in support of his argument. Examination of those facts will show that street railways failed for economic and demographic reasons which had nothing to do with any plot by General Motors.

The fact that General Motors provided a modest amount of financial assistance (without any managerial control) to National City Lines, which had interests in some transit operations, did not have any effect on their decisions to convert from streetcars to buses. Since, however, the author has placed considerable emphasis on the investment in National City Lines and on the National City Lines litigation, it is necessary at the outset to place those matters in perspective. (The source for this brief summary, unless otherwise indicated, is the statement by GM printed in "Hearings, Senate Subcommittee on Antitrust and Monopoly, Committee on the Judiciary," 1955).

General Motors did not invest in National City Lines or any of its affiliated companies because it was interested in obtaining control over the operating decisions of transit operators. In fact, it would have preferred not to invest in National City Lines at all. City Lines was a customer which had borrowed $150,000 at the time it was first organized in 1936, but repaid the loan in 3 months after a public stock sale.

Thereafter, the investment which GM made in National City Lines in 1939, and subsequent investments in American City Lines (a National subsidiary), in 1943, and Pacific City Lines (beginning in 1938 when that company was also a National subsidiary) were made at the request of those companies, which had experienced difficulties raising money from other sources. (The grand total of GM's investments in all three companies was only $2.9 million.) Similarly, partial requirements contracts for GM buses were only negotiated after the customers themselves had requested them.

Notwithstanding the fact that the investments and the partial requirements contracts were negotiated at the request of National City Lines and notwithstanding the fact that General Motors' share of the City Lines' business was lower after the contracts than it was before, these contracts were found to be an antitrust violation. It is this to which the author and other witnesses have so repeatedly referred as the means GM used to eliminate streetcars.

The important thing, however, is not that the violation which was found involved a close point of law [in the National City Lines civil case, the court said: "Whether or not these practices are illegal under the antitrust laws turns upon nuances of circumstances which cannot be foreseen or determined in advance of the event. . . . The failure to cancel these arrangements as soon as they were called into question by the Government is also consistent with a bona fide belief of the defendants that there was nothing unlawful about the arrangements and the court is not prepared to say that in the state of the law at the time the complaint was filed this belief could not reasonably be entertained"], but rather that it had nothing at all to do with the replacement of cars by buses. (The author seeks to reinforce the misleading impression that the National City Lines case involved an illegal conspiracy to substitute bus for rail transportation, by referring to the Government's appellate brief in the case throughout as the "U.S. Streetcar Appellate Brief.") There is not one word in either the Government indictment in the criminal case or the complaint in the companion civil case which charges GM with unlawfully scrapping or eliminating street railway systems.

As pointed out in the opinion of the Seventh Circuit Court of Appeals (*U.S.* v. *National City Lines*, 1951), GM and the other defendants were acquitted of the charge that they had conspired "to secure control of a substantial number of the companies which provide public transportation service" in various parts of the country. The case therefore lends no support to the contention that it was GM, through National City Lines or affiliates, who induced these companies to abandon streetcars. Moreover, the opinion in the case actually pinpoints the basic flaw in the current accusations that General Motors, for ulterior motives, destroyed healthy streetcar systems:

In 1938, National conceived the idea of purchasing transportation systems in cities *where streetcars were no longer practicable* and supplanting the latter with passenger buses [emphasis supplied].

The statement in "American Ground Transport" that "GM extracted" contracts from transit companies requiring the purchase of gasoline-fueled equipment is similarly false. (It is also implausible on its face because the diesel buses, which GM was trying to sell, do not run on gasoline.) The only contract containing such a provision (which apparently was the basis of the Government's accusation) was negotiated by a midwestern oil company; GM had nothing whatever to do with it (*National City Lines* v. *United States*). Moreover, this supply contract did not apply at all to any cities in the State of California, which the author cites as his prime examples of the ruin supposedly wrought by GM.

It is appropriate to turn now to the facts about Los Angeles.

LOS ANGELES

The author claims that in 1939 Los Angeles was served by the "quiet" and "efficient" Pacific Electric interurban electric railway system. This system, he asserts, was complemented by the Los Angeles Railway, which operated streetcars in the downtown area.

In 1936, he charges, GM had organized National City Lines, a "holding company to convert the remainder of the Nation's electric transportation systems to GM buses." Then, in 1940, he claims National City Lines, acting through affiliated companies, and Standard Oil of California, "began to acquire and scrap portions of the $100 million Pacific Electric System including rail lines from Los Angeles to Glendale, Burbank, Pasadena, and San Bernardino." Then "having severed Los Angeles' regional rail links," he claims that "GM and its autoindustrial allies . . . motorized its downtown heart," by converting the Los Angeles Railway system from streetcars to buses.

The story sounds dramatic, but what are the facts? The truth is that both the Pacific Electric and the Los Angeles Railway began to abandon streetcars before GM was even in the bus business and long before National City Lines or any of its affiliated companies were even organized. Moreover, National City Lines had nothing whatever to do with severing "regional rail links," as the author claims.

Pacific Electric commenced the progressive abandonment of its own rail passenger service as early as 1917, fully 23 years before it is claimed that GM (and its "allied highway interests") "began to acquire and scrap portions of the $100 million Pacific Electric System." As reported in an 1958 article in the *Pacific Railway Journal:* "The establishment of bus lines as a substitution for unprofitable rail service began in 1917. . . . Times were changing in Southern California and since PE could not provide proper rapid transit, it had no alternative but to change with the times."

According to a history prepared by its former general attorney, the bus passenger mileage operated by Pacific Electric amounted to approximately 15 percent of the total mileage as early as 1926. By 1939, the year before it is claimed that GM had any role in acquiring part of the system, over 35 percent of the total passenger miles were on buses. Pacific Electric steadily expanded its motor-bus operations in the 1920s and 1930s. Karr wrote in his paper:

> The motor transit company which served local areas and reached as far as Bakersfield, Victorville, and San Diego was partially absorbed into the PE system in 1930. By 1936 PE had purchased all interest owned by Greyhound and the lines were wholly merged into the PE bus system.

It is undisputed that the rail passenger operations of Pacific Electric were a financial catastrophe. Thus, Karr reports:

> The rail passenger operations were never profitable with the exception of the year 1923 and the war years of 1943 and 1944. During those two war years rail passenger service was profitable; however, by 1946 the annual loss was $2,200,000. In 1947 the loss climbed to $3,426,000, and this loss was incurred on a gross rail passenger revenue of approximately $10.5 million. If these amounts are converted into today's costs, the amount of loss is not only substantial but simply impossible for private enterprise to bear.

In 1940 the California Railroad Commission (predecessor of the public utilities commission) in a decision which inter alia granted the application of the Pacific Electric Railway to abandon portions of its railway lines altogether and substitute bus service on other portions, stated:

> Most elementary dictates of good business require that an industry stand on its own feet and earn sufficient compensation for the service rendered to offset the cost incurred in providing such service. Over a period of many years Pacific Electric has not been operated on such a basis. . . . Collapse of the financial structure of Pacific Electric is inevitable without outside financial assistance if operations are continued on the basis as experienced during past years. . . .

One of the logical sources of reduced costs is substitution of motor coach service for rail lines which were constructed at large investments and designed to carry traffic far in excess of that which now presents itself. [May 14, 1940, emphasis added.]

The conversion of rail to bus operation was interrupted during the war, but resumed thereafter. In 1950, the California Railroad Commission authorized the substitution of bus service for rail on nine major lines serving outlying communities. Again, the Commission's opinion is instructive. It concluded that the company "cannot continue to operate its outmoded and obsolete rail facilities at the losses indicated in this record" and continued:

. . . we find it to be in the public interest to authorize the changes in service as provided in this decision. In so doing, we are taking into account applicant's commitment to provide new, modern motor coaches to replace the rail passenger facilities. . . .

The record clearly shows that the passenger rail operations of applicant have been conducted at a loss over a long period of time. *On the other hand, its motor coach service has been operated at a profit.* [May 9, 1950, emphasis added.]

Noting the nationwide scope of streetcar companies' problems, the Commission continued:

In reaching the foregoing conclusions, we have in mind the very serious financial and service problems which have been experienced since the war by practically all metropolitan mass transit utilities, including those publicly operated. The war apparently served to delay, but failed to halt, a definite trend toward abandonment of surface rail facilities in congested metropolitan areas and the substitution of motor coaches. [May 9, 1950, emphasis added.]

This story could be continued into subsequent years, but we believe the point has been adequately made. It might be worthwhile to add, however, that the conversion from streetcar to bus operations continued into the 1950s and 1960s when the system was run by Metropolitan Coach Lines, which had no connection whatever with GM, and later by the Los Angeles Metropolitan Transit Authority, a public agency.

The author ignores the fact that Pacific Electric itself and its successors converted from rail service to bus service for a period of four decades. Instead, he blames GM and its "auto-industrial allies" for purchasing parts of the Pacific Electric System and thereby setting in motion a process which "severed Los Angeles' regional rail links and then motorized its downtown heart." The "regional rail links" which GM, through an affiliate, was supposed to have severed were lines from "Los Angeles to Glendale, Burbank, Pasadena, and San Bernardino."

This accusation is totally inaccurate. Pacific City Lines, a company in which GM had an investment, did not acquire any interurban rail lines between Los Angeles and these points.

Pacific Electric did sell its operations in Glendale (1941) and Burbank (1944) to Pacific City Lines, but these were local bus lines. In Pasadena, Pacific Electric itself obtained authority from the railroad commission to abandon its local rail lines and bus service; thereupon a Pacific City Lines subsidiary substituted local bus service. There is no evidence that Pacific City Lines or any subsidiaries ever acquired transit operations in or to San Bernardino.

The interurban lines were not "severed" in 1940; some continued in operation until the 1950s. They were abandoned in stages by Pacific Electric or its successor, pursuant to authority granted by the Railroad Commission, because of their rundown and unprofitable condition and because of a lack of patronage.

So much for the "regional rail links"; what about the "heart"? The author blames American City Lines, a company financed in part by GM, for the conversion of the downtown Los Angeles Railway system from streetcars to buses. But, this system was operating buses prior to 1928, a full 15 years before the creation of American City Lines, and the further expansion of its bus services, with abandonment of trackage, continued into the 1930s.

In 1941, 2 years before the creation of American City Lines, the California Railroad Commission approved the application of Los Angeles Railway to convert additional lines from streetcar to bus service. The reasons advanced by the Commission are both instructive and, by now, familiar:

... New motor coaches of modern design with uniform high rates of acceleration and deceleration, high free-running speeds and trackless maneuverability in replacement of obsolete, slow, noisy, rail cars restricted to use of tracks located in the street center will expedite the freer flow of vehicular traffic and allow a more efficient utilization of the street surface. . . .

In arriving at a decision in this matter consideration must be given to the economic elements involved in addition to the service and facilities. Applicant [The Los Angeles Railway] has for a number of years earned insufficient revenue to defray the normal costs of operation, fixed charges, and equipment replacement requirements. As a result many of applicant's rail cars are obsolete and unsuited to the demands of present-day transportation requirements. The oldest type of equipment is used on the "A" and "10" lines for which motor coach substitution is proposed. . . .

Although there has been a rapid increase in population during the past decade in the Los Angeles area, net income of applicant decreased from $1,483,300 in 1920 to a deficit of $381,705 in 1939, a decrease of $1,865,005. . . .

The conversion of Los Angeles Railway from streetcars to buses was thus well underway, for sound economic reasons, before National City Lines or American City Lines were even organized.

Moreover, the Los Angeles Metropolitan Transit Authority, created by the State legislature to acquire Los Angeles Transit Lines and other transit operations in the area, saw fit to continue the conversions from rail to bus after taking over the properties in 1958. In its 1963 annual report, the authority stated:

One of the highlights of 1963 was the successful conversion of the five remaining local streetcar lines and two trolley coach lines to modern bus operation. This changeover was accomplished smoothly after a concentrated public information campaign to acquaint the public with the added convenience, comfort and efficiency of the new operations in their particular geographic area.

The rail transit systems of Los Angeles were singled out by the author as the showcase examples of successful enterprises which he claims were eliminated by the machinations of GM. It turns out that they were eliminated by economics. Their demise resulted from the same economic problems that affected their counterparts across the country and had nothing whatever to do with any plot hatched by General Motors. Compare this history with the testimony given by the accusing author at the hearing in response to the questioning of Hruska:

SENATOR HRUSKA: *(Referring to a map of the Pacific Electric System)* Isn't that wonderful. And yet it wasn't enough. It folded, didn't it?

MR. SNELL: It didn't fold, Senator. It was acquired by General Motors and destroyed.

[...]

SENATOR HRUSKA: And what did they put in its place?

MR. SNELL: The product they manufactured, GM buses using Standard Oil of California fuel and running on Firestone tires.

SENATOR HRUSKA: And was that more profitable than the electric system?

MR. SNELL: To the companies that manufactured General Motors buses and. . . . [From the transcript of hearings, February 26, 1974.]

NEW YORK

"American Ground Transport" states that in 1936 General Motors "combined with Omnibus Corp. in engineering the tremendous conversion of New York City's electric streetcar system to GM buses." Placing the responsibility for this conversion on General Motors is vital to the author's argument because he claims:

The massive conversion within a period of only 18 months of the New York system, then the world's largest streetcar network, has been recognized subsequently as the turning point in the electric railway industry.

Again, let us look at the facts.

The implication that the impetus for the 1936 conversion came from General Motors is without foundation. (It is not true, as the author of "American Ground Transport" states, that as a result of stock and management interlocks GM was "able to exert substantial influence over Omnibus," until well after motorization was completed. GM had no supply contract with Omnibus, no financial investment in the company and no common directors in 1936.) Public dissatisfaction with the streetcar had been mounting for years. As early as 1920, Grover A. Whalen, then Commissioner of Plant and Structures in New York City, was reported to have expressed the following views:

The outstanding fact . . . is that the motor bus is more economical than the streetcar, the fundamental reason being that the only capital charge is for the bus and garage. . . . the bus not only stands up against the trolley car but it literally runs away from it, that is, it gives better and quicker service. In fact, buses have cut the running time between given points from 20 to 50 percent. . . .

In concluding his remarks, Commissioner Whalen emphatically said that the trolley car can be relegated to the limbo of discarded things and that the motor bus is the vehicle best adapted to the requirements of surface transportation in cities. [*Electric Railway Journal*, Jan. 17, 1920]

In 1930 a representative of a leading civic organization stated:

The substitution of motor buses for streetcars in midtown and downtown Manhattan has been for years the aim of practically every civic organization within the borough, but heretofore operating, financial, franchise and political complications have stood in the way. ["Buses to Replace Trolleys," *Little Old New York*, Sept.–Oct. 1930]

In 1929, ten civic organizations had petitioned the board of estimate and apportionment "for the removal of streetcar lines from 8th Avenue and Central Park West and the substitution of bus lines."

Operating companies and elected public officials were also supporters of the conversion from trolleys to buses. As Mayor Fiorello La Guardia said:

Bus operation in place of trolleys is not only a boon to the citizenry of New York in that it provides faster, more flexible and more comfortable transportation but also brings with it other gratifying attributes. It reduces noise, keeps traffic moving faster, and eliminates the danger of wet rails when the weather is bad. . . . Madison Avenue, since the substitution of buses for trolleys, has become one of the show boulevards of the world. Real estate values have been enhanced and *no one is mourning the passing of the streetcar.* ["The Bus Comes Back to Broadway," 1936; emphasis supplied]

Statements of this kind demonstrate that conversion was advocated long before GM appeared on the scene and by people who could not possibly be accused of participating in some plot against the welfare of the transit-riding public.

The superiority of buses is indicated by the fact that each conversion from streetcars had to run a gauntlet of approvals by the New York City Board of Estimate, the New York City Board of Transportation, the New York State Transit Commission and the New York State Public Service Commission. In each such conversion the approval of those four regulatory agencies was given after consideration of all the arguments presented by both bus and streetcar proponents at public hearings. Approval of each such conversion was granted because of the belief, as stated by William G. Fullen, then chairman of the transit commission, that "the substitution of the up-to-date flexible motor bus for the heavy fixed rail trolley . . . will prove of great benefit to the people of this city and particularly, to the traveling public." ("The Passing of New York's Pioneer Street Railway," 1935.) As Mr. Fullen further pointed out, the conviction of the regulatory agencies that buses were superior was shared by the general public. "Statistics show a complete acceptance by the general public and their approval of the change." ("The Bus Comes Back to Broadway")

If the memories of those who once used the streetcars are now insufficient to explain why the public favored the bus, the reasons can easily be found in the literature of the time. It was recognized that buses are vastly more flexible:

Surface traffic conditions no longer can tolerate the presence of streetcars. Buses are flexible. They can weave their way in the traffic. They do not block other traffic by taking on, letting off passengers under the wheels of other traffic. They take their passengers at the curb, where timid persons, or persons who cannot "step lively" by reason of age or infirmity, can board the bus without danger. ["Buses to Replace Trolleys"]

It was recognized that streetcar operations were suffering from the financial consequences of a loss in patronage and that buses provided greater cost efficiency and operating flexibility:

The congestion of vehicular traffic is increasing so fast that trolley cars are moving more and more slowly, and the public is learning to avoid them. The result is that the surface lines of Manhattan have shown tremendous decreases in traffic during the last six years....

Surface car companies of Manhattan are in a bad way financially and are unable to make the expenditures necessary to maintain their equipment in the proper condition. The loss of traffic has cut off profit and it seems a fair inference that this condition will continue. What hope, therefore, is there that they can render satisfactory service hereafter? ["Does Manhattan Need the Surface Cars?," *Harlem Magazine*, Jan. 1929]

The president of the Third Avenue Transit Corp. pinpointed an important advantage of buses from an operator's view:

Street surface transit lines mainly carry people to and from rapid transit lines and railroads, most of whom ride only a short distance.... The ability to turn back buses in short service at points which may be varied from time to time permits flexibility in the matter of schedules. This is particularly desirable in view of our short-haul business. ["Third Avenue Transit Starts Reconversion," *Bus Transportation*, Dec. 1946]

The same source cited by the author in his reference to the rapid conversion of the New York system also summed up the financial advantages of bus systems succinctly:

... The average large bus can be operated for about four-fifths of the cost of running a trolley. The ratio of capital investment to annual gross revenue greatly favors the bus. You can install a bus line with an investment not much greater than the first year's gross take, or about a dollar-for-dollar ratio.... When New York City Omnibus threw nearly 800 buses into the dying arteries of New York Railways, the overall gain in revenue passengers as against the trolley (April 1935 against April 1936) was almost 62 percent. ["Yellow Truck & Coach," *Fortune*, July 1936]

The fact that the conversion of New York continued unabated until the last streetcar disappeared in 1957 is evidence by itself of the continued belief of civic associations, operating companies, elected public officials, and regulatory agencies in the superiority of the bus. Mayor La Guardia summarized the attitudes which led New Yorkers to embark on this course as far back as 1936:

There will be many changes for the better in New York City this year but I venture to predict that few will be more welcome than the substitution of buses for trolley cars on the Broadway–Seventh Avenue line.... The city is now ... reaching the point where soon its main thoroughfares will have thoroughly modern buses replacing antiquated trolleys. ["The Bus Comes Back to Broadway"]

Three years later, Mayor La Guardia's attitude remained the same:

Removal of the remaining obsolete and traffic-obstructing trolley lines from 42nd St. and other congested thoroughfares in Manhattan and the Bronx was reported by Mayor La Guardia to be in sight. . . .

"This plan," said the Mayor, "provides for a complete substitution of modern, up-to-date buses during a period of years on all trolley lines in the Third Avenue system within the city. . . ."

Removal of the B.M.T. trolley lines in Brooklyn is part of the Mayor's rapid transit unification plan, which is scheduled to go into effect early next year. [N.Y. *World Telegram*, Aug. 21, 1939]

OAKLAND

The city of Oakland, which is listed as one of the cities whose conversion to bus transit is attributed to GM, assumed a particular significance at the recent hearings because the basic theme was amplified by the leadoff witness, the mayor of San Francisco. He also attributed the conversion of the Oakland "Key System" to General Motors and added, in an accusation that understandably captured the attention of the media, that General Motors was responsible for delay and excess cost in the construction of the Bay Area Rapid Transit System (BART).

Relying on the fact that National City Lines had acquired the "Key System" in 1946, he testified in 1974 as follows:

Then in 1954, that is 8 years after their acquisition, at a time when we began to talk seriously in San Francisco about building a BART system, they announced their intention of abandoning the rail system, electric rail system across the bridge, abandoning it.

It is very difficult to escape the inference in the light of the total context that they did this for the very purpose of slowing up and making impossible the development of our BART system.

Nevertheless, regardless of the motive, the fact is clear. They pulled up the tracks. Now in BART we have had to spend $200,000,000 to create the same corridor in the form of a tube on the bed of the Bay.

The short and simple response to this accusation is that, whatever National City Lines may or may not have done in the 1950s, it has nothing at all to do with General Motors. All of GM's supply contracts with, and investments in, National City Lines were terminated in 1949. (The author's claim that GM "continued to acquire and dieselize electric transit properties through September of 1955" is not true.) It might be worthwhile, however, to look briefly at the Key System since it provides one more illustration of the real reasons for the discontinuance of rail systems.

The Key System's problems were those which by now should sound familiar. Initially, both the Key System and the Interurban Electric Railway Co. operated over the Oakland Bay Bridge tracks. In 1940, Interurban Electric was permitted by the California Railroad Commission to abandon its bridge rail service because of losses which Interurban described as "no longer endurable." Key continued to operate bridge rail services, but it also experienced losses.

Prior to 1946 when National City Lines obtained an interest in the Key System, the Oakland City Council had approved a number of contracts calling for the removal of tracks and repaving of streets. [One resolution in 1945, for example, pointed out that substantial portions of the tracks are in need of repair and are no longer useful.] Prior to 1946, the Key System also operated buses over the Bay Bridge.

Any rail abandonments and conversions which were made while the Key System was a National City Lines property were, of course, carried out only with the approval of governmental authorities. Moreover, the decision to scrap the tracks across the Bay Bridge was also a governmental one.

As early as 1947, a joint Army-Navy study team, designated by the U.S. Congress, concluded that a subway was the "best solution" to the crossbay transportation problem. Rail passage across bridges was disfavored because structural considerations severely limited the speed.

Subsequently, BART was established. In 1956, the executive secretary of BART told the State public utilities commission that the "best plan" for rapid transit service between Oakland and San Francisco called for the construction of an underwater tube. The alternative "minimum plan" of running trains across the bridge aroused opposition because it would require elevated lines on city streets. (San Francisco *Examiner*, December 2, 1957)

In April 1957, the State director of public works and the chief of the division of bay toll crossings, reported to the legislature that the existing tracks would have to be replaced, no matter what happened:

... any plan for leaving the tracks in place and paving over this area would be impractical and would subject the bridge to a serious fire hazard. ... after 18 years of use, the wooden ties are so badly worn they must be replaced if the present railway continues in operation or if a rapid transit system is developed. [Oakland *Tribune*, April 24, 1957]

The decision of the Key System to convert from rail to bus was specifically approved by public authority in November 1957. This conditional approval was made final early by the state public utilities commission in 1958. By unanimous vote the commission reaffirmed its order of March 12, 1957, and denied a petition asking for reconsideration of that decision.

The commission provided that the change to bus service should coincide with the start of the State program for revamping the Bay Bridge for all-vehicle use. And it set July 1 as final deadline for the change. (Oakland *Tribune*, Mar. 11, 1958)

In 1957, the Legislature of the State of California authorized funds for the remodeling of the bridge so that both levels of the bridge could be used for one-way streets, with full utilization by vehicles. In 1959, in a declaration of policy, the legislature found that:

The relief of vehicular congestion of the San Francisco–Oakland Bay Bridge can be obtained most efficiently and at the least cost in public funds . . . through providing an underwater rapid transit tube.

These governmental decisions may or may not have been wise, in the light of hindsight, but that is not the point. The point is that the accusations against General Motors are false. The streetcar tracks were removed long after GM had severed its connection with the local transit company, and in any event, the action was entirely the result of governmental determinations.

OTHER CITIES

The true facts about the cities of Los Angeles, New York, and Oakland, which have been selected as prime illustrations of the author's thesis that the demise of the streetcar was caused by GM, do not support the thesis at all. The same could be said, were time and patience available, of other cities throughout the country. We shall round out the demonstration of this point by looking briefly at Kalamazoo and Saginaw, Mich., and Springfield, Ohio, which the author claims were the "first targets" of GM's attempts to motorize city transit systems.

As the statement the author quotes from GM's former general counsel indicates, GM formed a subsidiary, United Cities Motor Transit Co., to provide funds to local transit systems for the purchase of buses. The motivation for this action is, however, obscured by the fact that the author has quoted selectively. On the same page as the passage he cites, there appears the following:

. . . For some years streetcar companies in small urban communities had been losing money and this, coupled with the depression following 1929, had resulted in the depreciation of rolling stock and an inability on the part of streetcar companies adequately to serve the public. The Yellow management thought that, if it built a small bus, a market could be created in the smaller communities where a bus could be operated more economically. . . .

Financial failure, of course, is precisely what spurred the conversion from streetcars everywhere. Buses were not a destructive force: they were largely credited by transit companies with staving off the collapse of many systems which survived.

GM did not invest funds in these systems for the purpose of prompting their change from streetcars to buses; the necessity of that step had already been determined by events. GM provided some capital to mass transportation systems which had nowhere else to turn. This is made clear in the statement by GM's general counsel upon which the statement from his report and italicized is the immediately preceding phrase which he [Snell] has omitted:

. . . *inasmuch as it is impossible to raise money through public issue of securities or outside sources* to develop motorized transportation, our company should initiate a program of this nature and authorize the incorporation of a holding company with a capital of $300,000 . . .

In each of the three cities listed as "first targets" for GM's effort, the electric street railway companies themselves had already applied for permission to convert from streetcars to buses before GM was on the scene, but there were no funds available. In Kalamazoo, the existing company had given notice that it could not survive as a streetcar company and itself suggested bus service. The city decided to seek bids from other companies. Bus operations were commenced by a new company in which GM had invested a total of $20,000. The rails were disposed of by the receivers for the old company to concerns entirely unconnected with GM. (Kalamazoo *Gazette*, June 14, 1932; June 10, 1933)

In Saginaw, Mich., the local transit company, which operated both streetcars and buses, was actually in receivership. It was unsuccessful in obtaining approval to operate buses exclusively and was directed by the Federal court in bankruptcy to suspend operations. A bus service was commenced by a new company which at the time had no connection with GM. This new company began its operation with rented buses and only later did it purchase buses from GM. (Saginaw *Daily News*, Oct. 9, 10, 1931)

In Springfield, Ohio, the streetcar company had been in receivership for 5 years. The receiver himself had asked for permission to substitute buses for streetcars. The city manager asked for bids nationally from anyone who could provide an adequate system and the only response was received from a company in which GM later invested a total of $30,000. The streetcar system was abandoned by court order upon application of the city which pointed out "that for a good period of time ... [it] has operated at a loss and it [is] unlikely that the property can ever be operated at a profit." The substitute bus operation proved to be profitable from the start and less than a year later local interests bought out GM at a profit. (Springfield *Daily News*, Aug. 1, Aug. 30, Sept. 13, Oct. 31, Dec. 6, 1933)

These tales of failure from the early depression years have a poignant ring. Change is not always painless and a certain nostalgia for the past is understandable. What is inexcusable, however, is the author's attempt to rewrite history in order to blame General Motors for the destruction of otherwise healthy and viable systems. What happened in Los Angeles, in New York, in Oakland, in Kalamazoo, in Saginaw, and in Springfield happened everywhere. The demise of the streetcar has been described eloquently by a writer who sincerely regretted their passing:

... Somewhat like a moribund whale, the trolley industry was so large that it kept growing even after it had begun to die. Passenger riding kept inching slowly upward until 1923, when the total hit 14 million rides annually. Then riding too began to slope steeply downward.

Buses were still rare at the beginning of the decade. In the whole country less than 75 buses were operated by street railways in 1920. But as tidings spread that buses could cut losses and even actually earn money, they came on in a thundering stampede. ["Trolley Car Treasury," 1956]

General Motors did not generate the winds of change which doomed the streetcar systems; it did, however, through its buses, help to alleviate the disruption left in their wake. Times were hard and public transportation systems were collapsing. GM was able to help with technology, with enterprise and, in some cases, with capital. The buses it sold helped give mass transportation a new lease on life which lasted into the postwar years. Then rising incomes and further dispersion into the suburbs both required and enabled people to rely more heavily on personal transportation. If General Motors had really been interested in destroying mass transportation and creating complete dependence on the automobile, it would hardly have put forth such energetic efforts to develop and promote the sale of buses. GM's experience as a manufacturer of other kinds of transportation equipment did not create a destructive "conflict"; it conferred a positive benefit on the entire community.

PART IV.—THE PAPER ON "AMERICAN GROUND TRANSPORT" IS REPLETE WITH ADDITIONAL FALSE AND DECEPTIVE STATEMENTS

As was stated at the outset, we do not intend to burden this subcommittee with a comprehensive list of false or misleading statements in "American Ground Transport"; the most significant ones, upon which its entire argument proceeds, have already been identified. We would, however, like to refer briefly to a few representative misstatements which demonstrate, if the previous discussion has not sufficiently done so, that this entire document is unworthy of the subcommittee's consideration.

Some statements are simply untrue. For example, the document states that all four domestic auto manufacturers maintain "separate nationwide networks of franchised dealers, each of which deals exclusively in one make of automobile." This is just not so and the error can be demonstrated by simple observation. In fact, of 13,150 GM dealers existing in December 1973, 2,200 held the franchise of at least one other manufacturer. [Further], it is stated:

> The 270-page bill of particulars filed by the U.S. Department of Justice on January 2, 1973, in the fleet buyers' litigation contained documented allegations that the chairmen of GM and Ford routinely participated in "summit meetings" whose purpose was to fix prices on automobiles.

Wholly apart from the inherent deception involved in citing unproven Government charges without mentioning that the defendants had been acquitted of them by a jury, the statement is false. Only one of the pages from the bill of particulars cited to support the statement even mentions "summit meetings" and they are therein described, not as meetings "whose purpose was to fix prices," but as meetings "to discuss future negotiations for labor contracts." The Government never contended that these labor meetings were illegal; it argued only that they could conceivably have provided an "opportunity" for improper price discussions.

As to this kind of purely speculative "opportunity" and any others which the Government lawyers could think of, the bill of particulars states:

The Government cannot specify any direct communications between representatives of GM and Ford in which there was a mention made of the elimination or reduction of price concessions.

The subcommittee has not been exposed to an innocent mistake here; it has been victimized by a deliberate effort to mislead.

Other statements appear to have been deliberately expressed in a way which leaves the reader with a totally false impression. For example, it is stated that:

. . . there are some indications that the Federal Government has sought to protect American automakers from competition with imports by imposing "voluntary" automobile quotas on foreign governments. . . .

The isolated news story referred to in support for this statement might literally be termed an "indication," but the fact is—as the author must well know—that the auto industry has historically been a staunch advocate of free trade and that no quotas on imported automobiles have ever been imposed.

Take another example. On another page, it is stated:

According to a recent estimate by the Federal Trade Commission, 9 million purchasers of domestic 1972 automobiles paid $2.1 billion, or more than $230 per car, in shared monopoly overcharges. . . .

There has been no such estimate by the Federal Trade Commission. The author is apparently referring to a rumored study by the FTC's economics staff, not by the Commission. The Commission has never seen fit to release this so-called estimate; all the information about it is based on leaked reports about its conclusions. Since the underlying document is unavailable, one cannot critically examine its basic assumptions, but they must have serious flaws because the conclusion is absurd.

This is bad enough, but the deception is compounded in a later excerpt, where the author states that "monopoly overcharges" on 1972 trucks are "estimated at more than $600 million." This "estimate" is the author's own calculation, based on the application to trucks of the same percentage "overcharge" apparently calculated for cars in the mysterious "estimates" by some FTC staffers.

Another example: the author states that "several cities led by New York have filed a lawsuit charging that General Motors sets higher-than-competitive prices for its diesel buses and receives millions of dollars annually in monopoly profits." The complaint to which he refers purports to be a class action which bears his name as counsel. Thus far no cities other than New York have "filed" anything—either to join in the action or bring suit on their own. The author's source, thus, is once more himself—and his statement is inaccurate.

Still another example: the author makes the following extraordinary statement:

By 1972, in a move which possibly signified the passing of bus transportation in this country, General Motors had begun converting its bus plants to motor home production.

Since he has devoted the previous 10 pages to deploring GM's conduct of its bus business and since he recommends that GM be ousted from the business altogether, the author's apparent distress is puzzling. It is also unfounded. In his haste to reach a sweeping conclusion, he neglected to find out that no "transit coaches" had been built in the GM plant re-equipped for motor homes for at least 25 years. Moreover, the implicit assumption that GM is the only company that sells buses in this country is, of course, totally incorrect.

CONCLUSION

The major thesis of "American Ground Transport" is that General Motors has had a destructive impact on mass transportation in this country. This thesis essentially rests on the claim that railroads only bought diesel engines because General Motors forced them to and the claim that streetcars disappeared only because General Motors was seeking a market for its buses. Both claims have been demonstrated to be untrue.

Because these false and damaging claims have been associated with the hearings of this subcommittee and submitted to it by a member of its staff, they have attracted far more attention than they otherwise would have done. Accordingly, we find it necessary to urge, as set forth in the "Introduction," that this subcommittee place an immediate moratorium on further distribution of the document which asserts them until the subcommittee is in a position to distribute, under the same cover, this reply by General Motors.

Bibliography

BOOKS AND REPORTS

Berton, Pierre, *The Impossible Railway*. Alfred A. Knopf, New York, 1972.

Best, Gerald M., *The Ulster and Delaware . . . Railroad Through the Catskills*. Golden West Books, San Marino, Calif., 1972.

Blake, Herbert W., *The Era of Streetcars and Interurbans in Winnipeg, 1881–1955*. H. W. Blake, Winnipeg, 1974.

Blanchard, Leslie, *The Street Railway Era in Seattle: A Chronicle of Six Decades*. Harold E. Cox, Fortyfort, Pa., 1968.

Bromley, John F., and Jack May, *Fifty Years of Progressive Transit: A History of the TTC*. Electric Railroaders' Association, New York, 1973.

Brown, Dee, *Hear That Lonesome Whistle Blow*. Bantam Books, New York, 1978.

Bruce-Briggs, B., *The War Against the Automobile*. E. P. Dutton, New York, 1977.

Caro, Robert A., *The Power Broker: Robert Moses & the Fall of New York*. Alfred A. Kropf, New York, 1974.

Cavin, Ruth, *Trolleys*. Hawthorn Books, New York and Ontario, 1976.

City of New York, Department of City Planning, "Financial Feasibility, LR Transit, 42nd Street Case Study," January 1979.

Clarke, Bradley H., *Trackless Trolleys of the Fitchburg and Leominster Street Railway Company*. Boston Street Railway Association, Boston, Mass., 1970.

Conklin, Groff, *All About Subways*. Julian Messner, Inc., New York, 1938.

Cudahy, Brian J., *Change at Park Street Under: The Story of Boston's Subways*. The Stephen Greene Press, Brattleboro, Vt., 1972.

———, *Rails Under the Mighty Hudson*. The Stephen Greene Press, Brattleboro, Vt., 1975.

Cunningham, John T., *Railroading in New Jersey*. Associated Railroads of New Jersey, Newark, N.J., 1951.

Cunningham, Joseph, and Leonard DeHart, *A History of the New York City Subway System Part I: The Manhattan Els and the IRT*. New York, 1976.

———, *A History of the New York City Subway System Part II: Rapid Transit in Brooklyn*. New York, 1977.

———, *A History of the New York City Subway System Part III: The Independent System and City Ownership*, New York, 1977.

Day, John R., *The Story of London's Underground*. Staples Printers Ltd., London, 1972.

DeNevi, Don, *Western Train Robberies*. Celestial Arts, Millbrae, Calif., 1976.

Dorin, Patrick C., *Commuter Railroads*. Superior Publishing Company, Seattle, Wash., 1970.

Duke, Donald, *PE—The Pacific Electric Railway*. Golden West Books, San Marino, Calif., 1958.

Easlon, Steven L., *The Los Angeles Railway Through the Years*. Darwin Publications, Sherman Oaks, Calif., 1973.

Farrell, Michael R., *Who Made All Our Streetcars Go?* By permission of Baltimore NRHS Publishers, Baltimore, Md., 1973.

Fausser, William W., *The Brooklyn and Rockaway Beach Railroad: The Canarsie Railroad*. New York, 1976.

Filey, Michael, Richard Howard, and Helmut Weyerstrahs, *Passengers Must Not Ride on Fenders: A Fond Look at Toronto—Its People, Its Places, Its Streetcars*. Green Tree Publications, Toronto, 1974.

Goodrich, Warren, *Change at Jamaica: A Commuter's Guide to Survival*. The Vanguard Press, New York, 1957.

Granick, Harry, *Underneath New York*. Rinehart and Company, New York, 1947.

Griswold, Wesley S., *Train Wreck!* The Stephen Greene Press, Brattleboro, Vt., 1969.

Hamilton, Ellis, *The Pictorial History of Railways*. Crown Publishers, New York, 1968.

Keats, John, *The Insolent Chariots*. Fawcett Publications, Inc., New York, 1959.

Klamkin, Charles, *Railroadiana: The Collector's Guide to Railroad Memorabilia*. Funk & Wagnalls, New York, 1976.

Krause, John, and Ed Crist, *Lackawanna Heritage 1947–1952*. Railroad Heritage Press, New York, 1978.

Lind, Alan R., *Chicago's Surface Lines*. Transport History Press, Park Forest, Ill., 1974.

———, *From Horsecars to Streamliners*. Transport History Press, Park Forest, Ill., 1978.

Middleton, William D., *Grand Central . . . The World's Greatest Railway Terminal*. Golden West Books, San Marino, Calif., 1977.

———, *The Interurban Era*. Kalmbach Publications, Milwaukee, Wis., 1961.

———, *North Shore—America's Fastest Interurban*. Golden West Books, San Marino, Calif., 1964.

———, *South Shore: The Last Interurban*. Golden West Books, San Marino, Calif., 1970.

———, *The Time of the Trolley*. Kalmbach Publications, Milwaukee, Wis., 1969.

———, *When the Steam Railroads Electrified*. Kalmbach Publications, Milwaukee, Wis., 1974.

Miller, John Anderson, *Fares, Please! From Horse-cars to Streamliners*. D. Appleton-Century, New York, 1941.

Moedinger, William M., *The Trolley . . . Triumph of Transport*. Applied Arts Publishers, Lebanon, Pa., 1971.

Moline, Norman T., *Mobility and the Small Town: 1900–1930*. The University of Chicago Press, Chicago, Ill., 1971.

Myers, William A., and Ira L. Swett, *Trolleys to the Surf*. Interurban Publications, Glendale, Calif., 1976.

The New York Subway: Interborough Rapid Transit. Arno Press, New York, 1904.

Pavlucik, Andrew J., *The New Haven Railroad: A Fond Look Back*. Pershing Press, New Haven, Conn., 1978.

Quinby, Cdr. E. J., *Interurban Interlude*. Model Craftsman Publishing, Ramsey, N.J., 1968.

Reed, Robert C., *Train Wrecks: A Pictorial History of Accidents on the Main Line*. Bonanza Books, New York, 1968.

Seyfried, Vincent F., *The Cross-Island Line: The Story of the Huntington Railroad*. Garden City, N.Y., 1976.

Southerland, Thomas C., Jr., and William McCleery, *The Way to Go: The Coming Revival of U.S. Rail Passenger Service*. Simon & Schuster, New York, 1973.

Sturholm, Larry, and John Howard, *All for Nothing: The True Story of the Last Great American Train Robbery*. BLS Publishing Co., Portland, Oreg., 1976.

Swett, Ira L., and Harry C. Aitken, Jr., *Napa Valley Route*. Interurban Publications, Glendale, Calif., 1975.

Theroux, Paul, *The Great Railway Bazaar: By Train Through Asia*. Houghton-Mifflin, Boston, Mass., 1975.

Walker, James Blaine, *50 Years of Rapid Transit*. The Law Printing Company, New York, 1918.

Walker, Jim, *Key System Album*. Interurban Publications, Glendale, Calif., 1978.

Warner, Sam B., Jr., *Streetcar Suburbs: The Process of Growth in Boston, 1870–1900*. Atheneum, New York, 1974.

Westing, Fred, *Penn Station: Its Tunnels and Side Rodders*. Superior Publishing Co., Seattle, Wash., 1978.

Ziel, Ron, *The Twilight of Steam Locomotives*. Grosset & Dunlap, New York, 1973.

———, and George Foster, *Steel Rails to the Sunrise: The Long Island Rail Road*. Hawthorn Books, New York, 1965.

Zimmerman, Karl R., *CZ: The Story of the California Zephyr*. Delford Press, Oradell, N.J., 1972.

NEWSPAPERS, MAGAZINES, AND TECHNICAL JOURNALS

Use was made of numerous newspapers, magazines, and technical journals. Some of these were the following:

NEWSPAPERS: Boston *Globe*, Boston *Herald American*, Boston *Phoenix*, Long Island *Press*, New York *Daily News*, New York *Post*, New York *Times*, Philadelphia *Evening Bulletin*, Seattle *Post-Intelligencer*, Toronto *Globe and Mail*, Toronto *Star*, Washington *Post*, Washington *Star*.

MAGAZINES AND TECHNICAL JOURNALS: *Electric Interurban Railways of America, Headlights, Innovation in Public Transportation, London Transport* (London Transport Executive), *Metro, Metro Memo, Metro News, Metropolitan Washington: The Board of Trade News, Modern Railroads, Motor Coach Age, Newhouse News Service, The News World, Passenger Train Journal, Rail Fan & Railroad* (recently merged), *Railway Age, Subways: A Special Publication of the Smithsonian Institution, Sunset, Trains, Trolleybus Bulletin, Washington Society of Professional Engineers: An Analysis of Simpson & Curtin's Report to the Mayor's Transit Study Committee of Seattle.*

Index

COPYRIGHT ACKNOWLEDGMENTS